The Future of School Board Governance

Relevancy and Revelation

Thomas L. Alsbury

ROWMAN & LITTLEFILLD EDUCATION
Lanham • *New York* • *Toronto* • *Plymouth, UK*

Published in the United States of America
by Rowman & Littlefield Education
A Division of Rowman & Littlefield Publishers, Inc.
A wholly owned subsidiary of The Rowman & Littlefield Publishing Group, Inc.
4501 Forbes Boulevard, Suite 200, Lanham, Maryland 20706
www.rowmaneducation.com

Estover Road
Plymouth PL6 7PY
United Kingdom

British Library Cataloguing in Publication Information Available

Library of Congress Cataloging-in-Publication Data

Alsbury, Thomas L., 1960-
   The future of school board governance : relevancy and revelation / Thomas L.
Alsbury.
      p. cm.
   ISBN-13: 978-1-57886-794-3 (cloth : alk. paper)
   ISBN-10: 1-57886-794-0 (cloth : alk. paper)
   ISBN-13: 978-1-57886-795-0 (pbk. : alk. paper)
   ISBN-10: 1-57886-795-9 (pbk. : alk. paper)
   1. School boards—United States. I. Title.

LB2831.A35 2008
379.1'531—dc22   2007052713

Contents

Part III: School Board–Superintendent and Authority Relations

Part IV: School Board Democratic Effectiveness

Part V: School Board's Role in District/Systemic Reform

Part VI: Relevance: School Board Influence on Student Achievement

Part VII: Revelation: School Board's Viability and Possible Future

Preface

Research about school boards and the governance of education has developed steadily, although not systematically, during the past decade or so. Rather, this research, principally the work of individual scholars in political science and in educational administration, has been diverse in its purposes, approaches, quality, and impact. (Webb, 1975)

These words of the National School Boards Association (NSBA) executive director are as true today as they were 30 years ago when they appeared in the foreword to the publication that resulted from the first invitational symposium on educational governance.

When, in 1975, NSBA convened the symposium of 14 scholars, organized around key topic areas that had been the focus of school board research, their desire was to disseminate what had been learned, provide service based on knowledge, and contribute to more effective governance of schools. It was the task of the scholars to review, analyze, and synthesize the research and to suggest directions for future studies.

At the invitation of NSBA, the symposium was chaired by Professor Peter J. Cistone, previously of the Ontario Institute for Studies in Education at the University of Toronto, who also made major research contributions to the understanding of school boards. Following the symposium, a book was published which comprised the papers presented, revised by the authors on the basis of discussions during the symposium, and subsequently edited by Professor Cistone. This book provided the most comprehensive and useful review of the school board field at that time and was intended to serve as a catalyst for research during the next decade.

The idea for this edited volume emerged among three members of a team of researchers who are working on the Lighthouse Research Project, a multi-phase, multi-year study of school governance and it's influence on student achievement. The project is currently in its third phase and is one of several cutting-edge initiatives to improve school governance led by the Iowa Association of School Boards (IASB) and the Iowa School Boards Foundation (ISBF, http://www.schoolboardresearch.org) under the leadership of Ron Rice, executive director of IASB. Mary Delagardelle, deputy director of IASB, executive director of ISBF, director of the Lighthouse Research, and my former graduate student; Hilary LaMonte, information manager and director of Phase III of the Lighthouse Research; and I were musing on Cistone's 1973 national symposium and the subsequent edited volume, noting 31 years had passed.

The result was the conception of a similar invitational symposium with the same title, "School Board Research: Main Lines of Inquiry," convened September 14–15, 2007, in an effort to ensure the field was well informed about emerging knowledge related to school board governance. Funding for the symposium was provided by the Iowa School Boards Foundation, the Wallace Foundation, the Iowa State Action for Education Leadership and Policy (SAELP), the Iowa Association of School Boards, and the Illinois Association of School Boards.

Fifteen scholars from across North America were invited to participate in the symposium and to each prepare a paper on a specific area of school board research. These papers were subsequently revised in light of the discussions in the symposium among attendees, who represented a balanced combination of current and prospective researchers, local and state school board members, and state and national school board association officers from 30 states and 2 countries.

Researchers and topics were selected intentionally, based upon the belief that research in a vacuum does little more than provide interesting information, but research that develops systematically, continuously building upon prior work, creates new knowledge. As a result, the presenter/authors represent the full range of school board researchers conducted from the late 1950s. Included are the developers of the two major theories of local school board governance, the chair/editor of the 1975 symposium/book, and current board researchers representing five generations and including two emeritus professors, six deans, eight department chairs, eight executive directors, and four chief editors of leadership journals.

The authors represent nearly 300 years of experience in school board and superintendent research collectively, with over 200 additional years of K–12 administrative experience in the field, providing a unique and unusual combination of theoretical and practical perspectives. Authors come from both the field of educational leadership and political science, representing a rare combination of academic perspectives not found in other volumes on school board leadership.

The chapters are intended to take the reader through a history and retrospective of school board research and governance theory development for the past 60 years, often told by the original theory developers, seminal researchers, and cutting-edge new researchers in the field of school boards, school policy, political science, and the superintendency. The authors also provide a current assessment of present trends and future possibilities in this field of research, as well as offer practical advice to currently practicing school board members and superintendents.

These chapters are presented in a time when school boards are under fire as never before. School boards have experienced the "rapid and profound transformation" that Cistone predicted in 1975, and today the board's loss of local power; pressure from federally mandated accountability requirements; mayoral takeovers in urban areas; growing charter, private, and home schooling; and escalating consolidation of districts truly threaten this uniquely American institution.

Present calls and funding for alternative governance approaches emphasize the need for school boards to respond and adapt to their local communities. In order to understand the pressures threatening boards today and possible practical responses, current board members need to have answers from past and current research. These chapters provide challenge and direction to current researchers and their subsequent study agendas and topics, as well as explanations and recommendations for serving board members and superintendents.

This volume, reflecting the original symposium, is organized into seven major themes that take the reader through the history of past theory and research that informs present-day and future studies, and reviews the changing roles of school board members and the related change in school board–superintendent relationships. The themes also provide for the sharing of cutting-edge research that not only confirms past governance theories but also expands them to demonstrate the efficacy of boards in the present context. The title of the volume is mirrored in chapters showing the *relevance* of boards by their influence on school reform and student achievement. Additionally, chapters discuss the *revelation*; that is, they reveal the school board's viability and possible future in an increasingly hostile environment where many are questioning the viability of locally elected boards.

In Part I, "History of School Board Governance Theory and Research," chapters review the development and evolution of empirical research supporting major local school board governance theories. Frank W. Lutz and Laurence Iannaccone provide an overview of the development of their own Dissatisfaction Theory of American Democracy, while also offering a general overview of how theories should be developed as well as cogent differences between how policy study and political research are used to support or refute theory today. They also provide practical implications and recommendations for school board members and superintendents currently in practice. Peter Cistone provides a retrospective of school board research themes from the time of the last national school board symposium held in 1975. The author concludes that few empirical works extend governance models past those originally crafted prior to the 1970s. The author recommends that further work is needed to better define variables in governance models but maintains the efficacy of elected school boards as one of the few remaining accessible democratic institutions in local communities.

Part II, "History of the Changing Roles of School Boards," comprises chapters that analyze the historical roots of the local school board and its evolution through the 19th and 20th centuries. Michael Kirst, codeveloper of a major theory on local school governance, the Input-Output Theory, reviews their theory's foundational framework for understanding the operation of local school boards within their political system. He also stresses how deeply embedded and unique locally elected boards are to American culture, and provides an overview of changing board roles—namely, the erosion of local decision-making control that threatens the current efficacy of urban boards, in particular. Lars Björk provides a discussion of how superintendent and board member roles and their relationships have been shaped by macropolitics and micropolitics in the local community. A general examination of the dynamic relationship between education and society explains historical changes and frames recommendations for board members and superintendents in negotiating turbulent political times.

Part III, "School Board–Superintendent and Authority Relations," is composed of chapters that discuss the latest research findings and the historical underpinnings surrounding the topic of school board member and superintendent relationships. Meredith Mountford reviews the ever-present conflict that has existed between boards and superintendents and posits four underlying psychological and social factors that explain these tensions. The author offers recommendations for board and superintendent training programs to address and help alleviate these conflicts. George Petersen and Lance Fusarelli discuss how the relationship of the board of education and district superintendent has influenced leadership and decision making, while also raising criticisms of the current governance structure of public schools. They concentrate on four trends reshaping the board-superintendent relationship—demographic changes, external threats and stress, the politics of personalism, and changes in superintendents themselves—and explore their potential strength in influencing the leadership of schools.

Part IV, "School Board Democratic Effectiveness," comprises chapters that discuss some of the common functions of school boards involved in cogent events such as elections, finance, and the legalities and politics of policy application. In each of these chapters the authors explore the extent that board behaviors mirror their democratic function. Frederick Hess provides one of the first substantive understandings of the electoral process of local school boards and the role they play in electoral outcomes by exploring how money and interest groups affect board elections. Carol Merz Frankel examines the phenomenon of foundations established by school districts to raise funds from citizens to support schools and how this relatively new alternative funding phenomenon is providing new political power to local citizens to control their schools. She also explores the effects of private foundation funding of schools on local and statewide student expenditure equitability issues. Finally, Barbara DeHart and DeLacy Ganley provide a descriptive case study of one reconstituted school board that exemplifies the type of values shift predicted by Iannaccone and Lutz's Dissatisfaction Theory. The new board opposed a legally required policy language change resulting in significant negative impacts on the community, school personnel, and more importantly, the students in the district.

Part V, "School Board's Role in District/Systemic Reform," is composed of chapters discussing how school boards can significantly influence district and school-level reform, subsequently impacting student success. The chapters highlight that, despite some who question the board's relevancy, school boards do indeed affect the districts they govern. Mary Delagardelle provides an overview of the Iowa Lighthouse study, one of only a few known to successfully demonstrate a connection between school boards and student success. The author presents evidence that school boards in high- and low-achieving districts are significantly different in their beliefs and actions and shows a relationship between board training, board members' beliefs about their role, and the achievement of students in schools. Theodore Kowalski explores traditional and proposed school board roles in relation to school reform and argues school boards should be held accountable for maintaining ongoing information exchanges with multiple publics, especially in conjunction with visioning, planning, resource procurement, and political support. The conclusion is made that although radical changes in local governance are improbable, the concept of relational communication can be applied to positively and significantly influence school reform efforts.

Part VI, "Relevance: School Board Influence on Student Achievement," comprises chapters presenting several recent and uncommon empirical studies indicating that school board stability and leadership can positively influence student achievement in local districts. Thomas Alsbury presents a longitudinal, quantitative study supporting the Dissatisfaction Theory and showing a significant relationship between high politically motivated school board turnover and student test scores in a single state. Sam String-field provides a case study exploring the actions of a single urban school board and its impacts over seven years; impacts were positive and essentially continuous. Written through the experiences of a member of the new board, this chapter attempts to explain the role of the board in achieving desired district reform.

Part VII, "Revelation: School Board's Viability and Possible Future," is comprised of chapters that describe studies conducted by political scientists and educational leadership researchers supporting the possible viability of alternative governance structures in high-population, urban school districts. Thomas Glass describes how constant intraboard conflict and superintendent turnover destabilizes urban districts already suffering from chronic underachievement and system instability and supports the argument to replace elected boards with appointed boards in these types of districts. Kenneth Wong and Francis Shen provide a description of a national study using multiple data sources to evaluate student achievement, financial management, and human capital in large urban school districts. Their results show a small but significant increase in student achievement among urban districts taken over by mayors with no additional pupil expenditures. They discuss mayoral takeover as a potential viable option for struggling urban districts.

This volume covers an array of theoretical discussion, historical retrospectives, and empirical study from a more diverse range of perspectives and academic disciplines than any other volume in the past 30 years. Although it represents much of our current knowledge on school boards, it is important to note the relatively few empirical studies conducted over the past several decades and the fact that theoretical extension in this arena has been scant. Most of the authors in this volume raise many questions, share concern over the paucity of school board research and national comprehensive surveys or data collection of school board members, and encourage further and more sophisticated research of school boards and school board members. It is hoped that this volume provides an overview of the cogent information surrounding school boards and school board theory, but more importantly will stimulate further research and care for researchers, policy developers, and practitioners influencing a continued and relevant future for locally elected school boards.

In every respect, *The Future of School Board Governance: Relevancy and Revelation* is the result of a collaborative effort by an impressive group of Iowa state school board association leaders and supporting staff and our sponsors mentioned earlier. All of us who participated in the symposium at which these papers were originally presented wish to express our gratitude to the collective team who made the symposium possible. To the contributors, those researchers who came out of retirement to provide us with a rich historical and theoretical perspective, those new researchers working hard to continue this line of research, and those who practice in field, I express my sincere appreciation for your commitment to preparing and presenting your papers for the symposium and this volume. I want to express special thanks and dedicate this volume to Dr. Laurence Iannaccone, whose own lifetime of studies and effort in recruiting and mentoring prospective researchers in this line of study has produced generations of school board researchers who continue to explore the relevancy and revelation of school boards today.

Thomas Alsbury
North Carolina State University
Raleigh, North Carolina
October 2007

Foreword: Tracing School Board Governance and Research: From Democracy and Effectiveness (1975) to Effectiveness with Accountability in a "Flat World" (2007)

William Lowe Boyd, Penn State University

As Tom Friedman (2006) has documented in his best-selling book *The World Is Flat*, the world has changed dramatically since the year 2000. Like many of our established institutions, American school boards now face a vastly changed environment and unprecedented challenges as they try to adapt and respond to 21st century conditions, including the far-reaching impacts of globalization. Beyond that, school boards have entered an era that I think can be called "effectiveness with accountability in a 'flat world.'" Here, I'm using Friedman's term, "flat world," as shorthand for not only the effects of globalization but also the *unique changes* in the environment of school boards that have occurred in recent years. In other words, not only have the barriers come down and "flatteners" emerged enabling globalization, as Friedman emphasizes, but unique developments have dramatically altered or "flattened" the environment in which school boards operate, breaking their monopoly on public education within their boundaries, further loosening their already tenuous grip on policy, and empowering citizens, parents, and staff members.

This changed environment is affecting school districts of all types and sizes—rural, urban, and suburban—and has occurred through a confluence, some might say a "perfect storm" of developments: the startling paradigm shift to outcome-based accountability, high-stakes testing, and sanctions (especially via the federally enforced "No Child Left Behind Act"); new and steeper expectations for district and school board leadership to improve student achievement and close the black-white achievement gap; increasing transparency and availability of school district data via the Internet and online databases and Web sites; the technological "communications revolution" empowering citizens and parents (the Internet, email, cell phones, Google, YouTube, etc.); the emergence of school choice (charter schools, cyber schools, home schooling, and the threat of vouchers); new rights and entitlements for special needs students; . . . and the list goes on. The $64 billion question (we used to say $64 *million* question, another sign of the vast changes that have occurred) is: Can the school boards of today—rooted as they are in the early 20th century, not the Space Age, meet these very steep 21st century challenges?

This timely book—a tribute to the initiative and insights of Thomas Alsbury and the Iowa School Board Foundation—addresses this and related questions, many of which face and challenge not just school boards but all the institutions of American democracy. In writing this short foreword for this book, I am drawing on the perspective I have developed over my career as an educator, which dates from 1957 and includes my participation in the 1975 school board research conference that provided the baseline for the 2007 school board research conference this book reports (which illness prevented me from attending).

In the title of this foreword, I've tried to hint at the stunning changes in the 30-plus years between the two conferences. By "From Democracy and Effectiveness (1975)," I mean that the 1975 conference was focused mainly on the issue of democracy and only secondarily upon effectiveness—this was well before the 1983 "A Nation at Risk" report which dramatically raised the effectiveness issue. In their important 1974 book *Governing American Schools*, which represented some of the best research we had at that time, Harmon Zeigler and Kent Jennings had forcefully raised the issue of democracy. Their book presented extensive empirical data from a national survey of school board members and superintendents that Zeigler and Jennings believed showed *undemocratic role reversal undermining effectiveness*, that is that school boards were more likely to represent their superintendent's views and preferences to the community than to represent the community's views and preferences to the superintendent. This conclusion, which I, among others, felt was insufficiently supported by their data, was the subject of considerable debate at the 1975 conference. The paper I presented on this topic became a chapter ("School Board-Administrate Staff Relationships") in the conference book (Cistone, 1975) and later, in revised and expanded form, an article in the *Teachers College Record* (Boyd, 1976).

For better or worse, there is less attention now to the need for democracy (either on school boards or in schools) due to our obsession with the threats of globalization, international competition, accountability, and high-stakes testing. This is the obsession I've tried to suggest in labeling the theme of the 2007 conference "Effectiveness with Accountability in a 'Flat

World'" (2007). Indeed, much of the huge challenge now facing American schools, and especially our high schools, revolves around the way globalization, outsourcing, and automation have radically transformed the world economy and alarmed business leaders and school reformers. Unfortunately, concerns about shortages of skilled workers and declining American competitiveness—and the related push for high-stakes testing and accountability—are overriding and obscuring the equally important civic and social challenges facing American schools.

A good example of this appeared in a recent listserve message to participants in Penn State's Prevention Research Center Seminar Series. Even though worthwhile in its own right, teaching social-emotional skills was thought to lack acceptability in schools "in the current political climate" if it did little to advance academic performance:

> In the current political climate schools are under tremendous pressure to show that students are making adequate academic progress. Often, preventive interventions are given lower priority as time and resources become more scarce. While most educators agree that social-emotional skills are critical for success in school, research that documents the link is important to empirically establish the fact. Recently, a meta-analysis by Duncan et al. (2007) in *Developmental Psychology* suggested that there [is] limited support for social-emotional skills as predictors of later academic performance. Given the implications of this article and the potential that members of the PRC might be asked about this study, we thought it would be useful to devote some time to a group discussion on the article [in the near future]. (Confer, 2008)

It is daunting just to try to compile an adequate list of the extraordinary changes in American education that now form the environment for school boards that I call "Effectiveness with Accountability in a 'Flat World'" (2007). To show more fully what our school boards now must contend with, and to stimulate discussion, I will close this foreword with a list of what I view as the most dramatic changes in the field of education since 1950 (Boyd, 2007). I wish our school boards and scholars the very best as they explore and endeavor to cope with these remarkable developments.

An Amazing List of Dramatic Changes in the Field of Education since 1950 (Boyd, 2007)

A far-reaching and momentous paradigm shift, from

- a focus on inputs to a focus on outcomes and accountability
- a "logic of confidence" to a "logic of consequences"
- report cards on kids to report cards on teachers, administrators, schools, districts, and states

- underserved special needs students with few rights to special needs students with entitlements; the revolution in special education (PARC decree; P.L 94-142; and IDEA)
- racial segregation to desegregation, pride in diversity, and an elusive quest for true integration
- students and teachers with few rights and little power to activist students and teachers
- weak teachers organizations to powerful unions
- top-down management to shared leadership
- lockstep seniority ladders and "all teachers are equal" to differentiated staffing and compensation of teachers; "pay for performance"
- local control of K–12 education policy to increasing state and federal control of education
- no federal control to No Child Left Behind
- local control of the curriculum to increasing calls for national standards
- disconnected goals, curricula, and tests to systemic alignment and systemic school reform (Smith and O'Day, 1991)
- "schools don't make a difference" to the equally invalid idea that "schools make all the difference" (Rothstein, 2002)
- acceptance of the achievement gap to rigorous requirements for AYP (Adequate Yearly Progress) by disaggregated at-risk populations of students (poverty, special needs, English language learners)
- opinion-based to evidence-based, data-driven decision making, evaluation studies, and "randomized controlled trials"
- professional control and restricted access to information to increasingly open systems and growing influence and control for external actors and citizens
- education as a "back-burner" issue to one of great political importance
- an impenetrable wall of separation between church and state to possibilities for financial aid to religious schools
- the separation of education from politics to increasing political control, privatization, "contracting out" the management of schools, and public-private partnerships with "blurred boundaries"
- mayoral involvement, state and mayoral "takeovers" of urban districts, and the use of noneducators as superintendents/CEOs
- "contracting out" the management of schools to Education Management Organizations (EMO) (i.e., "diverse providers," public, private, Non-Governmental Organizations [NGOs], and for-profits)
- transformation and institutional change in urban school governance (Boyd, Kerchner, and Blyth, 2008).
- temporary "windows of opportunity" for education reform to perpetual reform

- "A Nation at Risk" (1983), at first thought to be only a brief window of opportunity for education reform, to, as it turned out, Anthony Downs's (1957) "Issue-Attention Cycle" put on hold
- public education as a near monopoly to diversified school choice
- on-site schooling to cyber schooling and home schooling
- "disintermediation" of public education (Paul Houston, AASA president)
- public education as a "sacred cow" to "scapegoat" to a sweeping reexamination and redefinition of the concept of public education and of the means for its delivery (Boyd, 2007).

REFERENCES

Boyd, W. L. 1976. The public, the professionals, and educational policy-making: Who governs? *Teachers College Record* 77 (4): 539–577.

Boyd, W. L. 2007, April 12. *Insurmountable obstacles? The evolution of education policy and politics in the United States, 1950 to 2007.* Invited Presentation to the Politics of Education Association at the Annual Meeting of the American Educational Research Association, Chicago.

Boyd, W. L., C. Kerchner, and M. Blyth, eds. 2008, forthcoming. *The transformation of great American school districts: How big cities are reshaping public education.* Cambridge: Harvard Education Press.

Cistone, P. J., ed. 1975. *Understanding school boards: Problems and prospects.* Boston: D.C. Heath.

Confer, K. A. 2008. Listserve email message to participants in Penn State's Prevention Research Center Seminar Series, January 27.

Downs, A. 1957. *An economic theory of democracy.* New York: Harper & Row.

Duncan, G. J., C. J. Dowsett, and J. Brooks-Gunn. 2007. School readiness and later achievement. *Developmental Psychology* 43 (6): 1428–1446.

Friedman, T. L. 2006. *The world is flat: A brief history of the twenty-first century.* New York: Farrar, Straus, & Giroux.

Houston, P. 2001. Superintendents for the 21st century: It's not just a job, It's a calling. *Phi Delta Kappan,* 82 (6): 428–433.

National Commission on Excellence in Education (NCEE). 1983. A nation at risk: The imperative for educational reform. Washington, DC: U.S. Government Printing Office.

Rothstein, R. 2002. *Out of balance: Our understanding of how schools affect society and how society affects schools.* Chicago: The Spencer Foundation.

Smith, M., and J. O'Day. 1991. Systemic school reform. In *The politics of curriculum and testing,* ed. S. H. Fuhrman and B. Malen, 233–267. New York: Falmer.

Zeigler, L. H., and M. K. Jennings. 1974. *Governing American schools: Political interaction in local school districts.* Scituate, MA: Duxbury.

I

HISTORY OF SCHOOL BOARD GOVERNANCE THEORY AND RESEARCH

1

The Dissatisfaction Theory of American Democracy

Frank W. Lutz and Laurence Iannaccone

The Dissatisfaction Theory of American Democracy says simply that when the citizens of our democracy become dissatisfied enough with "things," they go to the polls and vote to change "things." Often the "things" they vote to change are the incumbent policy makers. On school boards, it is the incumbent school board members who are voted out. The newly elected board members often fire the old superintendent, and education policies change. The purpose of this chapter is to describe how this theory came to be while also saying something about policy, research, and theory in the politics of education.

In 1960, a new doctoral student at Washington University in St. Louis decided to run for a seat on a local school board in one of the more than two dozen St. Louis County school districts. He was about to begin a two-and-a-half-year doctoral residency with no idea of a topic or even a general idea of what his dissertation might be. Laurence Iannaccone, a new professor out of Teachers College, Columbia, became his advisor. Iannaccone suggested Lutz keep a careful journal of his experiences during the school board election and a diary of daily events should he be elected as a school board member. Lutz was also assigned a bibliography of readings of classical anthropological works in order to understand how ethnographic description was carried out. Thus began a long and rewarding personal and professional relationship between Iannaccone and Lutz, and the seeds of the Dissatisfaction Theory were sown (Lutz, 1962).

THE DISSATISFACTION THEORY OF
AMERICAN DEMOCRACY

We often hear the question, "What's in a name?" In this case, considerable. That question in this chapter is broken into three parts. First, *why* dissatisfaction? Why not satisfaction? When we speak of voter attitudes about any issue, if there is voter dissatisfaction, there is also voter satisfaction. So why not call it the Satisfaction Theory? It is because in American democracy there is, more often than not, sufficient satisfaction among citizens that they are willing to permit the present policy makers to continue in office. Often the voters just don't care; things may as well stay as they are. Often voters do not bother to vote. In fact, it is usual for only about 50 percent of the eligible voters to vote in any national election and a much lower turnout in state or local elections. Local school district elections usually fall below 40 percent, even as low as 15 percent or less. Citizens seem satisfied enough and they don't know much about the issues, don't care much, and thus do not vote (Menand, 2007). It is when the voters become dissatisfied enough that something happens to get the voters' attention. When they bother to vote, it may be a single issue citizens are dissatisfied about. Not infrequently there are several issues that separate and different publics are dissatisfied about. When enough dissatisfaction occurs, voter turnout becomes unusually high. As they are dissatisfied with policy and cannot vote against the policy, they vote against the incumbent policy makers.

In most school districts, voters cannot vote against the superintendent, so they vote against the incumbent school board members who appointed that superintendent. When voters succeed in ousting enough board members, the new board appoints a new superintendent, and policy changes. Community influence on their schools is at the heart of the Dissatisfaction Theory. The two foci of the theory are incumbent school board members and superintendent turnover. Thus, it is called the *Dissatisfaction* Theory.

Second, *why* is it a theory? It is a theory because it fits the common criteria for a theory. It is grounded in a careful description of the reality of incumbent defeat and superintendent turnover, the Robertsdale ethnography (Lutz, 1962). That description has generated numerous hypotheses submitted to falsification testing. When they met an acceptable statistical confidence level, they were integrated into the theory and that theory became capable of predicting events. Thus, it is a theory.

Finally, *why* add the phrase ". . . of *American* Democracy?" We believe American democracy is unique. In many democracies citizens are required to vote. Failing that, in some democracies citizens may be fined or even put in jail. In America, citizens are given the right to vote but also the right not to vote. As often as not the American voter chooses not to vote. Such a condition favors the status quo and retention of incumbents. But incumbents should beware. Citizens have a lifetime pass to the ballot box. They may use that pass whenever they wish, and when they are dissatisfied enough they vote and incumbents are at risk.

Of considerable importance is the fact that the American democracy was founded upon the notion and expectation that elected officials have a sacred trust to represent the people in *ethical* ways. In what we today refer to in many nations as democracy, corruption and graft are often rampant, expected, and accepted as a way of life. Such behavior destroys American democracy. When 60 percent or more of the American people disapprove of what the president and Congress are doing, the American democracy is in danger. That is the real danger America faces today. If the American voters become so jaded that they expect their elected politicians to be unethical, when they think that all politicians are "crooks," when they believe it makes no difference whom they elect because things still won't change—our American democracy will die.

The local school district and local school district governance are unique to America. Nowhere else in the world, except Canada, is education governed by locally elected school boards. As we have said before, local school boards are "the crucible of democracy" (Iannaccone and Lutz, 1995). Local school elections in America provide the closest example of democracy for the American people. They are, or could be, the classroom wherein citizens can learn and practice American democracy. Thus, we have the Dissatisfaction Theory of American Democracy.

BUILDING THEORY

Occasionally doctoral students, unfortunately with the approval of a dissertation advisor, choose ethnography or case study as their research tool simply because they are inept at statistical design. After all, anybody can observe and write a description of what they have seen, can't they? Often such research is haphazard and done at the convenience of the observer. Such descriptions are not research and they are not ethnography. Good ethnography or case study should be the start, not the end, of educational research and theory. In such a manner, research and theory are *grounded* in reality. The criticism of many education practitioners that research is not practical is, in part, the result of the lack of grounding of research in the real world of education. Good ethnography or case study grounds research in the reality of society and culture.

The Robertsdale ethnography is the heart of the Dissatisfaction Theory (Lutz, 1962). It was based on three years of the careful recording of every piece of data related to the election and board member experience of Prentice, who served on that board and became president. Notes were made during or immediately after phone calls, whether in the afternoon or at twelve o'clock at night. Visits to local schools, administrators, and citizens were recorded when they happened. All agendas were saved along with printed financial data. Notes were made of conversations and expressions of sentiment during meetings. Descriptions were recorded of every meeting immediately after meetings, sometimes at one and two o'clock in the morning. The point here is not to instruct in ethnographic methodology. Rather it is to indicate that the Dissatisfaction Theory *is* grounded in the politics of school elections and of school board and administrative public and behind-the-scenes politics.

This book is about education political and policy research and their implication for education practitioners. It therefore seems reasonable to ask, "How does good research, in this case education political research, get accomplished?" In the 1930s and 1940s, the best we had to train and advise prospective and new superintendents was the sometimes insightful recollections of retired administrators and, occasionally, a school board member. This advice was grounded in *one* person's experience, usually remembered decades after the events and colored by years of personal hurts, professional glory, and often secondhand reporting.

Let me give you an example of one such report that we find funny and probably close to accurate. At an executive board meeting during the 1930s, a big-city superintendent was being given an unusually difficult time by a particular member of his school board. After some lengthy confrontation, the red-faced Irish superintendent rose and in a loud voice exclaimed, "For a thousand bucks I'd resign from this damn job!" That was a lot of money during the Great Depression. The board member who had been engaged in the conflict, who was quite wealthy, rose, removed a fine leather wallet from his inside coat pocket, and said as he peeled off 10 hundred-dollar bills and placed them on the table before the superintendent, "Go ahead, Mike, pick them up." The still red-faced superintendent slumped back in his big leather chair in the walnut-paneled boardroom, speechless.

That true story is grounded in the unchanged political reality of superintendents and board members even today. It is humorous and somewhat informative. It tells us that the superintendent's life is not always a bowl of cherries, and that boards do not always protect the superintendent, at least not in private. But it is hardly theory and does little to tell a superintendent how to handle other confrontations with school board members, even though Mike may have learned not to say something if he was not prepared to live it. (For your information, Mike survived that one.)

The point here is to suggest how education political research is accomplished and theory emerges. Political theory in education is badly needed today if public education is to survive. Universities are, or should be, places of inquiry. Universities, as opposed to training schools, have the mission of contributing to knowledge and *educating* individuals. Some may disagree with that position, which is one of the major discussions in the history of the University, but that is not the topic here. We are expressing our bias as a point of reference for what is to come. Research only takes place when it is encouraged, motivated, and rewarded. Theory only emerges after some time of well-thought-out theorizing and creative hypothesis-generating, followed by well-designed testing and thoughtful integration into the theory.

The development of theory usually takes funding of some sort, although the Dissatisfaction Theory never received any outside funding. But research requires more. It requires a culture of inquiry. At a university, it requires a program of professorial recruitment that makes explicit the role of research expected in the faculty. It requires the recruitment of doctoral students to study *with* those professors and for both to engage in a line of research, not just a random set of opportunistic encounters with anticipated benefits.

FERTILE GROUND FOR CULTIVATING A THEORY

The Graduate Institute of Education (GIE) at Washington University in St. Louis was just such a place. Under the leadership of Robert J. Schaefer, the GIE grew and prospered during the late 1950s and early 1960s. Professors were recruited who had a deep interest in education, in research, and in students. Having had some experience at professorial recruitment, we are well aware of the possible pitfalls of those who look good and make it and those who just do not live up to their promise. Whether fortuitous or not, the selection of the individuals at the GIE was, at that time, everything one could expect and more. All professors did research and published and many won national awards. All were interested in students and were in their offices with open doors to talk to students; not just chairs and committee members, but the entire faculty was available.

Lutz's first university position after his dissertation was at New York University (NYU), where Daniel E. Griffiths was Associate Dean for Research and then Dean of the College of Education. Many recall that Griffiths has been called the father of the theory movement in educational administration. He was also the prime mover in the establishment of the University Council for Educational Administration and a driving force for research and publication in educational administration programs. Those years with Griffiths certainly reinforced the values established at the GIE. A set of fortunate experiences brought Iannaccone to NYU for two of those years. He and Lutz took the same subway and bus routes to and from work and spent one day a week working together. That resulted in two coauthored books and the beginning of the Dissatisfaction Theory.

There were six full-time doctoral students who interacted with each other every day. For Lutz, it was an unforgettable experience. Decades later, he was visiting with Schaefer, then a close personal friend. They were walking along a beach and Schaefer asked, "Whatever happened to the very conservative young man who came into my office one day a long time ago, and asked to be admitted to the GIE? He wanted to be a school principal, as I recall." Lutz responded, "You and the GIE happened." That is what a graduate education should be. It should be a life-changing experience. And that is how education research and theory get started.

As research study follows research study, as dissertation follows dissertation, as professors develop a line of research, and sometimes their students follow the same course, theory is generated. Some graduates go into practice, but others into a professorship. When one is very lucky, interests merge and students follow a professor's general line of research. In the case of the Dissatisfaction Theory, two individuals worked together for decades off and on, and with their students, to produce what has become known as the Dissatisfaction Theory of American Democracy. That has been a most rewarding experience for both of us. No less than eight of the other authors in this book represent five generations of graduate student progeny emerging from Iannaccone and Lutz's original student-teacher relationship. In addition, dozens of other students and students of students have done research contributing to the Dissatisfaction Theory.

The point of this rather lengthy description is that for the pursuit of research and theory in education and, particularly, for our purposes here, the politics of education, several things are required. A university must foster such a goal. It must recruit research-oriented professors who are themselves engaged in research and theory building. It must provide resources, including scholarships, in order to recruit good students who study with those professors. Professors must be on campus to mentor those students. Lines of research must be developed, not just random topics pursued. Professors need faculty colleagues that hold the same values and are interested in interaction with each other about each other's research. While there may be individual exceptions, the above is the best way to foster research and theory. Additionally, neither the politics of education, nor education in general, make progress and improve without good research and theory building.

DEVELOPING QUALITY RESEARCH

As noted above, the Robertsdale case is ethnography in the classic sense of the word. More accurately, it is an ethnography describing the culture of a public school board operating in the early 1960s. School board cultures have not changed all that much in the ensuing decades. They still make most of their decisions in private and enact them in public. In other words, they tend to be elite councils (Richards and Kuper, 1971). The Robertsdale ethnography's original framework of analysis was a social systems framework using the concepts of activities, interaction, and sentiment as its tools of analysis (Homans, 1961). It was soon to be the subject of political analysis.

It is unnecessary to review the important and appropriate uses of good theory. Simply stated, theory provides practitioners with a means of acting with a specified confidence in a wide variety of situations under specified conditions. However, everything that is labeled a theory is not a theory. Additionally, "thinking like a researcher" can assist practitioners in making better decisions. Proposing a practical solution in hypothesis form can avoid the disaster of riding one's policy into the dark abyss of disaster. If one asks the question "Will this work under these circumstances?" and then collects data related to that question, one may find a workable solution. However, we must remember that research should always pose the negative question describing how something does not work. Thus stated, one has some hope of disproving the negative statement and making corrections in the description of reality before it is too late to be of use to practitioners in the field. Conversely, to seek the preferred or selected policy answer is to assure a biased answer and to court a failed policy. Additionally, "all that glitters is not gold." That is, all that appears to be research is not research. Perhaps some recent trends in education research have pushed research beyond the line.

The notion that one's belief or value orientation, psychic state, or philosophical position creates reality is beyond that line. Political correctness can distort scientific fact and cloud reality. True, the purely positivist orientation of education research had marginalized minority views, conditions, and voices. But just because one believes it so, even when others agree, does not make it so. Falsification remains the heart of good research. Elsewhere Lutz has written, "The fact that each of the three blind men saw a different 'reality' when they 'saw' the elephant does not change the fact that there is a real elephant. Each, after observation, had an image of the animal in their minds that was 'true' for that observer. That did not change the truth about what is an elephant" (Lutz, Watt, and Combs, 2006, p. 295). It is a good thing that positivism is not dead in education research.

New paradigms of research methodology have opened new vistas and understandings about education. They are helpful. But they may not be what are properly called research and may, in some unfortunate fashion, impede that research. Some present practitioners of our trade have suggested that this is so but suggest that to say it could be political suicide in the profession. That is at the heart of the problem in the current social/political milieu. To "preach truth to the powerful" could be a professional disaster! But not saying what you believe may prohibit the honest pursuit of important questions and promote tolerance of wrong ideas.

The renowned anthropologist Claude Levi-Strauss has written that magic and science are not bad and good ways of understanding human cultures. Rather, they are alternative ways. He says, "It [magic] forms a well-articulated system, and is in this respect independent of that other system which constitutes science . . . It is therefore better, instead of contrasting magic and science, to compare them as two parallel modes of acquiring knowledge" (Levi-Strauss, 1962, p. 13). Paraphrasing Levi-Strauss, it may be better not to contrast the new paradigms with positivistic research but rather to compare them as two parallel systems of inquiry.

More recently in an article in *Scientific American*, Krauss and Dawkins, described by the editors as "two prominent defenders of science," discuss science and faith (Krauss and Dawkins, 2007, p. 88). Krauss takes the position that, while some extreme positions in faith damage science or make it difficult for science to inform humankind, both science and faith have a place in our culture. He says:

> I do not think we will rid humanity of religious faith any more than we will rid humanity of romantic love or many of the irrational but fundamental aspects of human cognition. While orthogonal from the scientific rational components, they are no less real and perhaps no less worthy of some celebration when we consider our humanity. [Dawkins replies:] As an aside, such pessimism about humanity is popular among rationalists to the point of outright masochism. It is almost as though you and others . . . relish the idea that humanity is perpetually doomed to unreason. But I think irrationality has nothing to do with romantic love or poetry or the emotions that lie so close to what makes life worth living. Those are not orthogonal to rationality. Perhaps they are triangular to it. In any case, I am all for them, as are you. (Krauss and Dawkins, 2007, p. 90)

In a same fashion, we are not opposed to the new paradigms. We think they make a contribution to our field. But we believe they are different from what we refer to as research. Further, we believe public education and knowledge about its politics and policies cannot move forward and improve without good research.

POLICY STUDY VS. POLITICAL RESEARCH

Our discussion of political research cannot end without some mention of our views about the difference between political research and policy study and the meaning for theory and practice. A decade or so ago, policy study in education began to dominate the stage in the politics of education. This paralleled major increases in federal funding and the accompanying regulations for local school districts and states. As big dollars became available, so did the regulations and the questions about the success of the policy and the wisdom of continuing the policy. Usually school districts were not required to adopt the policy—but if they did not adopt, they received no funds. Few local districts or states could afford that luxury.

However, the question of the success of the policy was often left to an agency funded either directly or by contract from the agency that formulated or administrated that policy. Examples are so numerous that our readers require no examples. Simply put, when policy study is funded by the agency either initiating or funding the policy, the effort is often to prove the success of the policy rather than to question it. To what extent would anyone trust a study of the effects of smoking done by the tobacco companies?

As discussed earlier, research should rest on the effort to falsify and test the null or negatively stated hypothesis. A declaration of support for a theory is made only after finding that our null hypothesis was wrong. Policy study too often thrives when it finds what the policy's initiators want to hear. The effort is often not to find what is wrong with the policy but to find that it is working. If you had just put millions of dollars into some public program, how likely would you be, as an elected official, to tell your constituency that those millions were money down the drain? This is not a matter of partisan politics; it is a matter of human nature.

Policy study can be and sometimes has been useful. But, generally, it must be independent in order to be useful and trustworthy. Like research, it should be independently funded. When all pharmaceutical research is done by the big, for-profit corporations, the health of the American people is at risk. When research about national education policy is funded by the agencies that set those policies, American public education is at risk. At the very least, let's be sure that policy study does not push political research off the stage of public education research.

DISSATISFACTION THEORY AND ITS APPLICATIONS FOR PRACTITIONERS

Before explaining how the Dissatisfaction Theory was developed, it is important to understand that the suggested competition between it and the two other theories about the governance of local education in America (Wirt and Kirst's input-output theory and Zeigler's continuous participation theory) in our view is misleading. The theories are not as competitive as they are complementary. Each explains a different aspect of the politics of public school governance. Each posits a somewhat different thesis about the nature of democracy and, therefore, comes to a different conclusion of whether or not local education, governed by elected local school boards, is democratic. That is where they may be seen as competitive. In our chapters

(Iannaccone and Lutz, 1995, pp. 39-43; Lutz and Iannaccone, 1993, pp. 78-81), we have explained the differences in some detail, so we do not go into the detail here.

Zeigler et al. (1974) sees democracy as a matter of competition for office and participation by the voters in the election process. Finding there is often little competition for membership on the board and usually very low voter participation, they concluded the governance process to be undemocratic. The Wirt and Kirst (1992) input-output model looks at the public demands and compares those to policies the board enacts. As these may be commensurate, they suggest that democracy has worked. They find, however, that the policies (outputs) are seldom what the public had demanded (inputs). Therefore, they declare the governance process of local schools is usually undemocratic.

The Dissatisfaction Theory uniquely looks at the process in a longitudinal (diachronic) fashion. It suggests that in all aspects of our democracy, the American voter is often uninterested, usually fairly satisfied, somewhat uninformed, and doesn't bother to vote. But we point out that when the American voters become dissatisfied enough, they go to the polls and vote out the incumbents and install new representatives who, they hope, enact more satisfying polices. This we claim is the essence of American democracy, and therefore not only is the politics of local school governance democratic, it is one of the few remaining grassroots example of that democracy.

Actually the three theories together describe the complete overview of politics in the American republic. Democracy works best when there is competition for office and the people vote in large numbers. It is to be hoped that through this process of electing representatives of the people, those elected officials enact the policies expected by the people who elected them. When that doesn't happen, the people may become sufficiently dissatisfied and motivated to go to the polls and vote out the incumbents who failed to provide the policy they wanted. They expect the newly elected officials to enact the policies they want, or the voters also turn them out. That is American democracy.

Returning to the development of the Dissatisfaction Theory, based on the Robertsdale ethnography we posited a set of revised statements that accounted for the data in the three-year study. These provided a springboard for a series of research studies in an attempt to falsify or, failing that, to verify the statements. In *Public Participation in Local School Districts* (Lutz and Iannaccone, 1978), many of these are systematically reported so are not reported here in detail.

The 15 years following the original ethnographic study were very productive for the Dissatisfaction Theory. In 1966, three dissertations were completed. All basically verified the proposition that incumbent school board member defeat followed socioeconomic changes and was significantly related to superintendent turnover (Freeborn, 1966; Kirkendall, 1966; Walden, 1966). All were completed on the West Coast. Moen (1971) confirmed that the same phenomena were true in the partisan elections in Pennsylvania. Thus we felt fairly secure in asserting that school superintendents were in jeopardy when there were episodic shifts in socioeconomic indicators in their communities followed by the defeat of incumbent school board members.

As these studies also offered a set of precursors to incumbent defeat, we felt we had something important to say, not only to the school board member who wanted to stay in office but very importantly to superintendents who wanted to keep their jobs. However, in that same year, LeDoux (1971) completed a study in New Mexico that called these relationships into question. The findings reported by LeDoux and Burlingame (1973) had to be somehow integrated into the theory if the theory was to stand. Several years later, Lutz (1975) suggested that the relationship of superintendent turnover to incumbent defeat might not be as strong in school districts where socioeconomic indicators are turning down as they are in school districts where they are turning upward. This, he suggested, might be because politicians in such "down" communities might be pressured to respond more appropriately and quickly to the changing conditions in their communities than do politicians in "up" communities.

Garberina (1975), in a study in Massachusetts, posited a relationship between incumbent defeat and superintendent turnover using a set of socioeconomic indicators describing the "up" or "down" socioeconomic conditions in each school district. Using these predictors he again found a significant statistical relationship between incumbent defeat and superintendent turnover. Thus, the theory was becoming more sophisticated and predictive. Essentially, it was now clear that school boards and their superintendents are more likely to recognize and respond to downward socioeconomic trends than they are to upward trends. Where boards did not respond, it seemed superintendents were sometimes perceived as having attempted to be responsive. In such cases, these superintendents were more likely to survive after incumbent school board member defeat.

During this same 15-year period, two other studies stimulated by the Dissatisfaction Model and the Robertsdale ethnography were completed. Noting the election returns reported in the tax battle in Robertsdale, Spinner (1967) completed a study of school financial elections in New York State. In the Robertsdale case, an episode was observed where Prentice led the district in an effort to increase the tax levy in order to increase teacher salaries and significantly add to the high school curricular offerings. The tax proposal was first defeated by a fairly large margin; a second attempt also lost but by less of a margin. Finally it succeeded as the total vote continued to increase, and the yes votes finally exceeded the no votes, which had remained stable through the three elections. The question explored in the Spinner research was whether this pattern was unique or could be typically expected if defeated tax issues were resubmitted.

Carter and Savard (1961) suggested that as voter turnout increased, fiscal school elections stood a greater chance of losing. The Robertsdale data suggested that while this was partially correct, it missed an important point: In elections where propositions to support needed educational efforts lost and were resubmitted to the electorate, the proposition was likely to pass as the turnout continued to increase. This, it was suggested, was because the electorate was originally poorly informed and had expected the issue to pass. Many "yes voters" had stayed at home. The yes voters' participation increased in subsequent elections until the issue finally passed. In future tax elections after the tax passed, the voter turnout returned to its original and stable pattern with lower voter turnout, and the issue usually passed.

Spinner tested this notion in New York State elections using percentage of turnout rather than actual no/yes response as a measure. What he found confirmed that the voter behavior in school tax elections described in the Robertsdale case was consistent with the voter behavior in the New York elections, thus increasing the scope of the Dissatisfaction Theory and expanding the meaning of the Carter research.

A second study conducted by Cistone (1970) recognized the relationship between what appeared to be a changing political culture in Robertsdale and turnover on the school board with incumbent defeat leading to superintendent turnover. He sought to explore the relationship between political values and political culture, and the type of governance in that political entity. Citizens in Pennsylvania's local municipalities had been given the opportunity to select whether they wanted the city manager or mayoral form of governance (similar to but not exactly like machine vs. reform, or public-regarding vs. private-regarding politics).

He explored the relationship between the choice of municipal governance and the degree of professional freedom that elected school boards gave their appointed school superintendent. He posited that communities choosing the city manager form would also select school boards that gave the appointed school superintendents a greater degree of professional freedom. In other words, the board members, like the general electorate, preferred professional control of the public's business. That hypothesis was confirmed at a statistically significant level. Thus, we could say that political cultures tended to dominate across different aspects of the political governance in the community. This congruence was the beginning point in the Robertsdale case. Only when socioeconomic and value changes had taken place, caused by changes in population size, had political change in the

Robertsdale school board occurred. Again the Dissatisfaction Model was enriched and supported.

One of the problems with the Dissatisfaction Theory, when it came to the practical politics of school board members and superintendents, was a matter of political timing. It was clear that when an incumbent school board member was defeated, the superintendent was in real trouble. Actually, it was already too late for that board member and very late for the superintendent to do much about it. *In Politics, Power, and Policy,* Iannaccone and Lutz (1970) have a chapter titled "Mene, Mene, Tekel, Upharsin"—roughly translated, "It is finished; you have been weighed in the balance and found wanting; your kingdom is divided." That was the problem. Although the chapter relates many events that led to the incumbent defeat and these events continued through the second defeat in Robertsdale, it suggests that once the first incumbent defeat had occurred, it was over for the incumbent superintendent and for school politics as it had occurred before.

The chapter notes the Walden study (1966), which demonstrated that one incumbent defeat was sufficient to predict the demise of the superintendent. "It was finished!" All that could be suggested was that school board members and superintendents, like all good politicians, should always keep their finger on the pulse of the public(s) and note changes in population, values, and voter sentiment and demands. Not bad advice in any case. Smart superintendents do not totally rely on the school board for their information about these matters, and school board members should not rely only on the superintendent for their information. That pattern is obviously circular, self-fulfilling, and self-defeating. Yet the problem remained: What is the best way to predict incumbent defeat of a school board member and the superintendent?

Thorsted (1974), working with Mitchell, developed the Thorsted index, using a ratio of indicators that seemed to predict political unrest and incumbent defeat. However, Hunt (1980), using socioeconomic data and an incumbent defeat index, failed to predict incumbent defeat in an Ohio school district. This was the first time since the LeDoux study that the relationship between incumbent defeat and superintendent turnover had been challenged. Wang and Lutz (1989) reanalyzed the Hunt data and using the same target election developed a formula that they called the "Dissat-factor." That formula is: Dissat-factor equals one minus the quotient of the number of seats available divided by the number of incumbents running plus the number of challengers. This enabled the production of a statistical model that would have predicted the target Ohio election results. Working with Texas school districts and using the Dissat-factor, Wang (1989) was able to predict incumbent defeat in a target election in Texas, again confirming the Dissatisfaction Model and strengthening the theory.

OTHER ISSUES TANGENT TO DISSATISFACTION THEORY

Superintendent Resiliency

Some other issues, not directly within the Dissatisfaction Theory, are of considerable interest, particularly to practitioners. As the theory is centrally concerned with superintendent turnover, some of our work has been interested in the issue of superintendent mobility. We begin here with Callahan's (1962) *Education and the Cult of Efficiency*, which established the concept of "superintendent vulnerability." This concept holds that due to the conflict between a professional superintendent trying to make good educational decisions and a school board making conservative fiscal decisions, superintendents are in a state of constant vulnerability that sometimes costs them their jobs.

Wisener (1996, p. 57) states that in a personal communication Iannaccone told her that "Vulnerability is an underpinning thesis of his and Lutz's 'dissatisfaction theory' work" and Lutz said that the explanation of superintendent vulnerability is central to the Dissatisfaction Theory. Vulnerability, however, may have played an unintended role in the development of the myth of the superintendent's role. It may have led to an attitude of "pity the poor superintendent," which fosters a solid position where the superintendent may retreat when in trouble and an attitude that the board should be working to help the superintendent instead of the superintendent working to help the board.

In a sample of 260 Texas superintendents who had changed their positions within the four previous years, Parker reported that mobility among these superintendents did not appear to be the pressured kind, or at least not the emotionally difficult kind suggested by the notion of vulnerability. She reports that most superintendents moved up and to better salaries and larger school districts. Not one reported that his or her move was due to disagreement over business valuing issues. Most who reported major issues with the board were from smaller school districts; and the issues tended to be over who should or should not graduate, hiring or firing a particular individual, or other "board involvement in petty matters" (Parker, 1996, p. 77).

Taylor began with a sample of 700 randomly selected members of AASA. Of these, 544 responded and 302 of these reported that they had changed positions sometime in their career. Surveying those individuals, Taylor found that "superintendents who experienced mobility, whatever the reason for that move, did not suffer great losses, in fact, tended to improve positions. Mobility is not explained by vulnerability unique to the superintendency" (Taylor, 1996, p. 155).

But mobility is not the same as vulnerability. Merrell interviewed, by phone, 115 of the superintendents who had returned questionnaires in the

Taylor (1996) study. While agreeing with Parker and Taylor about the lack of *loss* in superintendent mobility, she reported some very interesting findings. She concluded, "Political pressures remain an area of 'vulnerability' for superintendents and their families and serve to reaffirm the relevancy of Raymond Callahan's "vulnerability thesis" (Merrell, 1997, p. 118).

Both Merrell (1997) and Brinson (1998) report similar findings. Both found that in retrospect, spouses of retired superintendents, both male and female, reported satisfaction with having been in that role and that "it was all worth it." That finding is interesting, as the data are clear that perhaps the highest price paid in the pressure tank of the superintendency position is to be paid by the superintendent's spouse and children. So vulnerability remains a central issue in the Dissatisfaction Theory.

Sometimes superintendents keep their positions because board incumbents fail to fire them in the face of community opposition. Those incumbents then lose their seats on the board to challengers who after winning the next election usually fire the superintendent. Sometimes superintendents lose their jobs because boards are trying to satisfy an electorate who wants the superintendent fired. In either case, superintendents are clearly a central actor in the Dissatisfaction Theory.

School Voter Behavior

A second tangent issue to our theory is voter behavior in school financial elections. For various reasons the focus of our research has been school bond elections. In their article Lutz and Smith (1990), using a sample of 290 voters over the age of 50, describe older voter behavior in school bond elections. They report that older voters, unlike the well-believed myth, are not much different than their younger counterparts. They tend to think they should support public education and when they vote in bond elections they tend to vote yes.

Voters who were approaching retirement age showed a slightly lower degree of support until they reached retirement age, and from then on the majority of all voters over 65 reported voting for the bond issue. One hundred percent of all reporting who were over 75 reported voting yes. One might suggest, based on this study, that a minority of older voters, like all voters who are less informed, less directly involved, or less pleased about the issue, tend not to vote or vote no.

Riehl (1991) studied a random sample of 360 Catholics and 360 non-Catholics in north-central Texas. He found that Catholics reported a slightly higher voter turnout rate in both regular school elections and in bond referendums than did non-Catholic voters. They also tended to report slightly higher support for public school bond issues than non-Catholics. This again destroys a popular myth about voter behavior. In general he found that Catholics reported approximately the same voting behavior in school elections as did non-Catholics.

Lutz and Foerch (1990) looked directly at the ability of the Dissat-factor to predict bond elections. They found that when dissatisfaction was high, defeat of the bond issue was high. However, they also found that some dissatisfaction was necessary for the bond issue to pass. There was the possibility that dissatisfaction was related to some need addressed in the bond issue. Predictors of failure were school board incumbent defeat within the past nine years and also superintendent turnover in the past nine years. There was no relationship to the size of the bond issue proposed or the intended purpose. There was a small empirical, but not statistically significant, tendency for defeat to be linked to higher voter turnout. Perhaps this is because defeated issues are often not proposed again when voter turnout seems likely to increase again and issues seem to pass.

Lutz and McGehee (1994) took a bit more oblique tack. They looked at how voter psychological satisfaction might affect the election. Using the concepts of "hygienes" and "motivators" (Herzberg, 1959), they found that "hygienes"—for example, the tendency to hold that schools were safe and children were being educated—were sufficient to prevent voters from voting against the bond issue but not sufficient for them to bother to vote for it. They tended to stay at home. Voters who had "motivators"—for example, those working for the school district or having a child that played on the football team, in the band, or on the debate team—tended to vote for the bond issue. Voters lacking both hygienes and motivators tended to vote against a bond issue.

As motivators are more difficult and expensive to produce, school boards can be advised to concentrate on the hygienes, using their public relations programs and targeting the different publics in the district. Thus, long before Karl Rove, we were telling school boards and superintendents that to win school bond referendums they had to identify and pay attention to the individual and different publics in their school districts.

A POSTSCRIPT ON THE RESEARCH

An article by Alsbury (2003) describes a study employing both quantitative and qualitative data and analyses. While four previous studies reported by Weller et al. (1991) examined the relationship between incumbent defeat and superintendent turnover and failed to confirm the relationship, Alsbury replaced the routine method of using ex post facto data to classify the nature of incumbent defeat as either political or apolitical. Still, only one of four analyses done according to time periods demonstrated a significant relationship between the variables. What was wrong? Using case study data collection methods and analysis procedures, Alsbury chose the school district within the sample that seemed to produce the most deviant case among districts in the nonsignificant group. When he examined those data, it became clear that the actual district politics mirrored the conditions that the Dissatisfaction Model described.

Eleven turnovers on the board that had been categorized as school board member defeats without superintendent turnover in the original study were actually eleven apolitical school board member retirements from the board. The single superintendent turnover during the case study period followed a three-year period when there was increased voter turnout, more challengers, and three political defeats on the board. That is exactly what the Dissatisfaction Theory would have predicted. It was the quantitative data categorization that had failed. Alsbury suggests that his study actually supports the theory, and suggests

> the necessity of in-depth data analysis of all districts that do not seem to follow the Dissatisfaction theory model before making conclusions about the efficacy of the theory. . . . Future research of [the model] should include distinctions between political and apolitical school board and superintendent turnover. (Alsbury, 2003, p. 689)

At this point a lot has been said about the research that went into the development of the Dissatisfaction Theory. If one isn't convinced, there is a lot more information contained in works reported in the references and more could be found in an extensive literature search. Perhaps we can now turn to a few generalizations about the larger body politic and offer some suggestions as to how this theory might be used to assist practitioners and develop new research.

IMPLICATIONS FOR SCHOOL BOARD MEMBERS AND SUPERINTENDENTS

While we know of no research that directly demonstrates that the Dissatisfaction Theory accounts for phenomena in the general world of American politics, most of us can recall considerable political comment suggesting that to be the case. Probably without ever hearing of the Dissatisfaction Theory, political news commentators have discussed periods when major changes have occurred in our national political arena following periods of intense citizen dissatisfaction. Situations like Newt Gingrich's "Contract with America," when the Republican Party took control of the Congress and kept it for years, the Reagan era, and when Clinton after riding high fell to a historic low, allowing the current president to win the presidency and

Republicans to take control of both houses of Congress, all come immediately to mind.

More recently, political commentators have pointed to the low approval of President Bush, followed by the Democratic takeover of both houses of the Congress in 2006, as an example. Most political commentators suggest that after citizens judge events as sufficiently wrong, have expressed considerable dissatisfaction, and fail to get the change they demand, they go to the polls and vote the incumbents out of office. Then, perhaps, policy is changed. That is exactly what the Dissatisfaction Theory of American Democracy describes and predicts.

Founded in the crucible of the American democracy of the local school district, the model emerges as the best example of what democracy in America is all about. What follows are some suggestions that we offer to the practitioners who administer our schools and the school boards that govern them, with the hope that better governance might produce better education. It should be noted that the issue of school board influence on student success was recently confirmed by Alsbury (forthcoming), who found a relationship between incumbent defeat, superintendent turnover, and student academic achievement.

Some suggestions for school board members and superintendents based on the Dissatisfaction Theory of American Democracy include the following:

1. In spite of a "few bumps in the road," the Dissatisfaction Theory of American Democracy remains the best description of the politics of education in independent school districts in America. It proposes that when American voters become dissatisfied enough, they go to the polls and exercise their right to vote, and vote the incumbents who created the dissatisfying policies out of office. The model suggests that in this way the citizens of a school district can get what they want and therefore probably get what they deserve. After incumbent defeat, newly elected officials create more satisfying policies or risk defeat at the next election. This theory may also describe and predict general American politics.

2. Both superintendents and school board members should keep careful track of the population, socioeconomic, ethnic, and value changes occurring in their school districts. Simple labels may mask data and not be sufficient. Superintendent mobility is not always turnover caused by political pressures or dismissals. An incumbent's name no longer appearing on the roster in the public school report does not necessarily signify a political defeat of that board member.

3. Single-interest groups are groups that are interested in your schools, in one fashion or another. "Recognize the diverse and pluralistic val-

ues, aspirations, and wants represented within the community. [They are] . . . not to be shunned and beaten down but to be heard, understood, and helped [to feel somewhat important]" (Lutz and Merz, 1992, p. 53).

4. Some political pundits have suggested that local school boards have become irrelevant or actually harmful to needed reform and higher achievement in public education in the United States. Nothing could be further from the truth. Our model suggests that through the process described, citizens can change local education policy and obtain the level of education they choose and are willing to support.

5. Local school districts and local school boards are not only a historical tradition in our nation; they are the grassroots example of American democracy. The political process described in the Dissatisfaction Theory is the best approach to teach American governance, with school boards offering the most accessible classroom. It is immediately at hand, just at our fingertips. Public education is a matter of some interest to all citizens and of major importance to many. Give up local school governance *very* reluctantly! It is a grand example of exactly what our American republic is all about: the right to educate *all* of our children as "we the people" choose, and the right to govern ourselves in a free and equitable republic.

ADDITIONAL CONSIDERATIONS

The following is not offered based on research nor based directly on the Dissatisfaction Theory research as are the above suggestions, but rather on nine decades of working in the professorship; observing school practitioners and school boards; and teaching school administration, politics in education, and occasionally ethics. They are offered for your consideration based on just what school administrators often accuse professors of having too little of: practical experience.

1. Rules are made to be broken and sometimes should be broken if justice is to be served. The statement "You are right, but we cannot make any exceptions" always earns new political enemies. Still, indiscriminately breaking rules based on personal preference surely gets you into difficultly. So, don't make too many detailed rules. Rather, establish broad policy to cover the generalized case and allow qualified and knowledgeable administrators on the scene some situational latitude. These exceptions should always be officially reviewed and documented, rationally defensible, and used to determine if and how policy should be modified to improve the organization.

2. The claim to occupy the "moral high ground" can be dangerous. It suggests that you have the only morally correct decision and those who disagree are immoral. One cannot change such a decision without being seen as immoral, either then or now. Sometimes you may want to change a decision. You don't want to be seen as a "flip-flopper." Often the only decision that can be practically implemented is a choice between two or more poor but possible decisions. The good decision is no longer possible due to conditions beyond your control. An ethical decision is impossible. What is required is to have a working philosophy and make an ethically defensible decision within that philosophical framework.

3. Ethics is not a matter of following six or so simple two-line rules. Ethical behavior requires the development of a working philosophy used so that one can make decisions and then examine those decisions over time. One has to work at being ethical. It is not as simple as following a set of simple rules. Being ethical is always a work in progress and never a matter of self-affirmation.

REFERENCES

Alsbury, T. L. 2003. Superintendent and school board member turnover: Political versus apolitical turnover as a critical variable in the application of the Dissatisfaction Theory. *Educational Administration Quarterly* 39:667–697.

———. Forthcoming. School board member and superintendent turnover and the influence on student achievement: An application of the Dissatisfaction Theory. *Leadership and Policy in Schools* 7.

Brinson, K. H. 1998. The impact of the superintendency on the spouses and families of retired public school superintendents. Paper presented at the annual meeting of the American Educational Research Association, San Diego.

Callahan, R. E. 1962. *Education and the cult of efficiency: A study of the social forces that have shaped the administration of public education.* Chicago: University of Chicago Press.

Carter, R. F., and W. G. Savard. 1961. *Influence of voter turnout on school bond tax elections.* Washington, DC: Government Printing Office.

Cistone, P. J. 1970. Formal government structures and the school board–superintendent relationship. PhD diss., The Pennsylvania State University.

Freeborn, R. M. 1966. School board change and the succession patterns of superintendents. PhD diss., Claremont Graduate University.

Garberina, W., Sr. 1975. Public demands, school board response and incumbent defeat: An examination of the governance of local school districts in Massachusetts. PhD diss., The Pennsylvania State University.

Herzberg, F. 1959. *The motivation to work.* New York: John Wiley.

Homans, G. C. 1961. *Social behavior: Its elementary forms.* New York: Harcourt Brace.

Hunt, B. P. 1980. An inductive approach to the Dissatisfaction Theory in the governance of local school districts: Predicting incumbent school member defeat. PhD diss., The Pennsylvania State University.

Iannaccone, L., and F. W. Lutz. 1970. *Politics, power, and policy.* Columbus, OH: Merrill.

———. 1995. The crucible of democracy: The local arena. In *The study of educational politics*, ed. J. D. Scribner and D. H. London, 39–52. Washington, DC: Falmer.

Kirkendall, R. S. 1966. Discriminating social, economic and political characteristics of changing versus stable policy-making systems in school districts. PhD diss., Claremont Graduate University.

Krauss, L. M., and R. Dawkins. 2007. Should science speak to faith? *Scientific American* 297 (July): 88–91.

LeDoux, E. P. 1971. Outmigration: Its relation to social, political and economic conditions and the governing of local school districts in New Mexico. PhD diss., University of New Mexico.

LeDoux, E., and M. Burlingame. 1973. The Iannaccone-Lutz model of school board change: A replication in New Mexico. *Educational Administration Quarterly* 9 (3): 48–65.

Levi-Strauss, C. 1962. *The savage mind.* Chicago: University of Chicago Press.

Lutz, F. W. 1962. Social systems and school districts: A study of the interactions and sentiments of a school board. PhD diss., Washington University.

———. 1975. The role of explanatory models in theory building. *Educational Administration Quarterly* 11 (1): 72–78.

Lutz, F. W., and D. B. Foerch. 1990. The politics of passing local school bond elections. *Journal of School Business Management* 2 (1): 63–73.

Lutz, F. W., and L. Iannaccone, eds. 1978. *Public participation in local school districts.* Lexington, MA: Lexington Books.

———. 1993. Policy and policymakers in urban education. In *Handbook of schooling in urban education*, ed. S. W. Rothstein, 73–90. Westport, CT: Greenwood Press.

Lutz, F. W., and K. P. McGehee. 1994. Passing school bond issues. *Journal of School Business Management* 6 (1): 13–20.

Lutz, F. W., and C. Merz. 1992. *The politics of school/community relations.* New York: Teachers College Press.

Lutz, F. W., and M. D. Smith. 1990. How do older voters affect school bond elections? *Journal of School Business Management* 2 (2): 11–34.

Lutz, F. W., K. Watt, and J. P. Combs. 2006. *Practical theory in educational administration: Texas public school organization and administration, 2006.* Dubuque, IA: Kendall/Hunt.

Menand, L. 2007. Fractured franchise. *New Yorker* (July): 86–91.

Merrell, L. 1997. The effect of political vulnerability upon superintendents and their families. PhD diss., Texas A & M University.

Moen, A. W. 1971. Superintendent turnover as predicted by school board incumbent defeat. PhD diss., The Pennsylvania State University.

Parker, P. 1996. Superintendent vulnerability and mobility. *Peabody Journal of Education* 71 (2): 64–77.

Richards, A., and A. Kuper. 1971. *Councils in action.* Cambridge: Cambridge University Press.

Riehl, A. T. 1991. A study of voter behavior of Catholics in school bond referendums. PhD diss., Texas A & M University.

Spinner, A. 1967. The effects of the extent of voter participation upon election outcomes in school budget elections. PhD diss., New York University.

Taylor, R. R. 1996. Vulnerability and its effect on the mobility of superintendents. PhD diss., Texas A & M University.

Thorsted, R. R. 1974. Predicting school board member defeat: Demographic and political variables that influence board elections. PhD diss., University of California, Riverside.

Walden, J. C. 1966. School board changes and involuntary superintendent turnover. PhD diss., Claremont Graduate University.

Wang, L. 1989. School board election prediction in Texas. PhD diss., Texas A & M University.

Wang, L., and F. W. Lutz. 1989. The dissat-factor: Recent discoveries in the Dissatisfaction Theory. *Educational Administration Quarterly* 25:358–376.

Weller, D. L., C. L. Brown, and K. L. Flynn. 1991. Superintendent turnover and school board member defeat: A new perspective and interpretation. *Journal of Educational Administration* 29:61–72.

Wisener, B. F. 1996. Influence of Callahan's vulnerability thesis on thought and practice in educational administration, 1962–1992. *Peabody Journal of Education* 71 (2): 41–63.

Zeigler, L. H., L. H. Jennings, and G. W. Peak. 1974. *Governing American schools: Political interaction in local school districts.* North Scituate, MA: Duxbury Press.

2

School Board Research:
A Retrospective

Peter J. Cistone

It does not seem possible that more than three decades have passed since the National School Boards Association convened an invitational symposium in April 1975 on the theme "School Board Research: Main Lines of Inquiry." Fourteen scholars from across North America were invited to participate in the symposium and to each prepare a state-of-the-art paper on a specific facet of school board research.

The papers were subsequently revised, in light of the discussions in the course of the symposium, and compiled in a book titled *Understanding School Boards: Problems and Prospects* (Cistone, 1975). The chapters reviewed, analyzed, and synthesized disciplined inquiry into various dimensions of the school board and suggested the most promising directions for future inquiry.

The present chapter is intended to offer a reflective statement on the main themes and issues that marked the 1975 symposium and to suggest some promising directions for future inquiry on the school board. It is not intended to be a historical review of the research literature on school boards, but rather to serve the purpose of furthering the discussion and debate on the scope, quality, and impact of that research.

CHANGING CONTEXTS AND SCHOOL BOARD RESEARCH

Historically, school board studies tended to reflect the dominant ideology of educational governance that emerged out of the reform era early in the

20th century. The ideology held that education is and ought to be a unique governmental function requiring unique constitutional, statutory, political, and administrative arrangements. The ideology was so pervasive and powerful that it conditioned the agenda and nature of school board research. The deliberate isolation and autonomy granted to the educational system oriented research to the internal functioning of the school system without due consideration of the organization in interaction with its multiple environments within a system of polycentric power. There was a conspicuous lack of focus on the governmental aspects of school systems, on the political characteristics of school boards, and on the political behavior of either individual school board members or boards as collectives.

Beginning in the mid-1960s, the social and political environment of educational organizations has been evolving from placid-field to turbulent-field conditions. We noted in *Understanding School Boards* that the external environment of the school board, as of virtually all public organizations, was undergoing rapid and profound transformation. In the past, that environment was relatively stable and placid; today it is increasingly unstable and problematic. Consequently, the insularity that once characterized the school board is being eroded under the powerful impact of social, economic, and political pressures. Not only are these pressures impinging on the school board, they are constraining and shaping its behavior as well. The need to respond and adapt to the external situation is precipitating changes in the personality and character of the school board itself.

Since 1975, research on the school board has increased incrementally, if not systematically. Earlier studies, which were preoccupied with internal procedures of school boards, have given way to open-system approaches that explore the dynamic interrelationship of school boards and their environments.

Regrettably absent from the more recent development of school board research has been a deliberate debate on theoretical and methodological perspectives. Conceptual and theoretical development is clearly peripheral to the field of school board research. Just as there is no grand theory of politics or of educational governance, there is no grand theoretical framework concerning the school board as an institution of government. Merton's observation on sociology aptly applies to school board research today: "We have many concepts but fewer confirmed theories; many points of view, but few theorems; many 'approaches' but few arrivals" (Merton, 1957, p. 52). Despite the growing recognition of the complementary relationship between theory and empirical research, the inventory of school board studies empirically testing theoretically deduced hypotheses is small.

A noteworthy exception to this general "nontheoretical consensus" in the field of school board studies is the seminal conceptual formulation of Iannaccone and Lutz (Iannaccone and Lutz, 1970; Lutz and Iannaccone,

1978). Their "Dissatisfaction Theory," as they termed it, has guided much empirical research, which has both refined and challenged the original explanatory model.

In a discussion of the perceived limitations of extant research on school boards, Land inferred that the school board literature is "rife with conclusions and recommendations based on personal experience, observations, and opinions" (Land, 2002, p. 265) and a heavy reliance on anecdotal evidence rather than on well-designed research studies. The failure to operationalize variables was also seen as another methodological weakness in much of the literature. Yet another serious impediment to the development of a solid research base is the "failure of studies of educational governance to treat the school board as a discrete unit of analysis" (Land, 2002, p. 266).

The study of the collective behavior of school boards has not approached the level of precision or rigor found in studies of individual member behavior. Historically, studies of school boards have tended to examine the behavior of members as individuals but not the behavior of the school board as a collective. Moving from the level of individual behavior to the level of collective behavior engenders methodological and theoretical issues. But preoccupation with individual (micro-level) analyses to the neglect of collective (macro-level) studies, and vice versa, renders an incomplete understanding of the simultaneity of individual and collective action.

THE 1975 SYMPOSIUM: MAIN THEMES AND ISSUES

The papers presented at the 1975 symposium "School Board Research: Main Lines of Inquiry" were intended to review, analyze, and synthesize disciplined inquiry into various dimensions of the school board. They attempted not only to assess the state of the knowledge on the school board but also to project past and emerging trends and to suggest the most promising directions for future inquiry. They were primarily centered on substantive issues, but they did not neglect technical or methodological considerations, although these were of secondary importance.

At the time it seemed important to me, as the symposium chairperson, to reinforce with my fellow colleagues and presenters that the emphasis of the symposium was on the critical assessment of empirical research in the scientific tradition. However, we were agreed that disciplined inquiry, while it includes empirical research, is by no means limited to it. An understanding of the school board must include the historical, the cultural, the philosophical, and the pragmatic, not all of which may be accessible to the "scientific method." Therefore, empirical research notwithstanding, the symposium papers made judgments about the quality, meaning, and relevance of the knowledge produced through disciplined inquiry that employs various perspectives, methods, and techniques.

The symposium papers were organized around six main divisions that were constructed on the basis of perceived topical concerns in the body of disciplined inquiry into the school board at that point in time. Just as there was no overarching theoretical framework to guide school board inquiry at the time, there was no overarching framework governing the papers presented at the 1975 symposium. The six main divisions were titled, respectively: (a) The School Board as a Target of Research, (b) The School Board as an Institution, (c) The School Board and Authority Relations, (d) The School Board and Community Structures, (e) The School Board and Community Demands and Supports, and (f) Future Perspectives on School Board Research and the Viability of the School Board.

Despite the variety and range of perspectives that were articulated at the 1975 symposium, several cross-cutting themes and issues were discernible in the papers presented and in the discussions that ensued in the course of the symposium. In order to convey a sense of those themes and issues, we now turn to a summary and synthesis of a certain few of those papers, although such an approach does not do justice to the contributions made by all of the symposium papers.

The School Board as a Target of Research

In his assessment of school board research, L. Harmon Zeigler contended that the uncritical borrowing of concepts and methodologies from the social sciences generated problems for the field. In his paper, he called for the abandonment of the case study approach in favor of both longitudinal and comparative studies of school boards. He contended that the school board (not the individual school board member) should be the basic unit of analysis, and that the school board as an institution should be studied as it interacts with other units in the family of governments.

As indicated earlier, despite a growing awareness of the complementary relationship between theory and empirical research, much of the research on school boards remains more disposed to description, historicism, and chronology. With respect to the debate over approaches and methods, the crucial point is that both quantitative and qualitative studies are essential to building the body of research on school boards; neither one alone is satisfactory.

The School Board as an Institution

Since Counts's description of the socioeconomic composition of school boards (1927), there have been literally hundreds of studies on school board member recruitment. The typical study has treated recruitment as an aggregate variable, comparing the socioeconomic attributes of board members with the demographic profile of their communities and then drawing inferences about the boards' statistical representativeness.

In our own symposium paper on the recruitment and socialization of school board members, we noted that the research literature on recruitment and socialization was generally lean and particularly deficient on the topic of socialization. The etiology of this condition was related to several factors, not the least of which was the nature of the conceptualizations of these dynamic processes that had guided research in the past.

These conceptualizations tended to be either too institutional or too individual. In the former case, emphasis is placed on institutional variables, such as nonpartisanship, and inferences are drawn about their impact on individuals. In the latter case, emphasis is placed on individual variables, such as personal traits or characteristics, and inferences are made about their impact on institutions and institutional behavior. Both approaches are useful but either used alone is prone to faulty inferences.

Research studies on school member recruitment have not incorporated individual and institutional variables in the same analysis. What is known is that, compared with the general public, school board members come disproportionately from groups with high social status. They tend to be white, middle-aged, male professionals, married, with children in the schools, and active in the organizational and associational life of the community. Evidently, school board members are not chosen in proportionate numbers from all population groupings and are not demographically representative of the population at large.

On the basis of accumulated findings produced by hundreds of studies of the social composition of school boards over the past 75 years or so, the stability of the social profile is striking, particularly in the light of the sweeping transformations that have occurred in the social, economic, and political environments of school boards. That is to say, the profiles of the communities have changed, but the social composition of school boards has remained fairly constant.

In his treatment of school boards as sociocultural systems, Frank W. Lutz contended that culture is a critical concept to understanding and evaluating local school board behavior. The paper was organized around five propositions: (a) all educational decisions are either political decisions or have political implications; (b) local school boards are the decision makers regarding specific public education programs at the local level, regardless of the wide range of pressures from all levels; (c) local school boards are themselves sociocultural systems and behave in ways dictated by prescribed cultural parameters; (d) local school boards are elected or appointed to serve larger, more heterogeneous cultures (school districts) whose subcultures may have needs, values, expectations, and aspirations that differ from those of the school board; and (e) a monolithic decision-making system cannot effectively serve a heterogeneous culture and, further, any one decision made by the local school board will likely advantage one subculture of the school district while disadvantaging another in the heterogeneous culture. In other words, political culture—the collective orientation of a society toward the basic elements of its political system—accounts for variations in political patterns and policies, and influences the tone, style, and substance of educational governance.

The School Board and Authority Relations

Viewing local school districts in theoretical perspective, Edith K. Mosher explored the extent to which educational government is enmeshed in extended and complex "family relationships" with other levels and units of government. One promising initiative identified by Mosher was that researchers were seeking ways to integrate scattered, partial inquiries by developing conceptual maps of the complex world of educational government.

Intergovernmental relations in the latter half of the 20th century have been characterized by an elaborate and complex set of interactions among national, state, and local units of government. The notion of a distinct division of powers and responsibilities among governmental levels and units actually obscures the operational realities of educational governance. The American system is one in which powers and responsibilities are shared among the three levels of government—the local school district, the state, and the federal government. Each of the three levels maintains autonomy in some areas of educational policy, but in practice these autonomous levels of educational government interact and have a system of mutual obligation and dependence. Indeed, the concept of "dual sovereignty" refers to the degree to which each level of educational government acts as a relatively autonomous entity with separate sources of legitimacy and authority—in particular, the degree to which the local school district is independent of state educational authority.

The relationship between the school board and superintendent is the focal point for local educational policy making. There are other participants in the process: teachers, other staff, citizens and stakeholders, children, and personnel in other levels and units of government. The critical nexus, however, is the link between the board and the superintendent.

In his paper, William L. Boyd posits that the key variables that bear on the school board–administrative staff relationship are (a) community characteristics, (b) personal characteristics of school authorities, (c) school government characteristics, (d) school system characteristics, (e) type of issue, and (f) relevant resources. The paper addresses the weaknesses and imbalances in these relationships and suggests that the problems are most acute in larger and more heterogeneous school districts, although districts of all kinds experience the need to seek an appropriate and functional balance in such relationships.

In some cases, the resources of superintendents cause boards to defer to them in the allocation of authority—the "rank" authority of a board conceding to the "technical" authority of a superintendent. Conversely, if school boards were to maximize their main resource, formal authority, boards would emerge as the dominant partner in the relationship.

The School Board and Community Structures

When the American school board is studied as a political system, Frederick M. Wirt argued in his paper, one clear theme emerges: It is losing its power. The forces that have accomplished that diminution arise from both within and outside the district. According to Wirt, those forces are (a) the alteration of the intergovernmental context in which local schools operate, (b) a new intensity in the pressure-group context of the local schools, (c) an intensification of professionalism in the delivery of school services, and (d) the differentiating effect of political cultures when imposed upon the mosaic of American education. The spasms of change that ripple across the school system arise out of the interaction of these four forces, suggesting the need for a concept of social change that might serve to explain the diminution of the role and authority of the school board.

Wirt concluded his analysis by suggesting that the perceived decline of the school board may be an artifact of the skimpiness of our data and of our theoretical underpinnings. Boards have been overlooked in empirical research and denigrated for their importance, he observed, perhaps because of theoretical deficiencies in our study of them.

The School Board and Community Demands and Supports

In his exploration of school board responsiveness, M. Kent Jennings employed a variety of models in trying to assess the nature of responsive linkages between school boards and the public. He found the concept of responsiveness an extremely elusive one and the empirical base for generalization inadequate. He concluded that it is not simply a question of conducting more research but of doing the right kind.

Future Perspectives on School Board Research and the Viability of the School Board

In the concluding session of the symposium, Laurence Iannaccone responded to the papers that had been presented and offered several observations regarding a research agenda with a focus on local school governance. Specifically, those observations were as follows:

1. Under conditions of cultural pluralism and political diversity, can demands be articulated, aggregated without fundamental distortion, and transmitted to local school government?
2. We need to distinguish two different public interests in education and develop appropriate mechanisms for each. One is the universal and impersonal interest of the general society; the other is the particular, personal interests of pupils and parents.
3. Representation needs to be understood as a basis for combining professional and lay interests, as well as the two notions of the public interests cited above.
4. The role of political concepts, ideology, and culture is too little understood. Guidance is needed on the application of these concepts to define and resolve problems of political conflict in educational governance.
5. Finally, we need to know more about the linkage between the demographic basis of a school district's political cultures to the school board and the policy-making process.

What, then, is the future viability of the local school board? As Michael D. Usdan saw it, the school board will survive in some manner, shape, or form, although its basic responsibilities and capabilities must be assessed more realistically. The demise of school boards is not imminent, Usdan opined, but they do indeed confront questionable futures. If they are to remain viable in an increasingly complex and politicized environment, school boards must broaden and deepen their base of lay support through the creation of new linkages and mechanisms that facilitate citizen participation in school affairs.

CONCLUDING COMMENT

The local school board is a distinctly American invention. It has evolved from its beginnings in colonial New England to become the most characteristic feature of contemporary American governance. Notwithstanding the considerable increase in state and federal power and concerns about its capacity and viability, the school board remains a cornerstone of representative democracy at the local level. It is a critical domain in contemporary life and merits the disciplined efforts of scholars, researchers, and practitioners alike.

REFERENCES

Cistone, P. J., ed. 1975. *Understanding school boards: Problems and prospects.* Lexington, MA: Heath.

Iannaccone, L., and F. W. Lutz. 1970. *Politics, power, and policy.* Columbus, OH: Merrill.

Land, D. 2002. Local school boards under review. *Review of Educational Research* 72:229–278.

Lutz, F. W., and L. Iannaccone, eds. 1978. *Public participation in local school districts.* Lexington, MA: Heath.

Merton, R. K. 1957. *Social theory and social structure.* New York: Free Press.

II

HISTORY OF THE CHANGING ROLES OF SCHOOL BOARDS

3

The Evolving Role of School
Boards: Retrospect and Prospect

Michael W. Kirst

The school board—unique in American society and, indeed, in the world—has governed public education for more than two centuries. The school board, however, is currently experiencing intense criticism of its performance, and even of its very right to exist. Influential education commentators such as Chester Finn (1991) have labeled urban boards a "dinosaur left over from the agrarian past" and an education sinkhole that supports the status quo (Gehring, 2003). The dramatic 1989 decentralization of the Chicago school board to the school sites was an early sign of the current ferment over the board's role and structure. Chicago's partial school-based governance signaled a return to a school board structure that existed in the early 1900s—a structure that, ironically, had led to charges of corruption, inefficiency, and a lack of challenging curriculums. Mayoral takeover of a few big-city schools has eviscerated school board control and overturned the 1900–1920 reform that separated school boards from city government. States are taking over districts for poor finances or performance, and No Child Left Behind (NCLB) continues to label more districts as failing.

The concept of the local board originated in New England, where citizens at first controlled the schools directly through town meetings. By 1826, however, Massachusetts already had created a separate school committee divorced from the rest of local government, and the Massachusetts model spread throughout the nation. Horace Mann, a founder of the American school system, proclaimed that the common school was to be free, financed by local and state government, controlled by lay boards of education, and mixing all social groups under one roof (Tyack, 1974). The school board was to be nonpartisan and nonsectarian.

The dominant credo was that a group of locally elected laymen, chosen in a manner in keeping with local interest and state mandate, should control the schools. In the 1800s, most schools were rural, had little bureaucracy, and were controlled by hundreds of thousands of local board members. As late as 1890, 71 percent of Americans lived in rural areas, where the one-room school was typical. By the turn of the 20th century, as society moved into the modern era, big changes were in store for school boards. However, the legal basis of school districts has never changed. Boards are created by state government and act as an agent of the state for school policy and operations that the state chooses to delegate (Yudoff et al., 2001).

WHY DECIDE LOCALLY? THE HISTORICAL RATIONALE

There are numerous and conflicting positions on the question of how well local school politics meets the democratic ideal. An issue is whether local political control of schools is more democratic than federal or state control. In general, citizens have greater opportunity to affect policy in their local district than they do at the federal or state level. Local policy makers serve fewer constituents than state or federal officials and are much closer to citizens psychologically as well as geographically. It's time-consuming and difficult for citizens to get to the state or national capital.

Local school board elections provide a means to influence local education policy that is much more direct than an election for a state legislator, who represents many local school districts on a much wider variety of topics. In the thousands of small school districts, a significant proportion of the community residents personally know at least one school board member. Local media provide better information and can capture the attention of citizens more effectively than reports from a distant state capital. This is not to claim that local school politics even approaches the democratic ideal. Indeed, a Gallup poll revealed that 36 percent of a national sample of citizens knew "very little" or "nothing" about their local public schools. However, local school officials can better anticipate the zone of tolerance of local school constituencies than state policy makers can.

Most states are too large and diverse for uniform policies to be effective. State officials typically prescribe teacher certification requirements, but leave hiring and compensation issues to local decision makers. There are large areas, however, such as civil rights and equal opportunity, where local flexibility must be greatly restricted.

Another argument for expanding local discretion is based on the link between political efficacy and public support of schools: Citizens participate in politics more if they believe they can have an impact on policy. But we do not know how the arguments favoring local control link school boards to educational achievement of students because few data-based studies exist of board impact upon achievement (Land, 2002). The local level offers the best opportunity for efficacy; therefore, a reduction in local efficacy leads to less overall citizen participation in education policy.

I will now analyze numerous historical forces that have eroded local control of education.

The Reform of the Urban School Board: 1900–1920

Although rural districts continued to grow in number, big-city boards were the first to experience major changes in structure and roles that established the basic administrative structure and pattern of school policy making we have today. At the turn of the 20th century, a nationwide interlocking directorate of "progressive" university presidents, school superintendents, and lay allies emerged from the business and professional elites in the cities (Tyack, 1974). One of its aims was to emancipate the schools from partisan politics and excessive decentralization. The members of these groups saw political corruption as the prime cause of education inefficiency in large cities. Indeed, many city politicians at that time used the spoils system and awarded school jobs and contracts as political favors. Writer Lincoln Steffens and other muckrakers revealed how textbook publishers and contractors allied themselves with corrupt school trustees to require common books in all schools (Steffens, 1904).

A decentralized, ward-based committee system for administering the public schools provided opportunities for this political influence. In 1905, for example, Philadelphia's 43 elected district school boards had 559 members. The Minneapolis board had only seven members, while Hartford, with only a third as many people, had 39 school visitors and committeemen. Although great variations were present at the turn of the century, 16 of 28 cities of more than 100,000 population had boards of 20 members or more.

The reformers contended that board members elected by wards advanced parochial and special interests at the expense of the school district as a whole. The reformers charged, moreover, that because the larger school boards worked through numerous subcommittees, their executive authority was splintered. The reformers believed the prerequisite for better management was centralization of power in a professional educator, a chief executive who had considerable delegated authority from the board. Only that kind of system would make large-scale improvements and accountability possible, they said.

By 1910, conventional education wisdom had evolved among the educators and leading business and professional men who spearheaded the reforms. The watchwords of reform became centralization, expertise, professionalization, nonpolitical control, and efficiency. The governance structure needed to be revised so school boards would be small, elected at large, and purged of all connections with political parties and government officials such as mayors and councilmen. Ironically, though, it was sometimes a very small group of patricians who secured new charters from state legislatures and thereby reorganized the urban schools without a popular vote in the cities.

Urban school reform was part of a broader pattern of municipal change at the turn of the century. Reformers wanted not simply to replace bad men with good; they proposed to change the occupational and class origins of decision makers. Underlying much of the reform movement was the elitist assumption that prosperous, native-born white Anglo-Saxon Protestants (WASPs) were superior to other groups and thus should determine the curriculum and the allocation of jobs. It was the mission of the schools to imbue children of the immigrants and the poor with uniformly WASP ideals (Tyack, 1974, pp. 28–59).

One classic 1927 study showed it was the upper-class professionals and businesspeople who had both the desire and resources to be elected from the entire city. For instance, after St. Louis reformed its school board in 1897, the percentage of professional men on the board jumped from 4.8 percent to 58.3 percent and big businessmen from 9 percent to 25 percent. The percentage of small businessmen dropped from 47.6 to 16.7 percent. These board members focused on board policy and were inclined to leave the details of administration to professionals. In sum, the decentralized boards had provided better representation of all economic classes but tended to intrude in many administrative details.

While most school boards are in suburban and rural areas where these city changes had much less impact, the variety of school board structures across the nation makes any generalizations difficult. Southern states created county boards in order to preserve segregation and aggregate county property values after the Civil War. Counties in Virginia and Maryland made the county education board fiscally dependent on the overall county government. Some cities like Providence, Rhode Island, and Trenton, New Jersey, preserved a major role for the mayor in controlling school expenditures. California, Illinois, and Arizona created separate school boards for grades K–8 and 9–12. In sum, so many school boards today (about 15,000) demonstrate such diverse structures and functions that our research base is narrow and shallow about what is actually happening at the local governance level.

A POLITICAL FRAMEWORK FOR UNDERSTANDING SCHOOL BOARDS

Given the turbulence and complexity surrounding school boards, it would seem hard to find patterns in what Henry James called the "buzzing, booming confusion of reality" (as cited in Wirt, Mitchell, and Marshall, 1988). These currents operate in thousands of school districts, erecting a truly indecipherable mosaic without some guide for explaining what transpires. What political framework of thought enables us to understand the nature of school turbulence? In short, is there a theory to describe and explain all this?

Theory involves suppositions and supporting evidence about the causes, consequences, and interrelationships of objects in reality. Causal theory of this kind is frequently found in the psychology of education and in the sociology of education, but seldom in educational administration. The most significant reason for the meager analysis of educational politics is probably the lack of theory and methodology. As political scientists pointed out 30 years ago, no single theory, simple or complex, guided it nor did agreement exist on the methodology. Despite the flood of politics of education work done since the 1970s, no overarching general theory generated any hypotheses that could be tested by acceptable methods in the crucible of political experiences. The politics of education is certainly not orderly for those who prefer scholarship that explicates established truths, but it is exciting for those who prefer to innovate in the development of theory and hypothesis.

Because scholarship, like life, is always some compromise with ideal requirements, I turn instead to one form of theory—heuristic. *Heuristic theory is not so much a predictive scheme as a method of analytically separating and categorizing items in experience.* It is a heuristic scheme or framework for political analysis that we employ in organizing the concepts and data of this book. This framework is termed *systems analysis*, from the ideas of David Easton, who emphasizes a "conceptual framework" or "categories for the systems analysis of politics" (Easton, 1965). The utility of systems theory is that, like all other heuristic schemes, it enables us at least to order our information or hunches about reality.

The Systems Analysis Framework

Easton's framework construes a society composed of major institutions or subsystems—the economy, the school, the church, and so on. Individuals interact with one another and these institutions in regular ways that constitute a distinctive culture. One of these institutions is the school board, operating within a broader political system. School boards decide among competing values and conflicting demands through their decisions and actions. School board decisions are generally accepted as authoritative, that is, legitimate. The values boards allocate may be material—a textbook, new buildings, or more teachers. Values allocated may also be symbolic, conferring status and deference on favored groups—for example, making Martin Luther King's birthday a school holiday. The link between the school boards

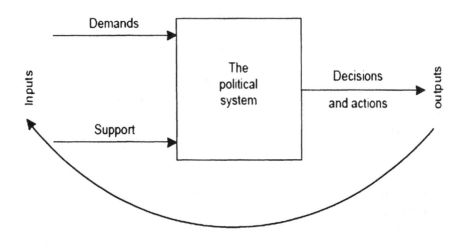

Figure 3.1.   A Simplified Model of a Political System
Source: Reprinted from *A System Analysis of Political Life* by David Easton by permission of the University of Chicago Press. © 1965 by the University of Chicago Press.

and their federal, state, and local environment (e.g., NCLB) is a key element. This interrelationship is one where *stress* in other subsystems like state government generates *inputs* of *demands* on and *supports* for school boards. Actors in the political system, like school boards, then reduce or *convert* these inputs into school board decisions or *outputs*. These in turn *feed back* allocated values and resources into the society where the process began. Figure 3.1 is a sketch of this set of interactions. These concepts seek to describe components of the dynamic, interactive political system that exists in any local school system.

The Model Illustrated for Schools

School boards allocate resources—revenues, programs, professionals—and they also allocate values, teaching Americanism. The interaction between schools and other subsystems can take two forms. The most obvious are *demands*, whose characteristics increase in today's political turbulence.

For example, a group wants a special curriculum, more parental authority, or more teacher power, and these wants are directed as demands toward school boards. A second form of interaction with the schools is *support;* that is, certain groups provide the school board with taxes or with intangibles, such as a favorable attitude toward education. The school board that receives such demands must deal with them carefully because it lacks resources to meet them all. In short, a gap exists between what all groups want and the resources to meet those demands.

In all times and places this gap is a powerful generator of social and political conflict. So school boards must act politically because they must choose which demands to favor and which to reject. The result of this decision is an *output*—for example, a school board resolution or a superintendent's program. Whatever form an output takes, all are alike in that they authoritatively allocate values and resources. After this policy decision, as the arrow at the bottom of Figure 3.1 implies, the school board output must be implemented in order to cope with the inputs that originally gave rise to it. For example, a demand for driver education generates a district program, implemented by the resources of personnel and material that organize the program.

A school board member must operate within this system in a way that shares much with the classical position of the politician. That is, he or she mediates among competing demands from school constituencies organized to seek their share of valued resources from the school system. All this occurs because allocations are always limited so that not all get what they demand.

The Concepts Defined

A more complete description of elements of systems analysis is appropriate here, beginning with the inputs, whether *demands* or *supports*. *Demands* are pressures on the board for justice or help, for reward or recognition. Behind these demands lies the human condition of longing for something that is in short supply. Resources are never plentiful enough to satisfy all claims— a condition of tremendous importance to all aspects of our society, particularly for the political system. *Supports,* on the other hand, are a willingness of citizens to accept school board decisions or the continued existence of a school board compared to mayoral or state takeover. A steady flow of supports is necessary if any political system is to sustain its *legitimacy* (i.e., the psychological sense that the system has the right to do what it is doing).

So vital is this input that all societies indoctrinate their young to support their particular system, a task that is part of the school's work but is also shared with family and peers. One point about today's school turbulence in big cities is that some parents withdraw support from the school board in seeking many types of reform. The whole process of strong demands and weak supports can be illustrated in the success of mayoral takeover in New

York and Boston. Clearly not all demands are converted into policy, for the political system is more responsive to certain values: those that are dominant in the larger society.

What inputs get through depends upon the values the conversion process reinforces or frustrates. They are also influenced by the values of the school board authorities operating within this flow of inputs. For example, some educators insist that maintaining discipline is a prime value of classwork, while others prefer to achieve intellectual excitement that often looks undisciplined. School boards responsible for running the political system constantly interact in the conversion process with those either outside or inside the political system. Their interactions often stem in part from role definitions imposed by the political system itself.

Such interactions generate certain pressures inside the political system— or *withinputs*—that in turn shape the conversion process and products. The result is a school board's commitment to a standard way of acting and believing that constitute a systematic way of life. That is a force contributing to its stability. It is also a force that generates challenge by those not benefiting from the outputs, as this book's chapter by Lutz and Iannaconne demonstrates. The outputs of the political subsystem, once achieved, require policy implementation that enhances the safety, income, and status of some while it also detracts from those of others. A resulting profile of public policy mirrors the local structure of power and privilege and tells us much about what values currently dominate the local political system.

Moreover, the authorized purpose of the board's output finds meaning in reality only through the process of *feedback*. This is the interaction of an output with its environment, becoming in time an established behavior—an *outcome*. Clearly, the gap between output and outcome becomes a major stimulus to future policy making. That is, the action of the political system may not result in desired outcomes such as improved test scores. Rather, because outputs can influence school district performance, they generate a subsequent set of inputs for more change to the school board through a *feedback loop*. That is, dealing with community conflict over low test scores causes a board response that subsequently generates new demands and supports from within the district. So a new round of challenge and response begins for the school board.

I will now summarize how the various concepts of political systems analysis have changed the school board over many years.

EVOLUTION OF SCHOOL BOARD ROLES

In 1920, board influence usually was restricted by a lack of time and independent staff, other than legal counsel. Board members often held demanding full-time jobs and could meet at night only once or twice a month. They rarely received objective criteria allowing them to question the professional judgments of the superintendent and his staff. Moreover, elections seldom provided board members with a specific mandate or policy platform, even though school boards had control of almost all the money. In 1920, public schools relied on local government for 83 percent of their funds, state government for 17 percent, and federal aid for less than 1 percent (National Center for Education Statistics, 2002, table 156.)

Before the mid-1960s, a description of the board's function required it most often to mediate major policy conflicts, leaving the determination of important policy issues to the professional staff. Even in mediating, they might do little. In the process, they often simply legitimized the proposals of the professional staff, making only marginal changes.

Although board members spent the bulk of their time on details of school operations, they did establish a policy zone of consent that made clear to the superintendent what was, and was not, acceptable. For example, a superintendent who tried to introduce bilingual education in a rural, conservative California district would discover that this program was outside the board's zone of consent. Not surprisingly, smaller districts with little population growth and a narrow spectrum of values and philosophies created more citizen satisfaction than did the larger units. Larger, more diverse districts often featured conflict between citizens who had lived in the district for many years, and better-educated parents who moved into the suburbs from the central city. This type of conflict was called the "locals" versus the "cosmopolitans" (Nunnery and Kimbrough, 1971).

Administrative centralization that occurred in city school boards had little impact upon rural boards. Rural boards, however, were greatly affected by a rapid school consolidation process that created larger schools with the capacity to offer a wide range of curriculum options. What was once an archipelago of districts in America—with each island having a board and community in harmony—has been fused into a system of larger, more varied districts. The 89,000 districts of 1948 became 55,000 five years later, 31,000 by 1961, and less than 14,000 by 2007. During the 1970s, on any given day, 3 districts disappeared forever between breakfast and dinner. Earlier in the 1960s, that many had evaporated between breakfast and the morning coffee break, with another 7 gone by dinner.

Educators, who believed bigger must be better, found that these larger districts offered more options but also created more conflicting viewpoints about school policy (Cistone, 1975). And while districts grew larger, boards grew smaller: Fewer board members were available to handle complex issues and represent a diverse citizenry. In the 1930s, a typical school board member represented approximately 200 people; by 1970, he or she represented 3,000 constituents. This expansion of their constituency base and the subsequent increase in diversity of values and interest became critical to school board members attempting to responsibly fulfill multiple roles within legislative, executive, and judicial branches of government.

Further, the composition of school boards did not keep pace with their burgeoning constituency. A 1989 survey conducted by the National Center for Education Information in Washington, D.C., revealed that school board presidents were 97 percent white, 71 percent male, in their late 40s, and had children at home. They had more education, made more money, and were more conservative politically than the average American. Since the 1930s, the major change in the composition of school boards as a whole has been the dramatic increase in female members from 12 percent in 1930 to 39 percent in 2002 (Glass, Björk, and Brunner, 2002). A national study of the roles of male and female school board members found women were more involved in curricular and other educational program issues than men; women also were less likely to delegate decisions to the superintendent. Males focused more on fiscal, contract, and management issues (McCloud, 1990).

SCHOOL BOARD CHANGES
DURING THE LATE 20TH CENTURY

By 1980, school boards had to juggle diverse and changing coalitions from within and without the school system. Although many school reforms such as new math disappeared, some reforms remained and created internal structural changes. Consequently, a partial legacy from the era between 1960 and 1980 was tremendous growth in the specialized functions of the school: More specialists were required in special education, bilingual education, nutrition, health, remedial reading, and other areas. Many of these new bureaucratic structural layers diluted the board's influence, because the specialists were paid separately by federal or state categorical programs.

The scope and intensity of recent state policy actions also make today's climate very different for local school boards. States change policy through statutes and regulations that have a standardizing effect. State assumption of the majority of school funding has limited flexible local resources. In addition, the focus of state policy making is no longer on categorical groups such as handicapped or minority students. Instead, it is aimed at the central core of instructional policy—what should be taught, how it should be taught, who should teach it, and how it should be tested.

From 1980 to 2000, many governors and legislators were impressed by arguments that local school officials had permitted academic standards to drop and were inattentive to the need for higher order skills and a more complex curriculum. Local school policy makers seemed to overemphasize basics such as rote mathematics and simplistic reading exercises. Conversely, global economic competition required a more adaptable work force equipped with a breadth and depth of knowledge that local officials seemed unable to provide.

State leaders turned for advice, in part, to an interstate network of policy activists. These reformers traffic in the "war of ideas" propagated by think tanks, and they use mass media, including newspaper columns and the Internet, to influence politicians. Many of these reformers supported the concept of state-driven curricular alignment—a concept that would allow states to guide the local curriculum and overcome the local board's capacity to thwart standards implementation. For example, reformers did not point out that the school board is the crucial agent for school improvement, and that state reforms should try to strengthen the local school board's capacity to bring about and monitor change. Rather, the reports implied that local boards should be bypassed (Danzberger, Kirst, and Usdan, 1992).

Many school boards take issue with the charge that they resisted change and higher academic standards. They contend that boards initiated and enacted most of the reforms in local districts before the state called for them. Indeed, a six-state study of 24 school districts from 1983 to 1989 found that in each state, local school boards had increased curricular standards before state laws were passed (Firestone et al., 1991).

School Board Control Squeezed from the Top and Bottom

As a result of these changing internal and external forces, the discretionary zone of boards has become progressively smaller. The board's discretion is squeezed from the top by increasing regulation from the legislative, administrative, and judicial arms of the federal and state governments. Private interest groups and professional reformers such as the Gates Foundation and the Education Trust have expanded their influence. Moreover, interstate groups including the National Governors Association and Business Roundtable have increased their sway, as have certain national interest groups such as the Council for Exceptional Children. All over the nation, networks of individuals and groups have grown, spreading their own isolated agendas and reform schemes including state school finance reform, testing, tougher academic standards, and specific reform programs.

Local boards also find their decision-making powers squeezed from the bottom by collective bargaining contracts advocated by national teacher organizations. Labor agreements grow incrementally and in cities encompass over one hundred pages. In the last three decades, local special interest groups, often springing from national social movements for the rights of the handicapped, minorities, and religion, also have increased in number and influence.

These recent interest groups and social movements differ from those of the 19th century, exemplified by Horace Mann, when a broader view of education needs existed. Current interest groups and think tanks help fragment school decision making and board agendas. Social movements and interest groups also tend to move decisions to the state or federal level, where some lobby groups are more effective. For example, Education Trust in Washington, D.C., was a prime mover for NCLB passage in 2001. Citizens go to their local school board and superintendent expecting redress of their problems only to find that decision-making power has shifted to the state or some other nonlocal level. The impression grows that no one is in charge of public education.

All of this certainly does not mean that local school boards are helpless or irrelevant. Rather, it means they cannot control their agenda or shape outcomes as they could in the past. Moreover, boards must deal with shifting and ephemeral intergovernmental and local coalitions that might yield some temporary marginal advantages. Consequently, current board members must be better politicians than in the past and be able to roll in and roll out of diverse interest-based coalitions. However, the growth of state and federal roles is not a zero sum game for school boards (Elmore and Fuhrman, 1990). Some federal and state programs can enhance central district curriculum and accountability impact.

PUBLIC SUPPORT FOR THE LOCAL SCHOOL BOARD

The American public still strongly supports local school boards, according to recent Phi Delta Kappan polls. The public wants to maintain the basic institutional role and structure of school boards. The public views school boards as the governance mechanism to keep schools close to the people and to avoid excessive control by professional educators or state authorities. In 2006, 55 percent of respondents to a national Phi Delta Kappan poll said school boards should have the greatest influence on what is taught in public schools; 26 percent preferred the state and 14 percent the federal government (Rose and Gallup, 2006).

A basic paradox exists: Support for the idea of the school board is coupled with widespread public ignorance of specific board roles and functions. Deep public apathy and indifference are common, as the tiny turnout for board elections in many communities demonstrates. This civic ignorance bodes even greater trouble for the future, when student populations become more diverse and creative leadership is even more necessary.

Studies found that local boards and board members interacted with general government only occasionally and seem to be isolated (in boards' and civic leaders' perceptions) from mainstream community political structures

(Howell, 2005). Little systematic communication takes place between school boards and other local governments, and boards are frequently mired in adversarial relationships with the municipal governments on which they must depend for money. In sum, more evolution is likely for this unique American institution.

MAJOR TRENDS THAT IMPACT SCHOOL BOARDS

The gradual shift in control from local school boards has progressed to a point where it is time to reassess historical decisions about what level of government should control what decisions. This chapter asserts the following:

1. The historical roots of the American education system are local policy, management, and financial control. This local control tradition is deeply embedded in U.S. political culture and continues to have strong public support. Americans have been dissatisfied with their schools for a century, although local control was not challenged until the last 40 years.
2. The total array of evolving influences on school policy has tended to drastically narrow the discretionary decision space of local policy makers and teachers over the past 40 years.
3. The shift in control to nonlocal levels can be attributed to several sequential but interacting forces, including (a) loss of confidence by higher authorities in local decision makers including elected school boards, teachers, and administrators; (b) the increased use of federal and state categorical grants; (c) changes in state funding and control patterns to enhance equity and place limits on local property tax spending; (d) growing legalization of education; (e) the tendency of NCLB and state accountability to centralize more authority than it decentralizes; and (f) federal and state concern about the role and impact of local unions.
4. The centralization of testing, curriculum, and instructional policy at the state and district level is narrowing teacher discretion in the classroom.
5. Collective bargaining is a major restriction on board discretion.
6. Despite the historic loss of local flexibility and initiative, the public prefers local control to state, federal, or professional control.

Nothing significant appears likely to reverse the trends eroding local school board control, and these trends may overwhelm governance at the local school board level. The current challenge is to rethink the institutional choices that we have made, through analyzing the purposes and mission of school boards and sorting out the level with the best capacity to serve the students. The federal or state role, for example, is often crucial when redistributive policies are needed in areas of civil rights and school finance. Typically, local politics precludes local board agreements that cause radical redistribution of resources within a district.

In order to decide whether we're allocating authority over education decisions in the most effective ways, we must look at why federal and state policy makers have lost confidence in school boards and their employees. For some politicians, the growth of unions has been a major factor. In a recent poll of American voters, school boards and parents were viewed as having the most power to change education, but the operational reality is different (Phelps-Deily, 2002).

TEACHERS ORGANIZE FOR MORE INFLUENCE

In the 1950s, teachers found themselves cut off from the school board and the public. Increasingly, they were being told how to conduct their classrooms by business managers, administrative assistants, subject matter coordinators, and department heads. At the same time, as education became big business, teachers were achieving a potential for power. After World War II, more parents wanted their children to have extensive schooling and the population of school-age children had increased dramatically. The country then spent more on education, and more teachers were needed. Between 1949 and 1970, the share of the gross national product devoted to education rose from about 3.5 percent to 8 percent. Where we had spent only $2 billion in 1940, we spent $50 billion in 1970, and over $100 billion in 1980. With this massive injection of funds into the schools, teachers grew in number from just over 1 million in 1940 to almost 2.5 million in 1971. By the mid-1970s, teachers were 1 million fewer in number than farmers, but substantially more numerous than teamsters, autoworkers, steelworkers, or doctors.

During the 1950s, teachers' perception of their proper professional role began to change. Once viewed as submissive, they now began to form unions, to engage in collective bargaining, and—despite laws in many states against strikes by public employees—to use the tactic of the strike. The number of strikes escalated between 1955 and 1975, from 35 to 114 in the single school year 1967–1968 and to 131 in 1969–1970.

Teachers' organizations also entered into federal electoral politics. In 1976, the National Education Association (NEA) endorsed a presidential candidate—Jimmy Carter—and spent $3 million on behalf of their endorsed candidates in federal elections. Not surprisingly, in 1979 President

Carter successfully pushed for a new cabinet-level Department of Education, something the NEA had much desired.

The late 1960s was the beginning of an intense period of implementing collective bargaining based on the private industrial union model. Between 1965 and 1980, in most states (except those in the Southeast and Mountain regions), teachers realized they needed collective bargaining. This was a major movement away from administrative and board dominance of governance. The outcome of collective bargaining is a written and time-bound agreement covering wages, hours, and conditions of employment. Unions want centralized agreements with school districts, and do *not* want to negotiate with each school, so unions are very wary of school-based management.

At the school site, the central school board's union contract language must be interpreted to apply to specific circumstances. This means that the principal, teachers, and union building representative must become very familiar with the terms of the central district contract. Yet even familiarity does not forestall many disputes about specific teaching arrangements. These disputes can lead to teacher grievances whose settlement can clarify the contract at the central district level.

What happens to administrator authority, particularly among principals, when teacher contracts filter down through the loosely coupled school system? A major study found that, although some provisions tightly limit the principal's freedom of action, others get redefined to fit the particular requirements at the school site. Johnson and Donaldson conclude that there is no evidence that school management was more effective before collective bargaining or that nonunionized states have improved teacher quality (Johnson and Donaldson, 2006). How the principal works with the union contract also affects teachers' respect for administrators. In short, having standards and expecting much of teachers earns principals tolerance and even respect from teachers when interpreting the contract. For teachers, a good school is more important than union membership, close observance of a contract, or control of the schools. Teachers like to be part of a winning team. But the central district teacher contract fundamentally alters and limits school board role and discretion with regard to both certified and classified employees.

THE CENTRAL OFFICE EXPANDS

The increasing complexity of school policy making tends to provide more influence to those who control detailed information and analyses of policy alternatives. The control of information highlights the role of the school bureaucracy vis-à-vis the superintendent and board. At this point, research has rarely progressed enough to differentiate the influence of the superintendent from her or his own staff. However, we do know a lot about this pattern in the urban schools. There, the central office staff has accumulated so much decision-making authority in such areas as curriculum, personnel assignment, and facilities, that the roles of outlying district administrators and building principals are significantly restricted.

Historically, the school principal is too involved with day-to-day management of the school to participate effectively in broad policy making. Central district administrators, in turn, are primarily concerned with ensuring that policies set down by central headquarters are followed by the schools in their districts. The local superintendent's impact in part comes from an orchestrating, or choreographing, external political role that develops a sense of mission for the bureaucracy and establishes a particular climate. Top officials at the central office are traditionally chosen from within the system by the superintendent or school board. In some districts, the board must ratify his or her recommendations, and a new superintendent cannot always bring in a large new team of top administrators. One case study found that 40 percent of senior staff work in a large district was devoted to meeting board member requests of administrators (McCloud, 1990).

Local Control at the School Site

Some boards opted to move partial control to the school site by developing policies to promote school site budgets, charter schools, and administrative decentralization. But full-blown school-based management (SBM) eludes boards in most districts. Education reform in the United States has been characterized as "tinkering toward utopia," so SBM keeps inching forward in a few localities while federal and state policies like NCLB grow simultaneously to centralize standards (Tyack and Cuban, 1995). Empirical evidence linking SBM to student achievement would help SBM spread, but so far decentralization changes have demonstrated only a limited impact upon pupil learning and instructional improvement (Wohlstetter, 1995).

School-based management also has been hampered by site-level capacity. Opponents contend that not much site-level administrative or teaching talent was waiting to be unleashed by school-based management schemes. Extensive capacity building is needed before school-based management can start, but few districts have been able or are willing to invest in more managerial professional development, including information systems and rethinking the principal's ubiquitous role. Recently, state governments have been intervening in NCLB failing schools and reconstituting them. But proactive school-based management by state governments is limited to extreme cases where schools have failed for many years. Rhetoric about restructuring and SBM as the symbol of school reform peaked in the 1990s but left little residue in today's schools.

Scholars do have ideas on how to make school-based management work, but there is a lack of agreement on who should control school-based management—teachers, parents, administrators, or all three of them. For example, the 1960s featured a discussion of community control by parents and citizens, but only in the 1980s were Los Angeles teachers given some priority in school site decisions. By 2000, Los Angeles was divided into several centrally managed geographic subunits, and SBM was de-emphasized.

If the school site should have the prime role in governance, then who should control school site decision making? Several alternatives are possible:

1. Under the concept of the principal as a site manager, the principal should control these resources and be held accountable for the success of the school. Success can be measured through school site performance reports that encompass pupil attainment measures, as well as the allocation choices made by the principal. This view of the principal as the site manager was reinforced by the school effectiveness literature's focus on strong site leadership.
2. Parents should control site policy because they are the consumers and care most deeply about policies at schools their children attend. Parents are less interested in central district policies that have no easily discernible impact on their children. The American philosophy of lay control implies that parent school site councils should deliberate and decide on school level policy and SBM.
3. Teachers should form a school site senate and allocate funds and personnel as well as decide instructional issues. Teachers cannot be held accountable for pupil performance if they do not control resource allocations but must instead follow standardized instructional procedures. SBM by teachers would also enhance the professional image and self-concept of teachers.

None of these rationales is sufficiently compelling that it should be the norm. Consequently, SBM should have "parity" of membership among teachers, administration, and parents so that they must reach an agreement through bargaining and coalitions. At the high school level, students may be included. All factions deserve a place at the table, and the best arguments should prevail. The growth of charter schools as part of local districts has provided a school-based control alternative, but not one that boards have much influence over. Indeed, school boards overwhelmingly oppose charter school expansion (Kirst, 2007).

OVERVIEW OF HISTORICAL TRENDS CONCERNING
SCHOOL BOARD ROLE AND CONTROL

A basic thesis of this chapter is that the discretionary decision zone of the local superintendents and the boards has been squeezed into a smaller and smaller area. In my view, local school district discretion will continue to shrink unless some measures are taken to restore public confidence in local authorities and increase their policy-making and instructional capacity. Specifically, local administrators and boards will continue to experience erosion in their once preeminent position in initiating policy agenda and controlling education. The local superintendent and administrative staff are often a reactive force trying to juggle diverse and changing coalitions across different issues and levels of government (Tyack and Cuban, 1995).

Part of the legacy of the past 50 years is a tremendous growth in specialized functions of the school, including administrative specialists in vocational education, driver education, nutrition, health, remedial reading, and so on. Many of these new structural layers with funding linked to federal and state resources diluted the influence of the superintendent and local board. Many local specialists are paid by federal or state categorical programs and are insulated from the board's influence by the requirements of higher levels of government. Their allegiance is often to the higher levels of education governance rather than the local community.

By 2000, increasing concern existed that the boards were trying to do too much even within whatever discretionary decision making they still had. Part of this concern stemmed from the need for more board focus on education standards, pupil achievement, NCLB, and state accountability. If the board continued overseeing the details of management and budgets, hearing citizen complaints about details of school operation, and being a judicial body, could the board also fulfill its new mission of raising standards and achievement (Danzberger, Kirst, and Usdan, 1992)?

SCHOOL BOARD ISSUES WITHIN THE LOCAL CONTEXT

Now that I have sketched historical trends, it is appropriate to examine boards within their local context. The major issue has been the relationship between the board and the superintendent. This issue begins with who is recruited and elected to the school board (Cistone, 1975).

The 1900–1920 reformers installed nonpartisanship as the dominant electoral pattern, and one result was a low voter turnout. Who is attracted and recruited to become a school board member? We know very little about recruitment because all we have are small databases about the actual process. For example, 25 percent of board members in 2003 said they lived

Table 3.1.   Length of Board Service

	Large Districts (25,000+)	Medium Districts (5,000–24,999)	Small Districts (less than 5,000)	All Districts
Less than two years	9.6%	8.7%	12.4%	10.6%
Two to five years	39.8%	42.3%	40.2%	41.0%
Six to ten years	32.5%	30.7%	29.4%	30.2%
More than ten years	18.1%	18.3%	18.0%	18.1%
Total Districts	83	300	378	761

Source: Frederick Hess and David Leal, *School house politics: Expenditures, interests, and competition in school board elections,* paper presented at the Conference on School Board Politics, Harvard University, October 15–17, 2003.

in a small town, and 16 percent in a rural area. Tables 3.1 and 3.2 provide a little insight by summarizing, from a national sample, board members' political views and length of service. Table 3.3 presents a national overview of board elections, board structure, and issues. Even though the 1900–1920 reforms featured at-large elections, by 2007 a majority of urban school board members are elected by subdistrict.

School Board and Superintendent Relationships

One of the major issues in board evolution is the pattern of interactions and roles between the board and the superintendent (Carol et al., 1986). Historically, the prevalent view is that the board should not cross the policy line and delve into the arena of administration. But these boundaries are often unclear and shift through four dominant patterns:

1. A strong superintendent, trusted by board members, dominates policy making and administration.

Table 3.2.   Political Views of Board Members

	Large Districts (25,000+)	Medium Districts (5,000–24,999)	Small Districts (less than 5,000)	All Districts
Liberal	18.7%	18.7%	12.9%	15.9%
Moderate	51.6%	46.2%	41.4%	44.5%
Conservative	24.2%	32.8%	40.9%	35.7%
None of the above	5.5%	2.3%	4.7%	3.9%
Total Districts	91	305	379	775

Source: Frederick Hess and David Leal, *School house politics: Expenditures, interests, and competition in school board elections,* paper presented at the Conference on School Board Politics, Harvard University, October 15–17, 2003.

Table 3.3.   Leading School Board Concerns

Percentage Listing Issue as "Significant" or "Moderate" Concern

	Large Districts (25,000+)	Medium Districts (5,000–24,999)	Small Districts (less than 5,000)	All Districts
Budget/funding	100.0	98.7	96.0	97.6
Student achievement	98.9	98.0	96.4	97.2
Special Education	93.3	93.4	85.2	88.1
Improving educational technology	84.3	90.7	85.9	87.5
Teacher quality	91.2	88.2	84.9	86.8
Parental support/ interest	88.9	81.0	77.3	79.8
Regulation	79.3	76.6	75.6	76.7
Drug/alcohol use	82.2	81.3	69.4	75.4
Discipline	81.3	78.4	68.8	73.7
Teacher shortage	95.6	76.9	65.3	73.2
Overcrowded schools	76.9	71.0	46.3	59.5

Source: Frederick Hess and David Leal, *School house politics: Expenditures, interests, and competition in school board elections*, paper presented at the Conference on School Board Politics, Harvard University, October 15–17, 2003.

2. A strong board that does not trust the superintendent dominates policy making and administration.
3. A mixture where the superintendent and board both cross over frequently into policy making and administration.
4. The textbook definition of separation of roles, where each participant knows what is expected and abides by those understandings (Carol et al., 1986).

The diversity of these local interrelationships is interesting, given that appointment of the superintendent is one of the most important decisions boards ever make. Superintendents' complaints about board micromanagement have not led to any statewide administrator legislative movement to reduce board management prerogatives.

SCHOOL BOARDS IN THE FUTURE

Despite the constant criticism of boards by some observers and analysts, I suspect most future board roles will remain intact and similar to the past. School boards are effective at defending the status at the state level. No state coalition has been able to undermine the board's existence on a statewide basis. Voters like the school board concept as it exists now.

Numerous options for radical change include the following:

1. Vouchers as the dominant state finance concept
2. Charter expansion to a large percentage of schools within a district or state
3. The board as a contractor for individual schools (e.g., the board operates groupings of common schools across multiple existing district lines)
4. State laws rewritten to restrict boards to policy-making bodies only
5. Widespread mayoral takeover of school governance
6. Direct state operation of individual schools using state regional offices

My hunch is that none of these options will become ubiquitous. Rather, school boards will continue to work on incremental improvements in their current role (McAdams, 2006). But the most likely contender to shake up a specific board's role and impact could be the spread of charters. Charters exceed 15 percent of enrollment in some suburbs of Phoenix, the District of Columbia, and Dayton, Ohio. This level of competition could alter the status of a particular board. School boards are part of a large coalition to fight charter expansion. But they are opposed by an impressive array of interest groups, think tanks, foundations, and wealthy individuals (Kirst, 2007).

In 1986, syndicated columnist Neal Pierce posed the political dilemma this way:

> I found it compelling to read how much the public believes in the need for school boards, how much it remains attached to the concept of grassroots educational self-governance. But it was equally disturbing to note, from this report, that the same public evidences essential illiteracy about the actual role and activities of school boards. Moreover, the public turns out in appallingly thin numbers to vote for the school boards it otherwise believes to be so essential. We are left with the disturbing question: If the school boards' popular constituency misperceives their role and doesn't care enough to exercise its franchise in their selection, how fully or forcefully will the boards ever be able to function? (Carol et al., 1986, p. 4)

I do not think much has changed in the past 21 years, nor is there a consensus on radical overhaul of this unique American institution. If school achievement does not improve after NCLB, school boards may be under more external criticism. Even if achievement increases, it is unlikely there will be conclusive studies linking pupil results to board decisions (Land, 2002). Probably we will witness a continuation of the major trends covered in this chapter, particularly the gradual loss of local board influence over education policy and operations to higher levels of government and expanded employee contracts.

REFERENCES

Carol, L. N., L. L. Cunningham, J. P. Danzberger, M. W. Kirst, B. A. McCloud, and M. D. Usdan. 1986. *School boards: Strengthening grass roots leadership.* Washington, DC: Institute for Educational Leadership.

Cistone, P., ed. 1975. *Understanding school boards.* Lexington, MA: Lexington/Heath.

Danzberger, J., M. Kirst, and M. Usdan. 1992. *Governing public schools.* Washington, DC: Institute for Higher Education.

Easton, D. 1965. *A systems analysis of political life.* New York: Wiley.

Elmore, R., and S. Fuhrman. 1990. Understanding local control. *Educational Evaluation and Policy Analysis* 12:158–171.

Finn, C. E. 1991. *We must take charge.* New York: Free Press.

Firestone, W., S. H. Fuhrman, and M. W. Kirst. 1991. State education reform since 1983: Appraisal and the future. *Educational Policy* 5 (3): 233–250.

Gehring, J. 2003. Essential or obsolete: Panel debates role of school boards. *Education Week*, October 29, 14.

Glass, T., L. Björk, and C. Brunner. 2002. *The study of the American school superintendency 2000: Superintendents in the new millennium.* Arlington, VA: American Association of School Administrators.

Howell, W. G. 2005. *Besieged: School boards and the future of education politics.* Washington, DC: Brookings.

Kirst, M. 2007. The politics of charter schools. *Peabody Journal of Education* 82 (3): 184–203.

Johnson, S. M., and M. L. Donaldson. 2006. The effects of collective bargaining on teacher quality. In *Collective bargaining in education*, ed. J. Hannaway and A. J. Rotherham, 111–140. Cambridge, MA: Harvard Education Press.

Land, D. 2002. Local school boards under review: Their role and effectiveness in relation to students' academic achievement. *Review of Educational Research* 72 (2): 229–278.

McAdams, D. 2006. *What schools boards can do.* New York: Teachers College.

McCloud, B. 1990. *Are there differences in male and female school board roles?* Columbus, OH: Ohio State Univ.

National Center for Education Statistics. 2002. *Condition of education.* Washington, DC: Government Printing Office.

Nunnery, M., and R. Kimbrough. 1971. *Politics, power, polls, and school elections.* Berkeley, CA: McCutcheon.

Phelps-Deily, M. 2002. Boards, parents seen as powerful. *Education Week*, June 5.

Rose, L. C., and A. M. Gallup. 2006. The 38th annual Phi Delta Kappan/Gallup poll: Of the public's attitudes toward public school. *Phi Delta Kappan* 88 (1): 41–53.

Steffens, L. 1904. *The shame of the cities.* New York: McClure, Philips.

Tyack, D. 1974. *The one best system.* Cambridge, MA: Harvard University Press.

Tyack, D., and L. Cuban. 1995. *Tinkering toward utopia.* Cambridge, MA: Harvard University Press.

Wirt, F. M., D. Mitchell, and C. Marshall. 1988. "Culture and education policy: Analyzing values in state policy systems." *Educational Evaluation and Policy Analysis*, 10 (4): 271–284.

Wohlstetter, P. 1995. Generating curriculum and instructional innovation through school based management. *Educational Administration Quarterly* 31 (3): 375–404.

Yudoff, Y., D. Kirp, B. Levin, and R. Moran. 2001. *Educational policy and the law.* 4th ed. Belmont, CA: West-Wadsworth.

4

Leading in an Era of Change: The Micropolitics of Superintendent-Board Relations

Lars G. Björk

During the past several decades, dramatic social, economic, and political changes in society have altered how public school districts are organized, governed, and led. Murphy (1999) characterizes the latter part of the 20th century as an era of ferment in which the education profession engaged in serious discourse on the nature of schooling in society, redefined its center to focus on learning and teaching, and reconfigured educational leadership. The new center emerged from a compelling need to improve the quality of American education and achieve social justice in society. Scholars agree that these fundamental changes may best be achieved by changing the culture of schools and engaging parents, community citizens, and interest groups in democratic policy- and decision-making processes. Understanding how these changes may affect superintendents' roles and the dynamics of super-intendent–school board relations remains a significant challenge to scholars and the profession. This chapter will briefly examine the dynamic relationship between education and society, the changing discourse of superintendents' roles, and the politics of superintendent-board relations.

EDUCATION, SOCIETY AND THE SUPERINTENDENCE

The integral relationship between schools and local communities is an important characteristic of the American education system (Cremin, 1988). Since the early colonial era, schools have been viewed as extensions of local communities and were inextricably bound together by economic conditions, notions of family, and religion, as well as the self-governance democratic ideal (Björk, 2005; Beck and Foster, 1999; Tyack, 1974). During the early 19th century (1820–1850), educational discourse was influenced by values that reflected a strong preference for local control, over centralized govern-ment and executive leadership. In addition, Protestant religious ideology ad-vocated that citizens should be numerate and literate in order to promote as well as share in the rewards of a redeemer nation (Brunner, Grogan, and Björk, 2002). At this juncture in American history, education was relatively uncomplicated, and local school boards played a direct role in supervising education programs and managing schools (Björk, 2005; Brunner, Grogan, and Björk, 2002).

Between 1820 and 1900, industrial and technological developments plus unprecedented levels of immigration fueled the rapid growth of cities and an abiding faith in corporate values of efficiency, productivity, bureaucracy, and scientific management (Beck and Foster, 1999). These changes had a profound impact on the nature of schooling. Rapid growth of cities in-creased the size and complexity of public schools and increased demands on school board members, who found it difficult to provide the manage-ment and supervision required to effectively run schools. In 1837, when district superintendents were hired in Buffalo, New York, and Louisville, Kentucky (Grieder, Pierce, and Jordan, 1969), superintendents' roles were largely defined in terms of being master educators who were assigned to monitor instructional programs and supervise teachers. Consequently, school boards shifted their efforts to focus on matters of governance and management (Kowalski and Björk, 2005).

During the middle of the 19th century, many prominent citizens and pol-icy makers expressed concern that marked differences in language as well as social, economic, and political experiences of immigrants would under-mine national unity. As a result, they viewed public schools as a vehicle for assimilation. This perspective bolstered support for Horace Mann, who per-suasively argued that creating a common school system would help unify a decentralized and increasingly diverse nation (Tyack, 1974; Tyack and Han-sot, 1982). The mission of common schools was to ensure that all children were numerate and literate, to transmit traditional cultural norms and val-ues, and to promote shared economic and political beliefs to support na-tional unity and progress. The expansion and standardization of school cur-ricula, enactment of compulsory school attendance laws, demands for increased accountability, and expectations for increased efficiency (Kowal-ski, 2003) changed the characteristics of public schools and increased the complexity of superintendents' work.

During the mid- to late 1800s, superintendents' stature as intellectual lead-ers in communities increased with their expanded role as teacher-educators. During this period many superintendents liked being cast as intellectuals rather than being characterized as managers or politicians and preferred leaving the business aspects of district administration to board members or to subordinate officials (Callahan, 1967). Many superintendents authored journal articles (Cuban, 1988) and later in their careers served as state superintendents, professors, and college presidents (Petersen and Barnett, 2003), which attested to their status among the nation's intellectual elite. In addition, their penchant to be viewed as intellectuals had a practical side in that it helped to shield them from community power elites who wanted to curtail their growing influence (Kowalski and Björk, 2005).

Toward the end of the 19th century, it was evident that local school boards and administrators were making every effort to align schools with "economic and social conditions of an urban-industrial society" (Cubberly, 1916, p. 126). In this milieu of industrial expansion and nationalist attitudes, concerns were raised that schools were not being operated as efficiently as successful businesses (Kowalski, 1999) and that instructionally oriented superintendents had insufficient knowledge and managerial skills to administer large, complex city school districts. Cuban notes that communities often engaged in heated community debates centered on "whether the functions of a big-city superintendent should be separated into two distinct jobs, i.e., business manager and superintendent of instruction" (Cuban, 1976, p. 17). This issue was resolved during the first two decades of the 20th century as the influence of American industrial and corporate ideology increased, leading to adoption of business management practices throughout society.

Tyack (1974) observed that school boards and superintendents embraced notions of centralized control and created large, comprehensive school systems. For example, they adopted new bureaucratic hierarchical structures that divided schools into grade levels (Goodlad and Anderson, 1963), defined the roles of principals and teachers and provided managerial oversight of school affairs through hierarchical chains of command, and instituted corporate governance and decision-making models; superintendents and principals viewed themselves as executives and employed business management perspectives (Björk, 2005). This transformation was supported by leading education scholars, including Ellwood Cubberly, George Strayer, and Franklin Bobbitt, who advocated adoption of scientific management in public schools (Cronin, 1973).

Although the stock market crash of 1929 and the Depression tarnished the image of captains of industry, through the corporate ideology and scientific management accrued during the preceding three decades the notion of the superintendent as a district CEO was resilient. Despite George Sylvester Counts's and other progressive scholars' criticism of efforts to insert business values into school administration and compelling arguments that it was inconsistent with the tenets of education in a democratic society (Van Til,

1971), these functions became inextricably embedded in the culture of school administration during the next several decades (Kowalski, 1999).

For example, local school boards expected superintendents to use concepts of efficiency and productivity to assess a wide array of district instructional and management tasks. Business management duties typically assigned to superintendents included budget development, administration, and oversight; standardization of rules, regulations, and policies governing operations; personnel management; and facility management. In addition, their image of district-level chief executive officers was reinforced by an increase in governmental control of education through official bureaucratic structures and by shifts of school boards' duties toward policy-making and governance tasks. In sum, the education enterprise unambiguously embraced the corporate management model, which had a profound and lasting effect on schooling and superintendent-board relations throughout the remainder of the 20th century (Tyack, 1974).

During the 1930s, the role of superintendent was influenced by significant economic and political changes occurring in the nation. For example, during preceding decades school boards primarily were responsible for engaging local communities, as well as for securing resources from city, county, and state levels of government. Although it was deemed inappropriate and unprofessional for superintendents to engage in political activities during previous eras (Björk and Lindle, 2001; Kowalski, 1995), the economic depression of the 1930s forced them to politically compete with other public agencies for scarce resources (Björk, 2005; Kowalski, 1999). In these turbulent circumstances, convictions regarding superintendents' serving as politicians and lobbyists were eclipsed by the compelling need to secure financial support for their districts.

In addition, many citizens adopted a populist stance, claiming that superintendents were excluding them from governance and decision-making processes (Kowalski, 2003) and called for restoring their liberties. Consequently, superintendents were forced to assume the mantle of democratic leader and directly engage the community. Although this move was symbolic for many, others saw that it was invaluable in mobilizing "the educational resources of communities" (Melby, 1955, p. 250) and galvanizing policy makers, employees, and other taxpayers to support school district initiatives (Howlett, 1993). In retrospect, the issue was not whether superintendents should be politicians, but how they would use politics to enhance their effectiveness (Björk and Gurley, 2005; Keedy and Björk, 2002). Thus, the political role of superintendents was defined by the changes in society and the need to acquire scarce resources, rather than being dominated by the apolitical rhetoric of the profession.

Between 1954 and 1970, increasing availability of information on the condition of public schools and widespread discriminatory practices contributed to a loss of faith in American education and school administrators. These circumstances contributed to pervasive public dissatisfaction with education and stimulated calls for local school boards and district superintendents to be more responsive to community needs. National issues including civil rights, demands for social justice, and effective education programs for children with disabilities generated political challenges at the local level and increased pressure on superintendents to more effectively communicate with parents, citizens, and interest groups. As public satisfaction with education plummeted, superintendents became increasingly vulnerable to political agendas of interest groups, state legislatures, and local school boards. Consequently, superintendents not only were expected to serve as democratic leaders and district spokespersons but were also asked to find ways to involve all stakeholders in district decision-making processes.

During the 1980s, public concern for the quality of education increased; however, at this juncture dissatisfaction was entwined with widespread perceptions that the national economy was in decline. The *Nation at Risk* (1983) report, as well as others that followed, was highly critical of public education and speculated that it had failed children and the nation's economy. Although economists did not view the academic performance of students as a major factor in slowing down economic growth (Björk, 1996), these popular reports were instrumental in launching the educational reform movement and politicizing how education problems were identified and solved. Interest groups, parents, and policy makers became increasingly strident in their calls for improving standards, test scores, and school choice plans.

The breadth and depth of these reform proposals compelled superintendents to increase their knowledge and capacity to engage in systemic change processes; understand distributed leadership; commit to achieving social justice; and build their capacity for analyzing community, board, and district power structures. During this era superintendents had to be effective "corporate" managers, skilled communicators, and adept politicians capable of maneuvering through a precarious and often unforgiving political landscape to survive in office.

National commission and task force reports released between 1986 and 2008 underscored the importance of educating all children, particularly those regarded as "at risk," and advocated providing support for families to improve the capacity of children to learn at high levels. These shifts underscored the importance of superintendents to serve as applied social scientists (Fusarelli and Fusarelli, 2005). Although superintendents had been expected to understand community social and economic contexts since the 1990s, it became increasingly important after Congress passed the No Child Left Behind Act (Björk, Kowalski, and Young, 2005). In this politically charged, high-stakes accountability environment, superintendents needed not only to understand community contexts but also to use research-based information in the design, development, and delivery of effective educational programs.

In addition, the notion that superintendents should serve as applied social scientists was embraced by critical theorists who agreed that engaging parents and citizens in policy- and decision-making processes was essential to ensuring social justice in public schools (Johnson and Fusarelli, 2003). They recognized that school superintendents were expected to contend with a wide range of contextual issues such as changing demographics, poverty, racism, drugs, and violence (Fusarelli and Fusarelli, 2005). These social and economic factors unquestionably influence the success of children in school and require that superintendents, who are at the forefront of ensuring that schools are socially just, have the knowledge and commitment to reduce their effects on student performance (Fusarelli and Fusarelli, 2005). Superintendents were expected to achieve socially just schools by involving parents and community citizens in policy- and decision-making processes. Although many superintendents recognized that working with community stakeholders would help them gain greater insights into problems and solutions, others found it uncommonly difficult to surrender control, appreciate dissent, and lead collaboratively.

Most policy analysts concur that since the mid-1980s effective school reform not only would require changing how schools are organized, managed, and governed but also would necessitate altering institutional cultures and underlying values and beliefs (Murphy and Louis, 1994). In making a commitment to democratic decision-making processes, superintendents would have to have good communication and conflict management skills (Carlson, 1996) as well as political acumen. Many scholars contend that communication and organizational culture, rather than being reserved for professionals in upper-level management positions, is pervasive (Conrad, 1994) and reciprocal, and influences behavior associated with building, affirming, and changing culture (Kowalski, 2005). In these emerging circumstances, superintendents' normative communicative behavior is influenced by several realities, including the need for them to lead the process of school reform (Björk, 2001a), to change district and school organizational cultures as part of the restructuring process (Kowalski, 2000), and to engage a wider range of political stakeholders in the reform process.

It is evident that schools are inexorably bound to local communities as well as to changes in the social, economic, and political life of the nation. Changes in these environmental contexts consequently influence the nature of organizational structures, administrator roles, and superintendent-board relations. In retrospect, five role conceptualizations have emerged that both describe and frame the work of superintendents: (a) *teacher-scholar* (1850 to early 1900s); (b) *organizational manager* (early 1900s to 1930); (c) *democratic leader* (1930 to mid-1950s); (d) *applied social scientist* (mid-1950s to mid-1970s); and (e) *communicator* (mid-1970s to present) (Kowalski and Björk, 2005). Although these five roles may be identified and help clarify the complexity of superintendents' work, effective practitioners often use them in concert to enhance their effectiveness. How superintendents enact these roles illuminates the political dimensions of their relations with local school boards.

SUPERINTENDENT AS EDUCATIONAL STATESMAN, DEMOCRATIC LEADER, AND POLITICAL STRATEGIST

Although superintendents eschewed the role of politician during the 19th and early 20th centuries, they were thrust unceremoniously into the fray during the turbulent post-Depression era of the 1930s. Americans embraced the populist notion that "public schools should practice and model democracy and re-establish symbiotic relationships with the communities in which they functioned" (Kowalski, 1999, p. 191). Consequently, between 1930 and the mid-1950s the role of the superintendent shifted to meet community expectations that they serve as *educational statesmen* (Callahan, 1967). Although this notion of superintendents is compelling, it may be useful to explore the philosophical roots of the term by examining Plato's notion of political statesman and Alexander Hamilton's ideal of the American statesman.

Plato asserted in his dialogue *Politicus* (Latin for "statesman"), written in 400 BCE, that the ideal form of government would be based upon "the supremacy not of law, but of the wise and kingly man." He makes an important distinction between an individual's knowledge and its application in government. Plato's notion of statesman is "one who really understands what is for the good of the commonwealth, and is right, and consequently makes the commonwealth better, whether by gentle measures or by sharp 'social surgery'" (Plato, trans. Taylor, 1961, p. 229). Plato refers to benevolent and skillful application of knowledge as the "art of politics," noting that the political statesman acts unilaterally and paternalistically in directing major functions of government in society, including military, rhetoric (i.e., diplomacy), and education.

As it is applied in education settings, Plato's statesman determines who is educated and what knowledge best meets the needs of society. He uses a weaving metaphor to elaborate the role of a statesman, describing him as a master weaver culling out the bad material from the good and using the best to construct the nation's social fabric. Plato's notions of statesmanship in a democratic society, particularly with regard to who rules and who benefits, must be balanced with the knowledge that in ancient Greece privileges of citizenship were reserved for the few rather than the many (Björk and Gurley, 2005). The autocratic nature of Plato's concept of statesman may be inappropriate in its application to a democratic society that is broadly representative.

Although Alexander Hamilton embraced the notion of centralized authority and shared Plato's belief that a statesman must base actions on expert knowledge and to serve as an architect for the common good, he believed a statesman had to be a "true politician" who was aware of the needs of and responsive to two primary constituencies: commoners and the economic elite (Miroff, 1993, p. 27). Hamilton was an aristocrat, and his vision was "rooted in disenchantment with and distrust of the American people . . . [who were] incapable of making good use of political freedom" (Miroff, 1993, p. 30). His notion of statesman and views of a democratic society in regard to who rules and who benefits are paternalistic and privileged the upper classes.

Scholars concur that superintendents' work is highly political in nature and note that during the past several decades it has increased both in its relevancy and intensity. Although the role of "educational statesmen" (Callahan, 1967) or "negotiator statesmen" (Cuban, 1976) describes one of the most important roles that superintendents must play, the term does not reflect the complexity and intensity of district politics fueled by unrelenting calls for educational reform, demands for accountability, expectations for providing a broader range to more students with fewer resources, and heightened levels of interest-group activity. A comprehensive analysis of the discourse on the superintendency between 1820 and 2001 by Brunner, Grogan, and Björk (2002) found that the reality of their work did not match the rhetoric surrounding the term *statesmanship*. Later, Björk and Gurley (2005) commented that this term is not and may never have been an appropriate role conception for American superintendents. They note that the superintendents' role was not about being a knowledgeable patriarch who benevolently managed school systems for the few, as Plato's statesman suggests. Neither is it like Hamilton's conception of the political statesman who was an elite expert, aloof, and adeptly manipulated constituency groups to benefit the privileged classes.

Instead, Björk and Gurley (2005) proposed that the American superintendency was grounded in the populist belief that public schools were intended to serve the public. In this regard, superintendents were expected to honor the public's lawful claim to its schools, manage them efficiently, and ensure that students became literate and numerate and participated in the social, economic, and political life of the nation. As noted by Brunner, Grogan, and Björk (2002), superintendents are leading in dramatically changing contexts, and consequently discourse surrounding their work suggests that present roles are being modified and new roles are emerging. They believe that in the future superintendents must become adept as professional advisors to boards as well as skilled at working collaboratively with boards, citizens, and diverse interest groups. It is evident that a superintendent's role is neither like Plato's patriarch nor like Hamilton's elite statesman. Rather, it is a role that is being defined by uniquely American experiences, suggesting that in this century we may view superintendents as democratically oriented political strategists.

POLITICS AND THE SUPERINTENDENCY

The term *politics* commonly refers to decisions about how values and scarce resources are allocated in society or in an organization. Macropolitics and micropolitics are two broad dimensions of the politics of education that involve similar conflictual and cooperative processes involving individual and group interests, power and influence, strategic interaction, values, and ideologies (Ball, 1987; Blase and Blase, 1998). In the post–*Nation at Risk* era, the value of research on policy making and the politics of education increased as scholars studied state and federal reform initiatives (Marshall, Mitchell, and Wirt, 1989); the devolution of governance to the school level (Malen and Ogawa, 1990); micropolitics (Blase and Björk, forthcoming; Blase and Blase, 2002; Johnson, 2003); and the dynamics of educational reform (Fuhrman, 1993). Advocates for strengthening the policy focus of research on education persuasively argue that politics and policy making are closely linked, in that the objective of the former is to accomplish the latter (Johnson, 2003). In this regard, the study of superintendents' political role involved their influence on state-level policy (i.e., at a macro level) as well as internal organizational and school board politics (micro).

Since the early 1970s, scholars have made an effort to study, synthesize, interpret, and explain the nature of the politics of education and chart its evolution as a field of study (Björk, 2005; Johnson, 2003). Efforts to define the politics of education as a field of study generated renewed interest and empirical investigations into the role of superintendents as political actors as well as their relations with school boards (Björk and Lindle, 2001; Blase and Björk, forthcoming). Initially, the nature and direction of these investigations were dominated by conventional political science perspectives and theoretical orientations including "behaviorism, pluralism, and elitism" (Johnson, 2003, p. 4).

During the 1950s, studies focused on structure, behavioral dynamics, and voting patterns in federal, state, and local education agencies. Scholars working during the 1970s and 1980s, however, felt constrained by traditional process-oriented frameworks and sought out a broader range of theories to help explain complex decision-making processes in public sector organizations and school districts. Consequently, the study of the politics of education moved from initial studies focused on electoral patterns, organizational processes, and local governance issues to a multidisciplined field of study that examined educational policy making and implementation at the state and federal levels of government (Berman and McLaughlin, 1978).

Micropolitics focuses on relations among individuals within organizations such as district offices and schools, as well as within groups attempting to influence the allocation of values and scarce resources through decision- and policy-making processes (Blase and Blase, 2002; Johnson, 2003). Blase and Björk (forthcoming) note that the study of micropolitics in education recognizes that a macropolitics influences micropolitical activities in organizations and communities. There is a lack of consensus in the field as to the conceptual parameters of micropolitics. For example, some scholars view micropolitics as occurring at the school level (Blase and Björk, forthcoming; Iannaccone, 1975; Malen, 1994); however, others contend that it can occur at any level of education and society (Morgan, 1986; Pfeffer, 1978).

Bachrach and Mundell bring considerable clarity to the discussion. They note that micropolitics "is not defined by its context but rather by its nature. That is, micropolitics (all levels) involves strategic contests among interest groups over different logics of action" (Bachrach and Mundell, 1995, p. 432) and thus can occur at many levels of organization and government. Blase provides a broad-based definition of micropolitics that includes conflictive as well as cooperative processes:

> Micropolitics refers to the use of formal and informal power by individuals and groups to achieve their goals in organizations. In large part political action results from perceived differences between individuals and groups, coupled with the motivation to use power to influence and/or protect. Although such actions are consciously motivated, any action, consciously motivated, may have "political significance" in a given situation. Both cooperative and conflictive actions and processes are part of the realm of micropolitics. Moreover, macro and micropolitical factors frequently interact. (Blase, 1991, p. 11)

Political action is the central mechanism that drives the organization, shapes its formal characteristics (structure, patterns of hierarchical authority), influences its informal, cultural elements (ideologies, decision making, power distribution), and social relations among participants (individual and group behavior).

MICROPOLITICS, SUPERINTENDENCY, AND EDUCATIONAL REFORM

Superintendent support is key to the success of educational reform (Björk, Kowalski, and Young, 2005). Research findings on the role of superintendents in facilitating and inhibiting reform provide insight into the use of power and micropolitical processes. For example, superintendents who are involved in instructional matters (Björk, 1996); serve as professional advisors to school boards (Björk, 2005); analyze Hispanic community power structures and cultural practices (Ortiz, 2001, 2002); coalesce Hispanic interest groups, build coalitions, and negotiate agreements (Owen and Ovando, 2000); assess constituent group positions and understand board power configurations (Skrla, Scott, and Benestante, 2001); build minority constituent coalitions (Grogan and Blackmon, 2001); and support the establishment of a professional climate for advancing teaching and learning, and effectively communicate with the public (Berends, Bodilly, and Kirby, 2003); contribute to successful educational reform efforts.

Although the role of superintendents is pivotal to the success of district-level school reform, they may also impede change through their decisions and practices. Scholars have examined the dark side of superintendents behavior, including the following: how they acquiesced to interest-group political pressure on a school board that undermined reform (Björk, 2001b); created widespread dissatisfaction in the community by changing their position on collective bargaining with unions (Riley, Conley, and Glassman, 2002); failed to provide adequate support and time for school-based decisions (Blase and Blase, 1994; Brown and Hawkins, 1988; Murphy and Louis, 1994); controlled release of test scores, which inhibited analysis of problems in low-achieving schools (Hoffman and Burrello, 2004); inhibited clarification of governance procedures to maintain control (Bondy et al., 1994); refused to support principals in conflicts with others (Crowson and Boyd, 1991); used contrived collegiality, for example, top-down mandates to create school-based collegiality among teachers (Hargreaves, 1991); and failed to remove structural and cultural barriers (sexist and racist practices) that limited professional advancement and marginalized black women principals (Bloom and Erlandson, 2003). In retrospect, it is evident that superintendents' use of formal and informal power can inhibit accomplishing educational reform.

THE MICROPOLITICS OF SUPERINTENDENT-BOARD RELATIONS

Since the early 1970s, researchers have investigated relationships between local school boards, communities, and superintendents as a way to understand how their roles are defined and redefined (Björk, 2005). Understanding this dynamic relationship as well as their responses to calls for educational reform provides a framework for understanding the use of formal and informal power and the micropolitics of superintendent–school board relations. Over the past quarter-century, school boards have been confronted by unrelenting public demands and government mandates to launch and sustain education reform initiatives focused on improving student academic performance. During this period, policy-making authority has shifted to state levels of government and decision making has devolved to local schools while resources have declined (Björk, 2005; Björk and Keedy, 2002; Johnson, 1996).

Despite these shortcomings, school board meetings continue to serve as political forums in which individuals and groups openly express real needs and reconcile their differences through open debate, negotiation, and compromise. This school governance perspective affirms their role as stewards of education in local communities and a commitment to building social capital and civic capacity in a democratic society (Björk, 2005; Björk and Gurley, 2005). Given the political nature of communities and the penchant of interest groups to use power to influence school board deliberations, decision outcomes may facilitate as well as impede school reform efforts.

Alsbury (2003) and Björk (2005) found that school board political configurations are influenced by changes in community values, interest-group coalitions, and school board power structures. Mountford (2004) found that the way school board members define power is related to their motivation to serve. In addition, Shipps (2003) acknowledged that the composition of multiple interest-group coalitions will often determine school board meeting agendas, policy-making processes, and outcomes. Feuerstein and Dietrich (2003) found that political turbulence in local communities and interest-group conflict frequently impede board efforts to develop and implement education reform initiatives. Furthermore, Louis and King (1993) discovered that reform efforts were impeded because a school board's need for accountability information required teachers to share negative data about reform that potentially threatened the school board's willingness to continue its support.

However, in a longitudinal study of school district reform, Björk (2001b) found that boards advanced educational reforms by engaging community interest groups and building consensus. These studies provide insight into the complexity of board policy- and decision-making processes, as well as difficulty in instituting educational reforms. As Mangham states, "[S]o significant is the collection of forces which underpin behavior in organizations that it is surprising that any changes ever manage to be promulgated let alone implemented" (Mangham, 1979, p. 122). Using a micropolitical lens to understand these dynamics may facilitate accomplishing reforms.

DISCUSSION

During the past several decades, local school boards and superintendents have been confronted with unrelenting calls to reform public schools. As the locus of policy and decision making shifted to states and schools, school boards and superintendents experienced increasing pressure from citizens, parents, and interest groups. These circumstances contributed to reconfiguring their respective roles and patterns of interaction as well as how they engage parents, citizens, and interest groups. Blase and Blase (2002) observe that micropolitics is useful to understanding the political culture as well as the use of formal and informal power by key actors in this dynamic relationship. Although research findings on organizational structures, practices, and processes provide insight into the changing nature and complexity of superintendent–school board relations, micropolitics provides a theoretical basis for explaining as well as predicting district-level behavior.

REFERENCES

Alsbury, T. 2003. Superintendent and school board member turnover: Political versus apolitical turnover as a critical variable in the application of Dissatisfaction Theory. *Educational Administration Quarterly* 39 (5): 667–698.

Ball, S. J. 1987. *The micro-politics of the school: Towards a theory of school organization.* New York: Methuen.

Beck, L., and W. Foster. 1999. Administration and community: Considering challenges, exploring possibilities. In *Handbook of research on educational administration,* ed. J. Murphy and K. S. Louis, 337–358. San Francisco: Jossey-Bass.

Berends, M., S. Bodilly, and S. Kirby. 2003. New American schools: District and school leadership for whole school reform. In *Leadership lessons from comprehensive school reform,* ed. J. Murphy and A. Datnow, 180–210. Thousand Oaks, CA: Corwin Press.

Berman, P., and M. McLaughlin. 1978. *Federal programs supporting educational change.* Vol. 3, *Implementing and sustaining innovations.* Santa Monica, CA: Rand.

Björk, L. 1996. The revisionists' critique of the education reform reports. *Journal of School Leadership* 7 (1): 290–315.

———. 2001a. Preparing the next generation of superintendents: Integrating formal and experiential knowledge. In *Advances in research and theories of school management and educational policy.* Vol. 6, *The new superintendency,* ed. C. C. Brunner and L. Björk, 19–54. Greenwich, CT: JAI Press.

———. 2001b. The role of the central office in decentralization. In *Twenty-first-century challenges for school administrators,* ed. T. Kowalski and G. Perreault, 286–309. Lanham, MD: Scarecrow Press.

———. 2005. Superintendent-board relations: An historical overview of the dynamics of change and sources of conflict and collaboration. In *The district superintendent and school board relations: Trends in policy development and implementation,* ed. G. Peterson and L. Fusarelli, 1–22. Greenwich, CT: Information Age.

Björk, L., and K. Gurley. 2005. Superintendent as educational statesman and political strategist. In *The contemporary superintendent: Preparation, practice and development,* ed. L. Björk and T. Kowalski, 163–186. Thousand Oaks, CA: Corwin Press.

Björk, L., T. Kowalski, and M. Young. 2005. National reports and implications for professional preparation and development. In *The contemporary superintendent: Preparation, practice and development*, ed. L. Björk and T. Kowalski, 45–70. Thousand Oaks, CA: Corwin Press.

Björk, L., and J. C. Lindle. 2001. Superintendents and interest groups. *Educational Policy* 15 (1): 76–91.

Blase, J. 1998. The micropolitics of educational change. In *The international handbook of educational change*, ed. A. Hargreaves, 544–557. London: Kluwer.

Blase, J., and L. Björk. Forthcoming. Micropolitics of educational change and reform. In *The international handbook of educational change*, ed. A. Hargreaves. New York: Springer.

Blase, J., and J. Blase. 2000. *Empowering teachers: What successful principals do.* 2nd ed. Thousand Oaks, CA: Corwin Press.

———. 2002. The micropolitics of instructional supervision: A call for research. *Educational Administration Quarterly* 38 (1): 6–44.

Bloom, C., and D. Erlandson. 2003. African American women principals in urban schools: Realities, (re)constructions, and resolutions. *Educational Administration Quarterly* 39 (3): 339–369.

Blumberg, A. 1985. *The school superintendent: Living with conflict.* New York: Teachers College Press.

Bondy, E., D. Ross, and R. Webb. 1994. The dilemmas of school restructuring and improvement. Paper presented at the annual meeting of the American Educational Research Association, New Orleans.

Brunner, C. C., M. Grogan, and L. Björk. 2002. Shifts in the discourse defining the superintendency: Historical and current foundations of the position. In *The educational leadership challenge: Redefining leadership for the 21st century*, ed. J. Murphy, 211–238. Chicago: University of Chicago Press.

Callahan, R. E. 1967. *The superintendent of schools: An historical analysis.* ERIC Document Reproduction Service No. ED010 410.

Carlson, R. V. 1996. *Reframing and reform: Perspectives on organization, leadership, and school change.* New York: Longman.

Conrad, C. 1994. *Strategic organizational communication: Toward the twenty-first century.* 3rd ed. Fort Worth, TX: Harcourt Brace College.

Cremin, L. 1988. *American education: The metropolitan experience.* New York: Harcourt Brace.

Cronin, J. M. 1973. *The control of urban schools: Perspective on the power of educational reformers.* New York: Free Press.

Crowson, R. L., and W. L. Boyd. 1991. Urban schools as organizations: Political perspectives. In *Politics of education yearbook*, ed. J. G. Cibulka, R. J. Reed, and K. K. Wong, 87–103. London: Taylor & Francis.

Cuban, L. 1976. *Urban school chiefs under fire.* Chicago: University of Chicago Press.

———. 1988. *The managerial imperative and the practice of leadership in schools.* Albany: SUNY Press.

Cubberly, E. 1916. *Public school administration.* Boston: Houghton Mifflin.

Feuerstein, A., and J. Dietrich. 2003. State standards in the local context: A survey of school board members and superintendents. *Educational Policy* 17 (2): 237–256.

Fuhrman, S., ed. 1993. *Designing coherent educational policy.* San Francisco: Jossey-Bass.

Fusarelli, B., and L. Fusarelli. 2005. Reconceptualizing the superintendency: Superintendents as social scientists and social activists. In *School district superintendents: Role expectations, professional preparation, development and licensing*, ed. L. Björk and T. Kowalski. Thousand Oaks, CA: Corwin Press.

Goodlad, J., and R. Anderson. 1963. *The nongraded elementary school.* New York: Harcourt Brace.

Grieder, C., T. M. Pierce, and K. F. Jordan. 1969. *Public school administration.* 3rd ed. New York: Ronald Press.

Grogan, M., and M. Blackmon. 2001. A superintendent's approach to coalition building: Working with diversity to garner support for educational initiatives. In *The new superintendency*, ed. C. C. Brunner and L. Björk, 95–114. Amsterdam: JAI Elsevier Science.

Hargreaves, A. 1991. Contrived collegiality: The micropolitics of teacher collaboration. In *The politics of life in schools: Power, conflict, and cooperation*, ed. J. Blase, 46–72. Newbury Park, CA: Sage.

Hoffman, L., and L. Burrello. 2004. A case study illustration of how a critical theorist and a consummate practitioner meet on common ground. *Educational Administration Quarterly* 40 (2): 268–289.

Howlett, P. 1993. The politics of school leaders, past and future. *Education Digest* 58 (9): 18–21.

Iannaccone, L. 1975. *Educational policy systems: A study guide for educational administrators.* Fort Lauderdale, FL: Nova University Press.

Johnson, B. C., and L. D. Fusarelli. 2003. Superintendent as social scientist. Paper presented at the annual meeting of the American Educational Research Association, Chicago.

Johnson, R. 2003. Those nagging headaches: Perennial issues and tensions in the politics of education field. *Educational Administration Quarterly* 39 (1): 41–67.

Johnson, S. M. 1996. *Leading to change: The challenge of the new superintendency.* San Francisco: Jossey-Bass.

Keedy, J. L., and L. G. Björk. 2002. Superintendents and local boards and the potential for community polarization: The call for use of political strategist skills. In *The promises and perils facing today's school superintendent*, ed. B. S. Cooper and L. D. Fusarelli, 103–127. Lanham, MD: Scarecrow Press.

Kowalski, T. J. 1995. *Keepers of the flame: Contemporary urban superintendents.* Thousand Oaks, CA: Corwin Press.

———. 1999. *The school superintendent: Theory, practice, and cases.* Upper Saddle River, NJ: Merrill-Prentice Hall.

———. 2003. *Contemporary school administration.* 2nd ed. Boston: Allyn & Bacon.

———. 2005. Evolution of the school district superintendent position. In *The contemporary superintendent: Preparation, practice and development*, ed. L. Björk and T. Kowalski, 163–186. Thousand Oaks, CA: Corwin Press.

Kowalski, T. J., and L. Björk. 2005. Role expectations of district superintendents: Implications for deregulating preparation and licensing. *Journal of Thought* 40 (2): 73–96.

Louis, K. S., and J. A. King. 1993. Professional cultures and reforming schools: Does the myth of Sisyphus apply? In *Restructuring schooling: Learning from ongoing efforts,* ed. J. Murphy and P. Hallinger, 216–250. Newbury Park, CA: Corwin Press.

Malen, B. 1994. The micropolitics of education: Mapping the multiple dimensions of power relations in school politics. *Journal of Educational Policy* 9:147–167.

Malen, B., and R. Ogawa. 1990. Community involvement: Parents, teachers and administration working together. In *Education reform: Making sense of it all,* ed. S. B. Bachrach, 103–120. Boston: Allyn & Bacon.

Mangham, I. L. 1979. *The politics of organizational change.* Westport, CT: Greenwood Press.

Marshall, C., D. Mitchell, and F. Wirt. 1989. *Culture and educational policy in American states.* London: Falmer Press.

Melby, E. O. 1955. *Administering community education.* Englewood Cliffs, NJ: Prentice Hall.

Miroff, B. 1993. *Icons of democracy: American leaders as heroes, aristocrats, dissenters, and democrats.* New York: Basic Books.

Morgan, G. 1986. *Images of organizations.* Beverly Hills, CA: Sage.

Mountford, M. 2004. Motives and power of school board members: Implications for school-board-superintendent relations. *Educational Administration Quarterly* 40 (5): 704–741.

Murphy, J. 1999. *The quest for a center: Notes on the state of the profession of educational leadership.* Columbia, MO: University Council for Educational Administration.

Murphy, J., and K. S. Louis, eds. 1994. *Reshaping the principalship: Insights from transformational reform efforts.* Thousand Oaks, CA: Corwin Press.

National Commission on Excellence in Education. 1983. *A nation at risk: The imperative for educational reform.* Washington, DC: Government Printing Office.

Ortiz, F. 2001. Using social capital in interpreting the careers of three Latina superintendents. *Educational Administration Quarterly* 37 (1): 58–85.

———. 2002. Executive succession processes and management success for Latina superintendents. In *The promises and perils facing today's school superintendents,* ed. B. Cooper and L. Fusarelli, 21–40. Lanham, MD: Scarecrow Press.

Owen, J., and M. Ovando. 2000. The superintendent as political leader. In *Superintendent's guide to creating community,* 32–44. Lanham, MD: Scarecrow Press.

Petersen, G. J., and B. G. Barnett. 2003. The superintendent as instructional leader: History, evolution and future of the role. Paper presented at the annual meeting of the American Educational Research Association, Chicago.

Pfeffer, J. 1978. The micropolitics of organizations. In *Environments and organizations,* ed. M. W. Meyer, 29–50. San Francisco: Jossey-Bass.

Plato. Circa 400 BCE. *Politicus.* Trans. A. E. Taylor. London: Thomas Nelson, 1961.

Riley, V., S. Conley, and N. Glassman. 2002. Superintendents' views of new and traditional collective bargaining processes. In *The promises and perils facing today's school superintendents,* ed. B. Cooper and L. Fusarelli, 77–101. Lanham, MD: Scarecrow Press.

Shipps, D. 2003. Pulling together: Civic capacity and urban school reform. *American Educational Research Journal* 40 (4): 841–878.

Skrla, L., P. Reyes, and J. Scheurich. 2000. Sexism, silence, and solutions: Gaining access to the superintendency; Head hunting, gender, and color. *Educational Administration Quarterly* 36 (1): 44–75.

Skrla, L., J. Scott, and J. Benestante. 2001. Dangerous intersection: A meta-ethnographic study of gender, power, and politics in the public superintendency. In *The new superintendency*, ed. C. C. Brunner and L. Björk, 115–131. Amsterdam: JAI Elsevier Science.

Tyack, D. 1974. *The one best system: A history of American public education.* Cambridge, MA: Harvard University Press.

Tyack, D. B., and E. Hansot. 1982. *Managers of virtue: Public school leadership in America.* New York: Basic Books.

United States Department of Education. 1991. *America 2000: An education strategy.* Washington, DC: Government Printing Office.

Van Til, W. 1971. Prologue: Is progressive education obsolete? In *Curriculum: Quest for relevance*, 9–17. Boston: Houghton Mifflin.

Wirt, F., and M. Kirst. 2001. *The political dynamics of American education.* Berkeley, CA: McCutchan.

III

SCHOOL BOARD–SUPERINTENDENT AND AUTHORITY RELATIONS

5

Historical and Current Tensions among Board-Superintendent Teams: Symptoms or Cause?

Meredith Mountford

The relationship between school boards and superintendents in American public schools has been fraught with controversy since their inception in the mid-1800s. This relationship has been notoriously characterized as tense and conflict laden, and largely because of this, board-superintendent teams today are often characterized as dysfunctional. While board development programs and superintendent preparation programs continue to try to educate board members and superintendents on their roles and responsibilities, the problems associated with school boards and superintendents have continued to exist for the past 200 years. Such persistence suggests perhaps that training and education programs for board members and superintendents have only been addressing the symptoms of something else. And until the source of those symptoms is identified and addressed head on, school boards and superintendents will likely remain largely dysfunctional.

This chapter briefly reviews the historical development of school boards' and superintendents' evolving roles and relationship over the last two centuries. Several historical and current sources of tension between school boards and superintendents commonly cited in the literature are also reviewed, and findings from a recent study suggesting the sources of tension commonly cited in board and superintendent literature are perhaps only symptoms of deeper, underlying psychological and sociological root causes. Ultimately, the purpose of this chapter is to elucidate some underlying root sources of tension between school boards and superintendents so that educational leadership and school board development training programs can begin to address some of the underlying root sources of the tension rather than just simply addressing the symptoms.

A BRIEF HISTORY OF THE CONFLICT BETWEEN SCHOOL BOARDS AND SUPERINTENDENTS

In 1789, Massachusetts passed legislation that authorized towns to employ special committees designed to supervise schools; they had extensive powers and responsibilities, including making curricular decisions, employing staff, choosing textbooks, building schools, awarding diplomas, and establishing administrative structures needed to operate the schools. These administrative structures primarily came in the form of local superintendents, who had some assigned duties and responsibilities, but the local board retained the majority of control (Callahan, 1975; Campbell et al., 1985). Formal authority over schools at the state and federal level was almost nonexistent (Callahan, 1975; Education Commission of the States (ECS), 1999).

However, in 1837, while traveling for pleasure abroad, Horace Mann, state superintendent of Massachusetts, visited several European school systems. During his trip Mann kept detailed accounts of his findings. His report back to the State of Massachusetts indicated that Prussia's school governance model was the best he had seen (Callahan, 1975). Mann believed the success of Prussia's system was due to its high level of supervision within each district. The kingdoms in Prussia had been divided into several districts, and each district had a commissioner. Mann concluded that schools having district supervisors brought the districts to higher levels of student achievement (Callahan, 1975; Campbell et al., 1985). After Mann made this discovery, he made sure that the low scores from tests administered by the boards of education to all public school students were made public, to ensure that people would begin to question the efficacy of boards of education and seek new governance models.

Next, Mann created a committee to study this issue. The committee issued a report, which suggested that those running for school board seats did not have the purest of motives and were not concerned with increasing student achievement. For instance, part of the report stated:

> The basic problem is that the schools are being run by a school board of twenty-four men who are not paid for their labor, and who share a responsibility which when broken into fragments presses no one. Who must on the common principles of human nature, be made willing to hold this office by every variety of motive, from the highest and purest love of usefulness, down to a mere personal purpose of coining its privileges and opportunities into dollars and cents? (*Common School Journal*, 1845, cited in Callahan, 1975, p. 23).

While Mann did not seek to abolish school boards, he did attempt to weaken the credibility of them by arguing that superintendents for individual school districts should be appointed. Mann and his committee successfully argued their case; subsequently, geographical areas were divided into school districts and a superintendent appointed (Callahan, 1975). This model of school governance spread across New England and eventually throughout the United States.

Throughout the Civil War, superintendents became increasingly agitated by their lack of real authority in terms of making systemic change without the approval of often large and growingly diverse boards of education. Therefore, superintendents engaged in heated debates with scholars and school board members over who should have the final authority in decisions regarding all aspects of school operations (Cuban, 1988). As Callahan states, "Their [superintendents'] objective was to change the system so that the superintendents had the power, the prestige, the salary, and the security which they thought they needed and deserved" (Callahan, 1975, p. 25). The superintendents who pushed the issue advanced their interests by promoting themselves as educational experts and protectors of democracy. They cited corrupt politicians in an attempt to convince Americans that school board members were corrupt. The situation has been described as follows:

> The writings and the speeches of the superintendents show a gradual increase in frustration over their lack of power and an increasing militancy and boldness in their recommendations for change. They were angered whenever a prominent superintendent was arbitrarily dismissed, and they were angered and aroused as the evidence of corruption by school board members was increasingly publicized. (Callahan, 1975, p. 27)

This debate dragged on until 1895, when school boards were reduced in size and superintendents were given complete control of instructional programming. Then in 1916, Elwood Cubberly, dean of the School of Education at Stanford, wrote a textbook commonly used in educational administration departments at that time across the country, which strongly supported Mann and his followers. He profiled the type of person that would be a "desirable type" to be on a school board. He indicated that citizens such as professional businessmen and bankers would be good and "efficient" school board members, but retired or unsuccessful businessmen would not make good board members. He maintained that these board members would spend too much time muddling the daily operations of the schools (Callahan, 1975). School boards were to decide policy, but the responsibility for the operations of the schools was handed over to the administrators. Therefore, while the number of decisions made by the administration increased, the number of decisions made by the lay boards decreased (ECS, 1999).

However, even with the school governance system changed, between 1915 and 1960, complaints about school board members and lay governance continued. Most of these complaints came from influential scholars. In a report published in 1929 by George Counts concerning the socioeconomic representation of people on school boards, Counts concluded that school boards were composed of mostly affluent, white-collar citizens; thus, the working-class citizens were not well represented on lay boards of education (Callahan, 1975). Counts's conclusion raised concerns for school officials, school board chairs, and scholars. Discussion of this criticism of school boards continued, and further research suggested that inequality in socioeconomic representation on school boards, in fact, did exist (Callahan, 1975; Tucker and Zeigler, 1980).

During the 1950s the federal government began to heavily intervene in school governance, after math and science scores on standardized tests of American school children steadily declined. As the federal interest in education grew, so did the bureaucracies that oversaw them. Each state education department became a "holding company" for collection and distribution of state and federally funded programs (ECS, 1999, p. 10). School boards and superintendents had few if any decisions to make with regard to state and federally funded programs within their district. It was at this point that the state and federal government began to take many of the legislative decisions (policy decisions) away from school boards, and their powers further diminished.

State and federal involvement continued throughout the seventies and began to increase after *A Nation at Risk* was published in 1983. The government became increasingly involved in legislating decisions at the local level. Today, state and federal educational agencies make many of the legislative decisions once made by local school boards. In the new millennium, school boards make fewer and fewer decisions but are held increasingly accountable for student performance and achievement, as are superintendents and principals in light of the No Child Left Behind (NCLB) legislation. In addition, school boards must rely heavily on the superintendent to keep them informed of changes in state and federal mandates. In fact, the NCLB legislation of 2005 includes 588 mandates that school administrators and boards are required to file a report on with the federal government.

While it seems logical that boards and superintendents have a common adversary to contend with, their relationship still remains rocky. Recently several reports have been published in an effort to help boards come together and become more collaborative partners, such as Goodman and Zimmerman's report that stated:

> Strong, collaborative leadership by local school boards and school superintendents is a key cornerstone of the foundation for student achievement. If this

country is serious about improving student achievement and maximizing the development of all its children, then local educational leadership teams—superintendents and school board members—must work cooperatively and collaboratively to mobilize their communities to get the job done. (Goodman and Zimmerman, 2000, p. 1)

While such advice may easily be given, in order to appreciate the complexity of following through on this advice, it is important to review and understand the specific issues frequently cited as obstacles to school board members and superintendents working as collaborative teams. To that end, the following section reviews nine specific issues commonly cited in superintendent and school board literature as the sources of tension for school board member–superintendent teams.

SCHOOL BOARD MEMBERS AND SUPERINTENDENTS: SYMPTOMS OF A TROUBLED RELATIONSHIP

Within school board and superintendent literature, several reasons are frequently cited as sources or causes of controversy and conflict among school board members and superintendents. Historically the sources of tension between boards and superintendents have been reported as (a) confusion over roles and responsibilities, (b) power struggles, (c) questionable motives for board service, and (d) equality of representation. These sources of tension still persist today, but with increasing complexity. In addition, new sources of controversy between boards and superintendents have recently been reported, such as (a) changes in philosophical orientation among new generations of board members, (b) disparate beliefs and attitudes, (c) increasing state and federal accountability, (d) increasing resistance for service, and (e) public apathy toward education. In the next sections, each of these nine commonly cited sources of tension will be described in more detail.

Role Confusion

Perhaps the most commonly cited reason for a lack of cohesion on school board member–superintendent teams—both historically and currently—is role confusion (ECS, 1999; Glass, 1992; Glass, Björk, and Brunner, 2000; IEL, 1984; Kaplan, 1989; National School Boards Association, 1996). Originally, school boards had total governance authority over the operations of the schools; presently their role has shifted to policy making. However, school boards rarely initiate policy because policy is most often formulated by the state or the superintendent (Glass, Björk, and Brunner, 2000) and brought forward to the board only after its formulation. In fact, Zeigler and

Jennings conducted one of the most comprehensive studies of school boards and concluded that

> School boards have largely ceased to exercise their representative and policy-making functions; for the most part they do not govern, but merely legitimate the policy recommendations of school superintendents. Thus, according to this view, the public, democratic control of education has been reduced to little more than a sham. (Zeigler et al., 1974, p. 85)

Because superintendents, the state, and increasing federal initiatives have usurped school board members' primary function as policy makers (Carver, 1997), board members understandably become confused as to where their energies should be funneled. Sometimes this confusion leads to board member micromanagement and can become a catalyst for controversy that severely weakens trust and collaboration between the superintendent and his or her board.

Power Struggles

In addition to role confusion, researchers have advanced that some school board members who are interested in exerting control or wielding power rather than seeking all possible sources of input before collaborating with their board colleagues or coming to a consensus on an issue create turbulent intra-board relationships (Danzberger, 1987; Danzberger et al., 1992). In some circumstances, power struggles emerge between board members who seek to advance local, state, and federal initiatives to ensure district accountability and those who wish to simply advance their own agendas (Boyd, 1975). In other circumstances, power struggles emerge when board members attempt to control staff, faculty, or even the superintendent in order to see their own agendas, or views, satisfied.

School board members do not hold formal power as individuals. Their power lies only with the entire group of school board members. They are not expected, nor encouraged, to make decisions as one, but rather are expected to collaborate with their board colleagues when a decision needs to be made. Yet, while expected to collaborate with their colleagues around decision making—potentially the most important part of their job—board members receive little to no training on how to engage in collaborative decision making, and even worse, many of their superintendents have not had this training either (Mountford and Ylimaki, 2005). Collaborative decision making is a skill that requires knowledge and practice of the process (Pounder, 1998). Yet board members who may or may not have had experience with collaboration are expected to cede individual decision-making processes to group processes from the moment they join the board.

Questionable Motives for Service

In 1958, Neal Gross's research on motivations for school board membership indicated that citizens interested in quality education should elect school board members who have the *right* motivation for serving. Citizens interested in quality education, he indicated, were those who wished to serve out of a sense of civic duty, rather than out of a desire to gain political experience or represent some political group (Boyd, 1975). Board members who run out of a sense of civic duty, Gross suggested, would be more likely to make decisions based on the common good of the students within a district. However, other studies investigating motives for board membership have also suggested that many board members run for board seats for reasons that are less than altruistic.

Empirical studies on the motives for board service have found that some school board members are motivated to serve on boards for reason of power acquisition rather than altruism or the promotion of the common good. McCarty and Ramsey (1971) found that people were motivated for both personal, altruistic, and a mix of these two types of motives. Several years later, a student of McCarty's (Alby, 1979) found five primary reasons people were motivated for board service: (a) a specific problem that needed correction, (b) civic interest, (c) recognition or prestige, (d) a need to belong, or (e) the board member had been recruited (Alby, 1979). He concluded that about half of the board members in his study had been motivated for service for personal reasons, and the other half had been motivated for service for altruistic reasons.

Equality of Representation

The first appointed board members were often elite members of society, were referred to as "selectmen," and were responsible for overseeing virtually every aspect of schools. However, it was argued by Samuel Adams that these selectmen perpetuated elitist attitudes already present in public schools and would continue to do so if board seats remained appointed positions rather than elected positions (Callahan, 1975). Samuel Adams warned of the potential problems brought on by having only elite members of the community represent student and community interests, and moved most states to an electoral process rather than an appointed process for board service. Two hundred years later, school districts across America still elect school board members who accurately reflect the demographics of the student populations they are intended to represent.

Several research studies have recently noted the lack of representativeness on school boards (Glass, Björk, and Brunner, 2000; Hess, 2002; Zimmerman, 1992). The 2000 Study on the Superintendency stated, "Unrepresentative governing bodies have long been a problem in the United States, with Blacks and women having been the most grossly underrepresented group" (Glass, Björk, and Brunner, 2000, p. 35). Zimmerman (1992) and others have studied this representation phenomenon at various levels of government and found similar findings to Glass, Björk, and Brunner. While it can be argued that school boards should represent the demographics of the greater community and taxpayers, it is the students who are most directly affected by school policies, and therefore, governing bodies should represent the demographics of the student population.

A New Generation: Changes in Philosophical Orientation

McCurdy (1992) believed that changes in the philosophical orientation of new board members have added to a lack of cohesion on school boards. He pointed out that because the majority of board members today are from the baby boomer generation, they are more likely to push for change that benefits their own demographic group. Profiles of people from this generation suggest baby boomers push hard for change, will not accept the status quo, and do not support decisions they do not own. Therefore, according to McCurdy, controversy among school board members is a result of the way the baby boomer generation of school board members has been socialized. An individual board member may push hard for change—but not necessarily for change that meets the needs of the district.

A report issued by the Institute for Educational Leadership (IEL) (1986), which profiled school board members from 14 states, indicated the philosophical orientation of board membership varies considerably from past orientations. Traditionally, board members saw themselves as institutional trustees (Danzberger et al., 1992). But now, greater numbers of citizens are serving for more personal reasons. This dichotomy of purpose sets up opposing philosophical orientations for membership that can have a profound impact on the interactions of the board, the amount of involvement school board members have in district decision making, and whether or not board members and superintendents will base their decisions on the goal of increasing student achievement or the goal of advancing their personal agendas (Danzberger et al., 1992).

Disparate Beliefs and Attitudes

Beliefs, interests, or agendas can often dictate a particular style of decision making and/or approach to leadership by school board members. In a study conducted by Eulau and colleagues in 1959, school board members demonstrated three primary styles of decision making—trustee, delegate, or politico. The trustee style of decision making is described as following one's own conscience, the delegate style is following the instructions of a represented party, and the politico style is making decisions using a trustee style or delegate style based on the particular circumstance. Complicating matters further, Tallerico (1989), studying school board members in six different districts, found that

> board member behavioral inclinations ranged from passive acquiescence to proactive supportiveness to restive vigilance. In other words, some board members function largely in a political world where compromise and special interests dominate, while others weigh information in relation to community interest. (cited in Kowalski, 1995, p. 45)

Such disparate decision-making styles and beliefs among school board members and the superintendent can create difficulty in building strong leadership teams at the district level (Boyd, 1975; Danzberger et al., 1992; Gross, 1958; Johnson, 1996; Kowalski, 1995) and can further complicate already highly complex decision-making processes (Kowalski, 1995; Tallerico, 1998).

Textbooks describe school boards as legal entities that have authority only when members act as a group in accordance with state constitutions. In the real world of practice, however, "superintendents readily recognize that boards are five or seven or more distinct individuals—each behaving on the basis of personal beliefs, interest, or causes" (Kowalski, 1995, p. 44), yet forced to act collaboratively while making decisions.

Clearly school boards, consisting of members with disparate beliefs and interests, and coming from different generational profiles, with different styles of decision making, contribute to decision-making processes wrought with disparities. In addition, Kowalski (1995) suggested these disparate beliefs would create muddled expectations for superintendents and likely ensure some type of role conflict between school board members and superintendents.

Increasing State and Federal Accountability Systems

Zeigler et al. (1974), Goodman and Zimmerman (2000), and Education Commission of the States (ECS) (1999) reported that contemporary school board members feel devalued because the state has become increasingly involved in local district decisions and has simultaneously increased the level of district accountability. In fact, the ECS (1999) maintains that, even though board members are encouraged to be creative in their decision-making processes and advised to play an active role in setting policy that will result in increased student achievement, decisions made outside the parameters of state or federal legislation can wind up getting the district penalized by state or federal government agencies. Therefore, boards find themselves frequently "rubber-stamping" the superintendent's recommendations in order to safeguard the district from sanctions or penalties.

Increased Resistance for Board Service and Apathy

Many of the tensions described above have caused some citizens to be reluctant to run for school board and many seated board members have become apathetic about their roles and responsibilities. Board members react differently to these tensions; some push harder to advance their own personal agendas, some fight back, and some become increasingly apathetic toward their roles and responsibilities and ultimately resign. Low numbers of school board candidates, low voter turnout at school board elections, and the short tenures of board members due to frequent and rapid resignations by school board members is indicative of the apathy toward school board service and the public's general disinterest in improving American education (ECS, 1999; Lutz and Merz, 1992; Zeigler et al., 1974). Even those citizens still interested in improving education within their local communities are reluctant to serve on school boards because they are not interested in volunteering their time and efforts to simply rubber-stamp the recommendations of the superintendent (Goodman and Zimmerman, 2000; McCurdy, 1992) or continually sign off on state-mandated policies. Consequently, even apathetic reactions tend to divide boards and place additional stress on board-superintendent relations.

When considering the commonly cited sources of tension between school boards and superintendents, it is important to note that most of these sources of tension have been written about empirically and anecdotally as problematic for more than two centuries. In that time, few, if any, of these tensions have been resolved. For example, role confusion, questionable motives for service, and equality of representation were cited as sources of tension among board and superintendent teams in the mid-1800s. Even though board development programs have focused specifically on these issues in an effort to alleviate them, they still persist today. This causes one to question whether the cited sources of tension are really not the sources of tension themselves, but rather symptoms of other, and perhaps, deeper underlying causes (Kowalski, 1992).

The remainder of the chapter is devoted to sharing findings from a study that suggested deeper psychological and sociological (psycho/social) factors as the potential root or primary causes for the myriad of tensions commonly associated with school boards and superintendents.

UNCOVERING THE PRIMARY SOURCES OF TENSION

As a former superintendent accustomed to working with both functional and dysfunctional school board members, I was interested in better understanding what motivated citizens to become board members. Therefore, I conducted a pilot study that investigated motives for school board membership and whether motive had any impact on the way board members approached decision making at the board table. Findings from this study suggested that while motives did play a role in the way board members approached decision-making processes (Mountford and Brunner, 2001), several other factors also impacted board members' approaches to decision making. Therefore, I conducted a larger study on board members which analyzed, again, their motives for service, but this time investigated three other factors that had emerged from the pilot study: conceptions and uses of power, the way board members used their voice, and their desire for change (see Mountford, 2001, for the full study and detailed methods; Mountford and Brunner, 2001; Mountford, 2004).

Using qualitative methods (Bogdan and Biklen, 1992; Glaser and Strauss, 1967; Glesne and Peshkin, 1992; Lincoln and Guba, 1985; Spradley, 1979; Strauss, 1987), 20 school board members from the Midwest region of the United States were interviewed. Open-ended to semi-structured interview questions were used to find out more about board members' perceptions of the factors and how each factor was influencing the way they went about making decisions in their board member role. In order to validate self-reports given by board members, interviews were also conducted with two other board colleagues and the superintendent of each board member in the study, for a total of 70 interviews. Corroborating data, such as board meeting agendas, minutes, and newspaper accounts of board meetings, were analyzed and compared to interview data. Findings from this study suggested not only that each factor influenced the way board members approached decision making but also that the four factors studied appeared to play a significant role in adding to tensions they felt with board colleagues and/or their superintendents.

In the study, "micromanager" and "collaborator" best described the way board members approached decision making. When participant board members were asked how they approached decisions and how they gathered data to make decisions, some board members used language that suggested they issued directives and/or influenced staff and other community members directly. They saw their role as board member as being involved in the day-to-day operations of the board or influencing others' opinions rather than seeking input to make decisions. These board members' approach to decision making was categorized as micromanagement. McCurdy (1992) supports this categorization by finding that board members were likely to inquire into the minute details of district operations when attempting to make a decision about something.

Other board members reported that their approach to decision making involved seeking input from others, as opposed to influencing others, gathering data from multiple sources, forming committees to gather data, and working with other agencies to assist in problem solving. These board members' approach to decision making was categorized as collaborative. All of the board members in this study reported one or the other of these approaches to decision making to one degree or another, or some combination of the two.

Admittedly, such a small sample of board members—only 20 primary participants—is far too small to suggest that the patterns found among these 20 board members is generalizable. However, the small sample size did allow me to conduct the extensive types of interviews necessary to get to the bottom of how each of the factors or combination of factors was not only influencing their decision-making practices but also playing a role in their relationship with the superintendent and board colleagues. The next four sections of the chapter briefly examine information from the fields of psychology and sociology related to each of the factors studied: motivation, power, voice, and change.

Motivation

The American Heritage Dictionary of the English Language defines motive as an "emotion, desire, physiological need or similar impulse acting as an enticement to action." One of the most prominent researchers on motivation, David McClelland, defines motive as a "recurrent concern for a goal state, or condition, appearing in fantasy, which drives, directs, and selects behavior of the individual" (McClelland, 1971, p. 56). Most researchers interested in understanding motives are mainly interested in why people do what they do. Theories of motivation, then, are primarily concerned with why individuals behave the way they do (Cavalier, 2000; Hall, 1982; Stewart, 1982; Weiner, 1985). Motivation theory, depending on which theory one subscribes to, deals with why people do what they do in the realm of interpersonal, social, conscious, and/or unconscious contexts.

Research on what motivates citizens to become school board members suggests that individuals are motivated for school board membership for personal motives, altruistic motives, or some combination of the two (Alby, 1979; Cistone, 1974; Garmire, 1962; Goldhammer, 1955; McCarty, 1959; Mountford, 2001; Mountford and Brunner, 2001; National School Boards Association, 1996; New York Regents Advisory Committee, 1965; Zazzaro, 1971). McClelland (1975) and Cavalier (2000) both cast power as an integral part of understanding human motivation. Certainly, school board membership offers an individual the opportunity to experience positional and formal power within the community. In addition, school board membership offers an opportunity to be generative and to "exert influence upon the world and the environment, and the care of future generations" (Cavalier, 2000, p. 110). Therefore, a deeper understanding of the link between motivation and power is important.

Juxtaposing motivation theory with research focused on motivations for school board membership suggests that at least one element motivating citizens to become school board members is an acquisition of power. Further, the expression of this power would be different depending on whether citizens were motivated to join school boards for altruistic or personal reasons (Mountford, 2001; Mountford and Brunner, 2001).

Findings on Motives

Some of the personal motivations the school board members in this study gave for joining school boards were, but were not limited to, interests related to their own children, ego needs, a need to belong, prestige, a need for formal power, contention with existing leadership, and/or political advancement. Based on the narratives of the participants, the triangulated narratives, and the corroborating evidence, each participant was categorized as having a personal motive, altruistic motive, or mixed motive.

For example, one board member in this study was motivated to join the school board for two primary reasons. First, she wanted to improve the gifted and talented program because she felt her gifted sons were not receiving adequate services, and also, she was not happy with the current superintendent, board practices, or makeup of the board. Therefore, she was motivated both by the needs of her own children and by her concerns about existing leadership. She stated:

> At the time I originally was moved to run for the school board, it was very frustrating for me as a parent and educator because they, all the administration, were not only male but had been in the district for 20-plus years. Things just weren't changing according to what I was seeing happen in other districts. Particularly of course, in the area of gifted and talented, which was my passion . . . is my passion. I have two sons who are highly able young men and I was concerned about what was happening there. Plus, the board at that time only had one female member and she had been on the board for 12–14 years, she had been there quite a long time. [Board Member 9f]

Another board member, who happened to be a former administrator in the district, expressed unhappiness with the current superintendent and was motivated for board service because he thought he could do a better job administering the district than the current superintendent. He stated:

> I didn't at all agree with the new superintendent. He was not my choice for hire. Therefore, I was motivated to join the board because he either shaped up or he was going to ship out. [Board Member 2m]

During triangulation interviews, board colleagues and superintendents were aware of board members who had joined school boards for personal reasons. One board member acknowledged that there were board members who served for strictly personal reasons or issues, and elaborated on the difficulty in working with such board members. This board member stated:

> It [the difficult part of working with other board members] comes down to those that come on with a chip on their shoulder or something to take care of. "I've got a goal, I've got a reason, and I'm going to take care of this teacher one way or another." They come and find out its not that easy. I've heard that many times. They come on with their own agenda and that's all that they're interested in, and I've seen them on the village board, too, the same way. People have gotten themselves elected for one cause, and once they got it, or they won that cause or they lost it, they are off the board because they don't have other interests. [board colleague discussing Board Member 9*f*]

The narratives and triangulated data indicated that nine board members who were part of this study were motivated to join the school board for various personal motives.

Theoretically, altruistically motivated school board members have the good of all students in mind as well as the maintenance or improvement of the district or community as a whole (Alby, 1979; Mountford and Brunner, 2001; Sarason, 1995). Typical altruistic motives for school board service are the general concern for education and a sense of civic responsibility. Board members whose narratives, triangulated data, and corroborative evidence suggested that their motivation for membership was altruistic were categorized as board members who were motivated for board service for altruistic reasons. One board member said her motive for joining the board was to help make a difference in children's lives and the community. When asked why she ran for the school board, she responded:

> [I ran for school board] because you can make a difference and you do know that in the end you will have made a difference for kids and for our community, to be a better place. I guess that's what my motivation for membership comes down to. [Board Member 12*f*]

Another board member commented on the importance of keeping children at the center of decision making. She stated:

> My whole total reason [for being a school board member] is I want to be a part of the educational plan for the children. At meetings I like to write down and keep it in front of me when we're making decisions "What is best for the children?" Because I want to stay focused on the children. [Board Member 4*f*]

During triangulation interviews, board colleagues and superintendents commented on and seemed aware of some of the altruistic motives of board members who participated in the study. For example, a board colleague suggested that one board member was motivated to run for board because "She has a genuine commitment to kids" and "She has a good heart."

Findings from the study show that 11 board members were categorized as having altruistic motives for board service. In addition, other studies examining the motives for school board service suggest that board members who have been recruited have neither personal nor altruistic motives for board service (Alby, 1979; Cistone, 1974; Garmire, 1962; Goldhammer, 1955; McCarty, 1959; National School Boards Association, 1996; New York Regents Advisory Committee, 1965; Zazzaro, 1971). However, of the two board members in this study who had, in fact, been recruited for service, both were ultimately categorized as having personal motives for board service.

Motives, Decision Making, Relationships

Within literature from the field of psychology, there is evidence suggesting that motives play a large role in decision making. Robert Cavalier (2000) specifically studied the link between motivation theory and its impact on decision making. Cavalier believed that decisions stem primarily from operational and thematic systems. Within the operational system, decisions are a result of an assessment of strategies. These strategies involve a sense of interaction and evaluation that leads an individual into a thematic system. Decisions made within the thematic system are based on either one or a combination of the ego-gratification motive, self-actuation motive, and/or altruism motive.

Understanding the multidimensional nature of motivation, it would be a stretch to believe that board member decision making could be predicted by simply using motives as a basis for prediction. However, earlier studies have shown a connection between motivations for school board membership and the implications these motivations have on decision making. In 1958, Gross linked motivations for school board membership with a board member's ability to adhere to professional standards. In 1959, McCarty linked a board member's motivation for service with the amount of friction a board endured during decision making, and Alby (1979) linked a board member's motivation for service with the type of operations a board would likely use.

The findings from this study also showed a relationship between motives and decision-making processes of board members. Nine out of 11 board members in this study who were motivated for altruistic reasons made decisions using a collaborative approach. That is, those board members in the study who had joined the board for altruistic reasons tended to seek input about decisions, were very committee based, and tried to build consensus when attempting to make decisions. Conversely, six of the nine board members in the study who were initially motivated for board service for personal reasons also tended to make decisions by not simply relying on the information from colleagues, constituents, or the superintendents but also delving into the minutiae of an issue to discover information for themselves. While perhaps, at face value, this is a thorough way of getting information, such involvement by board members can often cause tension for superintendents and staff members, setting up power struggles between a board member and the others within the district.

Power

The phenomenon of power and influence involves a dyadic relationship between two or more agents at micro and macro levels outside of or within any organization.

> Processes of power are pervasive, complex, and often disguised in our society. Accordingly one finds in political science, in sociology, and in social psychology a variety of distinctions among different types of social power or among qualitatively different processes of social influence. (French and Raven, 1959, p. 253)

In other words, power is an ever-present force typically invisible to the eye but easily detectable by the psyche.

Within organizations, those who have the most explicit and formal power are generally those who have the highest levels of positional status. However, implicit power also resides within the informal subdivisions of an organization (Natemeyer and McMahon, 2001). Interestingly, while power differentials are present between all individuals, and many people constantly strive to attain more power, power differentials are rarely the subject of conversation within decision-making forums, even though it has been suggested by some researchers that the ontological conception of power held by an individual can influence the way an individual wields power and makes decisions (Brunner, 2002).

In the area of educational leadership, Brunner and Schumaker (1998) examined the relationship between superintendents' conceptions of power and their leadership style. Brunner and Schumaker, drawing from definitions of power found in the political and social sciences, categorized conceptions of power held by individual superintendents as "power over" (controlling or dominating), "power with" (collaborative), or "mixed" (some combination of power over and power with) (Arendt, 1972; Ball, 1993; Brunner, 1995; Clegg, 1989; Dahl, 1961; Follett, 1924; French and Raven, 1959; Lasswell and Kaplan, 1950; Simon, 1953; Wartenberg, 1990; Weber, 1924; cited in Brunner and Schumaker, 1998).

Brunner and Schumaker's (1998) research showed a relationship between the way superintendents conceived of power and the way they tended
to approach their leadership role. Brunner concluded that superintendents
who defined power as control or authority (power over) tended to use a
"top-down" approach to leadership. Those participants who defined power
as shared tended to be more collaborative (power with) in their approach
to leadership. As Brunner (1998) put it,

> when superintendents in the study defined power as power with/to, they were
> more able to support and carry out collaborative decision making. The more
> strictly their definitions adhered to power as coming from or with others, the
> more capable they were as collaborative decision-makers. (p. 81)

As noted before, research from the field of psychology suggests a relationship between power and motive (Cavalier, 2000). McClelland (1975)
not only links power and motives, but goes further to posit an interrelationship between power, decision making, and motive. In fact, McClelland
suggested that motives were often centered on attaining achievement goals,
often inclusive of gaining more power. He states:

> Since [leaders] are primarily concerned with influencing others, it seems obvi-
> ous that they should be characterized by a high need for power, and that by
> studying the power motive we can learn something about the way effective
> managerial leaders work. (McClelland, 1975, p. 255)

Substantial research on the relationship between motives for board
membership and the need for power are notable in the literature describing
particular elements involved with motives for school board membership
(Alby, 1979; Cistone, 1974; Garmire, 1962; Goldhammer, 1955; New York
Regents Advisory Committee, 1965; Zazzaro, 1971). Researchers have long
believed there is some danger from board members motivated to join the
school board for power attainment and suggest that such motives can and
likely will influence their leadership styles.

Findings on Power

Several of the methods used in the study drew from Brunner and Schumaker's (1998) and Brunner's (2002) previous research on superintendents, their use of power, and how that influenced their leadership styles.
Brunner asked superintendents how they defined power, made decisions,
and got things done. These same three questions were used with board
members as a part of the interview protocol. Narrative data from the interviews, like Brunner's data, demonstrated a close relationship between the
way board members defined power and the way they approached decision

making. However, as discussed earlier, in this study, the terms *micromanagement* and *collaborative* were used to describe board member leadership behaviors to parallel literature on school board decision-making processes (Kowalski, 1992; McCurdy, 1992).

Findings showed that about half of the 20 board members in the study defined power as "power with." For example, one board member defined power as "the ability to reach a common goal that will benefit others," another defined power as simply "sharing." The other half of the board members defined power as "power over," using words such as "control" or "domination" within their definition. For example, at least two board members defined power as "the ability to get others to do what you want them to do."

Power, Decision Making, and Relationships

Findings related to power from the study showed that the same nine board members who had defined power as "power over" were the same board members who used micromanagement as their approach to decision making, and the 11 board members who defined power as "power with" approached decisions collaboratively. In other words, the same board members who believed power to be something shared were more likely to utilize decision-making processes that were collaborative in nature than those board members who considered power to be something accumulated and wielded over others. In the latter case, and not unlike board members with personal motives, board members who tended to wield power over others also tended to self-report and be considered by others to be micromanagers.

This finding is significant in two ways. First, this finding establishes a strong relationship between conceptions of power held by school board members with approaches to decision making. This is the first time this particular relationship has been determined among school board members. Secondly, this finding is important because it not only tests Brunner's (2002) theory on the link between conceptions of power and decision making found in samples of superintendents, but also proves a similar relationship exists in samples of school board members. To some degree, the finding sets up a predictable behavioral pattern which could potentially be used by boards and the community when boards hire a new superintendent or the community elects a new school board member.

Voice

Voices of board members are often involved in debate rather than dialogue, and board members are frequently accused of using their voice to

Table 5.1. Gender, Ethnicity, and Income of School Board Members and Students

| | Gender | | Ethnicity | | | |
	Male	Female	White	African American	Hispanic	Other
Board Members	61%	39%	85.5%	7.8%	3.8%	2.3%
Students	51%	49%	74%	16%	9.1%	.09%

wield influence over others rather than to use their voices to actively seeking input (Campbell et al., 1985; Danzberger and Usden, 1992; Goodman and Zimmerman, 2000; McCurdy, 1992). Debate is sometimes characterized as argumentative or means "to beat down" (Jaworski, 1996, p. 110), whereas dialogue refers to an exchange of opinions or "to converse," which involves both talking and listening. Another form of voice is demographic representation.

Table 5.1 shows a comparison of gender and ethnicity of school board members and students. While the gender of students across the nation is fairly evenly spread, with 51 percent of students male and 49 percent female, there are more male board members (61 percent) than female board members (39 percent). The table also shows that the majority of board members and students are white (85.5 percent of board members and 74 percent of students). However, the percentage of white board members is 11.5 percent, greater than that of white students.

While the lack of representation for females and minorities on school boards is obvious, among those who hold seats on boards, it is less obvious to distinguish whose voices are heard or privileged at the board table. The findings of the study presented in this chapter sought to provide a broader examination of school board member voice, than simply demographic representation. Therefore, in the study "voice" was defined as how verbal school board members were at the board table and within the community and whether they believed, or as reported by others, their voices were heard equally by their superintendent and their board colleagues.

Findings on Voice

Because board member debate and dialogue results in decisions being made for the school community, in the study it was important to better understand how the board members perceived their own use of voice as well as the perceptions held by their board colleagues and superintendents as to how the board members used their voices during decision making.

Seventeen of 20 board members self-reported and were reported by others to be highly vocal in varying degrees. For example, when one board member was asked how much vocal influence he had at the board table, he stated:

> Well, I am more vocal than most. I am not afraid to share my opinion. I think that everybody's opinion counts, and that's why you're here to represent different aspects and different sides to a situation, so if I don't share my opinion, then what value am I bringing? So I do share my opinion, so I am probably one of the more vocal board members, and when it comes to influence I feel I have a considerable amount of influence on the board. [Board Member 24m]

Only 3 of the 20 board members in this study considered themselves to be or were reported by others as having less voice at the board table. The term "low vocal" was used to describe individuals who reported they felt silenced by other board members and/or their superintendent. For example, one board member felt she had been silenced by other board members and the superintendent during the beginning of her board service. She stated:

> So at the next meeting, I brought this issue [a policy issue] up again. I was yelled at more loudly and more severely than I had ever been yelled at in a public arena in my life. "What did I think I was doing? Did I think nobody had been doing their job for past 30 years? What was I thinking to dare ask for a policy manual?" My own father never yelled at me that loudly. [Board Member 8f]

While the board member expressed feeling silenced on the board, her colleagues and superintendent did not consistently agree. In fact, in almost every situation where a board member had self-reported being silenced, their colleagues and board superintendents almost always disagreed. For example, the superintendent of board member 8f said the following about her:

> There are times when it's one of her issues, and she is verbal, she's very ineffective. The board just kind of shakes their heads saying, we already know where you are. Nine out of 10 times she lays back, she says her piece, it's very effective and helpful in terms of clarifying board's positions, and then there are other times when she'll get some public discussion of something that does not serve her or the board very well. [superintendent describing Board Member 8f]

Voice, Decision Making, and Relationships

Ten of the 20 board member participants in this study who were characterized through interviews and corroborating data as being moderately to highly verbal approached decisions collaboratively. However 7 of the 20 board member participants who were moderately to highly verbal used micromanagement as their approach to decision making. Of the three board members in the study characterized as being less vocal or silent, two approached decisions collaboratively, whereas board member 8f, who had earlier reported feeling as though she had been silenced by her board colleagues and superintendents, approached decisions as a micromanagement.

Change

Change, depending upon context, was simplified for the purposes of the study to simply represent the amount or type of change board members were interested in making when their board service began. It is important to note here that change was not used to represent whether or not board members had been successful implementing any changes; instead, change represented the board member participants' desire to initiate change when first joining the board. Conversely, "status quo" was used to describe board members who expressed little or no desire to initiate change but instead expressed an interest in maintaining the existing conditions or current state of affairs within the district (*The American Heritage Dictionary of the English Language*, 1984, p. 1260).

Further, selections of *change* and *status quo* to represent change initiation among board members were grounded in findings from McCarty and Ramsey's (1971) study on the operations of school boards, which suggested that school board members from different types of communities attempted to initiate different amounts of change upon first joining a school board, and McCurdy's (1992) profile of school board members, which stated that most school board members today come from the baby boomer generation and are therefore very interested in initiating change.

Findings on Change

Findings related to board members' desire for change indicated that 16 of the board members in the study were either extremely or moderately interested in changing something or in change in general when they first became board members. Only four board members in this study reported that they were not interested in making any specific change or change in general and thought the district was doing fine.

Board members in the study who indicated they wanted to initiate change typically expressed desire to change something specific or expressed a concern that the district needed change in general. For example, one board member who wanted change in general stated:

> I was interested in seeing things done a little differently . . . I think some of that is an understanding how things need to be done. I continue to feel like I want to do some fine-tuning. If it were all left to me, there are still some changes that I would make. [Board Member 23*m*]

While this board member had wanted to make many general changes in the district, board members also expressed desire to make specific adjustments. The changes they expressed were frequently tied to their motives for service. For example, Board Member 8*f*, who had earlier reported feeling silenced by the superintendent and her board colleagues, said the following thing about the specific change she wanted to make when she joined the board:

> When I first got on the board I started a crusade to create a policy manual for the district, and that stirred very deep emotions in the existing board and from the district administrator whose position was to never write anything down. [Board Member 8*f*]

Superintendents and board colleagues were generally well aware of board members who had a high desire to initiate change and what this desire to initiate change brought to the board table. One board member commented on other board members who join with strong desire to initiate change, and what they are likely to face:

> A couple times we have had new board members who have come on thinking they are going to change the world. And then you find out that there is so much more to being a school board member that you don't have any control over whatsoever—between state rules and regulations, laws governing open meetings, all that kind of stuff. There's not as much as you think you can control as what you actually do get to have a say in. [board colleague of Board Member 9*f*]

These narratives about change make it clear that board members who join the board with a specific change in mind typically have a high desire to implement that change. Further, interviews with board members also elicited a perhaps obvious but important link between three of the four factors examined: change, motive, and decision making.

Change, Decision Making, and Relationships

The link between a board member's desire to change something specific and his or her motive for service is perhaps very obvious, and the two frequently correlated among the board members in the study. Further, evidence from the study suggested that change and motive also play an integral role in how board members approach decision-making processes. The superintendent of one board member clearly demonstrates how the combination of a personal motive and a high desire to change something specific can lead a board member to engage in micromanagement. Regarding this board member's approach to decision making, the superintendent stated:

He pushes hard at committee. He pushes hard one-to-one with me. His style is to stop by the office and deal with issues that way. He's in the building a lot . . . I see that car pull up, I know he's coming in, and I know it's because of something he wants done or taken care of. So he's very specific about that, otherwise I don't see him much, but when I do see him, it's always, he has an agenda and wants something done [superintendent of Board Member 23*m*].

Not surprisingly, board members who wanted to make a specific change as soon as they came onto the board and had expressed personal motives for service tended to micromanage as their approach to decision making. However, and somewhat surprisingly, the same profile also held true for board members who came onto the board with no specific changes in mind; they expressed personal motives and tended to use micromanagement as their approach to decision making. In fact, all of the board members in the study who were interested in protecting the status quo or who were not interested in initiating change when first joining the school board were more likely to have been initially motivated for board service for personal reasons, were more likely to have defined power as power over, used micromanagement as their approach to decision making, and were fairly verbal.

UNDERLYING PSYCHO/SOCIAL FACTORS: THE ROOT CAUSES OF SYMPTOMATIC TENSIONS?

The findings of the study showed that power, motivation, voice, and change all played an integral role in the way board members carry out their board roles, make decisions, and relate to their colleagues and superintendent. To be sure, the study showed that each of the four psycho/social factors—motive, power, voice, and change, both in isolation and in various combinations—influenced board member behaviors, particularly behaviors related to decision making. Further, from these findings, the way psycho/social factors in the study have manifested or serve as aggravators to the nine commonly cited tensions among school board/superintendent teams also becomes more obvious.

The following section of the chapter discusses how psycho/social factors influence board member and superintendent behaviors, independently as well as in combination with the three other factors. Within each discussion, and shown in Table 5.2, many of the tensions commonly associated with school board superintendents, which each of the psycho/social factors can lead to or serve as a root cause for, are also discussed. Finally, in an effort to not only point out a problem but also suggest solutions, the chapter concludes by suggesting ideas for refocusing and subsequently reforming board development and superintendent training programs. Suggested changes to these programs are in an effort to address the four psycho/social factors head on and as a piece of foundational level training, rather than continuing with programs that appear to be focusing on symptoms of the problem rather than their actual causes.

Motives and Tensions

As mentioned earlier, about half of the board members in the study were motivated to join the board for personal reasons, and about half for altruistic reasons. However, a unique finding of this study suggested a board member's motive for service was strongly related to a desire for change. Board members who were motivated for personal reasons typically pushed hard for a specific change, particularly when first joining the board. Further, the study showed motivation for school board service was also related to power, voice, and decision making. That is, board members who expressed personal motives for service *and* expressed a "power over" conception of power tended to seek opportunities to micromanage and exert influence over others, which led some board members to feel voiceless during the decision making.

Table 5.2 shows that motivation for board service is a factor associated with almost all of the tensions commonly associated with school board–superintendent teams—the most obvious being "questionable motives for board service." Historically, individuals' motivations for school board service have been scrutinized for fear they may come onto a board with personal and often hidden agendas (Boyd, 1975; Garmire, 1962; Gross, 1958; McCurdy, 1992; Zazzaro, 1971). Congruent to earlier research, in the study personal motives did appear to be an influence on how board members carried out their roles. Conversely, and on a more positive note, the study's

Table 5.2.   Underlying Psycho/Social Root Causes of Symptomatic Tensions between School Boards and Superintendents

Historical and Current Tension	Underlying Psycho/Social Root Cause
Role Confusion	Power, Motivation, Change
Power Struggles	Power, Motivation, Change, Voice
Equality of Representation	Power, Change, Voice
Questionable Motives for Board Service	Power, Motivation, Change
Changes in Philosophical Orientations of New Generations of Board Members	Change, Voice
Disparate Beliefs and Attitudes	Motivation, Change
Increasing State and Federal Accountability	Power, Motivation, Change, Voice
Increasing Resistance for Board Service	Motivation, Change, Voice
Apathy	Power, Motivation, Change, Voice

findings also suggested that more than half of the board members in the study were motivated to join the board for altruistic reasons. The study also found that board members motivated for altruistic reasons tended to seek input about decisions and were very committee based and tried to build consensus when attempting to make decisions. However, without attention to the cracks in the systems, particularly for new board members, even altruistically motivated board members can easily career off course. Consider the following scenario:

Assume a board member's altruistic motive for joining a school board is centered on trying to help bring about positive changes to the district. Then, upon joining the board, the altruistically motivated board member is quickly informed that his or her primary role is that of policy maker. Fairly unclear about how to go about this "policy making" in order to help bring about the desired improvements, the new board member begins to take on other smaller roles or responsibilities, often related to the types of improvements the board member not only desires, but can see the progress of his or her labor. Most often, these improvements are in the area of district operations rather than policy. In addition, the new board member now finds himself or herself most often rubber-stamping policy made by others (superintendent, state, or the federal government), since in reality, very few districtwide and meaningful policies come directly from school boards.

In the prior scenario, several of the tensions associated with boards/ superintendents come to life. For example, confusion and/or perhaps disagreement over roles and responsibilities is evident. The new board member quickly becomes less focused on policy and more focused on the day-to-day operations of the district, perceived to some as micromanagement. Micromanagement, in this case, is a result of the board member's disenchantment with the primary role of policy maker—or in this case, as in many others, "rubber-stamper." To be sure, symptoms of such disenchantment could include the board member's attempt to renegotiate, overtly or covertly, his or her primary role—often misunderstood as role confusion. Instead, this might be best characterized as power struggles with the superintendent related to the services the board member wants to provide, which are in direct conflict with what he or she is allowed to provide in his or her role of policy maker. Ultimately, this power struggle can lead to disenchantment with board service entirely, resulting in apathy and potentially early resignation. In fact, theory attempting to explain the excessive turnover rate of board members suggests that most board members who resign prior to their term limit do so for personal, moral, or financial reasons (Chance and Capps, 1992; Fist and Walberg, 1992; Mitchell and Spady, 1983).

Personal motives for board service, particularly hidden agendas, can obviously lead to many of the commonly cited tensions on board-superintendent teams. However, given that more than half of the board members in the study were motivated to join a school board for altruistic reasons, it becomes crucial that school board training and superintendent training programs address the issue of how these board members, who appear to possess a natural sense of collaboration and consensus building, can be nurtured. Currently, many board training programs draw a deep line between policy and operations of the district. Board members are told that the operations of the district are the superintendent's purview and they are to stay within policy-making activities. Yet, given that policy making has been, for the most part, taken out of the hands of local control, what exactly is left for members to do?

Power and Tensions

In terms of power, the study's findings suggested at least half of the board members not only conceptualized power as control and/or domination, but their conception of power was directly related to their decision-making style. Board members who defined power as "power over" used micromanagement as their approach to decision making, and board members who defined power as "power with" used a collaborative approach when making decisions. To be sure, having a school board with almost half interested in controlling others (perhaps even the superintendent) clearly sets up tensions related to power struggles, which frequently characterize board-superintendent relationships. Conversely, board members who defined power as "power with" were more likely to have joined boards for altruistic reasons and approached decisions collaboratively, yet still felt as though their voice carried influence.

These findings suggest that a profile of boardsmanship does exist and if nurtured, through training directly addressing power differentials, may begin to diminish many of the commonly cited sources of board tension such as power struggles, disparate values and beliefs, and equality of representation. Recently, "findings from the Iowa Light House study resulted in a description of five main board roles related to improving student achievement" (Alsbury, 2007, p. 9). One of those findings suggested that school boards able to behave collaboratively and build consensus around decisions had an overall healthier school climate than boards who were frequently engaged in conflict or power struggles. Other studies have also found that increased student achievement is one of several positive distal outcomes of school districts with a healthy climate (LaRocque and Coleman, 1993; Rutter et al., 1979).

Voice and Change

Findings from the study demonstrated that while most board members in the study felt they had some degree of voice on the board, others expressed that they felt dominated and/or oppressed by board colleagues and the superintendent. The Iowa Lighthouse study (2002) found that some board members expressed fear of being stifled by the superintendent and that their lack of understanding of their board roles could result in a federal or state takeover. In another study on the characteristics of school boards from across the country (Ivory and Acker-Hocevar, 2007), many rural board members reported often being represented by a vocal minority voice and driven by self-serving agendas that dominated the public forum.

These findings clearly represent the existence of an inequality of voice on school boards, adding to the preexisting demographic inequality of board composition noted earlier. Such imbalances can and do contribute to many of the other commonly cited sources of tension for school board–superintendent teams such as power struggles, role confusion, and increased state and federal oversight.

Similar to voice, findings from the study presented in this chapter also demonstrated that most board members joined the board in order to make a specific change. Only three board members from the study wanted to make general changes or wanted to protect the status quo. In fact, all of the board members in the study who were interested in a specific change or in protecting the status quo when first joining the school board were more likely to have been initially motivated for board service for personal reasons, defined power as "power over," used micromanagement as their approach to decision making, and were fairly verbal. Such a finding sets up myriad tensions around board service.

The high desire and specificity of the change most board members want to make, coupled with micromanagement tactics to bring about that change, could easily lead to tense school board–superintendent relationships such as power struggles or role confusion. In fact, Grady and Bryant (1991) surveyed 80 Nebraska superintendents and found that conflict between superintendents and board members irreparably damaged their professional relationships. Among other things, role confusion was cited as one of the problems of their relationship.

Findings from the study presented in this chapter suggest a link between four psycho/social factors—motivation, power, voice, and change—and the commonly cited sources of tension between and among school board members and superintendents. Most of the nine commonly cited tensions—role confusion, power struggles, questionable motives for service, inequality of representation, increasing resistance to service, and apathy—appear to be more directly influenced by one or more of the four psycho/social factors. It could be argued that the three remaining commonly cited tensions—disparate beliefs and attitudes, changing philosophical orientations of a new generation of board members, and increased oversight from state and federal government—certainly have tangential ties to the underlying psycho/social factors.

Finding the primary source of a disease is only the first step in curing it. Symptoms of a disease will continue to present as long as the source remains untreated. However, by directly treating the source, the symptoms will diminish. Metaphorically speaking, as long as the underlying psycho/social factors (the source of the disease) that appear to be causing, or in some cases, at least aggravating tensions between school boards and superintendents (the symptoms), the dysfunctional school (the disease) will continue to exist as it has for more than 200 years. However, if superintendent preparation programs and school board development programs (the doctors) are able to work in tandem to address the primary source of the disease, school boards may one day become asymptomatic, fully functional governing boards.

TREATING THE DISEASE, NOT JUST ITS SYMPTOMS: BOARD AND SUPERINTENDENT TRAINING

Treating dysfunctional school governance is not an easy task. To be sure, many of the treatments already in place—such as workshops for new board members, seminars defining the roles and responsibilities of school board members, and policy governance—address many of the major symptomatic tensions associated with school governance (Iannaccone and Lutz, 1970). Yet, even though a number of similar types of school board and superintendent training programs have come and gone over the last 200 years, "school board operations have remained stable and the outcomes of schooling (student achievement results) have not improved" (Grissmer et al., 2000, as cited in Alsbury, 2007).

According to Alsbury, "school board associations must move away from traditional training for boards and provide guidance about how boards and superintendents can interact with each other and how they can interact with district staff around educational issues and areas that directly impact student learning" (Alsbury, 2007, p. 27). Yet, at the same time, a recent study conducted by Kowalski (2006) found that the chief complaints put forth by superintendents centered on issues related to power, motivation, and decision making, such as but not limited to pursuing single agendas, micromanaging, satisfying a need for power, and pursuing personal gains. Researchers seem to agree that for school governance to be effective, a reconceptualization of school board member and superintendent relationships, from a place of sacred boundaries and divisive roles, to a place of mutual respect and interdependence, is a necessary. However, this shift in relationship has not been sufficiently addressed by superintendent and school board training programs.

In some areas, university-based leadership preparation programs are beginning to move in this direction. Some programs have redirected their former androcentric, top-down, autocratic leadership curriculum, popular in the 1970s and 1980s (Young and McLeod, 2001), toward curriculum inclusive of more collaborative decision-making practices, parental and community involvement, flattened hierarchies, and operating under an ethic of care (Noddings, 1992; Rusch, 2004). As the country becomes increasingly pluralistic and a focus toward social justice has become more prominent, some university-based leadership preparation programs have articulated the need for school leaders to be inclusive of multiple perspectives and have asked aspiring leaders to step outside of a structural functional mindset and utilize leadership practices that are transformational (Marshall et al., 1996; Young, Mountford, and Skrla, 2006). In fact, anecdotal evidence from practicing administrators suggests that the role of educational leaders today is far too complex for traditional leadership training programs to be effective—the very transformational learning experiences that have shifted aspiring leaders' practices toward inclusiveness and collaboration in more progressive leadership programs (Mountford, Young, and Skrla, 2006).

Transformational learning experiences require outcomes that enable the learner to critically reflect upon, communicate, and shift, if necessary, preexisting assumptions, biases, and paradigms (Cambron-McCabe, Mulkeen, and Wright, 1991; Mezirow, 1990; 1991; 2000).

> Transformation learning theory suggests that transformative learning inherently creates understandings for participatory democracy by developing capacities of critical reflection on taken-for-granted assumptions that support contested points of view and participation in discourse that reduces fractional threats to rights and pluralism, conflict, and the use of power, and foster autonomy, self-development, and self-governance—the values that rights and freedoms are designed to protect. (Mezirow, 2000, p. 29)

Similar to many progressive universities who utilize transformational learning objectives with their aspiring leaders, if school board trainers could begin to refocus their energies toward transformational learning outcomes for school board members, the psycho/social factors that appear to be causing many of the tensions associated with school board–superintendent teams may be addressed. While some may still believe that training programs such as policy governance, delineating the roles and responsibilities of school board members and superintendents, and strategies for effective school boards will improve school governance, one only has to look at the outcomes of traditional board training over the past 200 years. Nothing has improved, but something must, if school boards are to maintain the little bit of local control they have left.

Findings from this study demonstrate that board members and superintendents experience negative and inequitable treatment from each other. To suggest that this negative behavior does not adversely influence student achievement and district climate, or perhaps more importantly, model oppressive ways of being to future generations, is to bury one's head in the sand. Transformational learning objectives directly target deeply held assumptions and biases, often related to power, motive, voice, identity, change, and decision-making practices. School board trainers and educational leadership preparation programs should consider transformational learning objectives when designing the training curriculum.

School boards and superintendents set the conditions under which our children learn and grow. They are also held increasingly accountable for these conditions. Training, then, needs to provide them with multiple cures for what ails them, not just one injection that relieves their symptoms for a short time.

NOTE

This chapter contains some condensed segments of a forthcoming book I am currently writing entitled *School Board Members: Attitudes and Beliefs*, under contract for publication with Rowman & Littlefield.

REFERENCES

Alby, T. 1979. An analysis of motives for seeking school board membership in selected communities in Wisconsin. PhD diss., University of Wisconsin, Madison.

Alsbury, T. 2007. Findings from the Lighthouse Study: Attributes of effective boards. Paper presented at the annual meeting of the American Educational Research Association, Chicago.

Arendt, H. 1972. *Crises of the republic: Lying in politics; Civil disobedience; On violence; Thoughts on politics and revolution.* New York: Harcourt Brace Jovanovich.

Bogdan, R., and S. Biklen. 1992. *Qualitative research for education: An introduction to theory and methods.* Boston: Allyn & Bacon.

Boyd, W. 1975. School board–administrative staff relationships. In *Understanding school boards: Problems and prospects,* ed. P. Cistone. A National School Board Association Study. Toronto and London: Lexington Books.

Brunner, C. C. 1998. The new superintendency supports a new innovation: Collaborative decision making. *Contemporary Education* 69 (2): 79–82.

———. 2002. Professing educational leadership: Conceptions of power. *Journal of School Leadership* 12:693–720.

Brunner, C. C., and P. Schumaker. 1998. Power and gender in the "new view" public schools. *Policy Studies Journal* 26 (1): 30–45.

Callahan, R. 1975. The American board of education. In *Understanding school boards: Problems and prospects*, ed. P. Cistone, 19–46. A National School Boards Association Research Study. Toronto and London: Lexington Books.

Cambron-McCabe, N. H., T. A. Mulkeen, and G. K. Wright. 1991. *A new platform for preparing school administrators: A report on the principles developed for the Professors of School Administration Program*. St. Louis: Danforth Foundation.

Campbell, R., L. Cunningham, R. Nystrand, and M. Usden. 1985. *The organization and control of American schools*. 5th ed. Columbus, OH: Merrill.

Carver, J. 1997. *Boards that make a difference: A new design for leadership in nonprofit and public organizations*. San Francisco: Jossey-Bass.

Cavalier, R. 2000. *Personal motivation: A model for decision-making*. Westport, CT: Praeger.

Chance, E. W., and J. L. Capps. 1992. *Superintendent instability in small/rural schools: The school board perspective*. Norman: University of Oklahoma, College of Education.

Cistone, P. 1974. The ecological basis of school board member recruitment. *Education and Urban Society* 25 (4): 439–440.

Clegg, S. R. 1989. *Frameworks of power*. London: Sage.

Dahl, R. 1961. *Who governs?* New Haven, CT: Yale University Press.

Danzberger, J. 1987. School boards: The forgotten players on the education team. *Phi Delta Kappan* 36 (9): 53–59.

Danzberger, J., M. Kirst, and M. Usdan. 1992. *Governing public schools: New times, new requirements*. Washington, DC: Institute for Educational Leadership.

Danzberger, J., and M. Usdan. 1992. *School boards: Strengthening a grass-roots American institution*. NSSE. Berkeley, CA: McCutchan.

Education Commission of the States (ECS). 1999. *Governing America's schools: Changing the rules*. Report of the National Commission on Governing America's Schools. Denver: ECS.

Fist, P., and H. Walberg. 1992. *School boards: Changing local control*. Berkeley, CA: McCutchan.

Follett, M. P. 1924. *Creative experience*. New York: Basic Books.

Garmire, L. 1962. A study of the attitudes of school board members as they relate to the reasons for seeking office. *Oregon School Study Council Bulletin, School of Education, University of Oregon*.

Glaser, B., and A. Strauss. 1967. *The discovery of grounded theory: Strategies for qualitative research*. Hawthorne, NY: Aldine de Gruyter.

Glass, T., L. Björk, and C. Brunner. 2000. *The study of the American school superintendency 2000*. Arlington, VA: American Association of School Administrators.

Glesne, C., and A. Peshkin. 1992. *Becoming qualitative researchers: An introduction*. White Plains, NY: Longman.

Goldhammer, K. 1955. Community power structures and school board membership. *American School Board Journal* 5 (3): 23–25.

Goodman, R., and W. Zimmerman. 2000. *Thinking differently: Recommendations for 21st-century school board superintendent leadership, governance and teamwork for high student achievement*. Educational Research Service and New England School Development Council.

Grady, M., and M. Bryant. 1991. School board turmoil and superintendent turnover: What pushes them to the brink? *School Administrator* 48 (2): 19.

Hall, J. 1961. *Psychology of motivation.* Philadelphia: Lippincott.

Hess, F. 2002. *School boards at the dawn of the 21st century: Conditions and challenge of district governance.* A report prepared for the National School Boards Association. School of Education and Department of Government, University of Virginia.

Iannaccone, L., and F. Lutz. 1970. *Understanding educational organizations: A field study approach.* Columbus, OH: Merrill.

Iowa Association of School Boards. 2002. *Iowa school board member attitudes/beliefs about student achievement.* Des Moines: Iowa Association of School Boards.

Johnson, S. M. 1996. *Leading to change: The challenge of the new superintendency.* San Francisco: Jossey-Bass.

Kaplan, G. 1989. *Who runs our schools?* Washington, DC: Institute for Educational Leadership.

Kowalski, T. J. 1995. *Keepers of the flame: Contemporary urban superintendents.* Thousand Oaks, CA: Corwin Press.

———. 2006. *The school superintendent: Theory, practice, and cases.* 2nd ed. Thousand Oaks, CA: Sage.

LaRocque, L., and P. Coleman. 1993. The politics of excellence: Trustee leadership and school district ethos. *The Alberta Journal of Educational Research* 39 (4): 449–475.

Lasswell, H., and A. Kaplan. 1950. *Power and society.* New Haven, CT: Yale University Press.

Lather, P. 1991. *Getting smart: Feminist research and pedagogy with/in the postmodern.* New York: Routledge.

Lincoln, Y., and E. Guba. 1985. *Naturalistic inquiry.* Thousand Oaks, CA: Sage.

Lutz, F., and M. Merz. 1992. *The Politics of school community relations.* New York: Teachers College Press.

Marshall, C., J. Patterson, D. Rogers, and J. Steele. 1996. Caring as a career: An alternative perspective for educational administration. *Educational Administration Quarterly* 32 (2): 271–294.

McCarty, D. 1959. School board membership: Why do citizens serve? *Administrator's Notebook* 8 (1).

McCarty, D., and C. Ramsey. 1971. *The school managers: Power and conflict in American public education.* Westport, CT: Greenwood.

McClelland, D. 1971. *Assessing human motivation.* Morristown, NJ: General Learning Press.

———. 1975. *Power: The inner experience.* New York: Irvington.

McCurdy, J. 1992. Building better school boards. *Administrator Relations.* Arlington, VA: American Association of School Administrators.

Mezirow, J. 1990. Toward transformative learning and emancipatory education. In *Fostering critical reflection in adulthood: A guide to transformative and emancipatory learning,* 354–375. San Francisco: Jossey-Bass.

———. 1991. *Transformative dimensions of adult learning.* San Francisco: Jossey-Bass.

———. 2000. *Learning as transformation: Critical perspectives on a theory in progress.* San Francisco: Jossey-Bass.

Mitchell, D. E., and W. G. Spady. 1983. Authority, power, and the legitimization of social control. *Educational Administration Quarterly* 19:5–33.

Mountford, M. 2001. Motivations for school board membership, conceptions of power, and their effects on decision-making. PhD diss., University of Wisconsin, Madison.

———. 2004. Motives and power of school board members: Implications for school board–superintendent relationships. *Educational Administration Quarterly* 40 (5): 704–741.

Mountford, M., and C. C. Brunner. 2001. Motivations for school board membership: Implications for superintendents. In *The new superintendency: Advances of research and theories of school management and educational policy*, ed. C. C. Brunner and L. G. Björk, 135–152. London: Elsevier.

Mountford, M., and R. Ylimaki. 2005. Conceptions of power held by educational leaders: The impact on collaborative decision-making processes. *Journal of School Leadership* 15 (7): 411–436.

Mountford, M., M. Young, and L. Skrla. 2006. Equalizing critical theory in educational leadership programming. Paper presented at the annual meeting of the American Educational Research Association, San Francisco.

National School Boards Association (NSBA). 1996. *Becoming a better school board member: A guide to effective school board service.* Alexandria, VA: NSBA.

New York Regents Advisory Committee. 1965. *Board of education service.* New York: New York Regents Advisory Committee.

Noddings, N. 1992. *The challenge to care in schools.* New York: Teachers College.

Pounder, D. 1998. *Restructuring schools for collaboration: Promises and pitfalls.* Albany: SUNY Press.

Rusch, E. A. 2004. Gender and race in leadership preparation: A constrained discourse. *Educational Administration Quarterly* 40 (1): 16–48.

Rutter, M., B. Maughan, P. Mortimore, and J. Ouston. 1979. *Fifteen thousand hours: Secondary schools and their effects on children.* Cambridge, MA: Harvard University Press.

Sarason, S. 1995. *Political involvement and the political principle: Why the existing governance structure of schools should be abolished.* San Francisco: Jossey-Bass.

Simon, H. 1953. Notes on the observation and measurement of power. *Journal of Politics* 15:500–516.

Spradley, J. 1979. *The ethnographic interview.* Orlando, FL: Harcourt Brace Jovanovich College.

Strauss, A. 1987. *Qualitative analysis for social scientists.* New York: Cambridge University Press.

Tallerico, M. 1998. The dynamics of superintendent–school board relationships: A continuing challenge. *Urban Education* 24 (2): 215–232.

Twentieth-Century Fund Task Force. 1992. *Facing the challenge: School governance.* New York: Twentieth Century Fund Press.

Van Maanen, J. 1988. *Tales of the field: On writing ethnography.* Chicago: University of Chicago Press.

Wartenberg, T. 1990. *The forms of power: From domination to transformation.* Philadelphia: Temple University Press.

Weber, M. 1924. *The theory of social and economic organizations.* Glencoe, IL: Free Press.

Weiner, B. 1985. *Human Motivation.* New York: Springer-Verlag.

Young, M. D., and S. McLeod. 2001. Flukes, opportunities and planned interventions: Factors affecting women's decisions to enter educational administration. *Educational Administration Quarterly* 37 (4): 430–462.

Young, M., M. Mountford, and L. Skrla. 2006. Infusing gender and diversity issues into educational leadership programs: Transformational learning and resistance. *Journal of Educational Administration* 44 (3): 264–277.

Zazzaro, J. 1971. What makes boardmen run? *American School Board Journal* 111 (9): 17–21.

Zeigler, L., M. Jennings, and G. Peak. 1974. *Governing American schools: Political interaction in local school districts.* North Scituate, MA: Duxbury Press.

6

Systemic Leadership amidst Turbulence: Superintendent–School Board Relations under Pressure

George J. Petersen and Lance D. Fusarelli

A great deal of time and thought has been devoted to superintendents and school boards and reexamining issues of school governance. Local boards of education are evidence of the fundamental relationship between schools and local communities. Entrusted by the public, boards of education are charged to work with the district superintendent to protect the public interest and to ensure a high-quality education is provided to each student. This form of governance mirrors America's long-standing traditions of local control and democratic decision making.

During the past several decades, the press for reform has changed the landscape of district politics and decision making at the local level. Johnson (2003) noted that the publication and media attention given to *A Nation at Risk* and subsequent reports launched what is arguably the most intense and sustained effort to reform education in American history. Heightened public scrutiny sparked a myriad of questions about the quality of education our children were receiving, and subsequently queries were also raised about the effectiveness of school district governance—more specifically the functions of school boards, their relationship with the district superintendent, and their role in policy making, as well as issues of power, effectiveness, and compatibility with modern reforms (Kowalski, 2006). The popular, public, and unrelenting dissection of public schooling has created a state of turbulence and pressure. According to Usdan et al.:

> District leaders are in an arena that is perpetually besieged by a *potpourri* of often conflicting forces: state laws and regulations, federal mandates, decentralized

school management, demands for greater accountability, changing demographics, the school choice movement, competing community needs, limited resources, partisan politics, legal challenges, shortages of qualified teachers and principals and a general lack of respect for the education profession. (Usdan et al., 2001, p. 26)

Advocates maintain that lay governance of schools by boards of trustees contributes to the unique strength of democratic decision making in public education by providing a responsive and accessible shared governance system to community stakeholders. Critics on the other hand question their usefulness and/or necessity, given the current social and political context of systemic reform mandated of schools. Whether effective or ineffective, school board governance plays a significant role in public education. The task of school boards in determining the general control and direction of the district, ensuring accountability, establishing processes for the articulation and adoption of policies, and providing community leadership are the building blocks of effective district leadership.

In this chapter, we explore the relationship of the board of education and district superintendent in an era of reform and eroding public confidence. We offer a brief review of extant literature and research examining the influence of this relationship on district leadership and decision making, while also presenting some recent criticisms of the current governance structure of public schools. However, the heart of the chapter concentrates on four trends we believe are reshaping this relationship: (a) demographic changes, (b) external threats and stress, (c) the politics of personalism, and (d) changes in superintendents themselves. We use these four trends as lenses to explore their potential strength in influencing, in any substantive way, relations between superintendents and boards of education and the leadership of schools.

THE SCHOOL BOARD AND
SUPERINTENDENT RELATIONSHIP

A substantial body of research exists indicating that a district superintendent's success hinges on the relationship he or she establishes with the board president (Allison, Allison, and McHenry, 1995; Campbell and Greene, 1994; Lunenburg and Ornstein, 1996; Petersen and Short, 2001; 2002) and board of education (Berg, 1996; Carter and Cunningham, 1997; Danzberger, 1994; Feuerstein and Opfer, 1998; Hoyle, English, and Steffy, 1998; Kowalski, 2006; McCurdy, 1992; Norton et al., 1996; Tallerico, 1989). Extant literature in this area has consistently asserted that a poor relationship between the superintendent and the board of education poses a threat to the district's ability to meet its goals and to engage in systemic reform. Poor superintendent–school board relations deter school improvement (Danzberger, Kirst, and Usdan, 1992), affect the quality of educational programs (Boyd, 1976; Nygren, 1992), increase conflict over district instructional goals and objectives (Morgan and Petersen, 2002; Petersen, 1999), weaken district stability and morale (Renchler, 1992), negatively influence the superintendent's credibility and trustworthiness with board members (Petersen and Short, 2001; 2002; Petersen and Williams, 2005), impede critical reform efforts, such as district restructuring (Konnert and Augenstein, 1995), collaborative visioning, and long-range planning (Kowalski, 2006), and eventually result in an increase in the "revolving door syndrome" of district superintendents (Carter and Cunningham, 1997; Renchler, 1992).

In a study of school board presidents, Petersen and Short (2001; 2002) found that a superintendent's credibility (trustworthiness and expertness), social attractiveness, assertiveness, and emotiveness are key components of successful superintendent leadership styles, enabling her or him to receive board support on multiple and often complex policy initiatives. A follow-up study by Petersen and Williams (2005) extended this line of analysis and drew upon social capital theory (human, social, cultural, and economic) to explain how superintendents can effectively lead school systems (and develop positive relations with school boards) amidst often-intense pressure to boost student achievement and eliminate the achievement gap while doing more with less money.

The importance of engaging with multiple policy makers throughout the community to initiate and sustain reform is now well established as an essential leadership behavior of successful superintendents (Fusarelli, 2005a). Although superintendents view themselves as professional educators and not politicians, nearly all adopt political strategies in dealing with board members, staff, and the community at large. Occupationally, superintendents may not be politicians, but all recognize their political work environment and maneuver accordingly. As Björk (2005) observed, the push for systemic reform forces superintendents to engage a wide array of community groups and generate broad-based community support for school improvement initiatives (see also Stanford, 1999). Increasingly diverse communities have multiple centers of power that superintendents and school boards must attend if they are to engage in systemic reform and school improvement. Grogan and Sherman (2003) note that superintendents, even those who are successful, lack enough personal power to single-handedly achieve their goals; they must work with and through others to operate effectively. Superintendents are required to develop relationships with a wide array of policy makers in diverse policy subsystems to build enough civic capacity to initiate and sustain multilevel systemic reform initiatives (Stone et al., 2001). Building and sustaining alliances with multiple civic actors, therefore, is not playing politics but rather an essential leadership skill.

While the relationship of the board and superintendent is pivotal in addressing reform and restructuring efforts, a critical component of success is intricately tied to the ability of the superintendent to influence critical policy decisions made by the board of education (Blumberg, 1985; Crowson, 1987; Zeigler, Jennings, and Peak, 1974). We know now that superintendents have considerably more control and influence in the establishment of the board agenda than previously thought (Petersen and Short, 2001), yet formal authority for policy articulation and decision making still resides with the board. Because of this, superintendents must, in most instances, attempt to sway the vote of each individual board member (Blumberg, 1985).

SCHOOL BOARD DECISION MAKING

It is evident that systemic reform is dependent upon a good working relationship between a superintendent and the school board; therefore, how school boards make decisions is a critical factor impacting that relationship. With their ability to create district policy, hire and fire administrators (in this case, the superintendent), approve the budget, tenure teachers, and negotiate teachers' contracts, the power of the school board to move the district forward or force it into bureaucratic gridlock is significant. Studies previously concentrated on issues of school governance and reform have continually emphasized the importance of the school board in the educational process of the district (Bullard and Taylor, 1993; Danzberger, Kirst, and Usdan, 1992; Fullan and Stiegelbauer, 1991; Wirt and Kirst, 2005). While school boards have power, they are usually unpaid, part-time, and untrained, and, except for the information presented to them by the superintendent or perhaps what they pick up informally, board members know little of the underlying issues for the scores of complex decisions requiring their approval at each board meeting (Cuban, 1976). Therefore, school boards often rely on the professional judgment of the superintendent in many educational matters. However, relying on the professional judgment of superintendents does not mean school board members are a group of "happy campers" under the gentle leadership of the superintendent. Björk and Lindle (2001) found nearly 1 in 5 superintendents identified their boards as factional, while slightly more than 1 in 10 have inert boards (i.e., boards that let the superintendent make all the decisions).

Boards of education are dependent upon an array of external social, economic, and political influences and their decisions are often predicated upon consideration of a host of factors they have little or no control over (Boyd, 1976; McCarty and Ramsey, 1971; Usdan, 1975). Numerous studies have classified board orientations as either hierarchical or bargaining (Tucker and Zeigler, 1980), elite or arena (Lutz and Gresson, 1980), political or professional (Greene, 1992) in examining their influence on decision making and school district governance. Findings from these as well as other investigations examining board behavior (Hentges, 1986; McCarty and Ramsey, 1971; Nowakowski and First, 1989; Scribner and Englert, 1977; Zeigler, Jennings, and Peak, 1974) have chronicled the often conflicting roles, responsibilities, and expectations of boards and their willingness or hesitancy to defer to the expertise of the superintendent in policy decisions. This dynamic continues to generate areas of tension in the margin of control and governance of the school district. Zeigler argues that because of the conflicting expectations, "school boards behave like typical schizophrenics. On the one hand, they willingly (indeed eagerly) give power away to the experts . . . On the other hand, they espouse an ideology of lay control" (Zeigler, 1975, p. 8). This factor continues to be a significant issue in the governance of school districts; research has indicated that the role of school boards in district governance depends primarily on their acceptance of the superintendent's claims to expertise in specific issue areas and secondarily on board orientation (Greene, 1992).

CRITICISMS OF BOARD GOVERNANCE

Although research has established the superintendent and board relationship as a fundamental component in the successful leadership of the school organization, more than a few authors beg the question, given the current dynamics and political landscape, concerning the pragmatism and necessity of boards of education. This line of inquiry includes district superintendents. Glass (2001) found only 30 percent of superintendents felt the current model of district governance should remain in its present form, with 68 percent indicating it should be seriously restructured or completely replaced. Increasingly, criticism of boards revolves around three issues: local representation, instability, and incompatibility with school reform.

Local Representation

One of the most stinging criticisms lies at the very heart of the democratic ideal, local representation. Several authors have noted that citizens feel boards no longer truly represent nor communicate with them (Danzberger et al., 1992) and membership often consists of power elites (Wirt and Kirst, 2005); more recently, boards are perceived as yet another instrument teachers unions and other politically organized groups use to exert undue influence in determining the membership of boards of education and the direction of schools (Moe, 2005). These problems, coupled with "single-issue" board members, help to foster negative opinions of boards as decision-making bodies and their orientation to represent the interests of all stakeholders.

Instability

The political nature of the superintendent–school board relationship has been identified as a substantive barrier to systemic school reform—specifically, the limited tenure of many superintendents and district leadership teams to implement needed changes (Kowalski, 2006). Glass (2002) in a study of board presidents found that 64 percent reported a turnover of three or more superintendents in the previous 10 years. Hess (2002) found 56 percent of sitting board members would not seek or were undecided about seeking reelection. This turnover in district leadership creates an environment where political and philosophical differences become more commonplace, often dividing communities and boards into competing factions and leveraging against substantive educational reform (Björk and Lindle, 2001; Kowalski, 2006).

Incompatibility with Reform

The mounting significance of accountability measures, academic achievement, changing social and economic conditions, alternative schooling, technology, diversity, equity, and the rapidly changing demographics of school districts in the United States have resulted in questions about the need and role of school boards (Finn, 1997; Fusarelli, Cooper, and Carella, 2002; Glass, 2001; Moe, 2005). Some scholars advocate that school boards refocus their attention and concentrate on facilitating and maintaining organizational relationships and policies that advance the technical core of curriculum and instruction and not issues of management (Danzberger and Usdan, 1994; Kowalski, 2006; Morgan and Petersen, 2002); other writers strongly question the role and utility of boards and view them as the paramount obstacle to systemic reform of the educational system. Elizabeth (2003) quotes Tom Glass, a professor and superintendent researcher at the University of Memphis, as proposing what he calls "a more drastic" model—abandoning school boards altogether and having the schools led by a superintendent who is part of the mayor's cabinet. Other critics, like Chester Finn, argue the current school governance structure perpetuates the status quo and actually prevents any substantive reform.

> We have a pretty clear understanding of what would work better, yet old-fashioned bureaucratic monopolies continue to insulate most U.S. public schools from change . . . Establishment interests wait for the opportunity to

slow down, weaken, or repeal key portions of the change they do not like. They have elephantine memories and the fiscal and political clout to reward friends, punish foes, and sway public attitudes. (Finn, 1997)

Demolishing traditional school boards and starting over is not a realistic alternative for a number of reasons. Most importantly, boards of education play a substantial role in the fabric of democratic decision making at the grassroots level. Consequently, if systematic reform is going to happen, it is dependent upon a positive and collaborative working relationship between boards of education and superintendents. Let's turn our attention to four trends we believe may result in a change in this relationship.

DEMOGRAPHIC CHANGES

Schools in the United States are becoming increasingly diverse, due in large measure to a massive influx of Latino students into the school system (Fusarelli, 2000). Since 1980, the Latino population "has increased at a rate five times that of non-Hispanic whites, African Americans, and Asians combined" (Howe, 1994, p. 42). Since 1980, the percentage of Anglo students in public schools has steadily declined relative to minority youth. Many districts "are still struggling with the challenges of serving these linguistically and culturally different students" (Gonzalez, Huerta-Macias, and Tinajero, 1998, p. xv). As districts across the country become more diverse, they are also becoming less wealthy. Nearly one in four children live in poverty, and the gap between rich and poor is widening.

Competing with this diversity and economic disparity is the fact that as the United States becomes increasingly non-white, it is also graying, particularly the Anglo majority. As a result, there is increased pressure to allocate scarce resources toward the care of the elderly (who, among other things, vote in record numbers), leaving fewer dollars available for education. Furthermore, the percentage of households with children is decreasing (20–25 percent nationwide, as low as 15 percent in some cities) (The Twentieth Century Fund, 1992). Like municipal, county, and state budgets, school district budgets are zero-sum games, where multiple demands compete for scarce resources. These trends do not bode well for school districts heavily dependent on local property tax revenue and contribute to tension between superintendents, school boards, and the communities they serve.

While politics has always been part and parcel of policy making in education, indications are evident that the demographic changes discussed here are contributing to a more divisive, politicized environment than has existed for at least a decade (for example, the 1990s was a decade of relative peace and prosperity). A "growing cultural divide among the citizenry" exists in the United States (Keedy and Björk, 2002, p. 105). Public education finds itself under attack from both the Left and the Right, and proposals (some radical, some not) covering everything from governance to choice have been adopted in states and locales throughout the country (see also Cibulka, 1999). Survey data from the most recent AASA Study of the American Superintendency revealed more than 57 percent of superintendents reported the existence of community interest groups actively engaged in debates over property taxes, curriculum issues, and school/community values (Glass, Björk, and Brunner, 2000). Across the nation, "schools boards—the traditional linchpin of American educational governance—are facing a serious crisis of legitimacy and relevance" (The Twentieth Century Fund, 1992, p. 1).

This situation often leads to conflict and turnover, although board turnover is not always (perhaps not even most often) due to community dissatisfaction with board members. Alsbury (2005) recommends superintendents pay close attention to community dissatisfaction and engage in continual two-way communication with board members and the community. By keeping their hand on the pulse of the community, superintendents should be more effective at responding to public concern and ensuring the success of leadership initiatives. The requisite organizational capacity necessary to implement and sustain systemic reform is not possible in districts with unstable governance and high administrator turnover. The dynamic political nature of many communities, where a relative handful of angry citizens can cause a superintendent's ouster (as opposed to broad community dissatisfaction), contributes to turnover and leadership instability, inhibiting systemic reform initiatives. Too-frequent turnover of superintendents and school board members makes initiating and sustaining comprehensive systemic education reforms problematic. As Bonnie Fusarelli (2005) observes, frequent superintendent-board turnover inhibits strategic planning and the implementation of systemic reform initiatives. Furthermore, it makes it difficult to develop sufficient institutional capacity to sustain effective learning organizations.

Stress and External Threats to Governance

The combination of the demographic changes places enormous pressure on superintendents and school boards to do more with fewer resources. Intense pressure for outcomes-based systemic school reform—including standards, accountability, budgets, and testing—has relocated much power and authority from superintendents and school boards to state legislatures and governors, state education departments, state and federal courts, and the federal government (Fusarelli, 1999; 2002a). Wirt and Kirst (2005) observe that within the last three decades, school boards have been steadily losing power as mayors, state legislators, and the federal government have usurped many of the roles and responsibilities of local school boards. State legislatures and governors, particularly through the National Governors Association, now play a powerful role in shaping local educational policy (Fusarelli, 2005b).

Although the impetus for increased state and federal involvement in education varies, common factors include pressure from the judicial system for greater equity in schooling inputs; economic concerns; the involvement of big business in education reform; impatience with ineffectual, incremental change; gubernatorial and legislative leadership; coalitional politics; the emergence of national policy networks; and an emergent institutional capacity to undertake reform (Fusarelli and Fusarelli, 2003; Mazzoni, 1995). As Kowalski observed, "increasing federal and state authority at the expense of local school board authority would diminish the stature of superintendents [as well as school boards] because their role would entail [or be reduced to] managing predetermined and pervasive policy" (Kowalski, 2005, p. xi), although it remains unclear how this trend affects the school board's relationship with the superintendent.

Throughout the United States, school districts are "constantly undergoing change, stress, and transition, as communities elect new school board members, new demands are made on schools, and key leaders come and go" (Natkin et al., 2001, p. 1). Furthermore, the external threat to public education has increased, with the emergence of charter schools, vouchers, tuition tax credits, contracting out educational services to private contractors, and a reinvigorated home schooling movement.

The question is how these external forces and governance trends, particularly the loss of local control over the past three decades, affect superintendent–school board relations. Fusarelli reported a conversation with a community school board member in New York City in which the board member "reiterated his belief that the growing mayoral and state influence in education policy making would make locally elected school boards obsolete in five years, since their decision-making powers have been steadily reduced by chancellors, mayors, and state legislators" (Fusarelli, 2000, p. 571). While this board member's pessimistic view is clearly erroneous, at least in suburban and rural areas where locally elected or appointed school boards are archetypal, his concern raises questions about how the steady erosion of local control impacts local school district governance.

Interest Groups and the Politics of Personalism

Some scholars argue that school boards (and therefore superintendent-board relations) have become increasingly politicized over the past 30 years, making effective district leadership more difficult (Björk, Bell, and Gurley, 2002). In AASA's most recent study, more than 90 percent of superintendents in large urban districts said interest groups exert political pressure on school boards (Glass, Björk, and Brunner, 2000). Most superintendents, including those in medium and smaller districts, acknowledge that interest groups are active in their communities (Glass, Björk, and Brunner, 2000). One significant change in interest-group activity with implications for superintendent–school board relations is the shift from centralized efforts to grassroots, individual lobbying (Goldstein, 1999; Opfer, 2001).

In her study of political conflict over evolution in Cobb County, Georgia, Opfer observes that "a by-product of this grassroots, individual participation is a politics of personalism" where extreme voices come to dominate public debate and affect superintendent and school board decision making (Opfer, 2005, p. 84; see also Fiorina, 1999). While this politics of personalism ("What's in it for me and my child?") is not new, it often conflicts with superintendents' and school boards' efforts to act in the best interests of *all* children. To mitigate this politics of personalism, Opfer (2005) suggests superintendents (and school boards) take measures to open up processes limiting participation and channeling participation in useful ways.

For their part, school boards must be cognizant of the individualistic, personalistic nature of interest-group activism and recognize that individuals who engage in such activities seldom represent the majority of opinion on school issues. If superintendents and school boards fail to recognize this trend, school policy risks becoming embroiled in "unnecessary conflict, animosity, delay, gridlock, and policy nonsense" (Opfer, 2005, p. 90). Drawing from Björk's (2005) research, as the influence of interest groups expands, scholars should focus more attention on studying the political dynamics of intensely factional school boards and should map out the political strategies superintendents use in dealing with such boards.

The Changing Face of the Superintendency

As if the demographic and contextual changes discussed above are not sufficient, within the last decade, in an attempt to improve often dismal school system performance, several states passed laws changing their certification requirements for superintendents, effectively permitting anyone—however trained—to become superintendent of a school district. The U.S. Department of Education, the Ford Foundation, the Carnegie Corporation, state governors, and legislators have been discussing and critiquing the training and preparation of school leaders (Olson, 2000). Several states, including Michigan, Tennessee, and Illinois, have either partially or totally eliminated requirements for superintendent preparation. For example, in Tennessee, superintendents need only citizenship and a college degree (in any field of study) (Kowalski and Glass, 2002). Many policy makers believe training in business, politics, or the military is sufficient preparation to lead school districts (Maher, 1988; Murphy, 1992).

Even though this movement remains small (less than two dozen school boards have chosen nontraditional superintendents to lead their districts), these nontraditional leaders are becoming increasingly common in large urban school systems. Several of the largest districts in the country—New York City, Los Angeles, Chicago, Philadelphia, San Diego, Seattle, and New Orleans—with over four million students combined, have been or are being led by superintendents with no significant educational background, no advanced training in an educational administration preparation program, and no certification as a school administrator.

Former New York City Schools Chancellor Harold Levy was a senior vice president of Citicorp; Ray Romer (Los Angeles) was former governor of Colorado; Paul Vallas (Chicago, Philadelphia, and now New Orleans) had extensive experience in public administration and business; David Hornbeck (Philadelphia) was a former lawyer and minister; John Stanford (Seattle) was a former general and county executive. This trend of hiring nontraditional superintendents to run school districts reflects the belief that advanced training in educational leadership or administration is unnecessary to lead and manage a school district effectively, although these nontraditional leaders may have extensive training in military or corporate leadership.

Although only about 1 percent of superintendents nationwide are noneducators, about 15 percent of superintendents leading large urban districts come from outside the traditional education establishment (Council of the Great City Schools, 2003). The movement of noneducators into top leadership positions in schools has generated much controversy and rhetoric (on both sides) but little solid, empirical research to date. Under the mantle of superintendent as CEO, some policy makers believe military training in leadership, business expertise, or politics is sufficient to effectively lead school systems. Young (2005) asserts superintendents must have successful experience in education as both a school leader (administrator) and as an educator (teacher), although the true measure of leadership lies in the ability to place the right people in the right positions in schools. Young argues that the research evidence suggests non-traditionally-trained superintendents (the superintendent as CEO role conceptualization is particularly applicable here) are not as effective in leading districts as those who come up through the ranks and have licenses and degrees from university-based administrator preparation programs (see also English, 2004).

A paucity of research exists on the effectiveness of nontraditional superintendents in leading school improvement and creating high-performing learning systems. Paul Houston, executive director of the American Association of School Administrators (AASA), concluded that the performance of noneducators in leading school improvement is mixed (Council of State Governments, 2004). Observing the differences in culture between education, the corporate environment, and the military, Houston notes that many nontraditional superintendents are frustrated by the political aspects of the job. Research by Bonnie Fusarelli (2005) explores the issue of how traditional superintendent–school board relations are altered when noneducators (those from outside the traditional education establishment pipeline) become superintendents. Fusarelli found that although conflict can be expected when outsiders unfamiliar with the culture of education assume leadership positions in schools, the precedent history and pattern of superintendent–school board relations are important factors that can affect any superintendent's leadership initiatives, be the superintendent an insider or an outsider.

A tendency exists to assume that retired military leaders and some corporate executives would be more autocratic than educators who rose through the ranks of school systems and perhaps generate more conflict with school boards. However, little research exists to either support or disconfirm this hypothesis. Limited anecdotal evidence suggests such notions are overly simplistic and sometimes erroneous (Stanford, 1999). While it is assumed noneducators would lead school systems differently than those from the traditional educational establishment, researchers have yet to establish that outsiders are less conventional or more innovative than their traditionally trained peers (Public Agenda, 2003). Bonnie Fusarelli suggests, "it is not the fact that individuals are educational outsiders that makes the difference, but rather that they have the interpersonal qualities, political acumen, and leadership skills required to lead a school district and work with a school board" (Fusarelli, 2005, p. 131).

Fusarelli and Petersen observe that the rise of nontraditional school leaders to the superintendency has significant implications for superintendent–school board relations. Questions such as "What happens when an individual unfamiliar with the education culture and workings of school boards is chosen to lead a school district?" or "What happens when the board interferes in personnel decisions made by the superintendent?" have been inadequately explored in the empirical literature on superintendent–school board relations (Fusarelli and Petersen, 2002, p. 287). Veteran school administrators are used to board interference and experienced with collaborative governance. However, nontraditional superintendents, particularly those from the military and corporate environment, may not be used to having their judgment questioned or may not have worked in an environment where the formal lines of decision-making authority are not always clearly defined. Fusarelli and Petersen ask, "If understanding role differences is a major factor contributing to successful superintendent–school board relationships, then how easily will nontraditional superintendents unfamiliar with school processes and culture 'fit' or meld into the culture of school boards?" (Fusarelli and Petersen, 2002, p. 287).

For example, some board members believe themselves far superior to "mere educators" such as the superintendent (Carter and Cunningham, 1997). What happens when the superintendent isn't an educator? Conversely, some boards have a history of "passive acquiescence" (Tallerico, 1989, p. 218), characterized by board members who seldom question the professional expertise of the superintendent. This paradigm is reinforced by superintendents themselves, who since the 1940s have portrayed themselves as professional educators (Glass, Björk, and Brunner, 2000). Assuming that boards value (to some degree) professional school experience, are they as acquiescent when the district is under the stewardship of a superintendent lacking that expertise? Or would they be more likely to intervene in district issues such as curriculum and instruction?

For example, it is not inconceivable that a school board would hire a nontraditional superintendent for his or her business and management expertise (such as successfully running a multimillion-dollar corporation), yet be more likely to intercede in instructional affairs than if the superintendent had extensive school experience (in the classroom and in school administration). These avenues of inquiry are unexplored in the scholarly literature, in part because of the newness and relatively small number of nontraditional superintendents. However, as noted above, the number and visibility of such superintendents is a growing trend in educational leadership and governance, with possibly significant implications for board-superintendent relationships.

More research is needed on the "culture clash" that often occurs between superintendents and school boards with long histories of "uniqueness." Every school board in every community has a particular history, a way of doing things, which greatly affects (either positively or negatively) the leadership initiatives of superintendents. This local context plays a major role in shaping superintendent–school board relations (Burlingame, 1988). Bonnie Fusarelli's (2005) research underscores just how important a role a community's history and the history of school board–superintendent relations play in constraining a superintendent's leadership initiatives, affecting her or his leadership success, producing turnover, and undermining the sustainability of reform. As Kowalski observes, the dividing line or demarcation between board member as policy maker and superintendent as policy implementer is "frequently very thin, and at times, even invisible" (Kowalski, 2005, p. x). As Bonnie Fusarelli (2005) noted, some districts have such contentious, micromanaging school boards that superintendent longevity is impossible. Superintendents, be they veteran educators, corporate leaders, or retired military officers, all face the challenge to lead and deal with the politics of leadership in an increasingly hostile environment that complicates and frustrates efforts to engage in systemic reform.

Re-imaging Board-Superintendent Relationships and Governance

Recent research using social influence theory explores how district superintendents and school board presidents interact with each other in attending to their respective responsibilities in leading the school organization, specifically, looking at their relationship and its influence on issues of agenda construction and board decision making (Petersen and Short, 2001; 2002). As Petersen and Williams (2005) observe, little research has been conducted in this area, despite the fact school board presidents are often the most influential members of school boards. As such, the dynamic between board presidents and superintendents may be an influential factor in successful district leadership and improved educational outcomes for all students. According to Petersen and Williams, the board president–superintendent–school board dynamic (largely unmapped) is pivotal in school reform and restructuring efforts.

Additional theoretical and empirical research is needed to examine school board members' and superintendent's views of the current board-superintendent governance model and whether it is perceived as facilitating or impeding the leadership of the district and its ability to respond to the needs of children. Specifically, researchers need to more thoroughly investigate the attitudes and opinions as well as the covariance between boards of education, superintendents, their views of the current board governance model, and its influence on the district's responsiveness to student learning and accountability. Have the pressures and changes discussed in this chapter produced changes in the leadership patterns of districts? Perhaps they have made for more directive or, conversely, more diffuse leadership.

Indeed, school boards have been steadily losing power and authority over school governance for decades (Wirt and Kirst, 2005). This raises an interesting question. If the power of school boards has been curtailed in significant and important ways, then how do these changes impact the relations between superintendents and school boards? If school boards are steadily losing power, are superintendents gaining power and authority over educational leadership and governance? Disagreement exists among scholars on this point. For example, Wirt and Kirst (2005) assert that school boards, superintendents, and central office administrators have been losing power and authority over decision making since 1950 (for more than five decades). However, Glass, Björk, and Brunner (2000) view local policy making as a pendulum of power swinging back and forth between the superintendent and school board.

CONCLUSION

School governance is complex, often contradictory, requires exceptional commitment, and at times results in conflict. In the past decade, school boards and superintendents have taken center stage in the discussion about the quality of American education. Boards of education in particular, with their preoccupation with patronage and penchant for micromanagement, have been vilified for their ineffectiveness in a series of scathing national reports (see, for example, Danzberger, Kirst, and Usdan, 1992; Finn, 1997; The Twentieth Century Fund, 1992). Included among the host of recommendations for improvement is the establishment of local education policy boards, revision of school board election procedures, improved school board development, contracting out, improved board-superintendent relationships, or abolishing school boards altogether (allowing states to directly run schools).

It is unrealistic to believe school boards will be abolished any time in the next several decades. No matter how ineffective they appear (and, as many point out, problems with the educational system are not all the school board's fault), locally elected school boards occupy a vital place in American democracy (Wirt and Kirst, 2005). Furthermore, the erosion of power of local school boards does not mean boards are powerless; in fact, boards remain responsible for deciding many issues of school leadership, curriculum, organization, staffing, and governance—making simplistic proposals for eliminating or replacing school boards unrealistic and impractical. Indeed, if all our representative bodies were threatened with dissolution based on poor performance or general dissatisfaction, our democracy itself might not survive. School boards continue to enjoy widespread popular support, at least when suggestions to abolish the institution are made. School boards "provide local control and an accessible level of government. In a country committed to representative democracy, they provide citizen access that remote state and federal capitals cannot duplicate" (The Twentieth Century Fund, 1992, pp. 6-7).

Another study sharply critical of school boards agreed, stating that boards "enjoyed a great deal of grass-roots support and were viewed as an important mechanism for representative government" because they "dealt with two of the most important elements in citizen's lives: their children and tax dollars" (Danzberger, Kirst, and Usdan, 1992, p. 51). In addition, given the mixed success of state and mayoral takeovers of failing school districts, no concrete evidence exists indicting state departments of education or mayors do a better job running local school districts than current school boards. Thus, despite its shortcomings, it is unlikely the school board–superintendent governance model will be abolished in the near future. We do know that the trends and forces presented here continue to generate competing demands on policy-making arenas and these demands require superintendents and boards to respond with differing roles and solutions in their leadership of schools. Based on this, what, then, of the future of local school governance? In an era of significant pressure and change, what roles and responsibilities are likely of school boards and superintendents in the future? We believe the governance structures will evolve to fit the modern era.

REFERENCES

Allison, D. J., P. A. Allison, and H. A. McHenry. 1995. Chiefs and chairs: Working relationships between effective CEOs and board of education chairpersons. In *Effective school district leadership: Transforming politics into education*, ed. K. Leithwood, 33–50. Albany: SUNY Press.

Alsbury, T. 2005. Political and apolitical school board and superintendent turnover: Revisiting critical variables in the Dissatisfaction Theory of American democracy. In *The politics of leadership: Superintendents and school boards in changing times*, ed. G. J. Petersen and L. D. Fusarelli, 135–155. Greenwich, CT: Information Age.

Berg, J. H. 1996. Context and perception: Implications for leadership. *Journal of School Leadership* 6:75–98.

Björk, L. G. 2005. Superintendent-board relations: An historical overview of the dynamics of change and sources of conflict and collaboration. In *The politics of leadership: Superintendents and school boards in changing times*, ed. G. J. Petersen and L. D. Fusarelli, 1–22. Greenwich, CT: Information Age.

Björk, L. G., R. J. Bell, and D. K. Gurley. 2002. Politics and the socialization of superintendents. In *The changing world of school administration*, ed. G. Perreault and F. Lunenburg, 294–311. Lanham, MD: Scarecrow Press.

Björk, L. G., and J. C. Lindle. 2001. Superintendents and interest groups. *Educational Policy* 15 (1): 76–91.

Blumberg, A. 1985. A superintendent must read the board's invisible job description. *American School Board Journal* 172 (9): 44–45.

Boyd, W. L. 1976. The public, the professionals, and educational policy: Who governs? *Teachers College Record* 77 (4): 539–578.

Bullard, P., and B. O. Taylor. 1993. *Making school reform happen*. Boston: Allyn & Bacon.

Burlingame, M. 1988. The politics of education and educational policy: The local level. In *Handbook of research on educational administration*, ed. N. J. Boyan, 439–454. New York: Longman.

Campbell, D. W., and D. Greene. 1994. Defining the leadership role of school boards in the 21st century. *Phi Delta Kappan* 75 (5): 391–395.

Carter, G. R., and W. G. Cunningham. 1997. *The American school superintendent: Leading in an age of pressure*. San Francisco: Jossey-Bass.

Cibulka, J. G. 1999. Ideological lenses for interpreting political and economic changes affecting schooling. In *Handbook of research on educational administration*, 2nd ed., ed. J. Murphy and K. Seashore Louis, 163–182. San Francisco: Jossey-Bass.

Council of State Governments. 2004. AASA Director Paul Houston talks about the 'politics' of school leadership. January 16. http://www.csg.org/CSG/Policy/education/Dr.+Houston+interview.htm (accessed June 29, 2004).

Council of the Great City Schools. 2003. Urban school superintendents: Characteristics, tenure, and salary. *Urban Indicator* 7 (1): 1–7.

Crowson, R. 1987. The local school district superintendency: A puzzling administrative role. *Educational Administration Quarterly* 23 (3): 49–69.

Cuban, L. 1976. *Urban school chiefs under fire.* Chicago: University of Chicago Press.

Danzberger, J. P. 1994. Governing the nation's schools: The case for restructuring local school boards. *Phi Delta Kappan* 75 (5): 367–373.

Danzberger, J. P., M. W. Kirst, and M. D. Usdan. 1992. *Governing public schools: New times, new requirements.* Washington, DC: Institute for Educational Leadership.

Danzberger, J. P., and M. D. Usdan. 1994. Local education governance: Perspectives on problems and strategies for change. *Phi Delta Kappan* 75 (5): 366.

Elizabeth, J. 2003. School board reform elusive. *Pittsburgh Post-Gazette*, December 1. http://www.post-gazette.com/localnews/20031201boardsmainp2.asp (accessed August 12, 2007).

English, F. W. 2004. Learning "manifestospeak": A metadiscursive analysis of the Fordham and Broad Foundations' manifesto for better leaders for America's schools. In *Better leaders for America's schools: Perspectives on the manifesto*, ed. T. Lasley, 52–91. Columbia, MO: University Council for Educational Administration.

Feuerstein, A., and V. D. Opfer. 1998. School board chairmen and school superintendents: An analysis of perceptions concerning special interest groups and educational governance. *Journal of School Leadership* 8:373–398.

Finn, C. E. 1997. Learning-free zones: Five reasons America's schools won't improve. *Policy Review* 85. http://www.hoover.org/publications/policyreview/3573132 html (accessed August 12, 2007).

Fiorina, M. 1999. Extreme voices: A dark side of civic engagement. In *Civic engagement in American democracy*, ed. T. Skocpol and M. Fiorina, 395–425. Washington, DC: Brookings Institution Press.

Fullan, M. G., and S. Stiegelbauer. 1991. *The new meaning of educational change.* 2nd ed. New York: Teachers College Press.

Fusarelli, B. C. 2005. When generals (or colonels) become superintendents: Conflict, chaos, and community. In *The politics of leadership: Superintendents and school boards in changing times*, ed. G. J. Petersen and L. D. Fusarelli, 117–134. Greenwich, CT: Information Age.

Fusarelli, B. C., and L. D. Fusarelli. 2003. Systemic reform and organizational change. *Planning and Changing* 34 (3–4): 169–177.

Fusarelli, L. D. 1999. Education is more than numbers: Communitarian leadership of schools for the new millennium. In *School leadership: Expanding horizons of the mind and spirit*, ed. L. T. Fenwick, 97–107. Lancaster, PA: Technomic.

———. 2000. Leadership in Latino schools: Challenges for the new millennium. In *Marching into a new millennium: Challenges to educational leadership*, ed. P. M. Jenlink, 228–238. Lanham, MD: Scarecrow Press.

———. 2002a. The political economy of gubernatorial elections: Implications for education policy. *Educational Policy* 16 (1): 139–160.

———. 2002b. Tightly coupled policy in loosely coupled systems: Institutional capacity and organizational change. *Journal of Educational Administration* 40 (6): 561–575.

————. 2005a. Future research directions and policy implications for superintendent-school board relationships. In *The politics of leadership: Superintendents and school boards in changing times*, ed. G. J. Petersen and L. D. Fusarelli, 181–197. Greenwich, CT: Information Age.

————. 2005b. Gubernatorial reactions to No Child Left Behind: Politics, pressure, and education reform. *Peabody Journal of Education* 80 (2): 120–136.

Fusarelli, L. D., B. S. Cooper, and V. A. Carella. 2002. Dilemmas of the modern superintendency. In *The promises and perils facing today's school superintendent*, ed. B. S. Cooper and L. D. Fusarelli, 5–20. Lanham, MD: Scarecrow Press.

Fusarelli, L. D., and G. J. Petersen. 2002. Changing times, changing relationships: An exploration of current trends influencing the relationship between superintendents and boards of education. In *The changing world of school administration*, ed. G. Perreault and F. C. Lunenburg, 282–293. Lanham, MD: Scarecrow Press.

Glass, T. E. 2001. Superintendent leaders look at the superintendency, school boards, and reform. Education Commission of the States, Denver. http://www.ecs org/clearinghouse/27/18/2718.htm (accessed August 12, 2007).

————. 2002. School board presidents and their view of the superintendency. Education Commission of the States, Denver. http://www.ecs.org/clearinghouse/36/39/3639.htm (accessed August 12, 2007).

Glass, T. E., L. Björk, and C. C. Brunner. 2000. *The 2000 study of the American school superintendency: A look at the superintendent of education in the new millennium*. Arlington, VA: American Association of School Administrators.

Goldstein, K. 1999. *Interest groups, lobbying, and participation in America*. New York: Cambridge University Press.

Gonzalez, M. L., A. Huerta-Macias, and J. V. Tinajero, eds. 1998. *Educating Latino students: A guide to successful practice*. Lancaster, PA: Technomic.

Greene, K. R. 1992. Models of school board policy-making. *Educational Administration Quarterly* 28 (2): 220–236.

Grogan, M., and W. H. Sherman. 2003. How superintendents in Virginia deal with issues surrounding the black-white test-score gap. In *Educational leadership in an age of accountability*, ed. D. Duke, M. Grogan, P. Tucker, and W. Heinecke, 155–180. Albany: SUNY Press.

Hentges, J. T. 1986. The politics of superintendent-school board linkages: A study of power, participation, and control. *ERS Spectrum* 4 (3): 23–32.

Hess, F. M. 2002. *School boards at the dawn of the 21st century: Conditions and challenges of district governance*. Washington, DC: National School Boards Association.

Howe, C. K. 1994. Improving the achievement of Hispanic students. *Educational Leadership* 51 (8): 42–44.

Hoyle, J. R., F. W. English, and B. E. Steffy. 1998. *Skills for successful 21st-century school leaders: Standards for peak performance*. Arlington, VA: American Association of School Administrators.

Johnson, R. 2003. Those nagging headaches: Perennial issues and tensions in the politics of education field. *Educational Administration Quarterly* 39 (1): 41–67.

Keedy, J. L., and L. G. Björk. 2002. Superintendents and local boards and the potential for community polarization: The call for use of political strategist skills. In *The promises and perils facing today's school superintendent*, ed. B. S. Cooper and L. D. Fusarelli, 103–127. Lanham, MD: Scarecrow Press.

Konnert, W. M., and J. J. Augenstein. 1995. *The school superintendency: Leading education into the 21st century.* Lancaster, PA: Technomic.

Kowalski, T. J. 2005. Foreword. In *The politics of leadership: Superintendents and school boards in changing times,* ed. G. J. Petersen and L. D. Fusarelli, ix–xii. Greenwich, CT: Information Age.

———. 2006. *The school superintendent: Theory, practice, and cases.* 2nd ed. Upper Saddle River, NJ: Prentice-Hall.

Kowalski, T. J., and T. E. Glass. 2002. Preparing superintendents in the 21st century. In *The promises and perils facing today's school superintendent,* ed. B. S. Cooper and L. D. Fusarelli, 41–59. Lanham, MD: Scarecrow Press.

Lunenburg, F. C., and A. C. Ornstein. 1996. *Educational administration: Concepts and practices.* 2nd ed. Belmont, CA: Wadsworth.

Lutz, F. W., and A. Gresson. 1980. Local school boards as political councils. *Educational Studies* 11:125–144.

Maher, R. 1988. Are graduate schools preparing tomorrow's administrators? *NASSP Bulletin* 72 (508): 30–34.

Mazzoni, T. L. 1995. State policy-making and school reform: Influences and influences. In *The study of educational politics,* ed. J. D. Scribner and D. H. Layton, 53–73. Washington, DC: Falmer Press.

McCarty, D. J., and C. E. Ramsey. 1971. *The school managers.* Westport, CT: Greenwood.

McCurdy, J. M. 1992. *Building better board-administrator relations.* Arlington, VA: American Association of School Administrators.

Moe, T. M. 2005. *Teachers' unions and school board elections.* In *Besieged: School boards and the future of educational politics,* ed. W. G. Howell, 254–287. Washington, DC: Brookings Institution Press.

Morgan, C., and G. J. Petersen. 2002. The role of the district superintendent in leading academically successful school districts. In *The promises and perils facing today's school superintendent,* ed. B. S. Cooper and L. D. Fusarelli, 175–196. Lanham, MD: Scarecrow Press.

Murphy, J. 1992. *The landscape of leadership preparation: Reframing the education of school administrators.* Newbury Park, CA: Corwin Press.

Natkin, G., B. S. Cooper, L. D. Fusarelli, J. Alborano, A. Padilla, and S. Ghosh. 2001. *Predicting and modeling the survival of school superintendents.* Paper presented at the annual meeting of the American Educational Research Association, Seattle.

Norton, M. S., L. D. Webb, L. L. Dlugosh, and W. Sybouts. 1996. *The school superintendency: New responsibilities, new leadership.* Boston: Allyn & Bacon.

Nowakowski, J., and P. F. First. 1989. A study of school board minutes: Records of reform. *Educational Evaluation and Policy Analysis* 11 (4): 389–404.

Nygren, B. 1992. Two-party tune up. *American School Board Journal* 178 (7): 35.

Olson, L. 2000. Policy focus converges on leadership: Several major efforts underway. *Education Week* 19 (17): 1, 16–17.

Opfer, V. D. 2001. Beyond self-interest: Education interest groups in the U.S. Congress. *Educational Policy* 15 (1): 135–152.

———. 2005. Personalization of interest groups and the resulting policy nonsense: The Cobb County school board's evolution debate. In *The politics of leadership: Superintendents and school boards in changing times,* ed. G. J. Petersen and L. D. Fusarelli, 73–93. Greenwich, CT: Information Age.

Petersen, G. J. 1999. Demonstrated actions of instructional leaders: A case study of five superintendents. *Education Policy Analysis Archives* (7):18. http://epaa.asu.edu/epaa/v7n18.html (accessed August 2, 2007).

Petersen, G. J., and P. M. Short. 2001. School board presidents and the district superintendent relationship: Applying the lens of social influence. *Educational Administration Quarterly* 37 (4): 533–570.

———. 2002. An examination of the school board president's perception of the district superintendent's interpersonal communication competence and board decision making. *Journal of School Leadership* 12 (4): 533–570.

Petersen, G. J., and B. M. Williams. 2005. The board president and superintendent: An examination of influence through the eyes of the decision makers. In *The politics of leadership: Superintendents and school boards in changing times*, ed. G. J. Petersen and L. D. Fusarelli, 23–49. Greenwich, CT: Information Age.

Public Agenda. 2003. *Rolling up their sleeves.* New York: Author.

Renchler, R. 1992. Urban superintendent turnover: The need for stability. *Urban Superintendents' Sounding Board* 1 (1): 2–13.

Scribner, J., and R. Englert. 1977. The politics of education: An introduction. In *The politics of education: The seventy-sixth yearbook of the national society for the study of education, Part II*, ed. J. Scribner, 1–29. Chicago: University of Chicago Press.

Stanford, J. 1999. *Victory in our schools.* New York: Bantam Books.

Stone, C. N., J. R. Henig, B. D. Jones, and C. Pierannunzi. 2001. *Building civic capacity: The politics of reforming urban schools.* Lawrence: University Press of Kansas.

Tallerico, M. 1989. The dynamics of superintendent-school board relationships: A continuing challenge. *Urban Education* 24 (2): 215–232.

Tucker, H. J., and L. H. Zeigler. 1980. *Professionals and the public: Attitudes, communication, and response in school districts.* New York: Longman.

The Twentieth Century Fund. 1992. *Facing the challenge: The report of The Twentieth Century Fund task force on school governance.* New York: Author.

Usdan, M. D. 1975. The future viability of the school board. In *Understanding school boards: Problems and prospects*, ed. P. J. Cistone, 265–276. Toronto: Lexington Books.

Usdan, M., B. McCloud, M. Podmostko, and L. Cuban. 2001. *Leadership for learning: Restructuring school district leadership.* Washington, DC: Institute for Educational Leadership.

Wirt, F. M., and M. W. Kirst. 2005. *The political dynamics of American education.* 3rd ed. Richmond, CA: McCutchan.

Young, M. D. 2005. Building effective school system leadership: Rethinking preparation and policy. In *The politics of leadership: Superintendents and school boards in changing times*, ed. G. J. Petersen and L. D. Fusarelli, 157–179. Greenwich, CT: Information Age.

Zeigler, L. H. 1975. School board research: The problems and the prospects. In *Understanding school boards*, ed. P. J. Cistone, 3–16. Lexington, MA: Heath.

Zeigler, L. H., M. K. Jennings, and G. W. Peak. 1974. *Governing American schools: Political interaction in local school districts.* North Scituate, MA: Duxbury Press.

IV

SCHOOL BOARD DEMOCRATIC EFFECTIVENESS

7

Money, Interest Groups, and School Board Elections

Frederick Hess

INTRODUCTION

The issue of local school board governance has been a subject of debate, and more than a little ridicule, for over a century. Mark Twain, of course, famously opined, "God made idiots. That was for practice. Then he made school boards." In a more contemporary vein, one need not search hard to find the 2006 *Reuters* story entitled "Dead woman wins deadlocked vote by coin toss." Headlines routinely depict school board elections as alternately venal, conflict laden, or unimportant, in stories such as the *Fort Lauderdale Sun-Sentinel's* "Insults, Charges Mark Race for School Board," the *Modesto Bee's* "Campaign in District 3 Turns Nasty," the *Daily News of Los Angeles's* "School Board Still Stewing; Last Year's 'Nasty' Election Leaves Lasting Wounds," or the *Arizona Republic's* "School Board Seats Attract Few; Lack of Candidates in 17 Districts May Force Cancellation of Elections."

Nonetheless, the more than 100,000 board members serving on approximately 15,000 school boards constitute the largest group of elected officials in the United States and collectively oversee the expenditure of more than $500 billion a year. How they govern and how effectively they do so are serious questions deserving of systematic inquiry. As with any democratic body, that inquiry starts with understanding how they are elected. While elected boards have been both celebrated as pillars of democracy and assailed as anachronistic institutions, claims about board electioneering, responsiveness, and democratic accountability have been made on the basis of remarkably little data. Little is known about how much board elections cost, who funds board members, how competitive board elections actually are, or what interests are most active in board elections.

The contemporary reform debate has encompassed a variety of reform proposals, each premised on particular critiques of board behavior. Hill (2003) has proposed replacing traditional school boards with multiple, competing entities each free to sponsor "charter districts." Others have suggested school boards are ill-suited to the challenges of contemporary schooling and have advocated dismantling boards and replacing them with mayoral control or some similar arrangement (Broad, 2003). Still other thinkers have argued that the priority ought to be ensuring boards have the training and professional development necessary to enable them to play their governance role more effectively (McAdams, 2006).

The various prescriptions rest on assumptions regarding the nature of board governance and elections, but are typically handicapped by the dearth of evidence documenting how school board elections, decision making, and processes unfold in practice. The aim of this chapter is to provide a more substantive understanding of the electoral process. In particular, it seeks to deepen understanding of boards and the role they play by exploring how money and interest groups affect board elections. In this respect, it complements the earlier and more quantitatively sophisticated analysis of Hess and Leal (2005) by providing a more updated and less technical discussion of the dynamics of board elections.

While previous research provides insight into the link between factors like public opinion and local spending, it does not tell us much about the electoral mechanism itself or how it may influence the makeup and behavior of school boards. Using information collected from a national sample of more than 800 school boards and matched with district-level census data, an empirical inquiry into the role of money and interest-group activism in school board elections is possible. The focus is on five questions: How much money do board candidates spend on their campaigns? Which interest groups supply campaign funding? How active are various interests reported to be in board elections? How competitive are school board campaigns? And, finally, how do factors such as community context, electoral arrangements, and the presence of collective bargaining affect the role of key interests in board elections?

PREVIOUS RESEARCH

From early in the 19th century until the 1970s, political scientists produced a long tradition of scholarship on the nature and politics of school boards (Dye, 1967; Jennings and Zeigler, 1971; Meranto, 1970; Wirt and Kirst, 1972; Zeigler and Jennings, 1974). In the late 1970s, political science research on these questions dropped off precipitously, leaving the field primarily to education specialists and journalists.

A resurgence of political science interest arose in education in the late 1990s, with scholars particularly interested in the influence of teacher employee unions and the importance of "civic capacity" (often measured as the relative engagement of business, civic, parent, community, and civil rights organizations) (see, for example, Portz et al., 1999; Stone et al., 2001). Researchers have evinced particular interest in the involvement of interest groups (Feuerstein, 1998), minority communities and race-based organizations (Henig et al., 1999; Orr, 1999; Rich, 1996), and of Christian right and evangelical organizations (Deckman, 2004; Regnerus et al., 1999).

Previous scholarship has documented that board members receive sparse compensation and operate with limited professional support, presumably reducing the number of individuals interested in board service and the energy they expend to pursue the seat. As the *Arizona Republic* explained, when reporting that no candidates had filed to run for 28 open seats in 17 Maricopa County districts, "The lack of interest is . . . due to a variety of factors. First, the school board positions are unpaid. Then, those who get elected often face long hours and find themselves appealing targets for disgruntled parents and teachers" (Baker and Carroll, 2006). A national study of approximately 800 school boards found more than two-thirds of all school board members receive no salary; even in districts enrolling 25,000 or more students, most board members receive no compensation and less than a quarter are paid $10,000 a year (Hess, 2002). Meanwhile, one-third of all board members, and about half of board members in districts with enrollments of 25,000 or more, serve on at least three other local boards or committees in addition to the school board—suggesting they must juggle multiple demands on their time (Hess, 2002). Moreover, a study of 57 urban districts reported that 89 percent of the districts provided board members with neither personal staff nor office space (Hess, 1999).

Recent research has had some success shedding light on the factors that influence board decision making. In an extensive empirical study of school boards, Berkman and Plutzer (2005) reported from an analysis of 7,885 school boards (of which about 300 were appointed) that appointed boards were more responsive to popular preferences than were elected boards when they examined the correlation between public opinion regarding school spending and actual per-pupil district expenditures. Their work also explores how constituent characteristics like age and race influence the outcome of policy decisions on spending and educational provisions. In doing so, Berkman and Plutzer extended research examining how demographic, fiscal, and institutional forces affect board policy decisions on issues like school violence prevention policies, opportunities for public input into district governance, and spending on bilingual education programs (Hess and Leal, 2001, 2003; Leal and Hess, 2000).

In a provocative study, Campbell (2005) investigated the effect the demographic makeup of a school district had on the political engagement of its residents. In particular, he examined how "heterogeneity" (measured by economic, racial/ethnic, ideological, and religious factors) affected public participation. He found religious and ideological heterogeneity were statistically significant, and that people who live in communities characterized by greater religious and ideological heterogeneity attend local and school meetings less often than those who live in more homogenous communities. Campbell concluded that more diverse communities had fewer ties binding the citizenry, and residents in more homogeneous locales, consequently, felt more comfortable in public settings and more invested in public institutions. Campbell's work provides a valuable illustration of how research into the effects of context on school board electioneering, governance, and practice can help inform thinking about desirable reform.

Perhaps the most rigorous and extensive inquiry into school board politics has been Terry Moe's research examining the influence of teachers unions in California board elections. In two studies, Moe (2006) has reported compelling evidence that union power is often a deciding factor in board elections. In summarizing one study, Moe explained:

> A study of 245 California school district elections and the 1,228 candidates who competed in them during the years 1998–2001 . . . shows that, for candidates who are not incumbents, teacher union support increases the probability of winning substantially. Indeed, it is roughly equal to, and may well exceed, the impact of incumbency itself. (Moe, 2006, p. 65)

Moe explains a second study:

> Interviews with 526 school-board candidates (winners and losers) in 253 California districts reinforce the study of electoral outcomes . . . suggest[ing] that the teacher unions are typically the most powerful participants in school-board elections and that their power is common across districts of all sizes . . . They also provide evidence that union electoral clout has genuine substantive consequences: the candidates supported by the unions, as well as the candidates who win, are considerably more sympathetic toward collective bargaining than the other candidates. (Moe, 2006, pp. 65–66)

Of course, while such research documents the influence of teachers unions, the intensive focus on them has inevitably meant studying them in isolation (rather than as one of multiple competing interests), which limits the ability of such research to explain how influential they are relative to other actors. Thus, the ensuing analysis seeks to complement scholarship such as Moe's by providing a national look at key questions, including:

How does union activity compare to that of other key interests, particularly the business community or racial and ethnic organizations? How exactly do unions exert their influence, and do campaign contributions play a substantial role?

DESCRIPTION OF DATA AND METHODS

The data for this analysis were obtained from two sources: a 2001 national survey of school boards developed by the authors and 2000 U.S. census data. In 2001, we conducted the most extensive survey to date of a nationally representative sample of the nation's school boards. The survey instrument was developed in collaboration with the National School Boards Association (NSBA) and then distributed by the NSBA to a randomly selected board member in each of 2,000 school districts. A stratified random sample of school districts was drawn from the nation's 15,000 districts. Responses were obtained from 827 board members, yielding a response rate of 40.9 percent. Response rates were relatively stable across districts of different sizes (Hess, 2002).

The analysis focuses on four measures of school board political activity. The first describes the amount of money spent in the most recent board election by the respondent. The second examines the percentage of campaign revenue that candidates raised from a variety of local interest groups. The third examines the reported activism of these organized interests in board elections. The fourth provides data on the competitiveness of local board elections.

School board campaigns tend to be amateur affairs marked by imprecise record keeping and low levels of candidate interest or expertise in the particulars of fund-raising or campaigning. Although this makes the data less detailed and systematic than would be ideal, it does not pose a major problem. While this state of affairs undoubtedly reduces precision in the analysis, it is not clear how this limited level of candidate interest or knowledge would bias findings in any particular direction. The one potential source of bias would be if board members were systematically over- or underestimating their campaign spending, their financial support from a particular interest group, the activity of particular interest groups, or board competitiveness. However, this would require that board members all tend to misrepresent activity in the same direction.

The analysis is primarily an exploration of survey data describing the role of funds and interest groups in school board elections and how competitive those elections prove to be. Because it has long been argued to be a significant determinant of the power of employee unions, the analysis frequently considers whether the district is located in a state with a collective bargaining law.

Collective bargaining laws are potentially of interest because they strengthen the hand of unions by encouraging a larger union membership and a more central institutional position. Thirty-four states have laws that provide for collective bargaining by public school teachers.

To understand more fully how community and political institutions affect the role various interest groups play, the discussion also addresses the importance of various contextual factors. In addressing the determinants of interest-group influence, the discussion at times takes into account district size, the percentage of the district that is urbanized, the racial composition of the district, and the education of the district population. Other variables measure various local and state arrangements that influence the conduct of elections, the structure of the board, and the relative professionalism of the local school board (including whether a salary or stipend is paid to board members, the length of board member terms, and the number of hours board members spend on the job each week).

MONEY: HOW MUCH AND WHERE IT COMES FROM

How much money do board members spend to get elected? Popular conceptions tend to be colored by politics in high-profile urban districts where heated campaigns draw significant media attention. In the first two months of a fiercely contested 2007 Los Angeles school board election, for instance, candidates backed by Los Angeles mayor Antonio Villaraigosa squared off against those supported by the United Teachers of Los Angeles. In the first two months of the year, the competing sides provided more than $2.5 million in donations to their preferred candidates as they struggled for control of the seven-member board (Zahniser, 2007).

In light of the modest compensation board members receive and the multiple demands on their time, however, it would not surprise if such outlays were the exception. For example, in the 2006 board election in Charleston County, South Carolina, a district spanning over 1,000 square miles, the biggest-spending candidates spent close to $20,000, while one incumbent spent $450 campaigning for a seat on the nine-member board of the 35,000-student district. In Sarasota County, Florida, one incumbent bemoaned the fact that another candidate had raised $36,000, remarking, "I think it's gotten totally out of hand" (Babiarz, 2006). In that same Sarasota race, campaigning for a seat atop the 40,000-student district, 3 of the 10 candidates raised less than $5,000 and 2 others less than $10,000. Which of these figures represents the norm? Just how expensive and how intensively waged are school board elections?

To determine how much money is spent on the typical school board campaign, the survey asked each board member to indicate the total amount he or she spent in the last election. Because respondents might not be able to precisely remember the figure, they were offered a choice of five categorical responses: $0 to $999, $1,000 to $4,999, $5,000 to $9,999, $10,000 to $24,999, or more than $25,000.

The results suggest that the Los Angeles case is a dramatic departure from the norm, and even the bigger spenders in Sarasota appear to be atypical relative to the national norm. In the 2001 survey, more than 76 percent of respondents indicated they spent less than $1,000 in their last campaign. Only 10 percent of candidates reported spending more than $5,000, and only 1 percent reported spending as much as $25,000.

These results are decidedly influenced by the fact that most board members run in small districts. When examining only those districts with enrollment of 25,000 or more, the races appear moderately more expensive. In those districts, 25 percent of board members spent at least $10,000 on their last campaign, and 38 percent spent $5,000 or more. Of course, that means that, even in these districts, nearly two-thirds of candidates still spent less than $5,000. In districts with fewer than 5,000 students, 95 percent of candidates reported spending less than $1,000 and less than 1 percent reported spending even as much as $5,000. In midsize districts (with 5,000 to 24,999 students), 64 percent of candidates spent less than $1,000, while just 4 percent reported spending $10,000 or more.

It is worth recalling that the data were collected in 2001 and that spending is likely higher today. Whether any such increase approximates the 13 percent increase in the cost of living from 2001 to 2007 (amounting to no more than a few hundred dollars on average) or something larger is a question requiring further research. It is also worth recalling, however, that the survey respondents were all currently serving on school boards, meaning they were all *winning* candidates in their most recent election. Given the likelihood that winning board candidates spend more than the candidates they defeat (although this is speculation currently unsupported by empirical evidence), it is very possible the estimated spending figure is higher than the amount spent by the typical candidate. Surveying defeated candidates would likely yield even lower estimated levels of spending.

A 2005 survey conducted by the New York School Boards Association provides more confidence that the estimates reported here still reflect the norm. In the New York survey of 921 school board candidates, 95 percent reported spending less than $1,000, 4 percent that they spent between $1,000 and $4,999, 0.7 percent that they spent between $5,000 and $9,999, and just 0.2 percent that they spent more than $10,000 (New York State School Boards Association, 2005).

Except in the nation's largest districts, campaign contributions from recognizable interests appear to play only a small role in elections. In fact, 63 percent of respondents reported either they or their friends and family supplied more than half of the funds for their most recent campaign. In total, a reasonable estimation is that fewer than 20 percent of candidates received a majority of their funding from any combination of organized interests. Outside of the largest districts, little opportunity exists for organized interests to influence candidates through traditional campaign contributions of the size attracting so much attention in national debates. An illuminating example of how these numbers play out was provided by the expenditures in the 19-school St. Charles Parish, Louisiana, district during the 2006 election. In their final preelection filing, candidates were more likely to have raised $20 than $20,000. Second District incumbent Mary Bergeron topped all candidates in reported spending, with a reported total of $1,004. Her challenger Angela Fenerty, meanwhile, reported lending $7.85 to her campaign for advertising-related photo processing.

In the First District, former councilman Ellis Alexander reported expenditures of $900 for yard signs and $83 for a newspaper advertisement. His opponent Desmond Hilaire reported having not yet raised or spent any money. In the Eighth District race, Hank Shepard donated $1,400 to his campaign; opponent Al Suffrin raised $500 from contributors and lent his campaign $2,000. In the Seventh District, incumbent Steve Crovetto reported no fund-raising or loans, but spent $20 to become an honorary member of the Louisiana Sheriff's Association, while challenger Robin Triche Fields reported no contributions or expenditures (Scallan, 2006). The incidence of candidates personally providing a substantial portion of their campaign funds, evident here, is a common state of affairs.

Two other examples from 2006 races in New York help to provide a clearer sense of the amount of money candidates spend and what it is spent on. To win a seat on the Nyack Board of Education, Michael Lagana spent $6,300. The breakdown of spending included $600 for handouts and fliers, $4,000 for signs, $250 for a Web site, $1,200 for print and Web advertising, and $250 for miscellaneous expenses. To claim a seat on the Clarkstown Board of Education, Rhea Vogel spent $4,620. That included $398.01 for printer ink and paper, $1,276.98 for magnets and pads, $1,809.20 for a newspaper insert ad, $1,104 for stamps, $17.90 for a Web site, $10 for a Clarkstown voter list, and $4.64 to send registered mail (Weiner, 2006). The itemized expenditures and the attached amounts are almost quaint in an era of hundred-thousand-dollar races for the state legislature, and serve as a stark reminder of how informal and unsophisticated most board campaigns remain.

While the aggregate amount of spending is significant in its own right, examining the source of those funds may help explain the influence and import of competing interests. In particular, given popular concerns about the influence of interests such as teachers unions or the business community in

Table 7.1.   Reported Distribution of Campaign Funds by Source

Percentage of Total Funds Contributed	Teachers Unions	Business Groups	Religious Groups	Personal Funds	Family/ Friends
0%	82%	76%	97%	34%	49%
1% to 25%	12%	14%	3%	16%	16%
26% to 50%	5%	7%	0%	7%	16%
Over 50%	1%	3%	0%	44%	19%
N	425	437	392	608	552

educational affairs, just how dependent are candidates on these groups for their campaign support?

The survey asked respondents to report the percentage of money they received from teachers unions, business groups, and religiously affiliated organizations, as well as from personal sources and from family and friends. Respondents were asked to indicate whether more than 50 percent, 26–50 percent, 1–25 percent, or 0 percent of funds came from a particular source. This strategy was used to simplify the burden on board members who might not recall the details or who might not feel comfortable providing explicit information on the nature and source of their funding. Table 7.1 provides more detailed information for each source.

As noted previously, respondents reported the most common source of funding was personal resources, followed by donations from friends and family. In fact, 44 percent of respondents reported they provided more than half of their own campaign funding, and another 19 percent received more than half from their friends or family. Meanwhile, just 6 percent of candidates received more than a quarter of their funding from teachers unions, just 10 percent garnered that much from the business community, and no one received that much from religious groups. It can be inferred from these statistics that interest groups are playing, at best, a minor role in the funding of most school board campaigns.

While these general patterns are interesting, it is possible these groups play different roles in different districts. Are organized interests more active in some districts and do teachers unions or business interests contribute a larger percentage of campaign funding in some kinds of communities?

Hess and Leal (2005) report teachers unions tend to provide a larger percentage of candidate funds in larger, more urbanized districts. The percentage of funds contributed by the business community also tends to be highest in urban communities and more affluent districts. In districts with 25,000 or more students, 61 percent of candidates reported donations from employee unions and 67 percent reported such donations from the business community. In districts with fewer than 5,000 students, just 6 percent of board members reported employee donations and just 8 percent reported business donations. In midsize districts of 5,000 to 24,999 students, the corresponding figures were 27 percent and 37 percent. Thus, board members in larger districts supply a smaller percentage of their campaign funds than those in smaller districts and are more likely to have received contributions from organized interests.

Hess and Leal also reported business giving constitutes a higher percentage of candidate revenue in districts located in collective bargaining states. Given total spending was not significantly different in collective bargaining and non–collective bargaining districts, business groups may be more organized in collective bargaining states (as union activity may be more of a day-to-day concern for the business community) or might be more aware of the activity of the teachers union and consequently be more inclined to organize and engage in district affairs. Aside from collective bargaining laws, Hess and Leal found little evidence that context affects the degree candidates are reliant on business or contributions by teachers unions.

Of course, a significant problem with an analysis of interest-group campaign contributions is that the results only measure the money groups contributed directly to board candidates. Such calculations inevitably exclude expenditures groups might spend directly or "in-kind" contributions such as phone banks, literature, advertisements, or yard signs groups might independently provide. In fact, it is in precisely those communities where some groups—such as teachers unions or religiously affiliated organizations— exert significant influence or are capable of marshaling significant resources so that they may find it unnecessary (or even counterproductive) to make sizable contributions.

INTEREST GROUPS AND BOARD ELECTIONS

Contributions are an imperfect measure of interest-group activity in campaigns, especially in school board elections where the ability to provide "in-kind" support or access to community networks may matter far more than monetary contributions. Consequently, the survey also employed a second measure—the reported activity of several major potential actors—to examine whether the results reinforce the preceding findings. This measure is less than ideal, given its subjective cast, our inability to unpack just what board members have in mind when they refer to activity, and the fact that a fair bit of variation in how respondents gauge activity is likely (with some focusing primarily on visible exertions and others potentially taking into account behind-the-scenes efforts). Nonetheless, the metric does offer an opportunity to determine whether public officials perceive local interests to be engaging in activities (such as pamphleteering or erecting signs) that would not be reflected in inquiries regarding campaign contributions.

Respondents gauged the activity of six discrete interests in local school board elections: teacher organizations, parental groups, the business community, religious organizations, racial and ethnic groups, and school reform organizations. Some of these "interests," such as parental groups or "school reform" organizations, are rather vague and might convey a different meaning across communities. For that reason, responses relating to those groups ought to be regarded with due caution. Respondents indicated whether they regarded each of the groups as "very active," "somewhat active," "occasionally active," or "never active." It is worth noting that this question asked about "activity" rather than "influence" in order to focus respondents upon the actual behavior of each group rather than upon its broader reputed ability to affect board affairs.

Board members regard teachers unions as the most active organized interest group in local elections (see Table 7.2). Teachers unions were regarded as "very active" in 31 percent of districts and either "very" or "somewhat" active in 57 percent. On the other hand, business groups were deemed "very" or "somewhat" active in just 33 percent of districts and "not active" in 39 percent. Compared with the results in Table 7.1, these findings suggest the business community's involvement in board elections takes place largely through campaign contributions, while teachers unions and other employee unions are more likely to engage in electioneering beyond contributions.

In the majority of districts, neither religious nor race-based groups were thought to be active participants; less than 20 percent of respondents labeled either group as "very" or "somewhat" active in local board elections. Parental groups were regarded as "very" or "somewhat" active in the majority of districts, while school reform groups were said to be that active in barely 10 percent of districts. On the other hand, uncertainty about who is included in these latter two categories, what points of view they adopt, or how they choose sides in elections leave a great deal of ambiguity concerning the substantive significance of this finding.

Table 7.2.   Reported Levels of Interest-Group Activity (in percentages)

	Teachers Unions	Parental Groups	Business Groups	Religious Groups	Racial/ Ethnic Groups	School Reform Groups
Very Active	31%	19%	11%	5%	5%	4%
Somewhat Active	26%	33%	22%	12%	13%	9%
Occasionally Active	20%	35%	29%	28%	21%	24%
Not Active	23%	13%	39%	55%	61%	63%
N	724	730	730	709	696	640

Note that even the most active groups are reported to be very active in less than a third of districts, with even the teachers unions deemed "not active" or only "occasionally" active in more than 40 percent of districts. However, it is not clear whether this reflects a relative quietude that tends to pervade many school board races or whether the question was constructed in a manner that tended to influence the overall level of reported activity.

Is interest-group activity consistent across districts, or are various interests more active in certain communities? Hess and Leal (2005) found that the degree various interests are active locally is a product of contextual factors. They reported teachers unions, business groups, and race- or ethnic-based organizations were all reportedly more active in larger and more urban districts. In short, they concluded that as in the case of campaign spending, board elections in these districts are more politicized.

They also documented that increased African American and Latino student populations were associated with an increase in the reported activity of race- and ethnic-based organizations. Consistent with previous accounts suggesting more educated communities tend to be more active in school district elections, they found the activity of parent groups increased in concert with the percentage of the local adult population with a college degree (Stone et al., 2001).

In general, Hess and Leal (2005) also discovered the activity of teachers unions declines as the resources available to other constituencies increase. A greater concentration of African Americans or a more educated adult population was associated with lower rates of teachers union activity. They also found teachers unions were reported to be significantly more active in states with collective bargaining laws, while business groups were less active in states with collective bargaining. While the ability of unions to exert influence through the collective bargaining agreement might be expected to lead them to engage in less explicit electoral activity, it apparently does not. Further work is needed in order to more fully understand the dynamics at work.

In closing, it is worth noting one concern with the "activity" variable: the possibility the reported efforts of some groups may be underestimated because these groups are able to exert influence in ways so subtle visible activity is not necessary or evident. For instance, if teachers unions are able to win many of their demands regarding wages and working conditions through the collective bargaining process, they may not try to exert influence on routine school board decisions. In such a case, board members might tend to underestimate their "real" influence while overestimating it for a group more explicitly active in daily board affairs. Such a group may dislike the status quo and want change, but apparent activism would signify their limited access rather than reflect their actual influence. This issue cannot be readily resolved with available data and is a question requiring further exploration.

THE EXTENT OF POLITICAL COMPETITION

Democratic governance rests on the principle that elections hold public officials accountable. Competitive elections are thought to increase the likelihood officeholders are attentive to public concerns, while the absence of such competition is thought to breed lethargy and irresponsible policy making. The mere prospect of a competitive election has long been understood to serve as a check on publicly elected officials.

News accounts often depict school districts as stumbling along and providing undisciplined governance with little consequence. Reform advocates have suggested boards are hobbled by low levels of voter participation and by shapeless elections that—typically absent of the organizing principles of platforms, party identification, or competing agendas—tend to turn on personalities, neighborhood concerns, and flashpoint issues like school closings and bus routes (Feuerstein, 2002). In an effort to dilute the import of small but intense constituencies and to provide more coherent direction in elections, some observers have noted the possible merits of partisan elections or holding elections concurrently with national elections (Hess, 2003).

In a sophisticated analysis of South Carolina data, Berry and Howell (2005) concluded that the degree voters hold board members accountable for performance is uncertain and depends on factors such as turnout and interest-group influence. While it is foolhardy to pretend to know with certainty the consequences of any particular proposed reform, it is possible to examine the data and consider how various electoral arrangements appear to affect the extent of electoral competition.

Just how competitive is the typical school board election? Board competition was measured via several metrics, the first by simply asking respondents to rate the level of electoral competition on a four-point scale. The scale ranged from "not competitive" to "very competitive." Fifty-seven percent indicated that board elections were never or only "occasionally" competitive, while just 15 percent described the elections as "very competitive." The extent of competition appears to be much greater in larger districts. In districts with 25,000 or more students, elections were deemed "not competitive" just 2 percent of the time, "occasionally competitive" 43 percent of the time, and "very" or "somewhat" competitive 55 percent of the time. In districts with fewer than 5,000 students, on the other hand, elections were termed "not competitive" 16 percent of the time, "occasionally competitive" 48 percent of the time, and "very" or "somewhat" competitive just 36 percent of the time. On this count, midsize districts looked more similar to the largest districts than to the smallest ones.

Second, board members were asked whether they would describe their last election as "very difficult," "somewhat difficult," "somewhat easy," or "very easy." Just 6 percent of respondents termed their election "very difficult," while more than 70 percent said that it was "somewhat" or "very easy," and nearly half reported it was "very easy." Elections were reported to be somewhat more competitive in larger districts, with 48 percent of respondents in districts of more than 50,000 students terming their election "very difficult" or "somewhat difficult," compared to 25 percent in smaller districts. In short, candidates reported their own elections to be somewhat less competitive than the district norm. It is not clear whether candidates may be overestimating overall competition, overstating the ease of their own election, or reflecting the fact that victorious candidates generally have had an easier experience than is the norm for all candidates.

A third question asked how many incumbent school board members seeking reelection were unseated by challengers since January 1, 1997 (in other words, in the preceding four years). The answers ranged from zero to ten with a mean of 1.01. Given the mean number of elected board members was six and that some percentage of board members do not seek reelection, this suggests it is likely something like 20 to 30 percent of incumbents had been defeated in that time span. Clearly, this figure is only a very crude estimate and ought to be treated as a conjecture rather than as a reliable calculation. Nonetheless, some cause exists to treat this estimate seriously. A study of 57 urban school districts reported in 1999 "it is not unusual for an incumbent board member to be defeated" and that over half of the districts had at least one incumbent board member defeated for reelection between 1992 and 1995 (Hess, 1999, p. 67). Moreover, the estimate is not so very different from data on city council elections, where a survey by the International City Management Association found that between 15 and 20 percent of incumbent city council members were defeated in their bids for reelection in the early 1990s (DeSantis and Renner, 1994).

Finally, respondents were asked whether or not they had run as part of a slate in their most recent election. Given the atomizing tendencies of nonpartisan elections (90 percent of electoral systems in this data set were nonpartisan) and the lack of spending on board member campaigns, how prevalent are efforts to organize and run coherent teams of candidates?

Overall, respondents reported they had run as part of a slate in just 25 percent of the districts surveyed. The frequency board members had run as part of a slate was not dramatically affected by whether the district used a partisan ballot, with 23 percent of respondents in nonpartisan districts and 36 percent in partisan districts reporting they had run as part of a slate. In districts with more than 50,000 students, slates were actually slightly less common than in smaller districts, with 15 percent of candidates in relatively large districts reporting themselves to be members of slates, as opposed to 25 percent of those in smaller districts.

CONCLUDING THOUGHTS

The conventional wisdom regarding school board elections is exaggerated or inaccurate on several counts. While popular accounts suggest school board campaigns have become expensive and combative affairs in which candidates attract substantial funding from teachers unions or the local business community, and religious or civil rights organizations frequently play a leading role, the evidence suggests the reality is otherwise. In fact, the data paint a picture of school board elections that appear to involve minimal campaign spending, with few board members receiving even a quarter of their campaign funds from teachers unions or the business community, and in which neither religious organizations nor race-based groups are thought to play an active role in board elections.

More in line with expectations, the results also suggest teachers unions are generally the leading interest group in local board politics; union influence is greater in larger, more urbanized districts and in states with collective bargaining; and the influence of race-based groups increases with the size of the local African American and (to a lesser extent) Latino populations. Importantly, in accord with the extensive California research Terry Moe has conducted, teachers unions are reported to be the most influential interest group in the national sample of districts studied here, though they contribute less than a quarter of the funds raised by winning board members. In other words, unions are influential but they apparently exert their influence through methods other than monetary contributions. The most notable ways they operate may be through the votes of their membership and the ability to organize, arrange phone banks, distribute flyers, and undertake other such labor-intensive activities. Unions also have the ability to constrain district decisions through collective bargaining agreements and informal agreements regarding work routines and district practices (Hess and West, 2006). Operating in this relatively stealthy fashion, it is possible for unions to exert substantial influence without appearing to do so.

How much does the pressure brought to bear on boards by their constituents ultimately shape policy outcomes after the election? Given their amateur status in comparison to other political institutions (low pay, few staff, and a part-time commitment), board members might be thought to be highly vulnerable to the appeals and exertions of organized interests. However, because seats are not very desirable in terms of material gain or prestige, many members may not ultimately be all that concerned with responding to constituent pressure, or even with reelection. The present analysis simply cannot tell us much about how the politics and conduct of board elections shapes governance. That question is ripe for further research.

Urbanized districts appear to be significantly more professional, expensive, competitive, and influenced by interest groups than those in smaller districts. This finding, in particular, suggests it may be useful for reformers to think about crafting at least two distinct approaches to reforming board governance: one focused on the largest and most urban districts that constitute just a tiny percentage of all districts but enroll a vastly disproportionate share of students, and a second focused on the 99 percent of boards governing smaller districts. The finding that the existence of a collective bargaining law has little impact on union influence or political activity should also give pause to those who imagine abolishing collective bargaining would reduce union influence.

Understanding the role and significance of school boards necessarily begins from the recognition that the institution we see today is the legacy of awkwardly designed and unevenly implemented efforts at reform and consolidation over two centuries. School boards are not one entity, but are an amalgamation wrought by varying state political climates, adaptive institutional evolution, and local context. In fact, the vast majority of boards are neither the hyperpolitical bodies sometimes glimpsed in popular media accounts nor the apolitical entities that the Progressives sought to construct. Instead, they are amateur and informal, featuring weak and inexperienced members, and are pursued by candidates who lack much in the way of tools, resources, or organization. Not surprisingly, this state of affairs has afforded significant influence to most organized constituencies, especially in those communities where the stakes are highest and most readily observed.

From the standpoint of policy and practice, the ultimate question is whether this kind of politics is likely to yield focused or effective educational governance in the 21st century. The answer rests on normative and empirical foundations deserving of further and more thoughtful exploration than they have received to date. Would more professional boards and elections yield more disciplined government? Or would the result serve primarily to import unhelpful partisan divides or otherwise complicate district governance? Does shifting the shape of board elections, or adopting an alternative form of governance such as mayoral control, serve to lessen the influence of particular interests and enable boards to take the tough measures required to improve teaching and learning? Do school boards appear more productive or more accountable in those (predominantly smaller) districts that feature sedate contests and little competition or in more conflict-laden (and typically larger) districts? Finally, K–12 schooling is hardly the only sector that has grappled with the challenges of democratic control and board governance in recent years. What are the lessons scholars of educational governance might glean from experience with corporate boards or university governance? This is a potentially rich vein of knowledge barely tapped to date by K–12 thinkers.

In the final analysis, democratic institutions are only as effective and accountable as are the elections that govern them. Reformers who seek to understand and improve school governance and management can benefit enormously from more rigorous and more thoughtful examinations into board elections and school politics.

NOTE

The author would like to thank Thomas Gift and Juliet Squire for their invaluable research and editorial assistance.

REFERENCES

Babiarz, L. 2006. Board hopefuls shelling out cash. *Sarasota Herald-Tribune*, August 31, BS1.

Baker, L., and D. Carroll. 2006. School board seats attract few. *Arizona Republic*, August 24, 1.

Berkman, M. B., and E. Plutzer. 2005. *Ten thousand democracies: Politics and public opinion in America's school districts.* Washington, DC: Georgetown University Press.

Berry, C. R., and W. G. Howell. 2005. Democratic accountability in public education. In *Besieged: School boards and the future of education politics,* ed. W. G. Howell, 150–168. Washington, DC: Brookings Institution Press.

Broad, E. 2003. Remarks presented at The National Governors' Association Policy Institute, Marina del Rey, CA, April 4.

Campbell, D. E. 2005. Contextual influences on participation in school governance. In *Besieged: School boards and the future of education politics,* ed. W. G. Howell, 288–306. Washington, DC: Brookings Institution Press.

Deckman, M. M. 2004. *School boards battle: The Christian right in local politics.* Washington, DC: Georgetown University Press.

DeSantis, V., and T. Renner. 1994. Term limits and turnover among local officials. In *Municipal Year Book 1994.* Washington, DC: International City/County Management Association.

Dye, T. R. 1967. Governmental structure, urban environment, and educational policy. *Midwest Journal of Political Science* 11 (3): 353–380.

Feuerstein, A. 1998. Understanding interest group involvement in the process of educational governance. *Planning and Changing* 29 (1): 47–60.

———. 2002. Elections, voting, and democracy in local school district governance. *Educational Policy* 16 (1): 15–36.

Henig, J. R., R. C. Hula, M. Orr, and D. S. Pedescleaux. 1999. *The color of school reform: Race, politics, and the challenge of urban education.* Princeton, NJ: Princeton University.

Hess, F. M. 1999. *Spinning wheels: The politics of urban school reform.* Washington, DC: Brookings Institution Press.

———. 2002. *School boards at the dawn of the 21st century: Conditions and challenges of district governance.* Alexandria, VA: National School Boards Association.

———. 2003. Voice of the people. *American School Board Journal* 190 (4): 36–39.

Hess, F. M., and D. L. Leal. 2001. The opportunity to engage: How race, class, and institutions structure access to educational deliberation. *Educational Policy* 15(3): 474–490.

———. 2003. Technocracies, bureaucracies, or responsive polities? Urban school systems and the politics of school violence prevention. *Social Science Quarterly* 84 (3): 526–542.

———. 2005. School house politics: Expenditures, interests, and competition in school board elections. In *Besieged: School boards and the future of education politics*, ed. W. G. Howell, 228–253. Washington, DC: Brookings Institution Press.

Hess, F. M., and M. R. West. 2006. *A better bargain: Overhauling teacher collective bargaining for the 21st century.* Cambridge, MA: Program on Education Policy and Governance, Harvard University.

Hill, P. T. 2003. *School boards: Focus on school performance, not money and patronage.* Washington, DC: Progressive Policy Institute.

Jennings, M. K., and H. Zeigler. 1971. Response styles and politics: The case of school boards. *Midwest Journal of Political Science* 15 (2): 290–321.

Leal, D. L., and F. M. Hess. 2000. The politics of bilingual education expenditures in urban school districts. *Social Science Quarterly* 81 (4): 1064–1072.

McAdams, D. R. 2006. *What school boards can do: Reforming governance for urban schools.* New York: Teachers College Press.

Meranto, P. 1970. *School politics in the metropolis.* Columbus, OH: Merrill.

Moe, T. M. 2006. The union label on the ballot box. *Education Next* 3.

New York State School Boards Association. 2005. *The 2005 member services assessment.* Latham, NY: NYSSBA.

Orr, M. 1999. *Black social capital: The politics of school reform in Baltimore, 1986–1998.* Lawrence: University of Kansas.

Portz, J., L. Stein, and R. R. Jones. 1999. *City schools and city politics: Institutions and leadership in Pittsburgh, Boston, and St. Louis.* Lawrence: University of Kansas.

Regnerus, M. D., D. Sikkink, and C. Smith. 1999. Voting with the Christian right: Contextual and individual patterns of electoral influence. *Social Forces* 77 (4): 1375–1401.

Rich, W. C. 1996. *Black mayors and school politics: The failure of reform in Detroit, Gary, and Newark.* New York: Garland.

Scallan, M. 2006. Hopefuls foot own bills for campaign. *New Orleans Time-Picayune*, September 15.

Stone, C. N., J. R. Henig, B. D. Jones, and C. Pierannunzi. 2001. *Building civic capacity: The politics of reforming urban schools.* Lawrence: University of Kansas.

Weiner, R. 2006. Money talks in school races. *Westchester County (NY) Journal News*, May 30.

Wirt, F. M., and M. W. Kirst. 1972. *The political web of American schools.* New York: Little, Brown.

Zahniser, D. 2007. School board money frenzy; Massive cash gushing into campaigns backed by Villaraigosa could outdo the $2.3 million raised by Riordan. *LA Weekly*, March 1.

Zeigler, H. L., and M. K. Jennings. 1974. *Governing America's schools: Political interaction in local school districts.* North Scituate, MA: Duxbury Press.

8

Local School Foundations: Equity and the Future of School Funding

Carol Merz Frankel

Research on school boards over the years has demonstrated again and again the close connection between communities and their schools. The tension between local control and centralization has been obvious as costs rise and centralized efficiencies become available, yet local communities always seem to find a way to have a say in the nature of their schools. When we look at the effects of statewide funding for schools, the result of court actions in most of the states in the past 40 years, we may be able to see yet another area where local control manifests itself, and another set of challenges presenting itself to the education community. In this chapter, we explore the effects of statewide and local fund-raising supplements for schools and the implications for school districts. We also consider the possibility that statewide funding of schools actually decreases the total amount available within a state, and may also influence goals for equitable funding for schools.

For about 30 years, school districts around the country have been forming foundations to raise and receive donations from parents. At first these seemed to be extensions of traditional fund-raising by Parent Teacher Associations (PTAs) and booster clubs, but now with the emergence of hundreds of such foundations in the United States and millions of dollars raised, they seem to have taken on a very different character from previous school fund-raising vehicles (Lewis, 2003; Winter, 2004). No one really knows how many foundations exist or how much money they raise, but we do know approximately 100 such foundations in the United States each raise over $1 million annually (Lampkin and Stern, 2003). Foundations pay for supplies, equipment, field trips, and curriculum initiatives, but some also fund selected teachers' salaries (National PTA, 2004; Pohlig, 2002).

Questions are routinely asked about whether these foundations compromise equity in school districts, and whether the willingness of local citizens to lend financial support to schools could result in the state taking its responsibility less seriously. Rarely do policy makers ask whether the growth in these foundations is an indication that state-level funding stretches the public's ability to identify with schools and leads to their willingness to support a more locally controllable form of school support.

ALTERNATIVE FUNDING EFFECTS ON LOCAL CONTROL

A long line of research, grouped largely under the Dissatisfaction Theory of American democracy, has demonstrated the importance of, and in fact, the *inevitability* of local control of schools (Iannaccone and Lutz, 1970; Lutz and Iannaccone, 1978; Lutz and Merz, 1992). This work has indicated that citizens identify strongly with their local schools, know what they want the character of the schools to be, and are willing to support financially the schools matching their expectations (Lutz and Iannaccone, 2007). Moreover, hands-on participation in local governance is, identified by de Tocqueville (1834/1945) as the "taproot" of democracy and the way the public continually recreates the American system of democratic governance. The importance of local control would suggest that the consolidation of power at the state level could be politically perilous if it disadvantaged powerful local communities within the state.

In the 1990s, a financial situation occurred in California triggering alternative fund-raising in affluent school districts. Examining this phenomenon gave our research team the opportunity to look at funding foundations in a new light. In this unique and somewhat narrow context, we were able to address some of the questions raised about foundations. In addition to looking at the question of equity, we looked at the relationship of state and local funding of schools. In fact, we were able to consider the possibility suggested by Fischel (Clowes, 2000) that contributions to these foundations may be functioning as a voluntary tax similar to traditional local property taxes severely limited in earlier school equity efforts.

In the 1990s, the high-tech industry faced a major downturn. Although this affected the U.S. economy in general, the effects were more severe in California, and specifically in the Silicon Valley south of San Francisco. Unemployment rose and state sales tax receipts declined. California is particularly dependent on sales tax revenue, and the state found itself with a $30 billion deficit (Martinez, 2003). School districts received news that state funds would be severely curtailed. Districts with foundations in place were generally able to maintain their programs through stepping up their regular fund-raising. Districts without foundations started them, and raised local donations to replace the loss of state funds (Luna, 2003; St. John, 2003). School foundations raised millions of dollars and it became apparent foundation receipts could be a major part of the district budget and be used to fund all aspects of the educational program, including teaching positions.

As the number of school foundations increases and districts begin to rely more and more on this source of school funds, it is appropriate to ask several questions. First, why is this phenomenon happening? Second, is this compromising school equity? What are the implications for balance between state and local funding of schools? Finally, what are the implications for school governance in this situation? In this chapter, we review the history of school foundations and look at the circumstances leading to the unusual foundation activity in California in the 1990s. Based on a 2003 study of foundations in West Coast states reported here and briefly in Frankel and Frankel (2007) and other relevant research, we examine the willingness of citizens to tax themselves for schools and consider the implications for current school funding, governance, and equity policies.

WHAT IS A SCHOOL FOUNDATION?

School foundations refer to organizations qualified as public charities under 501(c)(3) of the Internal Revenue Code. For the purposes of this chapter we exclude those commonly known as Local Education Funds (LEF), which have a specific reform purpose to create new sources of support for low-income schools. LEFs were originally created with assistance from the Ford Foundation; most are presently members of the Public Education Network (PEN). They serve primarily large urban school districts and work in ways familiar to many usual philanthropic organizations. This chapter focuses instead on the smaller units created by the citizens of a school district to raise funds for the general educational purposes of the schools in the district. For our purposes we also exclude money raised at the individual school level through PTAs and money raised by special-purpose groups, such as the band or athletic booster clubs.

School foundations as described here began to arise in the 1970s, particularly in California and Massachusetts, the first states to enact tax caps limiting the amount of levied property taxes allowed. Historically, the property tax was the primary source of school funding, and these tax caps had immediate implications for school funding (Downes, 1992; Fischel, 1988; Silva and Sonstelie, 1995).

School foundations gradually began forming elsewhere. In a 1995 study (Merz and Frankel, 1995), foundation activity was found to be evident in a range of states, but very few foundations raised more than $100,000. Most used their contributions for teacher mini-grants, extra science equipment, musical instruments, and special art programs. Some funded instructional aides to assist in classroom instruction. A very few funded teaching positions, and these were usually half-time reading specialists or additional time for music, physical education, or art teachers who were partly funded by state money. It was concluded that these foundations did not constitute a threat to equity, because the amount raised was so small compared to total budgets of school districts. Foundations, even those raising modest amounts, were seen to be beneficial in many ways, because they created new ties between the community and the schools. At that time, school foundation money made very little, if any, difference in the student-to-teacher ratio of schools. Interestingly, California superintendents saw the community money as much more dependable than state funds, and when asked if they had to choose between foundation money or state money, all responded they would rely on the foundation money because they saw state money as unreliable (Merz and Frankel, 1995).

CHANGES IN SCHOOL FUNDING

Since 1995, many changes in the factors influencing school funding have occurred. More states have implemented equity requirements stemming from court decisions based on state constitutions (Lewis and Simmons, 2003). These equity decisions languished for many years as states resisted implementation, but now have been implemented one way or another in most states. The equity decisions have shifted the burden of funding schools from the local community to the state, and states have been required to distribute state education funds on an equal per-student basis across all districts.

These court decisions also had important implications for the total money available to schools across each state, but these influences were not seen immediately. It is clear that if existing funds were simply reallocated on an equal per-student basis, affluent districts receiving the benefits of taxing themselves based on their property values would receive less revenue for their local schools than they previously enjoyed. States generally made some provision for the local taxing effort in place before state redistribution occurred, and allowed some local tax measures to supplement state funds, but in general it did not make up for the loss in redistribution.

Shortly after equity decisions were implemented, states began to see a flurry of taxpayer revolts of varying magnitude, causing schools to compete harder for tax dollars. These have taken the form of tax roll-back initiatives, tax limitation measures, and spending caps. The most noteworthy was in California, where Proposition 13 severely limited property tax collections.

Fischel (1988) has been among the first to suggest *Serrano v. Priest* (1976), the equity decision in California, caused Proposition 13. He concluded that taxpayers saw decreased return for their tax dollars as their funds were redistributed across the state, leading to a dramatic decrease in their willingness to pay taxes for schools. We will return to this argument later, but it is important to note other effects from Proposition 13. For example, it left school districts with an impossibly high super-majority of 75 percent voter approval rate required for local tax measures.

Some of the implications from Proposition 13 were not immediately evident as California experienced an economic boom in the 1980s and 1990s. The full effects of tax limitation measures became clear when the stock market took a major downturn in 2000. States relying heavily on income tax and sales tax were especially hard-hit. For example, California had a noteworthy shortfall of $35 billion midway through their 2003 budget year (Martinez, 2003) and Oregon's lack of revenue for schools was even lampooned in the cartoon *Doonesbury* (Trudeau, 2003). Schools in these two states faced significant budget cuts in 2003–2004, cuts resulting in the loss of many teaching positions, larger class size, and the loss of entire programs. The town of Burns, Oregon, made the news on National Public Radio as they were to lose their athletic program—a radio broadcast of their games was the primary entertainment in the small, isolated community in Eastern Oregon (NPR, 2003).

CONTRIBUTIONS MAKE UP TAX SHORTFALLS

In the summer of 2003, it began to be clear that affluent school districts, many with long-established foundations, were raising enough local money to replace the money lost in state cuts. The *San Francisco Chronicle* (St. John, 2003) reported that in Los Gatos, a small school district just west of Silicon Valley, concerned parents mounted a phone campaign and raised enough money in six days to replace the 10 teaching positions they would have lost to state cuts. Similar levels of fund-raising had been occurring, albeit without the fanfare in the national press, in many of the school districts in such communities.

In the research reported here, and in Frankel and Frankel (2007), the team conducted a search of media reports of foundation activity, interviews with a number of people engaged in foundations, and an independent review of the Urban Institute data of IRS 990. The findings indicated a very different level of foundation support existing in the most affluent districts. Table 8.1 shows the level of fund-raising by foundations in a sample of affluent districts. It is apparent foundations significantly increased their collections in 2003, the year the state shortfall was so severe. Another interesting facet of

Table 8.1. Revenues of Selected School Foundations in Oregon and California, 2003–2005

| Foundation | Founded | Revenue in Thousands | | | Enrollment 2005 |
		2003	2004	2005	
A	1982	$970	$1,235	$1,701	2,133
B	1982	$1,076	$1,027	$920	2,628
C	1982	$1,357	$1,540	$1,671	4,036
D	1980	$1,846	$1,992	$2,302	1,417
E	1986	$1,303	$1,168	$1,780	6,953
F	1983	$1,506	$1,936	$1,719	451

Sources: Private Foundations' IRS 990, 2007; Ed-Data, 2007; District Profile, 2007.

the data was that foundations, well established by 2003, continued to raise increased revenues over the next few years.

School foundations, through this kind of activity, have established a different position in relation to state funding of public schools. These communities are no long simply adding enrichments to the basic program provided by the state, but are able to fund a different educational program in their schools, visibly different in the day-to-day instruction of children. These funds are, in function, serving as a voluntary tax to the school district to fund the kind of educational program they desire. In the Lake Oswego (Oregon) School District mentioned earlier, donations dropped off slightly after the first year of big state cuts, but in the next year donations picked up again to the $1.5 million level. The Web site includes the following explanation, "Since 1990, the state has allocated per pupil funding. This amount is below what is needed to sustain the high quality of schools this community feels is appropriate, and far below what the community used to raise through property tax" (Lake Oswego School District Foundation, 2007). The campaign chairman is quoted in the *Oregonian* as saying, "This is more than a one-time event. The public has come to grips with that . . . They are thinking differently" (Green, 2005, p. B1). We must think carefully about the implications of school foundations on this level. In California, the Hillsborough Schools Foundation clearly states its relationship to school funding, "Despite repeated fiscal crises and ongoing threats to public education funding, our schools have been able to continue important programs and keep class size down through the continued support of HSF, now an integral part of funding for our school district" (Hillsborough Schools Foundation, 2007). This support now makes up 18 percent of the school district budget.

How widespread is fund-raising at this level? It is difficult to get firm numbers on school foundations. A recent study by the Urban Institute reports 1,267 school foundations filed Forms 990 with the IRS in 2001 (Lampkin and Stern, 2003). Only organizations with gross receipts of $25,000 or more are required to file these forms, so this number excludes any foundation raising less than $25,000, and those not complying with filing requirements.

By far the largest amounts are raised by foundations in small, uniformly affluent districts. These districts often are "elementary-only" as opposed to unified school districts—it appears to be harder to raise large amounts of money from high school parents, perhaps because of the impending burden of college expenses. In fact, interviews with foundation directors suggest much of the money raised by high school foundations goes for scholarships. A sample of the top fund-raising foundations in California and Oregon are set out in Table 8.1.

IMPLICATIONS OF FOUNDATION ACTIVITY

What are the implications of this kind of fund-raising for public education? Assuming relatively few school districts are now able to raise supplemental money sufficient to fund teaching positions, is this enough of an issue to warrant concern? More important, what does this tell us about funding levels of basic programs on a statewide basis? And even more basically, what does this tell us about how citizens relate to their schools at the local and state level?

Some light can be shed on these questions, by returning to the equity decisions and the following tax caps. Several researchers (Fischel, 1988; Downes, 1992; Silva and Sonstelie, 1995), as noted earlier, have studied the relationship between equity decisions, spending caps, and tax caps, most notably in California where Proposition 13 passed on the heels of the *Serrano* decision equalizing school spending across the state. They concluded *Serrano* caused the huge decline in school spending, taking California from 11th among states in per-pupil spending in 1970 to 30th among states in 1990. When districts were allowed to tax themselves directly for their local schools, many communities were willing to tax themselves at a fairly high level because they wanted exemplary educational programs for their children, and they saw the quality of their schools to be a defining quality of their community. The level of school funding was often even reflected in increased value of their homes and property. However, after equity decisions were implemented, property owners saw their tax dollars going to the state to be returned to the local district at a lower per-student amount. If we concede the connection between tax caps and equity decisions, we would predict money raised at the local level and stayed at the local level would be significantly greater than funds being reallocated by the state. In other words, people will tax themselves at a higher level when they get immediate and visible returns on their tax dollar; if their tax results are diluted by sharing the revenue with other communities, their tax effort will be lower. In fact, education spending as a percentage of total state spending has dropped steadily from 28 percent in 1973 to 24 percent in 2001 (States get stingier, 2003).

It is this gap, between what a community would raise in taxes for its own use and what it would raise for equitable sharing across the state, that is tapped into most successfully by the local school foundations. From this conclusion, we can say the money raised by local foundations is not money otherwise available to schools under current legislation. What this tells us about these communities is they believe strongly in the value of education for their children. Most of these communities consist solely of residential property and small businesses. Although the residences may be quite high in assessed value, typically no large commercial or industrial property, historically yielding large amounts of tax revenue, is present. These are simply citizens willing to pay for the schools they want, consistent with the Dissatisfaction Theory.

Does school foundation activity lead to inequity in schools? We must answer honestly, yes. But then we must ask several questions: Is the compromise of equity significant enough to be of concern? Could we create policies to effectively prevent fund-raising at such a high level? And finally, what would happen if we were to somehow prohibit this kind of local fund-raising?

First, is the overall money raised enough to constitute a real threat to school funding equity? We do not know how many foundations exist or how much money is raised across the United States. We can make a rough estimate based on the Urban Institute data (Lampkin and Stern, 2003); for the year 2000, they found about 1,227 foundations excluding PTOs, booster clubs, any group whose sole purpose was scholarships, and Local Educational Foundations or members of PEN (see above in What Is a Foundation? for definition). In the 1,227, they found fewer than 40 percent of the foundations in California (as represented in membership in the California Consortium of Educational Foundations) to be included. If the same percentage were to hold for all states, one could assume that 1,227 is 40 percent of all foundations, giving us about 3,000 foundations. The Urban Institute also found the average raised by foundations was $452,000. Because foundations raised roughly half a million dollars, and these constituted 40 percent of all foundations according to the California figures, we could assume the other 60 percent raised less than $25,000 and were not required to report to the IRS (or raised too little to be of consequence here). Thus we have a rough figure of $200,000 raised per foundation.

Second, could we prevent this level of fund-raising? Most schools want to be able to raise funds at whatever level their community supports. Tax policies have long been shaped to encourage charitable giving. It would take draconian measures indeed to prevent this level of giving to local schools.

Most state funding litigation now is over adequacy of school funding, whereas 10 years ago most litigation was about equity (Lewis and Simmons, 2003). If states provided adequate funding for a basic education program meeting state standards, the public might accept the notion that affluent school districts could enrich their programs beyond these standards if they choose to do so. Michael Kirst, long an advocate of school equity, recently proposed California abandon their current school funding scheme and adopt a new plan guaranteeing adequate funding for schools to meet the state academic standards (2003). He further advocates that communities who want a program exceeding these standards should be able to tax themselves to provide it.

The scenario presented here raises a significant question about whether states will be able to raise enough tax money to provide adequate funding at the state level. It would appear taxpayers will not tax themselves at a high enough level to provide statewide the kind of education demanded by these affluent communities. It would appear citizens are willing to pay significantly for education in their own communities, but do not relate in the same way to state-level education. This phenomenon of local foundation funding is consistent with the Dissatisfaction Theory. Previous work on the theory (e.g., Lutz and Iannaccone, 1978) has demonstrated that local constituencies have the power to create major changes when they choose to do so. In light of the power of local constituencies as posited by the Dissatisfaction Theory, we will consider the consequences of the state restricting these foundation funds in order to preserve state equity.

If we could prevent this kind of local fund-raising to supplement state monies for schools, would it be wise to do so? We would suggest that even if we were able to prevent more affluent communities from enriching the programs of their local schools, it might be detrimental to public schools in general. Families in these communities have access to private schools and are financially able to send their children to the best of them; in fact, research in California by Downes and Shoeman (1993) suggests parents often choose private schools if they are not satisfied with public schools. If through their foundation, parents were able to create the kinds of public schools they wanted for their children, it may increase their support and constituency of public schools. These parents are some of the most influential voices in the policy arena. Because all parents benefit from an adequate level of school funding from the state, perhaps these well-to-do and influential voices would more actively advocate for appropriate state allocations for all public schools, if the issue were presented effectively.

In light of the current reality in public resources, even with our goal of equity, we should be cautious about promoting policies that may eliminate affluent families from public schools. Public schools should serve all kinds of families and all kinds of communities. Various sources indicate that levels of family affluence are beginning to form a bi-modal distribution (e.g., Leonhardt, 2003), with the constituent communities of our public schools gradually being made up of families with greater financial need. Schools could inadvertently become a primary social service agency, not the unifying common experience envisioned by Horace Mann and John Dewey as the foundation of our democracy. We could, in fact, develop an educational system more like England's, where an elite leadership class has historically been educated quite separately from the general population.

FOR ALL OUR CHILDREN

If statewide funding is to succeed, we will need to develop a sense of public stewardship for the schools in the whole state, in the same way the Dissatisfaction Theory illuminates stewardship in the local community for local schools. In moving toward statewide funding, we must realize we are working against a long-standing preference in this country for local control of schools. Rather than being concerned with local supplements, the case needs to be made clearly to the public that everyone gains when all schools in a state are adequately funded and high quality. People need to see that successful schools lead to better jobs and a better state-level economy.

Several kinds of foundations attempt to work more directly for equitable education beyond the local community. Florida has legislative matching support for foundations at the state level (Consortium of Florida Education Foundations, 2007). This is a very different kind of foundation, since Florida school districts are countywide, and are consequently so large none would qualify as the small affluent districts we have studied here. We may also look to the types of foundations in the Public Education Network mentioned earlier in this chapter. These serve largely urban districts with a range of needs and seek support from businesses and large charitable foundations. What these kinds of foundations can contribute to funding solutions has yet to be determined. Both of these kinds of foundations vest power in agents other than the local community—the state in one case, and business in the other. In the long run, the Dissatisfaction Theory would tell us it is the public, not business or state government, that must be satisfied.

If the public cannot be convinced to fund state education budgets, we may simply have to live with less than adequate school funding from the state. We would not come to this conclusion happily, but perhaps be forced to change what is expected from schools at the state level. The federal No Child Left Behind legislation has mandated states achieve adequate learning among all segments of their populations in areas of basic skills. We then may be moving to a system where the state responsibility ends after meeting only the basic curricular areas. However, no one would agree education is adequate or equitable if poorer children receive only language and mathematics instruction, while more affluent children receive a wide-ranging curriculum including science, social studies, music, art, and physical education. But that may be where we are heading.

At the least, we must begin a serious dialogue about what kind of education we want for children in our state, and ask if that is the same kind of education we want for our own children. We must then go on to consider how we intend to fund that education. At the root of this whole discussion must be the question: Do we consider all the children in our state to be our own children, and what level of responsibility are we willing to maintain for them? We return to the words of John Dewey, "What the best and the wisest parent wants for his own child, that must the community want for all its children" (Dewey, 1900). In this case, we should paraphrase, "What the parents most able to pay want for their children, that must the community demand for all its children." Perhaps the essential question is, Can a statewide sense of community be achieved? In doing so, however, are we giving up the participation in local governance that has been, in the words of de Tocqueville, the "taproot" of our democracy?

REFERENCES

Clowes, G. 2000. Barking up the wrong tree: An interview with William A. Fischel. *School Reform News* (February). http://www.heartland.org/Article.cfm?artId=11086 (accessed September 19, 2007).

Consortium of Florida Education Foundations. 2007. Annual report. www.cfef.net (accessed July 16, 2007).

Dewey, J. 1900. *The school and society.* Chicago: University of Chicago Press.

District Profile. www.ode.state.or.us/sfda/reports/r0045select.asp (accessed July 7, 2007).

Downes, T. A. 1992. Evaluating the impact of school finance reform on the provision of public education: The California case. *National Tax Journal* 45:405–419.

Downes, T. A., and D. Shoeman. 1993. School financing reform and private school enrollment: Evidence from California. Working paper No. 93-8. Evanston, IL: Center for Urban Affairs and Policy Research. Northwestern University.

Ed-Data: Fiscal, demographic, and performance data on California's K–12 schools. www.ed-data.k-12.ca.us (accessed July 8, 2007).

Fischel, W. 1988. Did Serrano cause proposition 13? *National Tax Journal* 42:465–472.

Frankel, S., and C. Frankel. 2007. The new fundraising: As school foundations grow in dollars and influence, are they compromising equity or saving public schools? *American School Board Journal* 194 (7): 30–33.

Green, A. 2005. On pace to set fundraising record. *Oregonian*, April 13.

Hillsborough Schools Foundation. 2007. www.hsf.org/aboutus/index and www.hsf.org/annualgiving/index (accessed July 16, 2007).

Iannaccone, L., and F. Lutz. 1970. *Politics, policy and power: The governance of public schools.* Columbus, OH: Merrill.

Kirst, M. 2003. How to fix California's schools. *San Jose Mercury News,* November 23. http://ed.stanford.edu/suse/news-bureau/displayRecord.php?tablename=notify1&id=162 (accessed July 26, 2007).

Lake Oswego School District Foundation. 2007. www.losdfoundation.org/about/faq (accessed July 16, 2007).

Lampkin, L., and D. Stern. 2003. *Who helps public schools: A portrait of local education funds 1991–2001.* Washington, DC: The Urban Institute.

Leonhardt, D. 2003. Time to slay the inequality myth? Not so fast. *The New York Times,* January 25. www.nytimes.com (accessed July 26, 2007).

Lewis, A., and T. Simmons. 2003. *Leading through litigation. Money matters: A reporter's guide to school finance.* Washington, DC: Education Writers Association.

Lewis, N. 2003. Making the grade: Public schools raise millions with sophisticated techniques. *The Chronicle of Philanthropy,* August 21. www.philanthropy.com/premium/articles/v15/i21/21001501 (accessed July 24, 2007).

Luna, C. 2003. Schools lean hard on old foundations. *The Los Angles Times,* June 8. www.latimes.com (accessed June 11, 2003).

Lutz, F., and L. Iannaccone. 1978. *Public participation in local school districts.* Lexington, MA: Heath.

———. 2007. Dissatisfaction theory of American democracy. Paper presented at School Board Research: Main Lines of Inquiry, A National Symposium of Scholars of School Board Governance, Des Moines, Iowa, September 14–15.

Lutz, F., and C. Merz. 1992. *The politics of school-community relations.* New York: Teachers College Press.

Martinez, A. 2003. The programmed disintegration of the golden era in the golden state. *The New York Times,* February 9. www.nytimes.com (accessed July 24, 2007).

Merz, C., and S. Frankel. 1995. *Private funds for public schools.* Tacoma, WA: University of Puget Sound.

National Parent Teacher Association. 2004. *National PTA education funding poll.* Chicago, IL: Author.

National Public Radio. 2003. Touchdowns vs. taxes. *Morning Edition,* November 14.

Pohlig, C. 2002. Schools look to parents for more money. *The Seattle Times,* October 30. www.seattletimes.com (accessed November 1, 2002).

Private Foundations' IRS 990. www.guidestar.org (accessed July 8, 2007).

Serrano v. Priest 18 Cal.3rd 728, 557 P.2d 929, 135 Cal Rptr 345 (1976).

Silva, F., and J. Sonstelie. 1995. Did Serrano cause a decline in school spending? *National Tax Journal* 48 (2).

St. John, K. 2003. Parents try to cover schools' budget gap. *San Francisco Chronicle,* May 22.

States get stingier on education. 2003. *Investor's Business Daily,* July 3.

de Tocqueville, A. 1834. *Democracy in America.* New York: Knopf, 1945.

Trudeau, G. 2003. *Doonesbury,* March 3.

Winter, G. 2004. Those bake sales add up, to $9 billion or so. *The New York Times,* November 15. www.nytimes.com (accessed November 15, 2004).

9

A Descriptive Case Study of Discord and Dissent: The Story of a School Board's Act of Noncompliance to State and Federal Law

Barbara DeHart and DeLacy D. Ganley

AN AUTHOR'S FOREWORD

As I sat on the stage and peered through the large potted ferns lining the proscenium, I could hardly believe what I was seeing. Even though I knew this meeting was going to be crowded and frenzied, I wasn't prepared for the emotions I began to feel. I was scared but also ready and excited for the evening's events. The scene was surreal: a packed room of over a thousand people. They were talking loudly and waving large signs above their heads. The room, which typically was used for school lunch and dances, was tightly filled. The bleacher seating at the back of the room reached to the ceiling, enhancing the sense that I was viewing "real theater." This really couldn't be a school board meeting, could it?

Police officers padded with the thickness of bulletproof vests paced anxiously in front of the stage, their eyes piercing through the "aura of the room," searching for anything out of the ordinary. This military-like presence created yet another barrier between the dais and the community. Additional uniformed officers were walking along the side aisles that were covered with student art. Plainclothed officers were also sitting among the crowd. The doorways were congested with late arrivals trying to enter the room, pressing against the officers, who were trying to adhere to fire code regulations.

The clock was about to strike 7:30 p.m., signaling the beginning of the meeting. I suddenly realized that someday I was going to tell this story, not just about tonight but about all the events leading up to this meeting and the related events yet to happen. I didn't know how the evening was going to unfold, but I knew in my heart that civil rights for all children were going to prevail, weren't they? This is, after all, America. Does a local school board simply have the power to not obey the law?

Almost two years later, in my new life as a faculty member at a small private graduate university, a colleague and I were having a conversation over lunch about the role of homosexuality in the school's mission of social justice. She noted there were many mixed feelings among faculty about whether or not homosexuality should be included in diversity discussions. I was surprised (but not really) that this question existed in higher education. After sharing my story with her, we decided to write the following case study. You may be surprised at the results.

INTRODUCTION AND OVERVIEW

This descriptive case study highlights the problems created when a three-two majority alliance was formed on the five-member board of trustees of the Northville School District,[1] a medium-sized (10,250 students), suburban/urban, elementary (PreK–8) school district in Southern California. The crisis began when the newly formed three-member board majority was presented with and then spurned a legal mandate to revise the district's Uniform Complaint Procedure Policy (UCPP). This mandated revision would have assured district compliance to new state and federal laws granting "protected class status" to transgender and transsexual students (herein referred to as transgender/sexual students).

In California, the Uniform Complaint Procedure Policy (UCPP) delineates specific procedures for persons of "protected classes" to file a discrimination complaint against a public PreK–12 school district. The UCPP is called a "uniform policy" because all public PreK–12 districts in California are subject to the same laws and, accordingly, every district's UCPP is supposed to be identical to the others in terms of language and interpretation. As required by law, Northville's UCPP already extended protected-class status to students who experienced unlawful discrimination because of their ethnic group identification, religion, age, sexual orientation, race, ancestry, national origin, gender, color, or disability (physical or mental). The new mandated language changes being rejected by the board majority would, as dictated by law, now also extend protected-class status to transgender/sexual students and would therefore allow transgender/sexual students to file a discrimination complaint if they felt they had been harassed.

During school board meetings, the rhetoric of the board majority revealed its reluctance to protect the rights of other-than-heterosexual students. Questions asked included Where will little boys dressed as little girls go to the bathroom? What will prevent "these children" from becoming "Peeping Toms?" (Minutes, Special Meeting, February 26, 2004; Board Minutes, February 5, 2004). One board member publicly referred to transgender/sexual people as "trash" (Board Minutes, February 5, 2004). Another board majority member (who was, coincidently, a chaplain) fretted about the "sexual" and "homosexual agenda" and wondered how she would "answer to a higher power" if she were to vote in favor of revising the policy (Board Minutes, February 4, 2004).

Along with threatening the civil rights of transgender/sexual students, not being in compliance with state and federal laws endangered the district's financial viability. Put simply, the general rule of thumb is "No compliance, no funding." Following this logic, the California Department of Education (CDE) threatened to withhold all state and federal funding, estimated at over $51 million by district officials. The state superintendent of public schools (the chief of the CDE) repeatedly threatened sanctions against the district. In a letter to Northville's school board, the state superintendent warned he would "take all available steps to compel [the district's] compliance" and would "move with deliberate speed if you [school board members] challenge my authority" (April 1, 2004, letter to the Northville Board of Trustees).

Even after hearing these warnings and understanding the financial ramifications of being denied state and/or federal funds, the board majority held firm and continued to reject mandated language changes. The majority garnered support from conservative organizations and community members, as well as defending its perspective in the media.

The UCPP issue *crystallized* (Rae and Taylor, 1970, p. 24) preexisting political leanings amongst the board members. Unable to sway the majority, the two-person board minority became increasingly frustrated and embarrassed at its impotence. As the *cleavage* (Schattschneider, 1975) around the UCPP issue deepened, board interactions became increasingly contentious.

The district superintendent and district staff as well as the minority members of the board felt trapped by the board's decision. They saw the issue as being a civil rights matter. Attorneys from the CDE and the Northville School District agreed and advised the board in writing that to prohibit such a right was indeed illegal. Despite potential political fallout and the ire of the board majority, the district superintendent's publicly stated position was that any student who felt he or she had experienced discrimination in the district would be allowed to file a discrimination complaint regardless of whether or not that student was a member of a protected class (Board Minutes, April 1, 2004). With this position, she walked a fine line between insubordination and protecting the rights of students.

When the board majority's act of noncompliance became known to the public at large (thanks in large part to one of the board minority members writing an open letter to a county newspaper), many in the community objected vehemently to the majority's position. They understandably worried about the viability of their schools if the district were denied over $51 million in funding. Internet conversations abounded. Parents and community members gathered. Attendance at school board meetings ballooned to over a thousand. At these meetings people shouted, jeered, and waved poster-board statements. The media swarmed. Fearing unrest in the community, police initiated communications with the district resulting in a comprehensive safety plan for school board meetings, which included the presence of officers in bulletproof vests.

After four months of acrimony, the board majority voted to adopt the state's required language; however, (via addendums) it superimposed upon the revised policy its own unique definitions of key policy words. At first blush, it might seem that the board majority had ultimately acquiesced to the state's requirements because the body of Northville's UCPP had been revised to reflect the mandated changes word-for-word. As such, Northville's UCPP now read like everyone else's. But, unlike other districts, the board had added supplementary language to provide new/different meanings to key policy words. If one used the district's accompanying definitions, the policy's meaning was changed and would not technically extend protected status to transgender/sexual students.

Surprisingly to many, given the heavy warnings of the state superintendent of public schools, Northville's UCPP was accepted by the CDE. The state superintendent noted in a letter to the district dated April 19, 2004, that Northville's "proposal will technically resolve the non-compliance" issue. But he continued in this letter to "strongly caution the board regarding application of its newly adopted policy."

Not acknowledging the district's customized definitions but instead only recognizing this "technical resolution," the state superintendent claimed public victory. In a letter written to all California school district superintendents, the state superintendent explained he had brought the rogue district into compliance and no California public school district would ever be allowed to customize its UCPP or impose upon the policy its own definitions of key words (letter dated April 29, 2004). His letter did not mention that he neither forced the district in question to remove its customized definitions nor that Northville's added definitions changed the UCPP and therefore did not extend protection to transgender/sexual students (to this day, August 2007).

This descriptive case study is important for four main reasons: First, it narrates a story showing the importance of school board elections and the potential abuse of power of elected board members and, in doing so, serves as a call to action to voters. Second, it can be used as a tool for discussing issues of social justice and the politicization of education. Third, it contributes to the field of educational policy by examining the relationship among school board politics, educational law, and social justice. And, lastly, it speaks to the inconsistency and impotency of public school governance in California and beyond.

Methodologically, this qualitative case study draws upon participation-based research. One of the study's coauthors was Northville School District's superintendent during this period. Data was gathered through participant observation and organizational documents. Specifically, the case draws upon notes, recollections, and insights as well as upon a number of articles of public record, including Board of Trustee meeting minutes, correspondence, memoranda, and newspaper articles. The variety of data triangulates the research findings and provides balance to the data analysis. These methods assure that the case study that unfolds is an accurate story of the political passions and agendas of school board members in discord and dissent. With this said, we also recognize, as Bates notes in relation to his own work, "recollections [of the case], not surprisingly, differ" (Bates, 1993, p. 13).

For purposes of this chapter, the terms *conservative* and *liberal* are used to identify positions at opposite ends of a political spectrum as it relates to public education. In the context of this chapter, a *conservative* is one who rejects any federal and state involvement in public education as well as one who would advocate for a traditional "Back to Basics" approach to schooling. The term *Christian conservative* is used additionally to identify those conservatives who bring religious conviction into the political debate. For example, as used in this text, a *Christian conservative* would espouse that homosexuality is against God's will. By contrast, a *liberal* person might endorse collaboration between federal/state government and public education as well as advocate for an education system supporting the "whole child" (which includes meals and health care).

The case study below is in the form of a chronologically based narrative. It begins with a contextual history, explains the events directly leading up to the crisis, chronicles the most contentious four months, and provides a report of the current status of the case's main characters.

THE CASE STUDY

Contextual History of Northville School District

In 1947, the Northville School District was one of four districts named in a monumental and precedent-setting court case. In the context of this case, the California State Supreme Court determined ". . . in the field of public of education, the doctrine of 'separate but equal' has no place" (Chief Justice

Earl Warren as cited in Robbie, 2002). The case associated with this ruling
was filed by the parents of a dark-skinned Latina student of Mexican descent who was refused admittance to her white-populated neighborhood
Northville school by the school principal. The parents appealed the principal's decision to the Northville School District's school board, but the principal's decision was upheld. After a subsequent failed appeal to the County
Office of Education school board, the case ultimately made its way to the
state Supreme Court, where segregation was deemed unlawful for the first
time in U.S. history.

As Judge Albert Lee Stephens wrote in his decision, "By enforcing the segregation of school children of Mexican descent against their will and contrary to the laws of California, respondents have violated the federal law as
provided in the Fourteenth Amendment to the Federal Constitution" (as
cited in Robbie, 2002). Fellow justice Judge Paul J. McCormick stated, "A
paramount requisite in the American system of education is social equality"
(as cited in Robbie, 2002). This powerful ruling (predating *Brown vs. the
Board of Education* by seven years) desegregated all California schools as well
as other public institutions in California (e.g., public pools, theaters, etc.)
and kick-started national discussions on segregation that ultimately contributed to the *Brown vs. the Board of Education* decision.

Between 1947 and the early 1990s, Northville's school board leadership
reflected a variety of political positions, as was true of most school districts
in the United States. Sometimes the trustees approved what might be considered liberal policies, other times conservative. Schlesinger (1992, as cited
in Deckman, 2004) would likely suggest such an ebb and flow in school
boards is typical and, furthermore, provides the healthy debate that defines
American society.

By the early 1990s, conservative Christian politics had found stronger
footing in America. However, according to Deckman (2004), America has
had a long history of conservative school board politics. Deckman cites
many examples of conservatism, including the era of the Scopes case (of
1925) and the 1950s McCarthyism, and argues that the conservatism of the
1990s was not a new phenomenon. Ralph Eugene Reed, the first executive
director of the Christian Coalition, graced the cover of *Time Magazine* on
May 15, 1995: "The right hand of God: Meet Ralph Reed, 22. His Christian
Coalition is on a crusade to take over U.S. politics—and it's working." Reed
believed candidates who had a Christian agenda should veil their religious
orientation in order to be elected but then, once in public post, pursue their
Christian agendas. He was quoted in a 1992 *Los Angeles Times* interview as
saying,

> It's like guerilla warfare. If you reveal your location, all it does is allow your op-
> ponent to improve his artillery bearings. It's better to move quietly, with stealth,

under cover of night. You've got two choices: You can wear [camouflage uniforms] and shimmy along on your belly, or you can put on a red coat and stand up for everyone to see. It comes down to whether you want to be the British Army in the Revolutionary War or the Viet Cong. History tells us which tactic was more effective. (Deckman, 2004, p. 83)

With this statement, the term *stealth candidate* was born and, many would argue, political elections became a battleground for such guerilla-style warfare. Given schools have such a profound impact on shaping the norms of society, school board elections became a focus for the Christian Coalition as well as other conservative Christian organizations (including Citizens for Excellence in Education, the Education Alliance, the National Association of Christian Educators, and the National Council on Bible Curriculum in the Public Schools) (Deckman, 2004).

Reflecting the milieu of national politics, a three-person majority was elected to the Northville School Board in 1994, campaigning on conservative (but not necessarily Christian) issues. All three candidates campaigned upon a three-item platform of anti-bilingual education, pro–parents' rights, and Back to Basics. At least one of these board members shared with the district superintendent she had received "board training" from a conservative Christian organization.

The trend to elect politically conservative members to the Northville School Board sustained a three-to-two conservative majority throughout the 1990s. But it was the election of 2002 that ultimately precipitated the events of this case study. In this election, an ultraconservative Christian community member (called herein by the pseudonym Mrs. Barrins) was finally elected to the Northville Board after having run several times prior. Even before being elected, Barrins was well known by school personnel. Earlier, as a parent of a child in Northville schools, Barrins would routinely visit school and district administrators. Sometimes she objected to pictures of Martin Luther King Jr. being hung during Black History Month (February), requesting instead that additional pictures of George Washington and Abraham Lincoln be displayed to emphasize President's Day (over Black history). Claiming she was "anti-anti-bullying," she argued that children who deviated from the norm could benefit from peer coercion (what she called "witnessing"). Barrins objected to cooperative learning, advocating instead for curriculum delivered by the teachers to children sitting in rows. According to her, the job of the teacher was to disseminate information; the job of the student was to be recipients of information. Administrators reported that during her visits, she (on more than one occasion) pounded the table and emotionally stated, "God has sent me to save these children." She was one of only a few community members who routinely addressed the board at its meetings. Ironically, given her passionate convictions, Barrins never campaigned on these issues. Her campaign rhetoric instead focused upon Back to Basics and phonics. It could be argued that she was a stealth candidate, as described by Deckman (2004).

In the months following Barrins's hard-won election in 2002, her voting pattern and commentary revealed her conservative Christian zeal. So far politically to the right compared to any other member of the board (even in comparison to two other conservative Christian board members), her commentary was often rejected and deemed extremist by all her board peers. As such, during her first year, Barrins did not greatly impact board decisions, which often resulted in four-to-one votes. She was, in essence, fairly marginalized.

Then the situation changed. In December 2003, the board was presented with an "information item" regarding language changes necessary to keep policy current with mandated state and federal law. An *information item* on a school board agenda is an agenda item that provides contextual information and/or data to help board members prepare for future *action items*, those agenda items upon which votes are rendered. This was a routine agenda item, yet it ultimately and surprisingly altered the political alignment of the board, divided the community, and launched a national conversation. Because of this issue, a board alliance was formed between Barrins and the two other conservative board members, Mrs. Martinez (a chaplain) and Mrs. Nazwisko (a former instructional aide in the district and an active community member). Now, Barrins was no longer marginalized. She had become a figurehead of the board's new majority.

The District Prepares for a Coordinated Compliance Review

The California Department of Education (CDE) monitors district-level compliance to state and federal laws through a procedure called a Coordinated Compliance Review (CCR). In California, these "audits" occur every four years and are implemented in the district and monitored by a team of three to five CDE staff who are experts in fields related to compliance issues. Although the review team could conceivably verify compliance with any of approximately 150 compliance issues, it usually provides each district with a list of specific items that will be the focus of a particular CCR. The items on these "focus lists" vary from audit to audit, yet the one item that remains constant and is inspected and verified every CCR is a district's Uniform Complaint Procedure Policy (UCPP), a policy aimed to provide recourse if a student's civil rights are violated. Laws mandate every district's UCPP match the state's UCPP requirements both in terms of language (it should be a verbatim match) and in terms of interpretation/spirit. Accordingly, every California public school district should have the exact same UCPP; this is why it is called a "uniform" complaint procedure. As a part of every CCR, the review team confirms this match.

There are two likely reasons a district's UCPP is inspected during every CCR. First, the state's UCPP requirements change fairly regularly to reflect new legislation. The CCR is the state's method for confirming the districts are aware of and responsive to these new laws. Second, the UCPP protects civil rights as mandated by federal nondiscriminatory laws. Accordingly, the CCR's examination of a district's UCPP is part of an accountability loop that makes sure school districts, the state, and the federal government all are on the same page.

In December 2003, in routine preparation for a CCR, the district determined the language of its UCPP needed to be revised to reflect recent changes in the Education Code (which reflect state and federal laws) in order to maintain appropriate and legal board policies in the district (which prided itself on being legally "squeaky clean"). Accordingly, changes to the policy would be needed in order for the district to clear its CCR and ultimately receive the "green light" for the allocation of state and federal funds.

Given that language is routinely deleted and/or added to district policies as new legislation is implemented into law, revising the policy should have been a fairly pedestrian task. Accordingly, as was typical, via an information item on the board meeting's agenda, the district superintendent brought before the district's five-person Board of Trustees the preexisting UCPP with the proposed new language inserted into the text in bold. If there had been language that needed to be deleted from the preexisting policy, the district superintendent would have lined out the outdated words. By stylizing the text in this way, the board was able to see the proposed revision in relation to the preexisting policy and could hone in on the specific language changes.

In this instance, the only proposed change to the preexisting policy was the inclusion of the word *sex*:

> The Governing Board recognizes that the district has primary responsibility for insuring that it complies with state and federal laws and regulations governing educational programs. The district shall investigate and seek to resolve complaints at the local level whenever possible. The district shall follow uniform complaint procedures pursuant to state regulations when addressing complaints alleging unlawful discrimination based on ethnic group identification, religion, age, sex, sexual orientation [sic], race [sic], ancestry [sic], national origin [sic], gender, color, or physical or mental disability, in any program or activity, that receives or benefits from state financial assistance. The district shall also follow uniform complaint procedures when addressing complaints alleging failure to comply with state or federal law in consolidated categorical aid programs, migrant education, child care and development programs, child nutrition programs and special education programs. (Summary of Title V, presented to the board at January 15, 2004, board meeting)

For the sake of being accurate, it should be noted that Northville's preexisting UCPP did not actually contain the words *sexual orientation, race, ancestry,* or *national origin.* The absence of these words from the district's UCPP was deemed a clerical oversight. Other district policies addressed the issue of sexual orientation, race, ancestry, and national origin and, accordingly, the board never questioned the inclusion of these words. The only "truly new" addition to the policy was the inclusion of the word *sex.*

Along with adding the word *sex* to the UCPP, the CDE was also requiring districts to adopt a new definition of *gender.* The CDE's new definition of *gender* now included "a person's actual sex or perceived sex and includes a person's perceived identity, appearance or behavior, whether or not that identity, appearance or behavior is different from that traditionally associated with a person's sex at birth" (Board Information, January 15, 2004). Accordingly, the CDE was saying that the word *sex* was determined by the anatomical features with which a person was born, but a person's *gender* referred to a person's self-identity or perceived identity, regardless of whether or not this identity matched one's anatomical parts. (The definitions of *sex* and *gender* are included herein because they later became a central focus to the case at hand.)

Combined, these two changes—the inclusion of the word *sex* and the redefinition of *gender*—resulted in the CDE extending protected-class status to transgender/sexual students, giving them the right to file a uniform complaint if they felt they had experienced discrimination and/or harassment. These changes were a response to the (California) School Safety and Violence Prevention Act of 2000.

The Board Reacts to the Proposed Changes

At its January 15, 2004, meeting, the Board of Trustees received a routine "first reading" of the revised UCPP. Typically, when there is a policy issue for board consideration, it is first put on the agenda as an *information item,* where the board simply receives contextual information and related data. Then there is a *first reading* and subsequent *second reading* that involves the specific language regarding the policy. Having a first and second reading allows the board to discuss the issue and provides time for community feedback. After these readings, an *action item* is typically brought to the board and voted upon.

It was at this meeting and with this agenda item that the alliance between Barrins, Martinez, and Nazwisko was born. Despite a previous two-to-one voting split, this issue galvanized the three. The newly formed Barrins/Martinez/Nazwisko alliance was united in its opposition to the proposed UCPP changes. Although not exactly aligned in their rationale, they had found common ground in their disdain against transgender/sexuals as well as their resentment of state and/or federal involvement in local politics. Barrins stated that altering the district's policy so transgender/sexual students were to have the right to file a discrimination complaint would "harm the morality of our kids" (Board Minutes, February 5, 2004). She asked, "Where will the little boys dressed as little girls go to the bathroom?" (Minutes, Special Meeting, February 26, 2004).

Martinez publicly fretted the proposed revision was part of "the sexual [homosexual] agenda" (Board Minutes, February 5, 2004). If the policy change were approved, she stated the board would have to "answer in the long run to a higher power" (Board Minutes, February 5, 2004). She claimed the issue was not about civil rights but about (deviant) "sexual choice" (Board Minutes, February 5, 2004). Nazwisko justified her "no" vote by saying the state did not have the right to tell the district what to do. Nevertheless, her bias was evident when she declared, "I'm voting no. I can't [with] a clear conscience, I cannot vote for this trash" (Board Minutes, February 5, 2004). Meanwhile, one of the two board members in favor of compliance urged her peers (in vain) to "not let our personal thoughts on some things get in the way of progress in education" (Board Minutes, February 5, 2004).

To some, board majority rhetoric was reminiscent of language used in the 1940s when the Board of Trustees of this same district took action to maintain the segregation of Latino children in area schools. As discussed earlier, the board's decision was overturned in 1947 in a ground-breaking legal case, *Mendez vs. Northville*, a case that ultimately desegregated California public schools seven years prior to *Brown vs. the Board of Education*. Reflecting upon the language used in both eras lends credence to the supposition that suggests a history of exclusion and prejudice had existed in the district.

Although personally appalled at the callousness the board expressed in not wanting to protect the rights of transgender/sexual students, the district superintendent (who had been appointed by the district's board seven years prior) was initially not overly concerned with the board majority's stance. She figured that surely the board majority would pass the revised policy once it realized the implications for student achievement such financial loss would cause. Ultimately she believed the issue would be resolved as part of the CCR. She was wrong.

The CDE Renders the District Noncompliant

Once the CCR got underway (in February 2004), the lead reviewer of the CCR team demanded an emergency meeting with the district superintendent in her office. In this meeting, the lead reviewer sought an explanation for why the UCPP had not yet been revised. The district superintendent explained that the board had already been fully apprised of the legal, financial, and moral ramifications of noncompliance but had not approved the mandated changes. Upon learning of the board majority's opposition, the lead reviewer insisted he immediately be able to speak with the board. He was confident he would be able to convince the board majority to change its "no" vote. He felt he would be able to garner the majority's support because of his own previous political position as a former fundamentalist Christian. Additionally, he thought he could explain the legal mandates in a clear, meaningful, and persuasive manner.

In response to the lead reviewer's request, a special board meeting was held on February 26, 2004. At this meeting, the lead reviewer of the CCR team reiterated that noncompliance put *all* of the district's state and federal funds at risk. At this meeting the animosity between the board majority and minority escalated, and the *cleavage* (Schattschneider, 1975) between the CDE and the board was widened. Despite the lead reviewer's efforts (and much to his own dismay as well as to the growing concern of the district superintendent and her staff), the board majority still would not budge. According to a timeline of events prepared by Northville's public information officer, the board still "declined to direct [district] staff to revise the policy" ("Timeline of Events Regarding the Uniform Complaint Procedure," prepared by Northville's public information officer, February 2004).

The CCR Team presented its Report of Findings at a public meeting in the end of February 2004. At this meeting, the review team explicitly reiterated the importance of the board responding to all its recommendations within a 30-day period. Accordingly, the district was given 30 days to submit a revised UCPP and be in compliance. It was not until the CCR's Report of Findings that the California Department of Education (an office led by the publicly elected state superintendent of public instruction) determined the district was noncompliant and, furthermore, that the board majority was taking a defiant, obstructionist, and illegal stance. With this determination now made, the CDE sent a barrage of threats to the district.

March 2004: Positions Become Further Entrenched and Fortified as the Number of Stakeholders Grows

In early March 2004, the board's act of noncompliance became public (thanks in large part to a minority member writing an open letter to a county newspaper). The local story was quickly picked up by the national media, and members of the board majority seized upon the opportunity to "sunshine" its perspective. Mrs. Barrins was a guest of Fox's *[Bill] O'Reilly Factor* and made appearances on CNN. Additionally, one of the two board minority members was also on Fox's *O'Reilly Factor*. The minority's position did not, however, receive the same amount of press as did the majority's.

The publicity attracted the attention of national players—including the ACLU (a nonprofit organization that advocates for civil rights) and the Education Alliance (a conservative Christian organization that supported the board majority's noncompliance and advocates for the privatization and/or elimination of public education). These parties helped to fortify and further polarize the board members' positions.

Financial Woes Accrue Due to the Board's Position

On March 23, 2004, the district received notification from the Bank of America rescinding approval of the district's credit application for moneys to fund its Certificates of Participation (COP) earmarked to complete the district's asset management plan. Making reference to the board majority's stance on the UCPP issue, the bank stated it would not release any money until the district was assured it would receive its routine funds from the CDE. The disintegration of this arrangement, which had taken over a year to secure, sparked fear among district administrators that other partnerships might also be in peril. (It also, of course, sparked fear that the district would not have the funds to fix facilities in need of repair.)

As the issue became more public and the parties' positions further *crystallized* (Rae and Taylor, 1970), there were other financial ramifications. In California, schools are served through a county office system. It is the responsibility of County Offices of Education (COE) to proactively and closely monitor school districts' budgets (as per California AB1200). In late March, 2004, Northville District's COE requested an official meeting. At this meeting, CDE officials told the district superintendent that if Northville were financially sanctioned by the CDE, Northville would not be able to pay its bills and/or meet its fiduciary responsibilities. If this happened, the COE would have to label the district "qualified," an unattractive ranking reflecting financial insecurity (memo to Board of Trustees from the district superintendent titled "Re: Letter of Credit," March 23, 2004).

Although many parents in the community were chagrined by the board majority's political stance, it was the financial repercussions that prompted them to protest the board's action. In March 2004, parents in the school community initiated a grassroots effort to recall Martinez and Barrins. Martinez and Barrins had two-and-a-half years remaining in their terms. The third majority member, Nazwisko, was up for reelection in November 2004 and, hence, it was deemed unnecessary to include her in the recall. They were banking on Nazwisko losing this reelection. It turns out that the grassroots group was correct about the non-reelection of Nazwisko, but the recall effort itself was stymied because only 6,800 of the 7,200 signatures required to initiate the recall were validated.

By this point, district personnel were preoccupied by the case. The looming threat of financial sanctions held the attention of everyone. Instead of focusing conversations around student success, the district community was mired in political rhetoric.

The CDE Sends Official Warnings

As the issue boiled on at the local and county level, the state via its department of education turned up the heat. In an April 1, 2004, letter to the board, the California Department of Education (over the signature of its chief, the state superintendent of public instruction) warned,

> If you refuse [to comply], I will take all available steps to compel your compliance. Such steps may include withholding consolidated application funds [of $11 million] from your district in the current and/or future fiscal years. It would pain me to do that, since any loss of funds potentially hurts the children of your district. However, I will move with deliberate speed if you challenge my authority.

In this same letter, the state superintendent of public instruction also questioned the morality of the board's act:

> As one elected official to another [sic], I frankly find your reluctance to protect all of your children disturbing. It is immoral and unconscionable for elected officials to condone discrimination in any form, and your actions not only condone it, they encourage it . . . If you object to the law, then strive to change it. Do not victimize the very people you claim you are serving.

In subsequent telephone conversations to the district superintendent, the CDE clarified that legally *all* state and federal funding was in jeopardy—not just the $11 million in categorical funds but also the district's $40 million in General Revenue Limit funds (the district's primary source of revenue). Combined, the district was at risk of losing $51 million—approximately 75 percent of its annual budget. Even after hearing the CDE's warnings, the board majority remained firm. They still declined to adopt the new language.

Tensions Rise at a School Board Meeting

On April 1, 2004, attendance at a school board meeting ballooned to over 1,200. Typically attendance ranged between 4 and 10 community members. Given the increased attendance, the meeting had to be held at a different location. This move required significant logistical planning and attention on the part of district personnel and police. This is one of many examples of how the attention and time of district personnel was commandeered by this case.

Worried the situation would turn violent, over 25 police (some in plainclothes and others in bulletproof vests) infiltrated the crowd and guarded the proceedings. At the time, the district superintendent wondered if she too should wear a flak jacket. After all, she was the one who had the task of monitoring a meeting where people shouted, jeered, and waved poster-board statements, aiming to talk over and out-shout each other. Members of the community booed and hissed whenever anyone from the board spoke. Local and national media swarmed.

At this meeting, the unusually large number of 43 community people exercised their right to speak to the board regarding its UCPP position. (Typically only one or two people from the public might speak at a board meeting.) Thirty-five of the community speakers protested the board majority's stance; eight supported it (Board Minutes, April 1, 2004).

Member upon member from the community asked the board to have respect for the law and respect for all types of people. Some community members spoke as parents of gay, lesbian, bisexual, and transgender/sexual children. Others spoke on behalf of their organizations and churches. Some spoke on behalf of the children attending schools now at risk of losing funding. When a transgender adult (male to female) from the community was speaking at this meeting, board majority member Martinez uttered in a stage whisper that the witness was "trash." Not surprisingly, this escalated already palpable hostilities. The transgender adult responded to Martinez by saying:

> I tried to be an ideal boy. So I played sports; I worked on the family farm; I joined 4H. I did everything most boys did . . . I thought that after I worked hard enough at being a little boy, I could overcome these feelings to be a little girl. I finally spent 22 years in the army as a commissioned officer, retiring as a major. I am not trash. I am a proud individual. (Board Minutes, April 1, 2004)

Approximately 200 to 300 people were not allowed into this meeting because of space limitations. (It was a first-come, first-seated kind of situation, and they simply arrived too late.) The vast majority of the group standing outside was from a Latino Christian church that supported the board majority's stance. In order to be equitable, the district superintendent asked the police to escort some of the group in so that they could voice their opinion. A few quotes from the board minutes include:

> (Following is the paraphrase provided by the translator): She says that she represents the Hispanic community that couldn't come in because there are so many people. She is for traditional families, and she is against her kids being taught homosexuality. (Board Minutes, April 1, 2004)

Another representative from the Latino church noted:

> You guys are the board members. You stand for what you believe and stay with that. Because even though there's a lot of people in here that are screaming and yelling against you, there's a lot of people outside who are praying for you. (Board Minutes, April 1, 2004)

The board majority also received support from a City Council member in a neighboring city with some of its schools in the Northville District. He urged the two board members in the minority to change their vote so that the board could send a unanimous message to the California Department of Education. He said:

> I am here to support the Board vote . . . I think it is important to recognize some issues that I haven't heard from a lot here: local control and one of conscience. If you don't owe the people your conscience, if you do not give them that, then you are nothing but a rubber stamp and [you] don't deserve to be elected. (Board Minutes, April 1, 2004)

The Board Majority Maintains Its Course of Action

On April 8, 2004, the board majority called a special, spur-of-the-moment board meeting. The president of the board (who was not in the majority) was given less than 24 hours advance notice of this meeting. The district superintendent was summoned less than 12 hours prior to the meeting. Typically, a special meeting is called by the board president or the district superintendent. In this instance, the meeting was called without the knowledge of either. It was not until the last legal hour that the board president and the superintendent were told about the meeting and given a prearranged agenda.

In this meeting, the board majority introduced and then called for a vote on a new action item that led to the firing of the district's attorney of 33 years. This veteran attorney had been recommending the board follow the law (revise the UCPP), and the board majority knew he was not looking for legal avenues to meet its position. Upon this surprise firing, the district superintendent proposed a recruiting process to find suitable candidates for the now-open position. No such process was needed, for the board majority had already preselected its candidate: a relatively unknown, fresh-out-of-law-school, local attorney with no experience in school law. This novice attorney (who was oddly in attendance at this non–publicly announced meeting) had founded the Education Alliance, an ultraconservative group committed to the privatization and the elimination of public schools. He was deeply sympathetic to the board majority's stance and was approved as the new district attorney on the spot. Accordingly, within a 10-minute period, one attorney was fired and another hired by a three-to-two vote.

The unnatural circumstances of the meeting's callings as well as the speed and seemingly predetermined nature of the actions taken at the meeting suggested to some that the board majority had developed the plan prior to the meeting. Strict open meeting laws (i.e., the Brown Act in California) prohibit public officials from discussing in private with one another agenda items or from lobbying each other for votes prior to public meetings. Suspicion by and accusations of some community members that the board majority had violated these open meeting laws triggered a time-consuming investigation by the county district attorney's office. With this suit, the district's focus was once again being pulled away from its students and their achievement.

As a response to what was happening in Northville, a state senator from the district's legislative area initiated a senate bill that would put school districts into state receivership if their elected boards ever refused to follow state law. Although as of this writing (August 2007), the bill has not yet been passed into law, the senator has pledged ongoing commitment to this legislation. Meanwhile, the two-person board minority became increasingly frustrated and embarrassed at its impotence. Not wanting to be associated with the board majority, they sought out public venues to differentiate their position from the board majority. Such public display of board dissension is atypical and further exacerbated the bifurcation between the camps.

Eventually the bifurcation of the board led to a request by the board majority to reorganize the board. The request was heeded and, at a May 6, 2004, board meeting, board majority member Nazwisko replaced the president of the board (who was in the minority). The stated reason for removal was "Dereliction of duty" (Board Agenda, May 6, 2004; Board Minutes, May 6, 2004). Interestingly, when the board was reconstituted (as a result of Nazwisko losing her reelection campaign in November 2004), the ousted president was reinstated.

The District Superintendent Goes to the State Capital

With the board majority's heels dug in, the district superintendent became highly concerned with the district's financial viability. The $11 million in categorical funds (which accounted for 15 percent of the district's overall budget) seemed most at risk because there was precedence that the CDE had withheld such funds in the past. Although there was no precedent, the CDE's additional threat of possibly also withholding $40 million in General Revenue Limit Funds escalated the district superintendent's sense of urgency.

Aiming to be proactive, the district superintendent and a high-level colleague from the County Office of Education flew to Sacramento (California's capital) to meet with the deputy state superintendent (the number two person at the California Department of Education) and the CDE's team of lawyers. In this meeting (and in subsequent telephone conversations), the district superintendent tried to objectively explain the steadfast determination of the board majority and the high degree of unrest in the community as a result of the board's noncompliant stance. She explained threats from the CDE would not easily assuage the board majority's position; they seemed unwavering in their position. The state superintendent of public instruction did not participate in these talks; the state superintendent later told the district superintendent that the CDE's attorneys had advised him not to talk to the district superintendent during these tumultuous times.

The Board Majority Shifts Its Argument

Although the actions and rhetoric of the board majority clearly indicated they would not support the civil rights of other-than-heterosexual persons, the three dissenting board members started to shift their argument from sexual orientation to the semantics of the definitions of the words *sex* and *gender*. As noted before, the word *gender* was already in the district's policy. In order to be in compliance, however, the CDE was now requiring the district's policy to include the word *sex*. As also discussed earlier, with both the words *sex* and *gender* now being required in the revised policy, the CDE provided clarifying definitions of these terms.

Unlike federal law and the CDE, the board majority believed *sex* and *gender* are synonyms and, accordingly, argued there was no need to alter the existing policy to include both words. But, legally, without the new language being added to the policy, transgender/sexual students would not be specifically identified as a protected class and, of course, without mirroring the CDE's language, the district would not be in compliance. To many it seemed personal bias was being (thinly) veiled via confusing and pedantic semantic discussions regarding the definitions of *sex* and *gender*. In short, talk of social justice and equity was being replaced by complicated discussions regarding word definitions.

On April 12, 2004, as a result of consultation with the district's newly hired attorney, the board majority finally (and reluctantly) agreed the district's UCPP would have to be revised to include the word *sex* (Board Minutes, April 12, 2004). Accordingly, the board voted to make its UCPP a verbatim match as had been required by the EDC's Education Code from the beginning. But, still not wanting to accept the state's mandated language, the board majority voted three-to-two to superimpose upon the revised policy its own unique definition of the word *gender*. For the purpose of the District's Uniform Complaint Procedures, the board said that *gender* would be defined as follows:

> "Gender" is the biological sex of an individual or the alleged discriminator's perception of the alleged victim's sex, and includes the alleged discriminator's perception of the victim's identity, appearance, or behavior, whether or not that identity, appearance, or behavior is different from that traditionally associated with the victim's sex at birth. The perception of the alleged victim is not relevant to the determination of "gender" for purposes of the Uniform Com-

plaint Procedure. It is the perception of the alleged discriminator which is relevant. (Board Minutes, April 12, 2004)

Notably, the CDE defines gender as "A person's actual sex or perceived sex and includes a person's perceived identity, appearance, or behavior, whether or not that identity, appearance, or behavior is different from that traditionally associated with a person's sex at birth" (5CCR section 4910(k), Legal Advisory written by CDE's general counsel to all county and district superintendents, April 2004).

The board's superimposed definition of *gender* changed the spirit of the policy and did not protect the rights of a transgender/sexual student (or a student perceived as being transgender/sexual). Accordingly, the board added the word *sex* to the District's UCPP (so its policy would be a verbatim match to the CDE's policy, as dictated by law) but also included its own unique definition of *gender* and, in doing so, negated the intent of the state's policy.

The board majority justified the inclusion of its own definition of *gender* by arguing that the CDE's definition of *gender* was ill-grounded because it was not in line with California penal code language. The board majority predicated its case on the idea that the penal code supersedes the education code and, hence, the language of the penal code should be applied to this situation. At this point, the heart of the issue became whose perception matters, the victim's or the discriminator's?

To summarize, on April 12, 2004, after over four months of teeth gnashing, the board approved its revised UCPP (which included, via addendums, its own definition of *gender*) and submitted it to the CDE for approval (Board Minutes, April 12, 2004). This submission was needed to address the noncompliance findings revealed by the CCR and was a response to the CDE's threats. (Clearly, though, the district had not met the CCR team's allotted 30-day deadline.)

The CDE Accepts Northville's UCPP

Despite its many threats to the district, the CDE accepted Northville's revision to its UCPP because it included (as required by law) the word *sex* (Letter from State Superintendent of Public Instruction to Board of Trustees, April 19, 2004). But, surprising to many within the district and to those handful of individuals in the know outside of the district, the CDE never required the district to remove the addendums that provided the unique definition of *gender*. Accordingly, to this day (August 2007), the district's UCPP is still accompanied by the addendums that redefine *gender* and, consequently, transgender/sexual students are still not (according to district policy) able to file a discrimination complaint if harassed. As such, the district was never completely forced into compliance.

Ironically, in an April 29, 2004, letter to all California public school districts, the CDE (over the signature of the state superintendent of public instruction) announced it had indeed brought the district into compliance. In this letter, the CDE noted the district had revised its UCPP. The letter, however, did not tell the whole story. It failed, for example, to mention that the CDE had not forced the district to remove its unique definition of *gender* and had, accordingly, allowed the board to customize its UCPP. Furthermore, the CDE admonished the district and stated that no California public school district would ever be allowed to write its own definitions to policy words (but, again, did not note that it had indeed allowed Northville to do just this). Although the CDE had publicly declared it would "respond with every legal means available" if any local educational agency attempted to adopt a rogue discriminatory policy, the CDE never used any legal means to force Northville to remove its illegal definition of *gender* from its UCPP.

Since no school funds were ever withheld nor was any legal action ever taken against the district, the board majority members expressed vindication. They agreed they won a moral victory because the district was never forced to delete its definition of *gender*. Additionally, they claimed victory because they were able to dominate educational discussions in California for over a six-month period, drawing attention to an issue of great personal concern.

EPILOGUE

In the fall of 2004, the board majority met with an attorney to start proceedings to file a lawsuit against the California Department of Education that would force the CDE to clarify any vague language in California Education Code/Title V terminology. If the board majority's lawsuit were victorious, the CDE would have had to rewrite its UCPP language so transgender/sexual students would not be offered protected-class status. The lawsuit, however, was never actually filed. After board majority member Nazwisko lost her November 2004 reelection, the board dropped this from their agenda.

To date (August 2007), no transgender/sexual student has ever filed a uniform complaint alleging discrimination or harassment in the Northville District. Accordingly, the issue has yet to be clarified through the legal system.

Current Status of the Players

In November 2006, just as Lutz and Iannaccone's Dissatisfaction Theory would predict, the remaining two members of the board majority, Barrins and Martinez, lost their seats on the board, as did one of the board minority members (the individual who had sent the letter to the press that precipitated the media frenzy). Three new board members were elected. Combined with Nazwisko's 2004 loss, only one of the board members who originally received the agenda item still remains on Northville's board (as of August 2007). The Dissatisfaction Theory proposes that when American voters become dissatisfied enough, they will go to the polls and exercise their right to vote and vote the incumbents who created the dissatisfying policies out of office (Lutz and Iannaccone, 2007, pp. 26–27).

During the years between Nazwisko's loss in 2004 and the election of 2006, Northville had three different district superintendents, far exceeding the national average for district superintendent turnover. In July 2007, the board appointed a new superintendent, a woman who was one of the last people hired by the district superintendent discussed here in this case. The district superintendent featured in this case is now the interim dean of the school of educational studies at a small private graduate university. She directs a doctoral program in urban educational leadership and teaches on issues regarding social justice as they relate to educational administration. She left the district in August 2004 of her own accord (she had announced her intentions to retire in October 2003, far prior to any of these issues arising). The CDE still forges ahead under the leadership of the same superintendent of public instruction. Pundits occasionally suggest the state superintendent might consider running for governor. Today, the Northville School District is focused upon student achievement and closing the achievement gap.

NOTE

1. Even though all of the information found in this case study is part of public record, the identity of the district is veiled. In places where a proper noun is absolutely necessary, a pseudonym (Northville School District) is used. Likewise, people are referred to by title (not name) or by pseudonym.

REFERENCES

Bates, S. 1993. *Battleground: One mother's crusade, the Religious Right, and the struggle for control of our classrooms.* New York: Poseidon Press.

Deckman, M. 2004. *The Christian Right: School board battles.* Washington, DC: Georgetown University Press.

Lutz, F., and L. Iannaccone. 2007. Dissatisfaction theory of American democracy. Paper presented at School Board Research: Main Lines of Inquiry, A National Symposium of Scholars of School Board Governance, Des Moines, Iowa, September 14–15.

Rae, D., and M. Taylor. 1970. *The analysis of political cleavages*. New Haven, CT: Yale University Press.

Robbie, S. 2002. *Mendez vs Northville: For all the children/Para todos los ninos*. (Video). Huntington Beach, CA: KOCE-TV.

Schattschneider, E. E. 1975. *Semisovereign people: A realist's view of democracy in America*. Fort Worth, TX: Harcourt Brace Jovanovich.

Schlesinger, A. M. 1992. *The disuniting of America*. New York: Norton.

Wong, K., and F. Shen. 2007. Education mayors and big city school boards: New directions, new evidence. Paper presented at School Board Research: Main Lines of Inquiry, A National Symposium of Scholars of School Board Governance, Des Moines, Iowa, September 14–15.

V

SCHOOL BOARD'S ROLE IN DISTRICT/SYSTEMIC REFORM

10

The Lighthouse Inquiry: Examining the Role of School Board Leadership in the Improvement of Student Achievement

Mary L. Delagardelle

INTRODUCTION

> Quality school board functioning is central to the effectiveness of schooling. In fact, the effectiveness of school board governance is the single most important determinant of school district success or failure.
>
> The Honorable Rod Paige, U.S. Secretary of Education

These were the opening remarks of the second annual Jacqueline P. Danzberger Memorial Lecture during the National School Boards Association annual conference (Paige, 2002). However, school boards have not typically sought or been encouraged to play an active role in most facets of instructional reform efforts leading to improved student achievement. Generally, boards and superintendents have been more comfortable leaving instructionally related matters solely in the hands of the professional staff.

With the increasing public demand for accountability, a new emphasis on the responsibility of the board, as a governing body, to create the vision and direction for student learning, to set policy, to provide resources for improvement efforts, and then to monitor the results of student achievement initiatives (Henderson et al., 2001a; 2001b) is gaining public attention. School boards are charged with decisions impacting what students learn, how students are taught, how learning is measured, how teachers are supported with professional development, how funds are focused on district priorities, and how effectively the community is engaged around student learning. While by their nature school boards are removed from the day-to-day work of teaching and learning, they control the conditions allowing successful teaching and learning to occur throughout the system.

The public cry for improved achievement and accountability in public schools and the traditional lack of board involvement in issues related to student achievement create an urgent need to clearly understand the leadership role of the board as it relates to improving student learning. A better understanding of how board members establish district priorities, how district priorities are influenced by the attitudes and beliefs of the board members, and what board actions most likely result in shared commitment to district priorities related to student learning is a critical need in the educational literature (Coleman and LaRocque, 1990; Delagardelle, 2006).

In order to elucidate the role of the school board and examine the possible influence of school boards on school system performance, this multiphase line of inquiry examined the leadership differences in high- and low-achieving districts, the beliefs and actions of board-superintendent teams, board members' perceptions about their roles and responsibilities for improving student learning, the influence of certain contextual factors and characteristics of board members upon those beliefs, and the relationship between the beliefs and actions of the school board and the capacity of the school district to positively impact student learning. The findings after nine years of study begin to shed light on the governance roles and responsibilities that may be necessary to positively impact student learning in schools and school districts.

SCHOOL BOARDS: AN AMERICAN TRADITION

From the beginning, the essential value of the public school in a democracy was to ensure an educated citizenry (Glickman, 1993). Public education is education for citizenship. Honoring the treaty between the public and their schools and delivering on this promise of public education requires consistent evidence of high and equitable achievement among the students in public schools.

In what has become an American tradition, school boards comprised of elected officials are the guardians of and policy makers for our nation's schools. Local school boards have been an integral part of the history of American public education. Across the nation, approximately 15,000 local school boards and 95,000 local school board members serve, with approximately 96 percent elected by their communities (Resnick, 1999). These local school boards provide the means for segments in each community to have a representative voice in how schools should educate their children. School board members, as elected officials, view their accountability and responsiveness to the community in a manner local staff cannot. The perspective of the citizen school board member adds a dimension of stewardship to the system.

In principle, school boards provide public stewardship and direction to local education; however, whether school boards in practice are effective bodies for leading local education improvement for improved student learning is the most debated issue (Resnick, 1999). While different views regarding the primary purpose of school boards are evident (Campbell and Greene, 1994; Eadie, 2003; Kowalski, 2006; Sarason, 1997; Schlechty, 1992; Simon, 1986), most agree the primary purpose is related to the teaching and learning of America's youth and share an expectation for school governors to establish coherent, attainable outcomes that reflect the community vision for education in a democracy (Campbell and Greene, 1994; Kowalski, 2006).

According to the Twentieth Century Fund Report (1992), local public school boards have been "the distinctive hallmark of American education for more than one hundred fifty years" (p. 17). In recent decades, however, school boards have been the target of criticism by those who perceive them as outdated and incapable of effectively leading educational reforms to improve students' academic achievement, particularly in urban areas (Carol et al., 1986; Danzberger et al., 1987; Danzberger et al., 1992; The Twentieth Century Fund/Danforth Foundation, 1992). Even as the present research was being conducted, the national headlines were riddled with stories about school districts in trouble and local school boards blamed for the inadequacies in public education.

Years of fiscal incompetence, corruption, and neglect have resulted in the New Orleans public school system being officially declared "broke" (Thevenot, 2005), and the first state board of education is taking over the daily operations of Arizona's "failing" schools by removing principals, replacing teachers, and even reorganizing districts (Kossan, 2005). In Florida, at the request of the state board of education, four private firms were formally vying to take over the state's most troubled and "chronically failing" public schools (Harrison, 2005). Since 1988, mayoral and state takeovers have occurred in no less than 40 cities (Wong and Shen, 2003), fueled by the perception of failing student achievement, political conflict, inexperienced teaching staff, low expectations for students, lack of a demanding curriculum, lack of instructional coherence, and poor management (Edelstein, 2006).

Despite the long-standing presence of local school boards in public education and the more recent concerns about the effectiveness of locally elected governing boards, very few data-driven studies on the effectiveness of school boards contribute to the discussion of their role in school improvement or student learning. Rather, opinion-based writings on the overall role of the school board in relation to student achievement dominate the literature and, at best, prescribe general categories of board behavior for effective boardsmanship rather than agreed-upon specific criteria for judging the effects of school board governance on school systems. This dearth of research-based information to guide the development and support of local school boards around best practices for policy-level leadership is what launched the Lighthouse Inquiry and what has sustained the continuation of the work over time.

OVERVIEW OF THE LIGHTHOUSE INQUIRY

The educational literature provides convincing evidence that some teachers generate higher student achievement than others (Brophy and Good, 1986), in some cases dramatically higher (Sanders and Rivers, 1996). Some schools generate higher achievement than others (Brookover et al., 1978; Mortimore et al., 1988), in some cases dramatically higher (Harkreader and Weathersby, 1998; Weil et al., 1984). Some curricula and instructional methods generate higher achievement than others (Bloom, 1984; Slavin et al., 1996; Wang et al., 1993), in some cases dramatically higher (Joyce et al., 1999). However, a key question left unanswered in the literature is whether or not some school boards generate higher achievement than others. And, if so, do they do so through patterns of organizational behavior that can be described and learned by others?

The Lighthouse Inquiry has demonstrated that school boards in high-achieving districts are different in their actions and beliefs from school boards in low-achieving districts. The research also provides emerging evidence about what school boards need to know and be able to do to function in a manner that has a positive impact on a school district's efforts to improve student achievement. This line of inquiry has evolved in a systematic approach through various phases of study, with each phase focusing on slightly different research questions. The phases and research questions guiding each phase are shown in Figure 10.1 and are briefly described in the following section.

Phase I—Original Lighthouse Study (1998–2000)

The original Lighthouse Study was an ethnographic study of school districts in a Southern state with a history of generating unusually high levels of student achievement, and school districts with similar characteristics but generating significantly lower levels of student achievement. The purpose of the study was to examine whether some school boards generate higher achievement than others and to understand the differences, if they existed, between school boards in the high- and low-achieving districts.

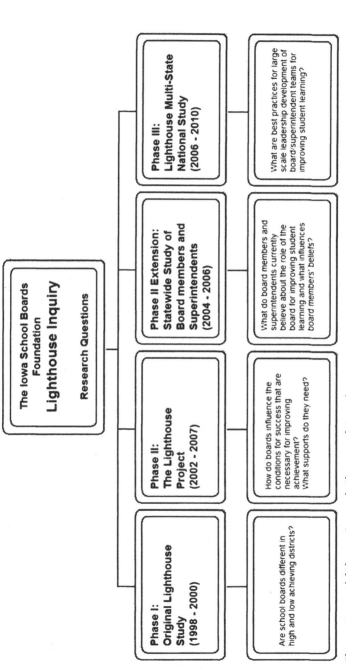

The Iowa School Boards Foundation
Lighthouse Inquiry

Research Questions

Phase I:
Original Lighthouse Study
(1998 - 2000)

Are school boards different in high and low achieving districts?

Phase II:
The Lighthouse Project
(2002 - 2007)

How do boards influence the conditions for success that are necessary for improving achievement? What supports do they need?

Phase II Extension:
Statewide Study of Board members and Superintendents
(2004 - 2006)

What do board members and superintendents currently believe about the role of the board for improving student learning and what influences board members' beliefs?

Phase III:
Lighthouse Multi-State National Study
(2006 - 2010)

What are best practices for large scale leadership development of board/superintendent teams for improving student learning?

Figure 10.1.   Lighthouse Research Phases and Questions

The researchers looked first for school districts with extremely different levels of student achievement but with very similar characteristics in such areas as the socioeconomic status of the students' families and the school district size. Individual interviews were then conducted with board members, superintendents, district-level administrators, principals, and teachers to learn about their school improvement efforts (what they were trying to improve, how they were trying to improve it, and what was influencing the change).

The findings from this phase of the inquiry concluded school boards in districts with a history of higher student achievement were different in their beliefs and actions from boards in districts with a history of generating low levels of student achievement. Boards were different in their beliefs about what was possible to expect in terms of student learning and in their beliefs about the district's capacity to impact the achievement of students.

Board members in high-achieving districts had more elevating views of their students' potential and more confidence in district staff's capacity to effect gains, whereas the board members in low-achieving districts were much more accepting of the status quo. The conversations in the low-achieving districts reflected a belief system that assumed the district was helpless to improve achievement because the factors "causing" low achievement were outside the control of the school district. They constantly made excuses for the current level of achievement due to external factors such as poverty, lack of student motivation, lack of parent involvement, poor instruction, losing the "good students" to nonpublic schools, etc. None of the districts were satisfied with their students' achievement, but board and staff members in the high-achieving districts rarely, if ever, made excuses.

The school districts were also different in relation to the presence of seven conditions for productive change. These conditions—connections across the system around the improvement work, a shared understanding of what it takes to change achievement, workplace support, professional development, a balance between districtwide direction and building-level autonomy, a strong community connection, and distributed leadership (see Table 10.1)—characterized the districts with higher levels of student achievement. The boards in these districts were more aware of the conditions and took more responsibility for ensuring these conditions were supported in ways that established effective norms of behavior and engagement in the improvement efforts.

This study became one of the first and only studies supporting a research-based connection between the work of the school board and the levels of student achievement. However, while the original study in the first phase of the research added information about differences between boards in high- and low-achieving districts, more specific questions about how they

Table 10.1.   The Seven Conditions for Productive Change

Conditions for Productive Change	Indicators in the Environment
-1- **Connections across the System** People working together because it is important to them to improve education for students.	• Shared decision making rather than mechanically making/mandating things happen. • Information flows in all directions with a high degree of involvement at all levels. • An ongoing emphasis on improvement (continuous effort to get even better) rather than seeing improvement as a way to solve a single problem or maintain the status quo. • People are connected across the system through involvement structures such as shared decision making and school improvement processes. • All people in the system are working together around a shared purpose that is important to them. • Collective efforts to improve because it's the right thing to do for kids—not because it's a mandate.
-2- **Knowing What It Takes to Change Achievement** A shared understanding about the type of learning culture needed to improve achievement and how to organize the district to make it happen.	Understanding the importance of key elements such as: • Using data and information to focus initiatives and select best practice strategies to improve instruction. • Various groups existing to support staff learning. • An intensive focus on implementation as well as a focus on effects for students. • Improvement efforts that are led and shaped by clear vision, goals, measurable targets, school improvement plans, teams, continuous study, processes for decision making, collective effort, etc. • Close alignment of curriculum/instruction and assessment. • A reasonable level of agreement, an adequate amount of professional development, the staff organized to work together to achieve implementation, a clear focus on teaching and learning. • Resources aligned to support implementation. • Improvement initiative is intentionally protected from fragmentation. • All parts of the system are aligned, coherent, and working together.

(continued)

Table 10.1. (*continued*)

Conditions for Productive Change	Indicators in the Environment
-3- **Workplace Support** Staff are supported in ways that help them succeed at improving student learning.	• Confidence in the ability of the system to improve learning for all students. • Restructured time to allow for collective study as part of the work day. • School staff organized into small study groups/teams that are connected to the larger community but responsible for one another. • Individual's work and results are public, scrutinized, supported, and responsibility is shared. • Staff feels efficacious and confident they can succeed.
-4- **Professional Development** An understanding of the purpose for and process of developing people as professionals.	• Professional development is an embedded feature of the workplace. • Professional development is structured as an ongoing inquiry into the focus area for improvement (reflective study of content, instruction, and effects for students). • Professional development is consistent with what research says it takes to change practice at the classroom level. • Instructional practice improves in ways that have a significant impact on student learning.

-5-
 A Balance between Districtwide Direction and Building-Level Autonomy
 Reliance on data to establish a balance between focus and direction from a district perspective with latitude at the building level—in order to achieve equity across the system.
	• Relentless use of data and information to determine districtwide needs and to help buildings determine their contribution to the districtwide effort.
	 • Focused alignment of improvement goals across the entire system.
	 • Use of action research processes, such as:
	   • Reliance on data and information to guide and monitor improvement efforts—internal and external information about student learning and the learning environment (which includes curriculum, instruction, assessment, available materials, etc.).
	   • The district is connected to the external knowledge base on teaching and learning.
	   • Regular monitoring of progress by monitoring implementation and effects for students.
	   • Actions are modified based on results.

Conditions for Productive Change	Indicators in the Environment
-6- **A Strong Community Connection** An understanding of how to generate community involvement and shared responsibility for improvement.	• There is a close connection to the community. • The distinctions between the professional and lay community are "blurred" because of level of involvement, support, and shared responsibility. • The community is involved in the functions of the district wherever possible. • The school district is responsive to community needs and wishes. • The community feels responsible for the success of the school district. • Staff and board regularly comment on the community support.
-7- **Distributed Leadership** Broad-based leadership to provide direction and focus for the improvement work. Strong but sensitive leadership, at all levels of the system, from dynamic leaders.	• Vigorous, integrative leadership is generated and supported at all levels. • The leadership in the organization keeps the focus on the few things the organization must do well in order to succeed. • There is a democratic process that holds the organization together around their improvement efforts. • Leaders are effective diagnosticians, problem solvers, and able to help others identify needs and create solutions.

became higher-functioning boards and the specific board actions that positively impacted the school district were still unanswered. These questions and others then became the research questions for the next phase of the Lighthouse Inquiry.

Phase II—The Lighthouse Project (2002–2007)

The second phase of the Lighthouse research became a five-year action research project examining the role of the local governance team in districtwide efforts to improve student achievement. The purpose of this phase was to build upon the findings of the first Lighthouse study and identify the ways local school boards influence the conditions for success necessary to improve student achievement. This project also sought to understand the types of development and supports school boards need in order to have a positive impact on district efforts to improve student achievement.

The researchers worked with the boards and superintendents in five pilot school districts in a Midwestern state over a period of five years while studying changes in specific conditions within the system that support improvement, changes in beliefs, and changes in student achievement. The preliminary analysis, after three years of collaborative work with the pilot districts, revealed significant information about key behaviors of the board-superintendent team that appeared to be positively influencing district efforts to improve achievement. As a result of this phase, the research team was able to describe five main roles of the board; seven key areas of performance boards assume as they carry out these roles; the knowledge, skills, and beliefs necessary to perform in these ways; and effective strategies for board development related to the board roles. Areas such as creating a sense of urgency, developing a districtwide focus for improvement, creating conditions within the system for success, monitoring progress, developing policies through a deliberative process, and developing a leadership continuum have influenced board behaviors as well as the practices and beliefs of district staff in these pilot districts. This phase of the Lighthouse Inquiry and the findings are discussed in more detail later in this chapter.

As the findings were unfolding during this phase of the research, new questions about the current status of board members' beliefs about their role, beliefs about student learning, and questions about factors that influence those beliefs began to emerge. In other words, what did most board members believe were important aspects of their role in relation to what was being learned in the Lighthouse Project? Are board members across the state similar in their beliefs to the board members in the pilot project? What factors influence the beliefs of board members? What are the implications for training and support to board members on a larger scale? A statewide study of board members' beliefs about their roles and responsibilities for improving student learning was initiated to begin examining these questions.

Phase II Extension—The Role of the Board in Improving Student Achievement (2004–2006)

This study investigated the beliefs of superintendents and school board members about the roles and responsibilities of local boards for improving student learning and the contextual factors or characteristics influencing those beliefs. The study utilized both qualitative and quantitative data collection and analysis techniques in sequential phases to survey board members and superintendents about the role of the board for improving student achievement, to determine factors influencing board members' beliefs about their role, and to study the differences among board members and superintendents with significantly different views about the role of the board. Data were collected through an online statewide survey, personal interviews, and documentation from 718 board members and superintendents and 375 school districts.

The results of this study revealed significant regional differences in board members' beliefs about their role, the importance they ascribed to responsibilities tied to improving student achievement, their understanding of systemic change, and their participation in board training. The results also established links between these differences and differences in student achievement. This mixed-methods study shed light on the need for and importance of leadership development for board-superintendent teams, implications for redefining board roles, and the overlooked importance of district-level governance on student achievement.

As the different components of the study uncovered specific board development needs during Phase II, new questions surfaced regarding large-scale study, implementation, and evaluation of best practices for governance teams. This became the focus for Phase III of the Lighthouse Inquiry.

Phase III—The Lighthouse Multi-State National Study (2006–2010)

The five-year action research during the Phase II project resulted in key information about the knowledge and skills boards need to function to enable school districts to improve student learning. But this is not enough. Continuing to build clarity about best practices for governance teams and developing systems for board development that can be delivered on a large scale remained as critical next steps and created the need for the third phase of the Lighthouse Study. This phase is a multi-year national expansion of the Lighthouse research, accompanied by a study of best practices of state school board associations and board-superintendent teams in multiple states for developing board leadership for improving student learning.

The purpose of Phase III is to build on and scale the learning from the Lighthouse Project across districts and states and to clearly define best practices for school boards and for the state associations supporting them. By working with the other states, the research team can learn, from an expanded implementation of the best practices identified in the Lighthouse Project, how and when the interventions are most effective, under what conditions those interventions are most effective, and how to efficiently and effectively provide systems of leadership development to school board–superintendent teams for large numbers of school districts.

Key questions for this phase of the study include: (a) What are the best practices of school board–superintendent teams for improving student learning? (b) What are the best practices for developing the knowledge, skills, and beliefs of school board–superintendent team leadership for improving student learning? (c) What are the most effective strategies for providing leadership development for all school board–superintendent teams across an entire state? (d) What does it take to create a statewide focus on improving student achievement and what supports are necessary to sustain that focus?

In this phase of the Lighthouse Study, state school board association staff replicate the key Lighthouse interventions in districts across their states with training, support, and monitoring by the Lighthouse research team. Other states are studying different interventions but collecting the same data each year to measure impact. This can allow for an ongoing analysis of the implementation of various interventions with data-based studies of impact on the school boards, school districts, and student achievement in order to identify best practices in board leadership and development.

The common data all states collect and monitor (at a minimum) include (a) changes in conditions within the culture of the school district that are critical for improving student achievement (Table 10.1), (b) beliefs about what is possible to expect and what has the biggest impact on student learning, and (c) statewide student achievement data indicating the current levels of student performance. The states participating in this phase of the study include California, Idaho, Illinois, Iowa, Kentucky, Missouri, Oregon, and Wisconsin. At the time of this publication, this phase of the research is in a very early stage of implementation and the researchers are continuing to seek funding.

A CLOSER EXAMINATION: SCHOOL BOARD LEADERSHIP AND STUDENT ACHIEVEMENT

Following Phase I of the Lighthouse Inquiry, which demonstrated that school boards in high-achieving districts were significantly different in their beliefs and actions from school boards in low-achieving districts, Phase II of the inquiry set out to understand more about the actions of local boards of education that positively impact school cultures and student outcomes and to understand how they learn to perform in those ways. The linkages between school boards and teaching and learning in classrooms are often misunderstood. School boards do not directly cause student learning. However, it would appear from findings of the Lighthouse research, as well as from the work of others (Coleman and LaRocque, 1990; LaRocque and Coleman, 1993), that the beliefs, decisions, and actions of school boards directly impact the conditions within schools that enable district efforts to improve achievement to either succeed or fail. These linkages are illustrated in Figure 10.2.

This phase of the research built upon the earlier study by identifying pilot school districts and providing technical assistance and support to the board, superintendent, and, in some districts, a districtwide leadership team in order to strengthen or create seven conditions for productive change (Table 10.1). The technical assistance focused on three key areas:

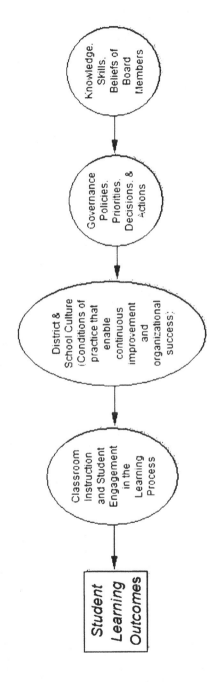

Figure 10.2. Key Linkages between School Boards and Student Learning

1. Developing a clear, compelling, and shared focus for school improvement and a belief that virtually all students can learn and succeed.
2. Using action research to improve the effectiveness of the system in helping students learn.
3. Developing leadership to support and sustain the improvement efforts.

The challenge was to move an entire district, a very complex system, from a set of deeply held assumptions, beliefs, and practices to a renewed focus on academic results and high levels of performance by all students.

The main premise guiding this phase of the research was the following:

> When local school board–superintendent teams generate a districtwide focus on improved achievement and engage local administrators and teachers in the creation of seven conditions that support continuous improvement, it should result in high and equitable student achievement and elevated beliefs across the system.

The key variables (generating a districtwide focus on improved achievement, creating or strengthening seven conditions that support continuous improvement, student achievement, and the beliefs of board and staff) defined the sources of data to be collected (Table 10.2). Although numerous types of data were collected for study, the three main sources included a districtwide survey related to the seven conditions for productive change, a districtwide survey of beliefs about what is possible to expect in terms of student learning and what it takes to improve learning outcomes, and annual student achievement data.

STUDY METHODS

The approach to the research process during this phase of the Lighthouse Inquiry involved members of the research team and members of the school district board and staff working together to define the achievement problem to be examined, cogenerate relevant knowledge about the problem, learn and study together, generate actions, and interpret the result of actions based on what had been learned (Greenwood and Levin, 1998). The research was carried out for the purpose of improving the conditions within the workplace, the beliefs of the board and staff, and the achievement of students. Therefore, action research methods, a form of research that generates knowledge for the express purpose of taking action to improve a situation and increase the organization's capacity to keep improving (Greenwood and Levin, 1998), were employed over five years in five pilot districts to shed light on the role of the board in district efforts to improve student

Table 10.2. Lighthouse Project Data Sources

1. Lighthouse Survey of all staff and board members' perceptions about the presence of the seven conditions
   a. 59 forced-choice and open-ended questions
   b. Years 1, 3, and 5
2. Beliefs Survey of all staff and board members
   a. 21 forced-choice and open-ended questions
   b. Years 1, 3, and 5
3. Focus Groups
   a. Questions related to beliefs and conditions
   b. Annually
   c. Board, superintendent, principals, district leadership team
4. Board Observations (during regularly scheduled board meetings)
   a. Quarterly in each pilot district
5. Policy Analysis and Relevant Revisions
   a. Pre/post
   b. New policies developed
6. Team Reflections on the Content and Process of Work in the Pilot Sites
   a. Ongoing collection
   b. Analyzed monthly
   c. Analyzed yearly
7. Participant Reflections on the Content and Process of Work in the Pilot Sites
   a. Ongoing collection
   b. Analyzed monthly
   c. Analyzed yearly
8. Achievement Data for Each Site
   a. Iowa Tests of Basic Skills and Iowa Tests of Educational Development
   b. A second measure of achievement in the focus area
   c. Collected and analyzed annually
9. Community Survey
   a. Formative—Year 3 only
   b. Randomly selected community members in each site
   c. 22 forced-choice and open-ended questions
      i. What they understand about what the district is doing to improve achievement
      ii. What they understand about policy
      iii. Perceptions of their role and connection
10. Initial Observations in All Sites
    a. Baseline observations
    b. Classroom based
    c. Most classrooms in four of five districts
11. Other Data Sources

Table 10.3. Description of the Participating Districts

District	Size	% Non-White	Student Enrollment	Poverty	Student Achievement
A	703	2%	Stable	22%	25% nonproficient
B	30,082	28%	Stable	48%	30–50% nonproficient
C	2,659	2%	Severe Decline	46%	20–30% nonproficient
D	703	8.2%	Stable	30%	25% nonproficient
E	972	11%	Significant Hispanic Increase	31%	30–40% nonproficient

learning. The five school districts selected to participate in the Lighthouse Project are described briefly in Table 10.3.

SCHOOL BOARDS CAN MAKE A DIFFERENCE

A preliminary analysis of data, completed at the end of Year 3, revealed results that school board leadership can make a difference in student success.

Significant Positive Change in Perceptual Conditions

The most significant changes in perceptions were associated with condition 4 (professional development) and condition 5 (balance between districtwide direction and building autonomy). Participants rated training (focused on instructional practices with support for implementation), collective participation in professional development, and the focus of professional development on instruction in the content area of greatest student learning need significantly higher in Year 3. Participants also rated the presence of a districtwide direction and focus for improvement and shared agreement about the importance of basing district and individual decisions on data significantly higher in Year 3. However, perceptions about the school district's connection to the community was the one condition that did not change significantly from Year 1 to Year 3.

Significant Positive Change in Beliefs

The most significant changes in beliefs from Year 1 to Year 3 included beliefs about the need for schools to be organized and structured differently in order to improve student learning, beliefs about the impact adults in the school can have on student learning, and beliefs about the importance of improving educators' knowledge and skills in order to improve student learning outcomes. The strongest beliefs at the end of Year 3 included beliefs about the importance of frequently monitoring student learning, beliefs about the importance of allocating resources to ensure children's earliest school experiences are successful, and beliefs about the importance of partnering with the community to improve student learning.

Significant Change in Conditions Necessary for Improved Achievement

Indicators with the most significant change from Year 1 to Year 3 (t=5.57–10.17) included the presence of distributed leadership, the presence of time for small groups to meet and work together to improve student learning, the presence of small working groups that exist to improve student learning, the sense of urgency for improvement created by district leaders, and the board's increased reliance on multiple sources of information when making decisions.

Significant Change in Achievement

In Year 3, significant gains on a measure of reading comprehension were seen at every grade level in one district, with an average of 94 percent of the students K–12 scoring average or above. In addition, four of the five sites showed statistically significant gains in student reading and/or math for at least two grade levels on the statewide norm-referenced measure of student achievement.

Additional Observations

Statistically significant differences that existed between role groups (board, administration, and teachers) in relation to their perceptions of the seven conditions had disappeared by Year 3. In Year 3, all role groups had very similar perceptions in relation to the presence of the seven conditions. In fact, on average, 91 percent of all staff and board members across all sites said a clear and focused goal in their district was to improve student achievement at the end of Year 3.

In four of the five sites, data show an increase of 48–90 percent of all staff and the board who could consistently describe the district's school improvement goals. In three of the five sites, the average amount of time spent in regular board meetings on policy and student achievement issues had more than doubled. The boards in all five districts are regularly allocating additional board work session time to focus exclusively on student achievement issues. Finally, by Year 3, staff and board members in all districts indicated strong agreement that local school boards can positively impact student achievement.

As a supplement to the data from the pilot sites, analysis of the statewide study (Phase II Extension) provided additional information about the current status of board members' beliefs and the effects of demographic differences between districts. In general, board members and superintendents have significantly different views about the role of the board, particularly as it relates to improving student learning. Board members in general identified responsibilities such as discussing student achievement at the board table, expressing confidence that staff can impact student learning, ensuring strong leadership exists, and monitoring student learning progress as most important for boards to do. In fact, board members in general identified responsibilities such as establishing criteria to guide staff in choosing initiatives, evaluating effectiveness of professional development, establishing and communicating a singular focus for improved student learning, and adopting and monitoring procedures for informing the community about student learning progress as less important for boards to do.

Factors such as the size of the school district, the length of time board members had served, the education level of the board members, the time they reported spending on board work, whether or not they had children in school, and the age of the board member had little or no relationship to how they perceived their role as a board member. Also, factors such as the financial health of the district, board member turnover, and percentage of low-income families within the school district did not explain the differences in board members' beliefs about their role.

Factors that did explain differences in board members' beliefs about their role included the region of the state where the board members lived and the amount of training they received. The region where board members participated in significantly less training and where board members expressed significantly lower beliefs about their role for improving student learning was also the region with the highest concentration of low-achieving districts.

Voices from the Field

With the project emphasis on establishing a districtwide focus on improving student learning and shared goals for the improvement of achievement, it was important to gather information about the collective understanding of what the district was trying to improve. Therefore, one of the survey questions asked the participants in the pilot sites to describe the current goal for improvement in their school district. The following quotes from staff and board members' responses to the survey item in one pilot district illustrate the kind of change that was observed across districts.

Year 1 responses to the question, "What are the improvement goals for this district?" included:

1. To enable all students to be successful learners both now and in the future.
2. To better educate students for their lifetime.
3. To do what is in the best interests of our students, by shaping the future of the world as we know it.
4. Helping students to do better.
5. To improve test scores.
6. To seek new challenges to continue the tradition of academic excellence and personal satisfaction.
7. To prepare students for college, work, life.
8. To make an impression on some test dreamed up by people who have little real experience in the classroom.
9. To allow our students to be the best that they can be.
10. So all students can experience success.

One year later responses to the same question, "What are the improvement goals for this district?" from participants in the same school district included:

1. Improve reading comprehension districtwide is the current initiative.
2. Improve reading comprehension through the use of new instructional strategies.
3. To improve the reading comprehension at all grade levels.
4. Improve reading and reading comprehension of every student.
5. All students will improve in reading comprehension.
6. Improve reading comprehension.
7. To improve comprehension scores in reading in all content areas.
8. Improve reading comprehension.
9. Reading comprehension (K–12) is the main improvement goal for our district.
10. Improve reading scores.

With approximately 80 staff and board members participating in the survey from this district of approximately 1000 students, over 97 percent of the responses mentioned the improvement of reading or reading comprehension as their current focus for improvement. This shift, from a very mission-driven district to districtwide clarity about the "most important thing to improve this year" as they carry out the mission, appeared to be critical for generating collective action and ultimately improving outcomes for students. The board played a key role in establishing the focus for improvement, clarifying expectations in relation to the improvement focus, protecting the district's improvement efforts from fragmentation, and aligning decisions and resources consistent with the needs in the focus area.

Knowing where to focus energy was not enough to ensure student learning improved. Actions consistent with the priority for improvement also became apparent in the data. Board-superintendent teams developed a renewed commitment to improving teaching in the area of greatest student learning need and ensured the professional development experiences of their staff members maintained this focus. The initial responses to questions asking participants to describe their professional development experiences over the past year included none of the characteristics of quality professional development that have been shown to impact teaching practices in ways that benefit student learning. Descriptions of their previous professional development experiences included references to motivational speakers or content that was not directly related to instruction as exemplified in the following quotes from respondents:

"Developing responsible behavior in students."

"One afternoon of attendance with professional speaker."

"Just what has been provided for us at the beginning of the school year . . ."

"Mr. Fitzgerald is about all that I can remember."

"Guest speaker on classroom discipline. Technology updates on grading system."

"Behavior management in the classroom, physical activity and nutrition, organizational skills."

"Teacher workshops at the beginning of the school year and a regional seminar."

"Motivational speakers were provided by the district."

"Learning workshops with handling student behavior."

"A state convention with inspirational speakers, hands-on workshops."

By the end of Year 3, 92 percent of the survey responses from the same district mentioned one or more of the characteristics of quality professional development with evidence of impact on student learning:

"The review of student data and the research and development of strategies to meet the needs of students."

"I have received further training in instructional reading strategies."

"Frequent teacher in-service times to learn about, practice, and discuss research-based reading comprehension strategies."

"Presentations by teachers, sharing data, reading/discussing a book, study teams."

"They were all related to the strategies we are to use to improve student reading comprehension."

"I meet weekly, sometimes daily, with my study team to improve on my teaching and student learning."

"Researched how to improve reading comprehension in my subject area."

"Shared and discussed experience in implementing reading strategies."

"Learning support strategies for the main comprehension strategies of inductive thinking and concept attainment."

"Most of them focused on teaching reading using inductive methods."

The results and quotes provided here represent only a few of the changes observed during the data analysis but provide a glimpse into the changing conditions within the participant school districts. The next step was to sort out the behaviors of the board members that may have contributed to the changes being observed within the culture of the school district.

WHAT DID THE BOARD MEMBERS DO?

The board-superintendent team assumed leadership responsibilities with a focus on systemic improvement. The board members in the pilot school districts were not passive "rubber stamps" of the superintendent's recommendations, but they were also not acting as if they were the professional educators. At the same time, superintendents did not view their boards as a necessary evil to be tolerated or merely "managed" in order to keep them from causing harm. Together, the board members and superintendents gained a sense of the leadership role the board could play and made substantial efforts to engage with each other as leadership partners without discounting the diverse perspectives and unique responsibilities each position brings to the team. The board members found a balance of active engagement in extensive dialogue about the district's focus and direction for improvement and a deep regard for the role of the teachers and administrators charged with moving the district in that direction. Finding and maintaining this balance enhanced the relationship between the board and the superintendent and the confidence they had in each other's ability to make a difference.

The board and the superintendent built a different type of relationship than is typical in many school districts. Positive, trusting relationships existed between the boards and their superintendents in all pilot districts—which, as in the original Lighthouse Study, appeared to be a necessary but not sufficient condition of the board-superintendent team. Boards and superintendents relied upon the positive trusting relationships to enable them to play strong, interdependent leadership roles, to examine and challenge each other's views, to study data and confront existing realities, to ask probing questions, and to scrutinize each other's performance in ways that strengthened and mobilized the entire team.

Roles of the Board

Five main functions or roles of the board surfaced as critical roles for boards to play as they interacted with district staff around their efforts to

improve student learning. First, the boards set clear expectations for the outcomes of the improvement work. Regardless of the specific area being discussed, the improvement of student performance or the improvement of
professional development, the boards worked to clarify expectations in
terms of the desired outcomes or results rather than the strategies the district staff would employ to meet the expectations.

With clear expectations for results, another role the board members
played was to hold themselves and the district staff accountable for meeting the expectations. The board members had to be willing to constantly
monitor progress and ensure corrective actions could be taken when the
progress was not adequate. However, their approach to monitoring was not
one of "mandate and hands off." Rather, it was a collective effort of shared
(albeit different) responsibilities for watching the progress and ensuring
success.

Another key role the board members played was to ensure the conditions
for success were present within the system. In other words, board members
had to be willing to support whatever it would take to meet the expectations that had been set. This type of reciprocal responsibility for the success
of the school district created a new dimension of *pressure* and *support* than
had been present in the districts previously.

The board members also found it important to build the collective will
of the staff and the community to improve student learning. In other words,
they needed to build a shared sense of urgency and a shared commitment
to ensuring all students learn well. And, finally, the board members found
it necessary to create time to learn together as a board team and engage in
extensive dialogue with each other in order to establish consensus about
what was most important to accomplish, to understand what it would take
to succeed, and to determine at what cost they were willing to pursue it.
Board members are not professional educators, but they did need to have
shared understandings about what was reasonable to expect and what it
would take to meet the expectations—and that required learning together
as a board team.

These five roles—setting clear expectations, holding the system accountable to the expectations, creating conditions for success, building the collective will to succeed, and learning together as a board team—became the
defining elements of the board's role from which seven key areas of performance emerged as the board members engaged in fulfilling these roles.

Seven Areas of Performance Related to the Roles of the Board

As board members played their role, they found it extremely important
to take responsibility for increasing public awareness of the current status
of student learning, point out critical needs, and build a "case for change"

to increase the sense of urgency for addressing the learning needs. This was often a difficult shift for board members, who were more accustomed to building public confidence by pointing out district strengths than attempting to build public confidence by pointing out areas of need and communicating what the district was going to do to address the needs. In order to perform this leadership function, they first had to challenge their own beliefs about what was possible to expect in terms of their student learning gains, then consistently and confidently mobilize the public, including district staff, to expect more.

A second performance area involved board members increasing their use of data to set expectations, determine and monitor indicators of progress, and apply pressure for accountability. This performance area was the most difficult for boards because they did not want to set the district up to fail and, therefore, were very reluctant to set measurable goals and targets that might expose any lack of success. Closely related to the need to apply pressure for accountability was the corresponding need to demonstrate unwavering commitment to the improvement efforts and ensure board actions and decisions reflected that commitment. This type of dedication required extensive learning, dialogue, and a willingness to stay the course.

The boards also realized that improving student achievement would be directly related to their support for quality professional development focused on the improvement of instruction. For most boards, this required significant changes in the allocation of resources (people, time, and money) and would not have happened without a clear understanding of the characteristics of quality professional development and a belief in the importance of improving the knowledge and skills of educators in order to improve student outcomes.

As board members increased their leadership role, they also had to support and connect with other district-level leaders to ensure a strong continuum of leadership was distributed across the school district. The relationship between the board and the superintendent, discussed previously, was extended to the district leadership team (usually consisting of central office administrators, principals, and teacher leaders from each building) to guide and protect the improvement efforts, monitor progress, and make midcourse corrections to accelerate progress. Whenever a breakdown in this leadership continuum occurred or a breakdown in the leaders' capacity to function effectively in their leadership role arose, the improvement work ceased to move forward.

Policies for guiding the decisions and actions of district staff have not been very effective in areas most directly impacting student learning (curriculum, instruction, professional development, assessment, etc.). Board members in the pilot districts believed sustaining the processes and structures of the improvement work playing out in their districts would depend upon written policies to provide continued guidance when key leaders or board members were no longer serving the district. However, they quickly realized that policies to guide and sustain the district work to improve achievement required a more deliberative process than the policy development process they used for existing policies. Board members collectively studied background information about the policy area, identified and prioritized expectations, determined measures of progress they would accept as evidence of success, identified support needs, and regularly monitored the implementation of their policy.

Finally, board members connected with the community to increase the community's involvement in and commitment to the school district's focus for improvement. The board members had to value the role of the parents and community in the education of students and be willing to engage the community in a more significant role than the compliance requirements for involvement established by the state department of education. Even though the community connection changed less than any other condition being monitored by the research team, several districts made impressive connections with the community that need to be developed, supported, and studied to determine impact over time.

While each of these seven areas of performance may have transpired differently in each district, many commonalities across districts existed. More information about the seven key areas of performance and the knowledge, skills, and beliefs board members identified as necessary to perform in these ways are provided in Table 10.4.

SUMMARY

Do some school boards generate higher achievement through patterns of organizational behavior that can be described and learned by others? Clearly, the initial findings in this line of inquiry would indicate they do. However, this is difficult for many to grasp. When we think about the educational system of a school district and its likely effect on students, we consider the elements of the system in terms of their proximity to the student. In the case of this study, the educational environment created in the classroom and the school is closest to the student and is likely to have the most influence. The conditions for change are more distal from the student and are unlikely to have a significant effect unless they affect the learning environment in the classrooms and schools. The governance processes are more distal yet and are likely to have a significant effect only when they affect the conditions for change and those in turn affect the educational environment (see Figure 10.2).

Essentially, the board-superintendent team operates "at a distance" from the learner. As they try to support student learning they must operate

Table 10.4. Key Areas of Board Performance and the Knowledge, Skills, and Beliefs of Board Members Associated with Each Performance Area

Key Areas of Board Performance	Knowledge, Skills, and Beliefs Necessary for Performances
Creating awareness of the need to improve—building commitment to the needs: • Creating clarity about the need • Increasing the sense of urgency • Focusing on improving achievement in a content area of need • Improving teaching as the key means to get there • Expecting more • Believing it's possible to achieve	**KNOW:** • Understand what's at stake if nothing changes (in relation to student learning) • Understand that improving teaching is the most important factor for improving student learning • Understand the importance of improving teaching in the content area of greatest student learning need • Understand what is possible to expect (schools that have beat the odds) • Clear understanding of the urgent status of student learning in their district, based on analysis of data • Clarity about learning gaps among subgroups of students that currently exist • Understand that boards make a difference (board leadership is critical for improving learning for all students) **DO:** • Confront current beliefs about what is possible to expect in terms of student learning (their own beliefs and the beliefs of others) • Communicate the urgency for improving student learning • Consistently communicate high expectations • Use data and research to identify highest priority area for change and define focus and targets for improvement • Consistently communicate the focus for improvement and model the adherence to the focus through board actions and conversations **BELIEVE:** • The current level of student achievement is not what can be expected—we can expect much more • How well students learn in school depends primarily upon what the adults in the school do • Improving the quality of teaching is the most important strategy for improving student learning • Virtually all children can meet grade level expectations • We have become complacent about the achievement of our students

(continued)

Table 10.4. (*continued*)

Key Areas of Board Performance	Knowledge, Skills, and Beliefs Necessary for Performances
Applying pressure for accountability: • Extensive use of data • Setting high expectations for improvement • Defining acceptable evidence of success • Monitoring progress	**KNOW:** • Understand the important role of pressure and support (accountability and reciprocal responsibility) • Understand key data analysis concepts • Understand the importance of monitoring both implementation and impact • Understand the school culture necessary for improving student learning (seven conditions necessary for productive change and continuous improvement) and key indicators of that culture • Understand the current status of achievement in the district and what needs to change • Understand what would be reasonable targets for improvement given the current achievement status **DO:** • Set improvement goals and targets that appropriately "stretch" the district improvement efforts • Identify the indicators the board will accept as progress toward the goal and/or targets • Regularly monitor progress toward the specific annual targets • Ensure conditions necessary for continuous improvement are present in the culture of the school and regularly monitor evidence of progress toward the learning culture for adults and students • Expect and support corrective action when progress is not evident (culture, implementation, and impact) • Regularly discuss implications of data reports and reference data in decision making and problem solving • Support decisions with good data and information (internal and external—cost and impact) • Ensure the districtwide comprehensive assessment system can provide answers to identified key questions about student learning **BELIEVE:** • Frequent monitoring of student learning is critical to improving teaching and learning

Key Areas of Board Performance	Knowledge, Skills, and Beliefs Necessary for Performances
	• Formative and summative (as well as up-close and distant) assessments of student learning are critical for monitoring progress

Demonstrating commitment :
• Creating board learning time
• Learning together as a board team
• Modeling a willingness to learn and innovate
• Engaging in extensive conversations among board members to understand different points of view among the board members and clarify what's important to the board as a whole
• Staying the course
• Taking actions and/or making decisions that demonstrate commitment to the focus area (resource allocation, time provision, calendar, negotiations, etc.)
	KNOW:
	• The role of the board for improving achievement
	• The public/governing role of the board in relation to democratic principles
	• Key principles of good governance
	DO:
	• Focus board meetings on the student learning improvement area
	• Talk to each other—when presentations are made to the board, balance the time asking questions of the presenter with meaningful dialogue among the board members to clarify shared understandings, implications, etc.
	• Commit extra board time for work sessions to focus on improvement and board learning
	• Demonstrate commitment to the learning priorities through:
	  • Negotiations
	  • Calendar development
	  • Budget setting
	  • Policy development and approval
	  • Superintendent selection
	  • Superintendent evaluation
	  • Et cetera
	• Evaluate the performance of the board based on the collective effort to monitor, support, and ensure the district improvement goals are met
	BELIEVE:
	• In order for student learning to improve, schools must be organized and structured differently
	• Schools cannot continue to do what they have always done and expect to get different results
	• Doing more of what we are currently doing will not result in significantly improved learning

Providing ongoing support for quality professional development: • Setting clear expectations (for the outcomes and process of professional development)	**KNOW:** • Characteristics of professional development (what it takes to change practice at the classroom level in ways that will have a positive impact on student learning)

(continued)

Table 10.4. (*continued*)

Key Areas of Board Performance	Knowledge, Skills, and Beliefs Necessary for Performances
• Creating time • Providing financial support • Celebrating success	• The board's role in relation to selecting initiatives and providing the professional development system to support them • The criteria to consider when approving and supporting initiatives to improve achievement • The implications of fully implementing potential initiatives to improve achievement (includes general understanding of what it will take for full implementation) **DO:** • Analyze the current professional development system in relation to what it takes to change practices • Consider initiatives to improve achievement from a framework of key criteria • Analyze the cost effectiveness of current and potential initiatives to improve achievement • Set clear/measurable expectations for the outcomes of professional development (improvement in student learning as the primary outcome) • Allocate resources to ensure a district infrastructure exists to support quality professional development • Allocate resources to ensure the success of approved initiatives to improve achievement • Monitor progress/success of professional development in relation to established outcomes **BELIEVE:** • In order to change outcomes for students, we must improve the knowledge and skills of the educators • School districts must focus major attention on improving professional practices in the classroom through high-quality professional development • Collaboration among adults is necessary for substantially improving student learning • Student achievement barriers, such as poverty and lack of family support, can be overcome by quality teaching
Supporting and connecting with districtwide leadership: • Providing strong district-level leadership from the board-superintendent team	**KNOW:** • The leadership role of the board • The importance of distributed leadership • The difference between leadership and management

Key Areas of Board Performance	Knowledge, Skills, and Beliefs Necessary for Performances
• Empowering shared district-level leadership through the creation and support of a district-level leadership team (central office administrators, principals, and teachers responsible for leading districtwide efforts to improve achievement) • Demonstrating a willingness and readiness to lead and let others lead	• The instructional leadership role of school administrators • The characteristics of leadership needed to lead for improved achievement—leadership needed for standards-based improvement • The importance of a narrow focus for improvement **DO:** • Establish clarity, systemwide, about the most important focus for improving student learning • Communicate consistently about the focus for improvement, the specific expectations/targets, and what the district is doing to improve achievement • Protect the work from fragmentation and distraction • Stay the course • Create a framework for receiving and responding to reports from staff regarding student learning and improvement initiatives during board meetings and work sessions to ensure productive and appropriate dialogue • Monitor progress regularly and ensure corrective action is taken and supported **BELIEVE:** • Leadership is either everywhere or it is nowhere • Leadership for improving teaching and learning is critical to school district success
Deliberative policy development: • Developing meaningful policies through deliberative processes in key areas related to the improvement of teaching and learning • Focusing policies on the desired outcomes/results (what the board wants accomplished) and the rationale (why it is so important to realize the outcomes) NOT how the outcomes will be met (not what the district will do to achieve the desired results)	**KNOW:** • The difference between discussion and deliberation • The importance of whole board deliberation throughout the policy development process (for policies directly impacting teaching and learning, or the seven conditions) • The role of policy for guiding and sustaining district improvement work **DO:** • Study background information related to the policy area • Identify greatest hopes • Prioritize expectations • Determine measures of progress/success for each expectation • Identify support needs for each expectation

(*continued*)

Table 10.4. (*continued*)

Key Areas of Board Performance	Knowledge, Skills, and Beliefs Necessary for Performances
	• Finalize priority expectations based on what can be monitored and supported • Regularly monitor policy implementation **BELIEVE:** • Local school governance is critical for ensuring the success of all students • Local school boards can positively impact teaching and learning • The actions and beliefs of board members are critical for district success

Connecting with the community and building the public will to improve achievement:
Establishing meaningful relationships and mutual partnerships with parents, community members, and groups or businesses within the community
	KNOW:
	• Understand the importance of the school and community connections
	• Understand there are different levels of community connection
	  • Informed
	  • Input
	  • Involved
	  • Engaged
	• Understand the board's role for ensuring the community helps decide and communicate what needs to change, why it needs to change, what can be expected, what it will take to get there
	DO:
	• Value the important role of the community in helping the district meet its improvement goals
	• Value the role of the school within the larger community (among other child-serving organizations) and understand the specific contribution of each organization
	• Consistently communicate the case for change and the vision for the future
	• Consistently communicate what the district is trying to improve, specific expectations, what the district is doing to reach the expectations, and how the community can help
	BELIEVE:
	• The school exists to serve the community
	• The community must be a partner with the school district in order for the school to improve learning for all students

through the organization since the actual work of educating is done by others. How to create these processes and how to shape them to affect the conditions for productive change and, in turn, the learning environment is just starting to become clear through the continuing Lighthouse research.

School boards matter. Solving the problems of public education depends upon the leadership of public schools (Waters and Grubb, 2004; Waters et al., 2003). Issues affecting the conditions of schools that enable productive change are issues of policy. School boards are critical players in the school change process and must be active leaders on behalf of the students in their schools. Without effective school board leadership, systemic change becomes impossible, and improvement in student achievement remains episodic, with only pockets of excellence sprinkled throughout public schools and school districts. How board-superintendent teams understand and carry out their roles can make the difference between dysfunctional leadership teams incapable of leading change and highly effective leadership teams that build districtwide capacity to ensure every student succeeds.

A great deal is already known about what it takes to improve the achievement of all students in classrooms and schools. Numerous studies and books have been written describing the characteristics of more effective learning environments. Numerous examples of schools that beat the odds and produce high levels of learning for all students exist. However, less is known about what it takes to lead an entire district to high levels of learning and sustain a culture focused on excellence and equity. Until recently, school boards have been excluded from the school reform literature and excluded from consideration as a unit of change or a key lever in the change process. This study and those that follow should open the door to understanding the critical leadership role of school governance. This understanding can then help establish the processes for creating conditions for productive change that impact the teaching and learning environment throughout the school district and, in turn, impact the learning of students in schools.

REFERENCES

Bloom, B. 1984. The 2 sigma problem: The search for methods of instruction as effective as one-to-one tutoring. *Educational Leadership* 41:4–17.

Brookover, W., J. H. Schwitzer, J. M. Schneider, C. H. Beady, P. K. Flood, and J. M. Wisenbaker. 1978. Elementary school social climate and school achievement. *American Educational Research Journal* 15 (2): 301–318.

Brophy, J., and T. Good. 1986. *Teacher behavior and student achievement: Handbook of research on teaching.* New York: Macmillan.

Campbell, D. W., and D. Greene. 1994. Defining the leadership role of school boards in the 21st century. *Phi Delta Kappan* 75 (5): 391.

Carol, L., L. Cunningham, J. Danzberger, M. Kirst, B. McCloud, and M. Usdan. 1986. *School boards: Strengthening grass roots leadership*. Washington, DC: Institute for Educational Leadership.

Coleman, P., and L. LaRocque. 1990. *Struggling to be good enough: Administrative practices and school district ethos*. Basingstoke, Hampshire: Falmer Press.

Danzberger, J. P., L. Carol, L. Cunningham, M. Kirst, B. McCloud, and M. Usdan. 1987. School boards: The forgotten players on the education team. *Phi Delta Kappan* 68 (1): 53–59.

Danzberger, J. P., M. W. Kirst, and M. D. Usdan. 1992. *Governing public schools: New times, new requirements*. Washington, DC: Institute for Educational Leadership.

Delagardelle, M. L. 2006. Roles and responsibilities of local school board members in relation to student achievement. PhD diss., Iowa State University.

Eadie, D. 2003. *Eight keys to an extraordinary board-superintendent partnership*. Lanham, MD: Scarecrow Education.

Edelstein, F. 2006. Mayoral leadership and involvement: An action guide for success. Paper presented at the U.S. Conference of Mayors, Washington, DC.

Glickman, C. D. 1993. *Renewing America's schools: A guide for school-based action*. San Francisco: Jossey-Bass.

Greenwood, D. J., and M. Levin. 1998. *Introduction to action research: Social research for social change*. Thousand Oaks, CA: Sage.

Harkreader, S., and J. Weathersby. 1998. Staff development and student achievement: Making the connection in Georgia schools. Paper prepared for The Council for School Performance.

Harrison, S. 2005. Failing schools takeover targets. *Miami Herald*, March 31.

Henderson, E., J. Henry, J. B. Saks, and A. Wright. 2001a. *Team leadership for student achievement*. Alexandria, VA: National School Boards Association.

———. 2001b. *Team leadership for student achievement: The roles of the school board and the superintendent*. Alexandria, VA: National School Boards Association.

Joyce, B., E. Calhoun, and D. Hopkins. 1999. *The new structure of school improvement*. Philadelphia: Open University Press.

Kossan, P. 2005. State decides to take over 11 "failing" schools. *Arizona Republic*, March 29.

Kowalski, T. J. 2006. *The school superintendent: Theory, practice, and cases*. 2nd ed. Thousand Oaks, CA: Sage.

LaRocque, L., and P. Coleman. 1993. The politics of excellence: Trustee leadership and school district ethos. *Alberta Journal of Educational Research* 39 (4): 449–475.

Mortimore, P., P. Sammons, L. Stoll, D. Lewis, and R. Ecob. 1988. *School matters: The junior years*. London: Open Books.

Paige, R. 2002. School boards: Holding the power and bearing the responsibility for educational leadership. Paper presented at the National School Boards Association Annual Conference—The Second Annual Jacqueline P. Danzberger Memorial Lecture, New Orleans.

Resnick, M. S. 1999. *Effective school governance: A look at today's practice and tomorrow's promise*. Descriptive Report. Denver: Education Commission of the States.

Sanders, W., and J. Rivers. 1996. *Cumulative and residual effects of teachers on future academic achievement.* Knoxville: University of Tennessee Value-Added Research and Assessment Center.

Sarason, S. B. 1997. *How schools might be governed and why.* New York: Teachers College Press.

Schlechty, P. C. 1992. Deciding the fate of local control. *The American School Board Journal* 178 (11): 27–29.

Simon, T. R., ed. 1986. *Fundamentals of school board membership.* Trenton: New Jersey School Boards Association.

Slavin, R., N. Madden, L. Dolan, and B. Wasik. 1996. *Every child, every school: Success for all.* Thousand Oaks, CA: Corwin Press.

Thevenot, B. 2005. School system is declared broke: Audit finds it went under during the past fiscal year. *Times-Picayune,* March 29.

Twentieth Century Fund/Danforth Foundation. 1992. *Facing the challenge: The report of the Twentieth Century Fund task force on school governance.* New York: Twentieth Century Fund Press.

Wang, M. C., G. D. Haertel, and H. J. Walberg. 1993. Toward a knowledge base for school learning. *Review of Educational Research* 63 (3): 249–294.

Waters, T., and S. Grubb. 2004. *The leadership we need.* Aurora, CO: Mid-Continent Research for Education and Learning.

Waters, T., R. Marzano, and B. McNulty. 2003. Balanced leadership: What 30 years of research tells us about the effect of leadership on student achievement. http://www.mcrel.org/topics/productDetail.asp?productID=144 (accessed 2005).

Weil, M., B. Marshalek, A. Mittman, J. Murphy, P. Hallinger, and J. Pruyen. 1984. Effective and typical schools: How different are they? Paper presented at the annual meeting of the American Educational Research Association, New Orleans.

Wong, K. K., and F. X. Shen. 2003. Measuring the effectiveness of city and state takeover as a school reform strategy. *Peabody Journal of Education* 78 (4): 89–119.

11

School Reform, Civic Engagement, and School Board Leadership

Theodore J. Kowalski

The information age was shaped by the rapid development of information and communication technologies and the emergence of a global economy. As America moved away from its long-standing manufacturing base, business and government elites expressed concerns that the country's unchallenged preeminence in commerce, industry, science, and technological innovation was being diminished. By 1983, they publicly declared the nation's welfare was at risk and blamed public schools for having contributed significantly to this national crisis (Hlebowitsh, 1990). More precisely, critics claimed the performance of public schools had reached a new low, an accusation that went virtually unchallenged even though no evidence was provided to support it (Hawley, 1988).

State-level change initiatives prevalent between 1983 and 1989, commonly referred to as *intensification mandates*, reflected an opinion that schools would improve appreciably if students were simply forced to work more diligently. Most education scholars were skeptical, primarily because they regarded school performance as an intricate entanglement of social, economic, and education variables. Their doubts, however, were ignored by most policy makers—that is, until it became apparent that intensification mandates would not be sufficiently effective.

By 1990, it became apparent that elites and educators had dissimilar convictions about school improvement strategies. The former viewed schooling primarily through an economic lens, a perspective that encouraged them to focus solely on excellence. The latter viewed schooling primarily through a social lens, a perspective that encouraged them to focus on excellence and equity (Kowalski, 2003). As educators achieved a greater voice in reform debates, they were able to make two essential arguments: *national and state reform initiatives would have limited success because the needs of students across schools differed substantially* (Metz, 1990) and *schools would not improve appreciably unless they were restructured* (Bauman, 1996). These two contentions unavoidably spawned questions about local district governance, a topic the elites literally ignored during the 1980s (e.g., Danzberger, Kirst, and Usdan, 1992).

The overarching purpose here is to examine linkages among school reform, citizen involvement, and the emerging need for school board leadership. These associations are framed by three conclusions:

1. School reform has been and continues to be an evolutionary process. Current efforts constitute a form of directed autonomy—a concept in which state government (a) sets broad improvement goals, (b) provides leeway to local officials (i.e., so they can determine how to meet the benchmarks), and (c) then holds local officials accountable for outcomes (Weiler, 1990).

2. Moving the locus of reform to the district level is supported by political and pedagogical realities. Politically, agreement on needed change is unlikely if employees and other stakeholders are excluded from school improvement discourse and decision making. Educationally, school improvement efforts are unlikely to raise school productivity significantly unless they address dissimilarities in student needs, across and even within local districts.

3. Pursuing reform locally should entail deliberative democracy—a process in which stakeholders collaboratively engage in visioning and planning.

Based on these conclusions, the argument is made that school board members should exercise leadership in revitalizing civic engagement in their communities. More precisely, they should facilitate collaboration, a process of deliberative democracy requiring them to use interpersonal communication.

The rationale for board members assuming a facilitative role begins with an analysis of three facets of board member behavior: individual orientations toward being a board member, diverse role expectations, and a board member's disposition toward being adaptive. Then the evolution of the modern school reform era is summarized demonstrating how evolving strategies have de facto resulted in new expectations for board members to be facilitative. Last, school board leadership in collaborative engagement is examined with emphasis placed on relational communication.

PO + RUA + AD = Behavior

Where:

PO = Personal orientation to being a board member (i.e., viewing board members more like trustees or more like delegates)

RUA = Role understanding and acceptance (i.e., being able to perform instrumental, representative, and facilitative roles as appropriate and necessary)

AD = Adaptations (i.e., the ability to alter orientation and the willingness to transition among role conceptualizations)

Figure 11.1.   Understanding Board Member Behavior

BOARD MEMBER BEHAVIOR

Generally, a board member's behavior is determined by an elaborate mix of the three factors displayed in Figure 11.1. The first dynamic, *role orientation*, is comprised of personal attributes, such as values, beliefs, needs, and ambitions. The second, *role conceptualizations*, is comprised of societal and institutional expectations that outline what board members are expected to do. The third, *ability and disposition*, determines whether individual board members are able and willing to change their personal behavior. Collectively the three variables help us to understand individual board member behavior.

Personal Orientation

Despite having received a great deal of attention in the literature, confusion and controversy over the ideal role of school board members has been prevalent (Campbell and Greene, 1994). As an extension of state government, local boards historically have had two broad responsibilities. The first has an external orientation (i.e., toward the community) and involves making decisions that represent the will of district residents, especially in matters not addressed directly by law and federal or state policy. The other has an internal orientation (i.e., toward the school district) and ensures administrative control of the district (through the office of the superintendent), especially in relation to fiscal control (e.g., budgets and taxes) and accountability (e.g., evaluation of learning outcomes) (Campbell et al., 1990). The National School Boards Association (2007) provides more specific role expectations that are identified as eight key actions: vision, standards, assessment, accountability, alignment, climate, collaborative relationships, and continuous improvement.

Trustee   **Delegate**

Focused on serving   Focused on serving
the needs of all   personal needs or
stakeholders and   the needs of
the general welfare   special interest
of the community;   groups; makes key
makes key   decisions politically
decisions rationally

Figure 11.2.   Board Member Orientation

Despite the existence of role expectations, overwhelming evidence indicates that many board members ignore or reject them, both with respect to what they do and how they behave. Behavioral dissimilarities are partly explained by personal orientation differences. As used here, an orientation refers to a general disposition toward school board service. Orientations are more easily understood when they are placed on the continuum shown in Figure 11.2.

At one extreme is a *trustee orientation* and at the other is a *delegate orientation*. The former characterizes board members who (a) act in the public interest rather than the selective interests of individuals and groups, (b) govern rationally rather than politically, and (c) restrict their involvement in district matters to setting policy (Zeigler, Jennings, and Peak, 1974). The latter characterizes board members who (a) act on the basis of personal interests or the interests of special groups, (b) govern politically, and (c) do not restrict their actions to policy making (McCurdy, 1992). Actually, few board members are completely delegates or trustees; rather, board members are inclined to behave in accordance with one extreme or the other.

Even before 1900, the literature presented the trustee orientation as the ideal, yet the concept was frequently misunderstood or rejected. Studying relationships between governance and school reform, Danzberger and Usdan (1994) concluded that school boards had become progressively more political and more directly involved in administrative functions after the 1960s. An intricate mix of factors elevated political behavior, but two of them—changing demographics and a growing distrust of government officials—ostensibly were the most influential. Since 1950, the population in many school districts has increased, gotten older, and become more racially/culturally diverse (Kowalski, 2008). This demographic pattern has caused philosophical and political fragmentation—a condition in which special interest groups compete with each other in an effort to satisfy dissimilar needs and wants (Cooper, Fusarelli, and Randall, 2004).

Fragmentation usually results in a confrontational approach to policy making, and this tactic incrementally decreases the public's confidence in

Instrumental Role

Focus on enforcement of
laws and state policy;
concerned with fiduciary
responsibilities and
accountability

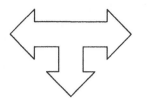

Representative Role

Focus on representing
stakeholders in making
key decisions; concerned
with providing a
representative form of
democratic governance

Facilitative Role

Focus on engaging all stakeholders in
making key decisions; concerned with
open communication allowing citizens
state, test, and debate values and ideas

Figure 11.3.   Board Member Role Conceptualizations

elected officials and professional administrators (Cooper, Bryer, and Meek, 2006). Studying New Jersey school board members, Greene (1990) found positive associations between board member political activity and two district variables (a high level of electoral competition and political complexity) and one personal variable (a board member's intentions to run for re-election). Based on his findings, he concluded that political realities faced by board members in many districts either encouraged them to adopt delegate-type behaviors or reinforced such behaviors.

Role Conceptualizations

Role conceptualizations also influence behavior. Whereas orientations are personal, conceptualizations are societal and organizational (Hanson, 2003). They are developed by a mix of state laws and local values; and since values within individual communities are increasingly disparate, role expectations gradually have become more ambiguous. For example, some citizens want board members to lead while others prefer they micromanage. Though role expectations are intended to be general—that is, they are neither absolute (Yukl, 2002) nor comprehensive (Kowalski, 2005)—they almost always influence behavior.

Over time, three distinct board member roles have emerged reflecting contemporary social, economic, and political realties. Shown in Figure 11.3, they are defined as follows:

1. *Facilitative role.* This perspective dates back to the beginning of public education in America and reflects the cherished value of liberty. Within a context of local control, board members were expected to work with

and not on behalf of constituents. Most notably, board members were expected to facilitate citizen participation, ensuring that stakeholders could directly influence important decisions. This conceptualization waned in popularity after school districts got larger, communities became more diverse, and other values, such as efficiency and equality, attenuated the importance of liberty (King, Swanson, and Sweetland, 2003). However, many small, rural districts continued to emphasize the facilitative role during much of the 20th century.[1]

2. *Representative role.* This expectation emerged as school districts became larger and more complex organizations, especially after 1900. The role directed board members to act on behalf of stakeholders, since participatory democracy had become impractical and too contentious (Callahan, 1962). Philosophically, this conceptualization is premised on three assumptions: (a) board members should behave as trustees; (b) they should have the knowledge and skills to make objective and effective decisions; (c) district stakeholders should accept and support decisions made on their behalf (Cronin, 1965).

3. *Instrumental role.* This expectation emerged as the governance of public education became more centralized. It emphasizes that school boards are legally an extension of state government, and board members are agents of state government. As such, boards have enforcement (e.g., ensuring that laws and state policy are followed) and fiduciary (e.g., setting tax rates, approving budgets, protecting public investments) responsibilities. Though aspects of this role date back to the emergence of state departments of education in the 19th century (Spring, 2008), the instrumental perspective became most prominent from 1950 to 1990, a period when landmark legal decisions, civil rights legislation, and state intensification mandates resulted in greater centralization of authority (Kowalski, 2006).[2]

Though these conceptualizations are distinct, they are not necessarily incompatible. The challenge for board members is not to select one role over the others but rather to be able to transition among them as situations require.

Ability and Disposition

Knowledge, skills, and attitudes also influence behavior. Ability pertains to knowledge and skills; that is, they constitute one's *capacity* to do what is expected. Dispositions are philosophical and anchored in values and beliefs (Guest, Hersey, and Blanchard, 1986); they constitute one's *willingness* to do what is expected. Ability and disposition are distinct factors. Thus, possessing knowledge does not ensure it will be used; conversely, having the will to do something is insufficient without the requisite knowledge and skills.

Research on organizations reveals that executives often err by targeting group behavior as the initial stage for change. As an example, the top executive determines that employees need to change the way they handle customer complaints. He sends a memorandum to employees outlining a new complaint procedure and orders them to begin implementing it on a given date. This approach to change is predicated on two assumptions: the employees have the capacity to follow the directive and they will act rationally to comply with it. However, studies of organizational behavior reveal that neither assumption is totally accurate (Hanson, 2003; Hoy and Miskel, 2005). In the case of school boards, for example, individual members differ substantially with respect to personal knowledge and skills, and individual members have the latitude to behave politically. Thus, efforts to alter the group behavior of school boards logically begin with efforts to change individual member behavior (Guest et al., 1986).

MODERN SCHOOL REFORM AND BOARD MEMBERS

The National Commission on Excellence in Education (1983) summarized its negative evaluation of public education in the highly publicized report *A Nation at Risk*. The authors asserted:

> If an unfriendly power had attempted to impose on America the mediocre educational performance that exists today, we might well have viewed it as an act of war. As it stands, we have allowed this to happen to ourselves. We have even squandered the gains in achievement made in the wake of the Sputnik challenge. Moreover, we have dismantled essential support systems which helped make those gains possible. We have, in effect, been committing an act of unthinking, unilateral educational disarmament. (National Commission on Excellence in Education, 1983, p. 5)

After the report was published, state government took a more central and active role in public education (Mazzoni, 1994). Would-be reformers intuitively concluded that diminished productivity was due to lazy and unmotivated students. Within two years, they also blamed incompetent teachers for dragging down productivity in public schools. This problem perspective led them to conclude that the negative slide could be reversed rapidly and inexpensively by forcing students and educators to do more of what they were already doing. Objective analysts, however, pointed out that the intensification mandates were largely political in that they were intended to mollify public dissatisfaction; consequently, the mandates rarely were connected to state funding policy. When confronted with this inconsistency, intensification proponents rationalized that reform could be achieved without additional funding—an explanation for which they provided little or no evidence (Hertert, 1996).

Most of the initial mandates, though state-centered, actually were developed by national networks consisting of a mix of elected officials and corporate executives, and they basically ignored the relevance of district governance (Wirt and Kirst, 1997). Traditional education interest groups and education scholars had relatively little influence on reform policy during the 1980s (Feir, 1995). School boards, administrators, and teachers were treated as instruments of change; they were directed to enforce mandates but not allowed to construct, critique, modify, or replace them (Kowalski, Petersen, and Fusarelli, 2007). By being indifferent to the minds and hearts of educators, the reformers actually encouraged principals and teachers to scuttle reform initiatives that conflicted with prevailing school cultures (Fullan, 2000).

Coercion has never worked well in public education, because reliance on laws, regulations, and mandates flies in the face of conventional wisdom (Finn, 1991). Educators have proven repeatedly that they can derail most mandates,[3] and their resentment toward being treated as nonprofessionals often prompted them to do just that. By the late 1980s, it was apparent that schools more often changed the mandates than the mandates changed schools (Tyack and Cuban, 1995).

Other factors also attenuated state-centered reforms promulgated during the 1980s. The following are the more prominent ones:

1. The problem responsible for the perceived decline in school productivity had been framed incorrectly. According to Cuban (1988; 1990), those setting the reform agenda viewed education problems as simple and solvable when in fact they are persistent dilemmas requiring hard choices involving conflicting values.
2. Reformers relied on myths to justify their biases. As an example, they frequently condemned the preparation of education professionals and the teaching profession's knowledge based on perspectives that were at best narrow and at worst incorrect (Pogrow, 1996).
3. Reformers thought that staff development would ensure that educators would implement their prescribed changes. However, this activity is only effective when the change initiatives being promoted align with educator values and beliefs (Fullan, 2000; Louis, Toole, and Hargreaves, 1999).
4. Many reforms were contradictory in nature (Orlich, 1989), disjointed, and unrelated to philosophical discourse about the purposes of schooling (Soltis, 1988), a condition that actually fueled community fragmentation (Fullan, 2000).
5. A national shift in civic engagement occurred after 1950 (Cooper et al., 2006), resulting in a loss of social capital (Putnam, 2000) and a

declining trust in government (Nye, 1997). Thus, state reform mandates often encountered political resistance from citizens who disagreed with and distrusted "big" government.

6. The reformers were either ignorant of or indifferent toward evidence indicating that student performance in schools was tempered by social and personal conditions. As an example, they rarely considered how circumstances such as hunger or abuse prevented learning (Smrekar and Mawhinney, 1999).

7. Perhaps most noteworthy, the reformers failed to consider the critical nexus between change and school culture. This oversight was explained by noted psychologist Seymour Sarason (1996). After studying public schools in the early 1970s and then again in the early 1990s, he concluded that little improvement had been achieved over two decades. The inertia, he concluded, was due to a pervasive, long-standing, negative institutional culture (i.e., a set of shared values and beliefs that influence teacher behavior). Reformers as well as educators, he pointed out, did not comprehend the power of school culture to thwart change. The disassociation between state mandates and school culture largely explains why the intensification strategy had little positive effect (Louis et al., 1999).

After studying these and other explanations as to why reforms had failed, several scholars (e.g., Henkin, 1993; Murphy, 1994) concluded that the locus of school improvement needed to shift and new strategies had to be deployed. They offered three primary suggestions:

1. Reform strategies had to be based on both vast differences in real student needs and resource disparities across districts and schools.
2. Reforms needed to be forged in the context of existing school climates so institutional culture could be diagnosed and improved.
3. School board members, superintendents, and principals had to provide leadership for school improvement.

These recommendations gradually gained acceptance after 1990, partly because they are supported by empirical evidence and partly because the political coercive strategies preceding them proved to be ineffective.

Currently, contemporary reform initiatives display a mix of the three strategies described below and outlined in Figure 11.4:

1. *State deregulation.* This tactic is nested in the reality that real needs differ across local districts and individual schools. It is based on the concept of directed autonomy described previously.
2. *Decentralization.* This tactic promotes flexibility and involves a redistribution of authority and legitimate power. It is based on the prem-

State deregulation
- State sets broad improvement goals
- Relaxes state mandates allowing local officials to tailor reforms to specific needs
- Holds local officials accountable for outcomes

Decentralization
- Authority is shared
- Citizens and educators are given greater power to influence decisions
- Intended to improve decision quality and acceptance

School restructuring
- Improvement requires major changes in schools, especially to institutional culture
- Requires objective analysis of operations in relation to outcomes
- Redesigns are determined by specific student/community needs

Figure 11.4.   Contemporary Reform Strategies

ise that reforms should be developed by educators and policy makers who are close to the teachers and students who will be affected (Brown, 1991). This strategy is epitomized by school-based councils, a concept that gained popularity in the late 1980s (Kowalski, 2003).

3. *School restructuring.* This tactic focuses on the reconfiguration of schools, most specifically, revamping school culture (Kowalski et al., 2007), and it is based on the conviction that schools are complex, unpredictable, and dynamic institutions (Louis et al., 1999). Therefore, organizational and operational structures need to be redesigned and power redistributed, most notably to ensure teacher professionalism and community involvement (Bauman, 1996).

Each of the three strategies has consequences for school boards. State deregulation requires local boards to forge (or at least approve) school improvement policy. Decentralization requires local boards to redistribute power and authority so that employees and other stakeholders can participate in making critical school improvement decisions. Restructuring encourages (or in some states, requires) local boards to first engage in collaborative visioning and planning and then to attain necessary levels of political and economic support for implementing needed changes.

BOARD LEADERSHIP

Leadership has been defined in many ways. A professor, for instance, asked his school administration students over a three-year period to define the term, and he received about 50 different definitions (Glasman and Glasman, 1997). Leadership often has been used incorrectly as a synonym for management. In fact, these two organizational roles are distinctively different. Managers make decisions about *how* things should be done; that is, they focus on controlling and using resources (Hanson, 2003). Leaders, on the other hand, make decisions about *what* should be done to improve an organization; that is, the role is focused on more abstract and intricate tasks such as visioning, planning, and consensus building (Kowalski, 2003). In the realm of organizational studies, scholars (e.g., Yukl, 2002) assert that both roles can be and often are assumed by executives (or administrators).

Clearly, local boards always have had managerial responsibilities and, no doubt, many boards also have engaged in leadership activities. The contemporary notion of board member leadership, however, relates to making choices about what should be done to improve schools. Two facets of this idea, facilitating civic engagement and communicating with the public, are crucial.

Facilitating Civic Engagement

In general terms, facilitation involves providing human and material resources that permit others to complete their assigned responsibilities. In the context of deliberative democracy, the process requires board members to intervene in school improvement planning directly and indirectly. As examples, direct interventions could include (a) setting policy that ensures citizen participation, (b) accommodating civic engagement by providing suitable meeting sites, (c) scheduling public meetings, and (d) moderating discussions at such meetings. Indirect interventions might include (a) promoting citizen involvement in the media and in discussions with stakeholders, (b) building a climate in the district that promotes civic engagement, and (c) serving as a role model for other stakeholders. As described previously, board member roles have two dimensions: knowledge and dispositions. To function appropriately in the facilitative role, board members must have an understanding of deliberative democracy, collaboration, conflict, and consensus building. And once they acquire this knowledge, they must come to believe in and value the processes.

Cooper et al. (2006) believe that minimally, leaders have a responsibility to answer five questions in relation to civic engagement:

1. Who should be involved?
2. Who should initiate the process?
3. Why are citizens given an opportunity to participate?
4. Where will the engagements occur?
5. How will citizens be involved?

Obviously, demographics influence the quantity and quality of facilitation needed, but no school district should dismiss deliberative democracy because of its size. Contrary to popular thought, this concept has been used effectively to construct collaborative visions, even in situations where the targeted population exceeds 100,000 (Weeks, 2000). Equally notable, it can and has failed in very small districts, especially when leadership was missing or insufficient.

Communicating with the Public

The importance of communication is framed by both the present information age and the realization that school reform, school culture, and communication are inextricably linked. Said differently, schools, and especially ineffective schools, do not improve unless their underlying values and beliefs are altered (Hall and Hord, 2001). For example, in a school where educators set low expectations for students, we should not expect improvement unless the values and beliefs underlying the low expectations are identified, challenged, and replaced (Fullan, 2000; Hall and Hord, 2001).

The critical nature of leadership communication in organizational change is well documented across all types of organizations (e.g., D'Aprix, 1996; Goodman, Willis, and Holihan, 1998; Quirke, 1996; Walker, 1997). Even in the realm of private corporations, studies reveal that most embattled CEOs shared a common characteristic—they were poor communicators (Perina, 2002). Studies of school administrators have typically produced the same conclusion (Kowalski, 2005; Kowalski et al., 2007), and scholars writing about civic engagement assert that the communicative behavior of leaders affects the quantity and quality of citizen participation (Cooper et al., 2006).

The instrumental role of board members has neither required nor encouraged civic engagement. Instead, it focuses on management decisions, and as such, it does not require two-way, open communication. Managers typically rely on a classical communication model, one in which instructions and commands are transmitted down the chain of command and only from one person to the person or persons below (Luthans, 1981). Closed, one-way communication is efficient and does build shared understandings (Hoy and Miskel, 2005).

The representative role encourages but does not require civic engagement. As noted previously, behavior in this role depends on personal orientation. Delegate-like board members typically communicate unevenly because they typically provide more information to their supporters than they provide to others. Board members with a political orientation typically treat information as a source of power, and thus, they use it to enhance their

Role conceptualization	Open, two-way communication
Instrumental role	Neither required nor encouraged
Representative role	Encouraged but not required
Facilitative role	Encouraged and required

Figure 11.5. Board Role Conceptualizations and Open, Two-Way Communicative Behavior

political strength (Kowalski, 2005). Conversely, trustee-like board members may be more likely to engage in open, two-way communication.

Only the facilitative role encourages and requires open, two-way, and continuous communication, because this communicative behavior is essential to civic engagement (Kowalski, 1995; 2003). Deliberative democracy in relation to school reform requires board members and superintendents to engage stakeholders in discussion of seemingly intractable governance, power, and organizational design problems (Carlson, 1996; Heckman, 1993). Moreover, these discussions must be conducted in social-political environments where many stakeholders, including principals and teachers, favor reform generally but resist change when it affects them (Sarason, 1996; Streitmatter, 1994). A comparison of role conceptualizations and communicative behavior is shown in Figure 11.5.

When facilitation is interfaced with communication, the need for *relational communication* emerges. This concept pertains to the manner in which information is exchanged and to perceptions of the exchange (Littlejohn, 1992), and it requires both of these aspects to be interpersonal. Interpersonal communication is a two-way process wherein persons influence one another's behavior over and above their organizational role, rank, and status (Cappella, 1987); in essence, all involved parties behave similarly to minimize power and authority differences that exist between or among them (Burgoon and Hale, 1984). In addition to being interpersonal, relational communication is symmetrical, meaning it is intended to benefit all parties involved (Grunig, 1989).

Complementary communication is the opposite of relational communication; it is one-way, directive, coercive, and designed to reduce opportunities for mutual influence and information sharing (McGregor, 1967). Its intent is to maximize differences among people, especially in relation to one person being dominant and other person(s) being submissive (Burgoon and Hale, 1984). Differences between these communicative styles are quite apparent; for example, board members exercising power over citizens communicate differently than do board members exercising power with citizens. When power is exercised collectively, the board member is a citizen acting collaboratively with other citizens. When power is exercised over citizens, the board member is an official directing others.

Regrettably, relational communication does not develop naturally. In fact, many highly educated individuals, and especially those in professions and management positions, are inclined to use complementary communication in an effort to underscore their legitimate (position-based) power and intellectual superiority. Complementary communication is normative in highly bureaucratic organizations because legitimate power is commonly used to control subordinate behavior (Hanson, 2003).

Engaging in relational communication, like other behaviors, depends on knowledge, skills, and dispositions. This point is evident in the concept's three domains.

1. *Cognitive domain.* To be an effective communicator, one must demonstrate that he or she knows and understands the basic field of communication (Larson et al., 1978). As an example, board members should have conceptual knowledge about the various ways that communication can occur and about the potential effects of their communicative behavior choices.

2. *Psychomotor domain.* To engage in relational communication, board members must be able to demonstrate their ability to apply communicative knowledge and understanding (Weimann et al., 1997). Application examples include the ability to encode and decode messages, use correct grammar, listen effectively, apply principles of nonverbal communication, communicate in context, work effectively with print and broadcast media, build credibility and trust, resolve conflict, and use appropriate technology to facilitate communication.

3. *Affective domain.* To apply relational communication, individuals must possess supportive attitudes and feelings about the process (McCroskey, 1982). This philosophical component is directly related to role orientation. As an example, trustees are more likely to value relational communication than are delegates. Spitzberg and Cupach (1984) describe this domain in terms of an individual's desire to communicate appropriately and effectively (in other words, personal motivation).

The nexus between relational communication and deliberative democracy is axiomatic. Having citizens state, test, and debate their values and beliefs publicly is essential but difficult and often contentious (Wirt and Kirst, 1997). For this level of discourse to occur, citizens must believe that board members value their opinions and value democratic decision making.

SYNTHESIS

The evolution of school reform strategies and societal transitions over the past three decades has placed school boards in a pivotal but difficult position. A mix of state deregulation, decentralization, and school restructuring strategies results in expectations that school improvement will be designed, carried out, and evaluated at the local level. Equally important, boards are expected to engage school employees and other stakeholders in meaningful discussions about what should be done to improve schools.

Given the current emphasis on local reform and civic engagement, the logical question is: *Why not reconfigure school boards by altering state laws?* This query actually was addressed about 15 years ago. One prominent proposal called for school boards to be transformed into educational policy boards. Recommended in two national studies issued in 1992—*Facing the Challenge* (funded by the Twentieth Century Fund and the Danforth Foundation) and *Governing Public Schools* (Danzberger et al., 1992)—it is based on a conclusion that school board members would not provide adequate leadership for school improvement as long as they were spending most of their time dealing with management issues (e.g., bus routes, employment matters, and maintenance issues). Thus, state legislatures were encouraged to enact laws that replaced traditional school boards with policy boards, and the role of the new governing body was defined by three parameters:

1. Policy boards would be restricted to setting broad policy guidelines, overseeing operations, and defining accountability standards.
2. Policy boards would not have quasi-judicial, fiduciary, and management responsibilities.
3. Eligibility standards (e.g., level of education) for serving on a policy board would be higher than those for serving on a school board. (Harrington-Lueker, 1993).

Though thoughtful, this proposal received little support, largely for two reasons. First, many citizens prefer that board members engage in management and oversee administrative decisions (Kowalski, 2001). Second, "school boards are deeply embedded in U.S. political culture, and proposals for radical change in their roles will encounter well-organized grassroots resistance" (Wirt and Kirst, 1997, p. 148). As amending the legal status of boards is highly improbable, change must be accomplished within current parameters of board authority. The logical objective, therefore, is to modify individual board member behavior by providing them with knowledge and by changing their attitudes about school reform and deliberative democracy.

In closing, the objectives here were to describe board member behavior in relation to the forces that produced the current reform environment and to demonstrate that board member leadership in the form of facilitation has become critical to school improvement. Meeting this role expectation requires board members to understand their actual and ideal behavior as facilitators and communicators. Board members also must possess requisite knowledge about and dispositions favorable of deliberative democracy. At the same time, however, they must continue to meet expectations embedded in their instrumental and representative roles. Thus, they must be able and willing to transition among their roles so that they can lead and be trusted while remaining sensitive and responsive to the political will of the people (Wirt and Kirst, 1997).

NOTES

1. A scene from the movie *Hoosiers* exemplifies this condition. In one scene, residents gather in a church and vote on a motion to dismiss the high school basketball coach.

2. Centralization was intended to produce uniformity in compliance with laws, an outcome that reduces the potential for litigation and reduces risk exposure to state government.

3. The two most dramatic changes in public education over the last 100 years have resulted from litigation (school desegregation) and legislation (laws protecting the rights of disabled students). Many analysts conclude these changes endure because of legal penalties for violating them. Conversely, major changes not protected by legal penalties often are resisted and then discarded.

REFERENCES

Bauman, P. C. 1996. *Governing education: Public sector reform or privatization.* Boston: Allyn & Bacon.

Brown, D. J. 1991. *Decentralization: The administrator's guidebook to school district change.* Newbury Park, CA: Corwin.

Burgoon, J. K., and J. L. Hale. 1984. The fundamental topoi of relational communication. *Communication Monographs* 51:193–214.

Callahan, R. E. 1962. *Education and the cult of efficiency.* Chicago: University of Chicago Press.

Campbell, R. F., L. L. Cunningham, R. O. Nystrand, and M. D. Usdan. 1990. *The organization and control of American schools.* 6th ed. Upper Saddle River, NJ: Prentice Hall.

Campbell, R. F., and D. Greene. 1994. Defining the leadership role of school boards in the 21st century. *Phi Delta Kappan* 75 (5): 391–395.

Cappella, J. N. 1987. Interpersonal communication: Definitions and fundamental questions. In *Handbook of communication science*, ed. C. R. Berger and S. H. Chaffee, 184–238. Newbury Park, CA: Sage.

Carlson, R. V. 1996. *Reframing and reform: Perspectives on organization, leadership, and school change.* New York: Longman.

Cooper, B. S., L. D. Fusarelli, and E. V. Randall. 2004. *Better policies, better schools: Theories and applications.* Boston: Allyn & Bacon.

Cooper, T. L., T. A. Bryer, and J. W. Meek. 2006. Citizen-centered collaborative public management. *Public Administration Review,* special issue, 76–88.

Cronin, J. M. 1965. The board of education in the "great cities," 1890–1964. PhD diss., Stanford University.

Cuban, L. 1988. How schools change reforms: Redefining reform success and failure. *Teachers College Record* 99 (3): 453–477.

———. 1990. Reforming again, again, and again. *Educational Researcher* 19 (1): 3–13.

Danzberger, J. P., M. W. Kirst, and M. D. Usdan. 1992. *Governing public schools: New times, new requirements.* Washington, DC: Institute for Educational Leadership.

Danzberger, J. P., and M. D. Usdan. 1994. Local education governance: Perspectives on problems and strategies for change. *Phi Delta Kappan* 75 (5): 366.

D'Aprix, R. 1996. *Communicating for change: Connecting the workplace with the marketplace.* San Francisco: Jossey-Bass.

Feir, R. E. 1995. *Political and social roots of education reform: A look at the states in the mid-1980s.* (ERIC Document Reproduction Service No. ED 385 925)

Finn, C. E. 1991. *We must take charge.* New York: Free Press.

Fullan, M. 2000. The three stories of education reform. *Phi Delta Kappa* 81 (8): 581–584.

Glasman, N. S., and L. D. Glasman. 1997. Connecting the preparation of school leaders to the practice of school leadership. *Peabody Journal of Education* 72 (2): 3–20.

Goodman, M. B., K. E. Willis, and V. C. Holihan. 1998. Communication and change: Effective change communication is personal, global, and continuous. In *Corporate communication for executives,* ed. M. B. Goodman, 37–61. Albany: SUNY Press.

Greene, K. R. 1990. School board members' responsiveness to constituents. *Urban Education* 24 (4): 363–375.

Grunig, J. E., 1989. Symmetrical presuppositions as a framework for public relations theory. In *Public relations theory,* ed. C. H. Botan, 17–44. Hillsdale, NJ: Lawrence Erlbaum.

Guest, R. H., P. Hersey, and K. H. Blanchard. 1986. *Organizational change through effective leadership.* 2nd ed. Englewood Cliffs, NJ: Prentice Hall.

Hall, G. E. and S. M. Hord. 2001. *Implementing change: Patterns, principles, and potholes.* Boston: Allyn & Bacon.

Hanson, E. M. 2003. *Educational administration and organizational behavior.* 5th ed. Boston: Allyn & Bacon.

Harrington-Lueker, D. 1993. Reconsidering school boards. *American School Board Journal* 180 (2): 30–36.

Hawley, W. D. 1988. Missing pieces in the educational reform agenda: Or, why the first and second waves may miss the boat. *Educational Administration Quarterly* 24 (4): 416–437.

Heckman, P. E. 1993. School restructuring in practice: Reckoning with the culture of school. *International Journal of Educational Reform* 2 (3): 263–272.

Henkin, A. B. 1993. Social skills of superintendents: A leadership requisite in restructured schools. *Educational Research Quarterly* 16 (4): 15–30.

Hertert, L. 1996. Systemic school reform in the 1990s: A local perspective. *Educational Policy* 10 (3): 379–398.

Hlebowitsh, P. S. 1990. Playing power politics: How a nation at risk achieved its national stature. *Journal of Research and Development in Education* 23:82–88.

Hoy, W. K., and C. G. Miskel. 2005. *Educational administration: Theory, research, and practice.* 8th ed. New York: McGraw-Hill.

King, R., A. Swanson, and S. Sweetland. 2003. *School finance: Achieving high standards with equity and efficiency.* 3rd ed. Boston: Allyn & Bacon.

Kowalski, T. J. 1995. *Keepers of the flame: Contemporary urban superintendents.* Thousand Oaks, CA: Corwin.

———. 2001. The future of local district governance: Implications for board members and superintendents. In *Advances in research and theories of school management and educational policy,* ed. C. Brunner and L. Björk. Stamford, CT: JAI.

———. 2003. *Contemporary school administration: An introduction.* 2nd ed. Boston: Allyn & Bacon.

———. 2005. Evolution of the school superintendent as communicator. *Communication Education* 54 (2): 101–117.

———. 2006. *The school superintendent: Theory, practice, and cases.* 2nd ed. Thousand Oaks, CA: Sage.

———. 2008. *Public relations in schools.* 4th ed. Upper Saddle River, NJ: Prentice Hall.

Kowalski, T. J., G. J. Petersen, and L. D. Fusarelli. 2007. *Effective communication for school administrators: An imperative in an information age.* Lanham, MD: Rowman & Littlefield.

Larson, C. E., P. M. Backlund, M. K. Redmond, and A. Barbour. 1978. *Assessing communicative competence.* Falls Church, VA: Speech Communication Association and ERIC.

Littlejohn, S. W. 1992. *Theories of human communication.* 4th ed. Belmont, CA: Wadsworth.

Louis, K. S., J. Toole, and A. Hargreaves. 1999. Rethinking school improvement. In *Handbook of research on educational administration,* 2nd ed., ed. J. Murphy and K. S. Louis, 251–276. San Francisco: Jossey-Bass.

Luthans, F. 1981. *Organizational behavior.* 3rd ed. New York: McGraw-Hill.

Mazzoni, T. L. 1994. State policy-making and school reform: Influences and influentials. *Journal of Education Policy* 9 (5–6): 53–73.

McCroskey, J. C. 1982. Communication competence and performance: A research and pedagogical perspective. *Communication Education* 31 (1): 1–7.

McCurdy, J. 1992. *Building better board-administrator relations.* Alexandria, VA: American Association of School Administrators.

McGregor, D. 1967. *The professional manager.* New York: McGraw-Hill.

Metz, M. H. 1990. Hidden assumptions preventing real reform: Some missing elements in the educational reform movement. In *Education reform: Making sense of it all,* ed. S. Bacharach, 141–154. Boston: Allyn & Bacon.

Murphy, J. 1994. The changing role of the superintendency in restructuring districts in Kentucky. *School Effectiveness and School Improvement* 5 (4): 349–375.

National Commission on Excellence in Education. 1983. *A nation at risk: The imperative for education reform.* Washington, DC: National Commission on Excellence in Education.

National School Boards Association. 2007. Key work of school board members. http://www.nsba.org/site/page.asp?TRACKID=&CID=121&DID=8799 (accessed July 30, 2007).

Nye, J. S. 1997. The decline of confidence in government. In *Why people don't trust government*, ed. J. S. Nye, P. D. Zelikow, and D. C. King, 1–18. Cambridge, MA: Harvard University Press.

Orlich, D. C. 1989. Education reforms: Mistakes, misconceptions, miscues. *Phi Delta Kappan* 70 (7): 512–517.

Perina, K. 2002. When CEOs self-destruct. *Psychology Today* 35 (5): 16.

Pogrow, S. 1996. Reforming the wannabe reformers: Why education reforms almost always end up making things worse. *Phi Delta Kappan* 77 (10): 656–663.

Putnam, R. D. 2000. *Bowling alone: The collapse and revival of American community.* New York: Simon & Schuster.

Quirke, B. 1996. *Communicating corporate change.* New York: McGraw-Hill.

Sarason, S. B. 1996. *Revisiting "the culture of the school and the problem of change."* New York: Teachers College Press.

Smrekar, C. E., and H. B. Mawhinney. 1999. Integrated services: Challenges to linking schools, families, and communities. In *Handbook of research on educational administration*, 2nd ed., ed. J. Murphy and K. S. Louis, 443–462. San Francisco: Jossey-Bass.

Soltis, J. F. 1988. Reform or reformation? *Educational Administration Quarterly* 24 (3): 241–245.

Spitzberg, B. H., and W. R. Cupach. 1984. *Interpersonal communication competence.* Beverly Hills, CA: Sage.

Spring, J. H. 2008. *American education.* 13th ed. New York: McGraw-Hill.

Streitmatter, J. 1994. *Toward gender equity in the classroom: Everyday teachers' beliefs and practices.* Albany: SUNY Press.

Tyack, D. B., and L. Cuban. 1995. *Tinkering toward utopia: A century of public school reform.* Cambridge, MA: Harvard University Press.

Walker, G. 1997. Communication in leadership. *Communication Management* 1 (4): 22–27.

Weeks, E. C. 2000. The practice of deliberative democracy: Results from four large-scale trials. *Public Administration Review* 40 (4): 360–373.

Weiler, H. N. 1990. Comparative perspectives on educational decentralization: An exercise in contradiction? *Educational Evaluation and Policy Analysis* 12 (4): 433–448.

Wiemann, J. M., J. Takai, H. Ota, and M. O. Wiemann. 1997. A relational model of communication competence. In *Emerging theories of human communication*, ed. B. Kovacic, 25–44. Albany: SUNY Press.

Wirt, F. M., and M. W. Kirst. 1997. *The political dynamics of American education.* Berkeley, CA: McCuthcan.

Yukl, G. 2002. *Leadership in organizations.* 5th ed. Upper Saddle River, NJ: Prentice Hall.

Zeigler, L. H., M. K. Jennings, and W. G. Peak. 1974. *Governing American schools: Political interaction in local school districts.* North Scituate, MA: Duxbury.

VI

RELEVANCE: SCHOOL BOARD INFLUENCE ON STUDENT ACHIEVEMENT

12

School Board Politics and Student Achievement

Thomas L. Alsbury

School boards are one of the last remaining examples of local democracy in action and represent a uniquely American institution (Twentieth Century Fund, 1992). However, some researchers have suggested that boards are so disconnected from the schoolhouse and citizen involvement in board elections so minimal that they have become obsolete mechanisms of democracy and have little, if any, influence on student achievement (Whitson, 1998; Wirt and Kirst, 1992). Some have even suggested that increasing the board's role in instructional matters creates an intrusion negatively influencing culture and even leading to a drop in student achievement (Peterson, 2000). However, the National School Boards Foundation (NSBF, 1999), supported by numerous anecdotal case study findings, contends that increasing school board responsibility for maintaining and measuring quality instructional programs has led to improved student success.

School governance researchers continue to seek empirical evidence for a link between school board stability and student achievement gains (Iannaccone and Lutz, 1970; Weninger and Stout, 1989; Wirt and Kirst, 1992). High turnover of school and district leadership has been shown to disrupt districts attempting to implement reform efforts, as a result of a lack of clear and stable direction, policy, goals, and resource allocation (Cunningham and Carter, 1997; Fullan and Miles, 1992; Grady and Bryant, 1989; Kowalski, 1995; Olson, 1995). Despite the movement toward a more centralized governance system and increased incidents of mayoral, city, and state takeovers of school board roles, most states still give significant statutory responsibility over districts to their locally elected school boards.

While no studies have been able to measure a direct link between boards and school improvement, some suggest the most powerful influence comes from the more indirect and difficult-to-measure loss of superintendent and principal morale, security, and continuity, resulting from politically motivated and frequent turnover on boards (Grady and Bryant, 1989; Olson, 1995). Several studies have analyzed how school board member stability can positively influence superintendent leadership, stabilizing mission and policy direction for building leaders and staff, and subsequently affect student achievement (Iannaccone, 1996; Johnson, 1988; Johnson-Howard, 1991; Land, 2002). However, empirical studies linking school boards to student achievement has remained nearly nonexistent.

REVIEWING THE LITERATURE

Overall, few studies have attempted to measure the school board's effectiveness in changing student achievement. This chapter focuses on one recent study (Alsbury, forthcoming) that supports the existence of a connection between school board stability and student achievement. Few studies have attempted to directly measure the influence of school boards on student success, because of the presence of too many unknown and difficult-to-measure intervening variables, and the perceived organizational chasm between boards and students. However, numerous studies have focused on the presence or absence of the supporting components in organizational governance models designed to demonstrate connections between boards and student outcomes.

Studies seeking empirical evidence to support particular governance theories and models have measured political participation at board elections, forced board turnover rates, superintendent–school board relations, and board influence on local policy. In order to better understand how governance models link boards and student achievement, Alsbury sought to test a frequently studied and unique model that highlights the connection between community, boards, and schools: the Dissatisfaction Theory of American Democracy.

SCHOOL GOVERNANCE THEORIES

As noted above, it is assumed by many that school board members do not influence student achievement because of organizational separation and disparate roles. In fact, many board members report spending little or no time in school buildings and are committed to maintaining a strict separation between their policy role and school operations, instruction, and personnel management (Glass, 2007). However, one need only look to the not infrequent debacle and bankruptcy of large corporate empires, brought down by failed corporate board oversight, to recognize that board decisions can and do have a significant influence on organizational health and production, and schools are no exception.

Just as in business, educational and political science researchers have devised models to describe the presence or lack of connection between school boards and student success. The most prominent such theories include the Decision-Output Theory (Wirt and Kirst, 1997), and the Dissatisfaction Theory of American Democracy (Iannaccone and Lutz, 1970). Mitchell (1978) and Iannaccone (1994) contend that these theories represent complementary but varying perspectives on board governance, with the Dissatisfaction Theory standing as the sole theory that recognizes significant and functioning linkages between the school board and student success.

THE DISSATISFACTION THEORY

While Lutz and Iannaccone's (1986) Dissatisfaction Theory may be complementary to other governance theories, it maintains several unique characteristics while attempting to describe the political environment through which board members and superintendents navigate. For example, the theory stands alone in its foundational premise that boards function in a democratic fashion and that citizens, through local school board elections, still influence their schools. This influence, the theory shows, is exercised through the election, defeat, and pressured resignation and retirement of school board members and the subsequent forced turnover of superintendents.

Most school governance theories generally cite the lack of community involvement and the relative unresponsiveness of school boards to citizens, supported by data like the general inactivity of the voters during most board elections. Other governance theories conclude that boards do not function in a particularly responsive or democratic fashion but tend to maintain the status quo and fail to recognize or respond to changing demands from their communities. The Dissatisfaction Theory of American Democracy (Iannaccone and Lutz, 1970), while conceding that communities often appear inactive and uninterested in board elections, points to sporadic, politically charged episodes where citizens take action against a school board and transform their school leadership and policy.

The theory's model, as shown in Figure 12.1, indicates that when community member dissatisfaction with their local school board reaches an unacceptable peak, increased political activism within a local community leads to a predictable series of events. During these episodes of heightened political activism, multiple contenders emerge in what is normally a sparse

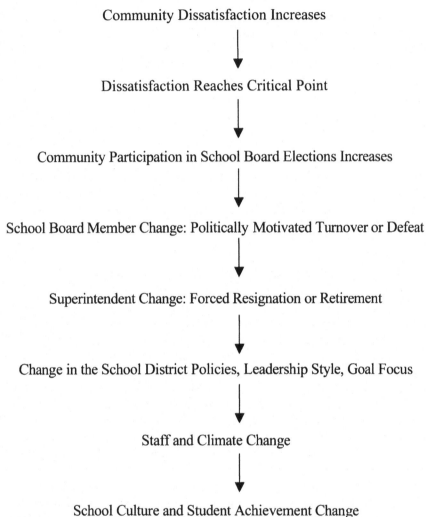

Community Dissatisfaction Increases

Dissatisfaction Reaches Critical Point

Community Participation in School Board Elections Increases

School Board Member Change: Politically Motivated Turnover or Defeat

Superintendent Change: Forced Resignation or Retirement

Change in the School District Policies, Leadership Style, Goal Focus

Staff and Climate Change

School Culture and Student Achievement Change

Figure 12.1.   Dissatisfaction Theory of Democracy Model. Shows the sequence of causal events linking school board turnover and student achievement change.

electoral field, voter turnout increases sharply, and the challengers' platforms and goals become increasingly diverse and incongruent with the incumbents.

As new board members are elected through outright defeat of incumbents or by filling a vacated seat emptied through pressured resignation or retirement, they often take office with a presumed mandate for change from the citizenry. New board members seated in this way typically promote viewpoints antagonistic toward district leadership and board colleagues, and commonly press for the replacement of the superintendent. New superintendents, hired as a result of politically motivated board reconstitution, typically make substantive changes under board directive, in an attempt to better respond to community dissatisfaction and demands.

In fact, Iannaccone and Lutz (1970) found incumbent school board defeat led to pressured superintendent turnover within three years. New superintendents typically implemented significant changes in school policy, procedures, and school programs. Indeed, these organizational changes seemed to placate the community and the outgoing school superintendent provided a convenient scapegoat for past grievances. Grady and Bryant (1989), however, found that frequent turnover of district leaders often results in the fragmentation of vision, goals, and procedures and negatively affects climate and culture, diminishing student performance (Deal and Peterson, 1999).

As in previous research, Alsbury's study focused on confirming the presence or absence of the links in the Dissatisfaction Theory model, specifically the link between school board and superintendent turnover and student achievement. These links are perhaps the most critical to the usefulness of the Dissatisfaction Theory, because unless leader turnover and the resulting policy change influences student achievement, the fact that citizens change their local board membership would be rendered irrelevant to school change.

Superintendent Turnover and Student Achievement

Few studies have focused on the link between superintendent turnover and its influence on student achievement. The studies that have attempted to make this connection, while not able to demonstrate a direct link between superintendent turnover and measurable change in student achievement, do seem to indicate an indirect but significant influence on school personnel, school culture, and teaching efficacy (Petersen, 2002; Bredeson, 1996; Bredeson and Kose, 2005; Morgan and Petersen, 2002; Petersen and Barnett, 2005).

In a case study by Johnson-Howard (1991), findings indicate that new superintendents hired as an outcome of politically motivated board turnover, and the forced resignation of their predecessors, changed policy in multiple areas including organizational structure, personnel, programs, finance, curriculum, student assessment, and facilities. Organizational changes included significant job reassignment, transfer of staff to alternate grade levels, transfer of school leaders to alternative buildings and positions, and school reconfiguration. Johnson-Howard (1991) noted that, in one district, the superintendent reassigned all administrators and all elementary teachers.

In addition, every district in her study decentralized decision making and established a community goal-setting process. Increased levels of parental involvement in making significant decisions were established throughout the district and in every school. In several districts, major philosophical shifts led to broad organizational restructuring such as the conversion of junior high schools to middle schools. In most districts, funding was decentralized and curriculum realignment and revisions were significant.

These cited examples represent only a few of the many significant changes made in all facets of the schools in Johnson-Howard's study—changes which, notably, were not random but intentionally encouraged by the newly configured school board. In fact, the new board was careful to select a new superintendent who agreed to initiate significant reform and change. This study's findings clearly demonstrate how community action through school board elections eventually resulted in organizational reforms substantial enough to influence building principals, teachers, school culture, and staff morale—all influential in altering student achievement.

Weninger and Stout (1989) similarly found that politically reconstituted boards tended to draft policy and press newly hired superintendents to change instructional programs, modify teacher evaluation approaches to increase accountability, press principals to remove poorly performing teachers, alter budget and resource allocations, increase community participation in significant decision making, and reconfigure staff and building leaders.

In an effort to determine whether new leadership following contentious board turnover may have an influence on student achievement, multiple case studies have identified and described the resulting district changes. These include not only technical changes, such as staff reassignment, building grade reconfiguration, and budget reallocation, but also paradigmatic shifts in values and beliefs such as equity, choice, quality, and efficiency. Deal and Peterson (1999) similarly noted that frequent superintendent turnover may diminish the ability for a district to establish a clear and positive culture; lead to inconsistent values, goals, and beliefs; and introduce instability and unpredictability.

Indeed, other studies have linked superintendent turnover and the resulting policy adjustments to a potential impact on student success (Merz, 1986; Weninger and Stout, 1989), while others do not support that conclusion (Disanti, 1988; Peterson, 2000). As noted earlier, the connection between superintendent turnover, policy change, and school success is a foundational theoretical imperative of the Dissatisfaction Theory—the sole governance theory describing elected school boards as exemplars of democratic governance in action, and defending their relevance.

Notably, the qualitative phase of the Alsbury study indicated that superintendents, following a politically reconstituted board, were more likely to implement major changes within their first year, including revisions in the district vision and goals, principal and teacher staffing, teacher evaluation and supervision, curriculum, testing, procedures, resource allocation, and programs. In this study, respondents indicated that personnel transfers, resource reallocation, and building reconfiguration dramatically disrupted school, staff, and student culture.

TURNOVER THAT MATTERS

It should be noted, however, that not all superintendent or board turnover would be expected to result in significant district change. Indeed, the Dissatisfaction Theory predicts that apolitical turnover would not generally result in the hiring of a superintendent with a dramatically different paradigm. This type of benign turnover would likely lead to the hiring of a leader with similar beliefs and values who would maintain the status quo.

Turnover in Small, Rural Districts

Despite the general presumption that increased superintendent tenure would promote positive school culture and increase student achievement, Alsbury's study found that the lack of superintendent turnover in smaller districts was linked to declining test scores. Superintendents managing to maintain a long tenure in school districts frequently accomplished longevity by avoiding change and reform in an effort to curry peace, diminish conflict, and keep their list of enemies as short as possible.

Another factor complicating studies of superintendent turnover is the presumption that most superintendents begin their career in small, rural districts and then move on to larger and more lucrative positions. If, in fact, we found a significantly higher number of apolitical turnovers in small versus large districts, it could conceivably complicate the analysis of turnover rates and thus the ability to draw conclusions in a study of this type. However, while the American Association of School Administrators' recent national superintendent study did indicate that leaders most often held their first superintendency in districts of 300 or fewer students (61 percent), the percentage of superintendents who started in larger districts was nearly identical (56 percent) (Glass, Björk, and Brunner, 2000).

This is partially explained by the fact that many superintendents' (43 percent) career paths take them from teacher to director or assistant superintendent and then to the superintendency within larger districts. Further opposing the presumption that administrators most often move from small to large districts is the fact that superintendents in districts of all sizes have virtually the same tenure of between five and six years, except in large urban districts where it is lower (Glass, Björk, and Brunner, 2000). Alsbury (2004b) confirmed this in a national study of superintendent turnover indicating that apolitical turnover in districts of 500 or fewer (62 percent) was not much different than in larger districts (55 percent).

Political Turnover Is the Key

Overall, the key to validly studying school board and superintendent turnover rests in the use of an appropriate definition of turnover. In fact, Alsbury's (2003) study argues that "turnover" must be defined as bona fide electoral defeat and forced resignation or retirement for both school board members and superintendents. Studies failing to confirm the Dissatisfaction Theory share the distinction of not defining turnover carefully, but considering all board and superintendent turnover as equivalent.

In fact, this point is seen when reviewing a series of quantitative studies attempting to demonstrate a significant relationship between school board and superintendent turnover. This series of doctoral studies from the 1970s through the 1990s concluded that no connection existed between board and superintendent turnover (Brackett, 1995; Chmara, 1989; Flynn, 1984; Kitchens, 1994; Krise, 1994; Ledoux, 1971; Poyourow-Ripple, 1990; Sullivan, 1990). These studies were conducted in no less than eight states, including Alabama, Oklahoma, Pennsylvania, North Carolina, Louisiana, Georgia, New Mexico, and South Carolina.

In fact, aside from case study confirmation of a strong link between school board and superintendent turnover, few quantitative studies supported this connection. Alsbury (2003), however, noted during his 12-year tenure as a school administrator that board members and superintendents frequently left the board voluntarily. This generally led to newly elected or appointed board members and superintendents possessing similar dispositions, beliefs, and goals. Occasionally, however, when community dissatisfaction led to defeat or forced resignation of a board member, the seated superintendent was generally at risk, resigned, or retired "under a cloud," and was replaced by a superintendent with a decidedly different set of values and goals. In fact, national surveys confirm that board members usually resign or retire for apolitical reasons, with only around 30 percent leaving as a result of political conflict or pressure from the community (Chance and Capps, 1992; Erickson and Keirnes, 1978; Hosman, 1990; Mitchell and Spady, 1983).

Additionally, board challengers who arise during a period of community dissatisfaction are usually more vocal about their desire to change the district in significant ways, including removing the current superintendent. Likewise, a new superintendent hired as a result of this board change usually felt the need to visibly change the school system in order to show the board that he or she had indeed followed the new public mandate for change.

Despite research findings and personal anecdotal experiences, Alsbury (2003) noted that most quantitative studies of the Dissatisfaction Theory had used *all* board and *all* superintendent turnover when running analyses to detect for a significant relationship between board and superintendent turnover. This was a potentially critical methodological error, considering that the Dissatisfaction Theory purports to describe only the unique pattern of events following the often infrequent political activity in the community resulting in school board defeat at the polls or pressured turnover. Only in those circumstances, the theory explains, would forced superintendent and subsequent policy change follow. Alsbury concluded that previous studies not distinguishing between political and apolitical board turnover were missing a critical variable that dramatically influenced their ability to draw valid conclusions (Mitchell and Thorsted, 1976; Rada, 1984). This was a significant concern, considering that most of these studies had concluded that the Dissatisfaction Theory, while effective in describing school governance in the 1960s and 1970s, no longer was valid.

Indeed, Mitchell and Thorsted (1976) discussed this point in their study, indicating that board and superintendent turnover was frequently not politically motivated and usually was not initiated by community dissatisfaction. In fact, Mitchell (1978) cautioned future researchers to take care in defining incumbent school board defeat when used as a cogent variable in studies of the Dissatisfaction Theory. Likewise, Iannaccone and Lutz (1994) noted the need to conduct longitudinal studies when studying the Dissatisfaction Theory, because community discord of enough intensity to result in board defeat, while occurring regularly in some districts, may occur very rarely in others. This infrequent political upheaval and the chain of events that follow distinguishes the Dissatisfaction Theory from other theories explaining local school governance.

This, they explained, is why other theories are complementary to the Dissatisfaction theory rather then contradictory. Other theories describe the normal political environment of school districts, characterized by minimal community involvement, causing these researchers to conclude that districts rarely operate democratically. This is why Iannaccone and Lutz (1994) note the danger in taking snapshot analyses of local district governance function, and Mitchell (1978) cautioned against assuming that all turnovers were congruent to incumbent defeat. Alsbury (2003) empirically confirmed both methodological requirements through a longitudinal, mixed-method study designed to allow for a distinction between political and apolitical school board turnover.

DO COMMUNITIES DEMOCRATICALLY INFLUENCE SCHOOL BOARDS?

Wirt and Kirst (1997) argue against the presence of measurable causal links between several of the components in the Dissatisfaction Theory model

focusing primarily on the lack of empirical evidence supporting the influence of community members on forced school board turnover or policy
change. Their Decision-Output Theory, for example, concluded that while
local citizens occasionally influence their school boards, parents and community members exercise little or no control over their schools.

Lutz and Wang (1987), in comparing the Decision-Output and Dissatisfaction theories, noted that each described the reality of local school governance from two distinct political viewpoints. The Decision-Output Theory
measures the responsiveness of school boards to public demands and the
level of public participation in school board elections and school board
meetings, as indicators of the extent of democratic function within the governance system. Lutz and Wang noted that the Dissatisfaction Theory instead "insists that the essence of democracy is the freedom to participate
. . . when the people are dissatisfied enough" (Lutz and Wang, 1987, p. 67).
The key factor in this theoretical perspective is the public's *opportunity* to
change the system, whether they choose to do so or not. Lutz and Iannaccone wrote that it was a theoretical focus on "liberty of opposition seen in
the capacity to unseat those in office" that makes the Dissatisfaction Theory
unique among school governance theories (Lutz and Iannaccone, 1978, p.
131).

While some governance theories suggest a weak or absent link between
the public and their local school governance, Alsbury (2003) found that, on
average, 30 percent of Washington State school board members turned over
in every election, with 25 percent of that turnover caused by defeat or politically motivated resignation and retirement. Over the eight-year study,
representing three school board elections, school board member turnover
occurred in 97 percent of the school districts, with 70 percent of the districts
experiencing three or more school board changes representing a change in
the voting majority. Additionally, superintendent turnover occurred in 74
percent of the districts over the course of the study. These numbers would
seem to indicate that while theorists debate whether school governance is
democratic, citizens are busy practicing democracy by replacing their school
leadership at a fairly frequent rate.

THE WASHINGTON STUDY

Alsbury's (forthcoming) mixed-method study was intended to determine
the presence of a significant relationship between (a) board turnover and
student test score change, and (b) superintendent turnover and student test
score change. The study employed two distinct phases. In Phase I, a survey
was administered to all the superintendents in Washington State (296). Of
these surveys, administered in 2001, 176 were returned (59.5 percent) with

only 162 of these districts reporting their test results and subsequently used in the analysis. The survey asked superintendents to indicate each school board member turnover by year from 1993 to 2001; whether the turnover was a retirement, resignation, or defeat; and the reason for the turnover.

The choices provided on the survey regarding why school board members retired or resigned included the most predominately reported reasons school board members leave as determined by research studies in this area (Erickson and Keirnes, 1978; Mitchell and Spady, 1983; Robinson and Wood, 1987). These choices were confirmed through the administration of a phone interview to a random, representative sampling of superintendents. Respondents could select as many of the listed options for why a board member left and also add independent reasons if they desired.

Statewide data on superintendent turnover were gathered from records at the Washington Association of School Administrators. All returned surveys were used in the study and were determined to have a high level of representation based upon district size, organizational structure, and geographic distribution. The Pearson Chi-square test for independence was used to test for a significant relationship between board turnover, superintendent turnover, and student achievement change. Data analyses were further disaggregating by district size, and student minority and poverty levels. No significant relationships were determined as a result of minority or poverty levels, but key findings did emerge when controlling for district size.

Washington State is comprised of only 10 percent districts with an enrollment of 10,000 or greater, with approximately 35 percent having an enrollment of 500 or fewer, and 80 percent enrolling fewer than 3,000 students. As a result, this study's findings and any subsequent conclusions necessarily focus on rural schools. Conversely, most studies of school boards have occurred in urban districts (Danzberger, 1992; Kirst, 1994; Wilson, 1994). While this study's findings cannot be generalized to urban districts, the significance is not broadly limiting considering that more than 50 percent of districts nationally enroll fewer than 1,100 students, over 90 percent enroll fewer than 6,400, and the majority are located in rural settings (NCES, 2002).

Another possible benefit of analyzing school board and turnover data from smaller school districts is the argument that these district leaders may have more direct and immediate influence on student achievement. In larger districts, superintendents and board members are separated from classroom instruction by numerous bureaucratic levels, possibly diminishing the ability to measure their influence on student achievement without controlling for an unwieldy number of contravening variables.

Because Washington State is a state of small school districts and because the degrees of separation between the central office leadership and the teaching staff may be important, the study utilized Maguire's (1989) approach for categorizing district size by organizational structure (OS). Each OS category represents an additional layer of administrative hierarchy between the central office leader(s) and the students. For example, a school district in Washington State with 250 or fewer students was composed of one superintendent who also served as the principal and might teach classes. Districts of 500 students typically employed one superintendent and one principal. As district enrollment increases, additional administrative layers are typical, adding complexity to the ability to detect any influence on students by school board and superintendent turnover. Survey returns were representative based on district size and organizational structure.

Defining School Board Turnover

As argued previously in this chapter, one of the key measured variables in this study was *politically motivated* versus *apolitical* school board member turnover. This confirmed Alsbury's (2003) findings that indicated the need to delineate between *all* turnover, *political* turnover, and *apolitical* turnover in studies of the Dissatisfaction Theory. Political and apolitical reason(s) for school board member turnover included on the study survey were defined operationally as shown in Table 12.1. Items A–H indicate *politically motivated* school board turnover, including defeat. Although respondents were invited to select multiple options to describe why the board member resigned or retired, less than 15 percent of the returns showed multiple selections. In order to take a conservative approach, the selection of even one politically motivated reason was characterized as politically motivated board turnover.

One potential concern over identifying the political or apolitical nature of board turnover through a survey given to superintendents is that respondents may report politically motivated turnover as benign, due to a lack of knowledge, a misinterpretation of the circumstances, or an intentional fabrication to protect the board member or the school district. It has been argued that respondents citing illness, satisfactory completion of service, or other options defined in the study as "apolitical" may indeed represent misidentified politically motivated departures.

However, several protective methods in the study as well as realities in the field suggest the reporting and classification are reasonably accurate. First, pre-survey instructions requested superintendents, if necessary, to confer with other longtime district administrators and other board members to determine the reasons a board member resigned or retired. They were also asked not to complete the survey unless they felt confident in their knowledge concerning the reasons for the board turnover. In fact, approximately 10 percent of potential respondents, located primarily in larger districts, declined to participate in the study due to a lack of confidence and an inability to corroborate the reasons for the turnover.

Table 12.1.   Frequency of Reasons for School Board Member Turnover Delineated by Political and Apolitical Turnover

Reasons for School Board Turnover	Number of Times Selected	Percent
Politically Motivated Reason		
Defeat	62	11%
A. Public pressure	18	3.3%
B. Dissatisfied with school programs	9	1.6%
C. Time wasted on unimportant matters	5	0.9%
D. Washington reform movement	0	0%
E. Conflict with other board members	25	4.6%
F. Teacher union	1	0.8%
G. Conflict with the staff	0	0%
H. Other politically motivated reason	2	0.36%
Total Political	122	22.26%
Apolitically Motivated Reason		
I. Too time-consuming	38	6.9%
J. Satisfied all my goals had been met	48	8.8%
K. Personal or family health	115	21%
L. Served long enough/someone else's turn	129	23.5%
M. Personal business sales to school	39	7%
N. Moved out of town or voter district	42	7.7%
O. Other apolitically motivated reason	15	2.7%
Total Apolitical	426	77.7%
Total Responses	548	99.96%

Second, it might be argued that superintendents and fellow board members who were aware of political pressure causing a board member turnover may have withheld the information or given inaccurate responses to save from embarrassment or protect against potential political or legal liability to themselves, the superintendent, or the district. However, because the survey was confidential, and resigning and retiring board member names were not requested on the survey, little reason existed for the superintendent, board members, or other informants to refrain from providing an honest assessment.

Finally, it is important to note that respondents were allowed to select multiple reasons, both political and apolitical, for a board member's departure. Respondents wanting to protect themselves or the reputation of the departing school board member might have been expected to give a mix of political and apolitical reasons for the turnover. However, very few survey returns indicated a mixed response; board turnover was characterized as decidedly political or apolitical in nature. The methods used for data collection and analysis, while not eliminating all potential error, certainly support the reliability of the findings.

Another concern raised may be in regard to the actual political and apolitical items used on the survey to indicate the reasons for departure. For example, the item "state/federal reforms" was counted in the study as a political reason for turnover; however, it may be argued that the respondent viewed this as an apolitical reason. Alsbury (2004a) discusses and defends, in detail, the levels or dimensions of political turnover possible. To help defend against this and other arguments, this study used several measures to protect the reliability of the survey. First, the most conservative options were selected as "politically motivated" turnover. By erring on the side of designating more turnovers as apolitical, the expectation would be a smaller chance that the significance analyses would find a relationship.

Second, survey items were not selected randomly, but were in fact taken from a preliminary randomly sampled phone survey and an extensive review of previous studies conducted on why board members retire and resign. Third, because respondents could, and typically did, mark multiple options, any errant interpretation about the nature of a single item would have been corrected by other, clearly understood items selected. Finally, respondents were provided with the option of adding their own "reason for turnover" if they desired; however, no significant number of respondents chose to do so.

Do Superintendents Know Why Board Members Leave?

Another potential problem with the study design is whether superintendents can be expected to accurately know why school board members left, at least well enough to characterize the turnover as political or apolitical. It should be noted that superintendents taking the survey who were relatively new to a district were instructed to seek out key informants such as building-level administrators, staff, and board members who had been present at the time of each of the board turnovers. Additionally, a follow-up qualitative study was conducted of randomly sampled districts. Researchers spent three days in each district interviewing past and present board members and central office personnel, and collecting school and newspaper documentation. Politically motivated defeats, pressured resignations, increased numbers of incumbent challenges, and high voter turnouts were verified by key informants and newspaper accounts, both confirming some public issue(s) that solidified the community's dissatisfaction with the seated board. In addition, board members who were politically pressured off the board were interviewed and confirmed the superintendents' survey responses.

For the vast majority of superintendents in the field, political pressures leading to board member entry and exit from boards as distinguished from the more common benign turnover is commonly known by not only the superintendent but often many members of the community. Superintendents quickly learn the value of political savvy and a talent for listening for and reacting to politically negative community comments. In fact, some superintendents manage to stay in their position longer than predicted during politically motivated board turnover because they detect the "coming storm" and begin disassociating themselves from at-risk board members before the crisis hits in earnest.

Further, it could be argued that the departing school board members themselves may be less reliable than their superintendent when reporting political pressures leading to a forced retirement or resignation. Additionally, politically contentious challengers make for excellent press. As a result, most politically charged school board races likely to lead to defeat or pressured turnover are usually well covered in the local media and evidenced by editorial letters of complaint, increased incumbent challengers, and other indicators of growing community dissatisfaction. It would be unlikely, in fact, for a superintendent to not be aware of politically motivated board turnover and its causes.

Tracking Student Achievement

In this study, student achievement was defined by tracking the cumulative English and math scores of cohorts of students over an eight-year period. The assessment, the Washington Assessment of Student Learning (WASL), is a criterion-referenced, performance-based assessment required for all 4th-, 7th-, and 10th-graders in Washington State.

Results on the WASL were obtained from the Web site of the Washington Office of Superintendent of Public Instruction (OSPI). Data of district-level WASL results have been available online to the general public since 1993. In addition, the state provides a growth unit of measure referred to as the Learning Index (LI). The LI is a composite measure of year-to-year achievement in reading and mathematics for each grade cohort that took the WASL. District LI scores for each student cohort were tracked from their 4th-, 7th-, and 10th-grade results to determine if their LI had significantly increased, decreased, or stayed the same.

DOES LEADER TURNOVER INFLUENCE STUDENT ACHIEVEMENT?

As described earlier, this study was designed to attempt to answer two main questions centered on whether school board and superintendent turnover are linked to student achievement change. Alsbury's earlier 2003 study already

Table 12.2. Chi-square Analysis of the Presence of a Significant Relationship between School Board Turnover Rates and School District Washington Assessment of Student Learning (WASL) Test Score Change. Tracked by Student Cohort Groups, 1993–2001.

| | Pearson Chi-Square Results | |
Type of School Board Turnover	Value	Significance
All Sized Districts (N=162)		
All Board Turnover	9.924	.447
Politically Motivated Turnover and Defeat	16.106	.041*
Districts of 500 or less (N=37)		
All Board Turnover	18.063	.054**

* Represents a high confidence significant value at < 0.05
** Represents a moderate confidence significant value at < 0.10

confirmed the link between politically motivated board and superintendent turnover, supporting the Dissatisfaction Theory. In this study, the first study question asked if school board turnover can be linked to student achievement. Table 12.2 shows no statistically significant association present when tracking multiple student cohorts' test scores over eight years and measuring against *all* school board turnover in all districts in the study ($p = .447$). Data were then disaggregated by district size, as defined by Maguire's (1989) OS categories, and in districts with an enrollment of 500 or less, a probability level of $p = .054$ was achieved. Although this probability level was not significant in terms of the preset study level ($p < .05$), frequently studies of this type accept a $p < 0.10$ as a moderate confidence level.

The second analysis in the study was to compare only *politically motivated* school board turnover to student achievement change in all districts in the study. Table 12.2 shows a statistically significant association ($p = .041$), indicating there exists a significant relationship between *politically motivated* board turnover and defeat and student test scores. This finding confirms Alsbury's (2003) earlier study indicating that controlling for politically motivated board turnover is critical in studies of the Dissatisfaction Theory. These results suggest that in districts of all sizes, board turnover caused by political turmoil, resulting from critical community dissatisfaction with the school board and/or district leadership, is linked to declining student test scores.

The second key question of the study centered on whether there existed a significant relationship between superintendent turnover and student test change. Table 12.3 indicates no relationship exists ($p = .783$) when including all districts in the analysis. However, when comparing superintendent turnover and student test scores in districts of 500 or fewer, significance is indicated ($p = .016$) at a high level of confidence. Further correlation test-

Table 12.3.   Superintendent Turnover Rate Compared to the School District's Washington Assessment of Student Learning (WASL) Test Score Change. Tracked by Student Cohort Groups, 1993–2001.

	Pearson Chi-Square Results	
Size of District	Value	Significance
All Sized Districts (N=159)	3.202	.783
Districts of 500 or less (N=36)	15.580	.016*

* Represents a very high confidence significant value at < 0.01

ing confirmed that in small districts where no superintendent turnover occurred during the eight-year study period, student test scores were more likely to be declining. Results from other disaggregated district sizes yielded no significance and were not included in the tables in this chapter for brevity's sake.

It should be noted that student test score change was measured from one to four years *following* school board turnover. Thus, already declining student scores were not necessarily a premeditating factor in community action to change the board. This was also confirmed by the qualitative phase of the study. Further it should also be noted that superintendent replacement typically occurred three years after the board turnover. Coupled with the results that superintendent turnover was not connected to the student test change, it appears the impacting variable was *frequent* school board turnover in small districts and *frequent politically motivated* turnover in all districts.

Complicating Contextual Variables

In any school district and community many contextual variables are present that may have contributed to student test change. During an eight-year study period and 162 different school districts, it is likely that teachers and principals, curriculum and programs, and perhaps even socioeconomics and other demographics may have changed in the community. However, it must be understood that the myriad of uncontrollable and unique contextual variables would add more and more randomness to the data and thus should result in lowering the probability that a significant relationship between the school board and superintendent turnover and student achievement would be detected.

The fact that a relationship was demonstrated supports the argument that school board and/or superintendent turnover does appear to be an important variable to include when measuring the causes of student achievement change. While the presence of contravening variables presents potential limitations to any study attempting to determine the causes for student achievement change, these findings support the notion that political board turnover influences student achievement.

CONCLUSIONS

Lutz and Iannaccone's (1986) Dissatisfaction Theory predicts that politically motivated school board member turnover results in a change in superintendent, and in substantive policy and organizational change throughout the district. Although numerous studies have measured the connection between the community and school board turnover, school board and superintendent turnover, and superintendent turnover and policy change, few studies have been able to link school board or superintendent turnover to student achievement directly (Land, 2002).

This study does, in fact, demonstrate a significant relationship between frequent politically motivated school board turnover and student achievement decline. In addition to providing empirical support for the Dissatisfaction Theory, the findings speak to the relevancy and importance of locally elected school boards. Further, the findings support the notion that nonurban communities continue to regularly exercise significant control over their local schools through school board elections, affirming the contention that school boards are not only still relevant but as democratic in their function as any American governmental institution.

School Boards Matter

Recently, the criticism targeted at school boards is increasing, with some calling for their elimination (Chubb and Moe, 1990; Finn, 1991; Harrington-Lueker, 1996; Olson, 1992; Streshly and Frase, 1993; Whitson, 1998). However, others believe school boards still provide a viable example of functional democracy—in fact, one of the few remaining examples in our local communities (Resnick, 1999). Study findings appear to be equally inconclusive concerning the efficacy and value of school boards. While some conclude that school boards are often ineffective and act more as an obstacle frustrating positive school reform (Peterson, 2000), other studies catalogue numerous examples of school boards' influencing, supporting, and even leading positive school change (Cotter, 2001; Parelius, 1982; Russell, 1997; Scott, 1991; Underwood, Fortune, and Cleary, 1985).

Findings in this study indicate that school board member turnover, especially politically motivated turnover, seems to be related in some way to student achievement. While the design of this study did not allow drawing clear conclusions of causality, it does support the relevance of school boards—their interconnectedness and potential for influence on their community and students.

Findings from this study do not allow us to conclude with certainty if declining student performance is caused by community dissatisfaction, the ensuing conflict with the local school system, or the subsequent instability brought on by frequent board turnover. It may be just as likely that the student performance is merely a symptom of a troubled community that finds its local school board or school leaders convenient officials to blame for a generally declining community. Either way, this study certainly dispels claims of irrelevancy, elitism, or disconnectedness of local school boards to their schools and communities. Smoley puts it simply when he notes, "A school board is part of the community it serves" (Smoley, 1999, p. 2).

In fact, it is evident that the school board and the schools are really a byproduct or microcosm of their community, especially evident in very small towns. Supporting this notion, it is not uncommon for the success of a school athletic team to lift the spirits and substantively change the culture, attitude, and even economic prominence of a local community. Conversely, negative community culture can not help but be mirrored in the school culture. Likewise, a troubled school with little positive to celebrate can negatively influence a community in significant ways.

Research indicates that communities need to be extremely dissatisfied before they will take action against a local school board. Therefore, when parents and community are at that high point of contention, poor performance in school may merely be a symptom of a larger dysfunctional environment, a negative learning culture that extends beyond the schoolhouse. In fact, Fullan (2001) denoted the singular importance of a positive culture to student achievement, while Sergiovanni (1992) refers to the importance of climate to the learning environment. This leads to several cogent implications of this study.

IMPLICATIONS

The School Board–Community Connection

The study lends support to the Dissatisfaction Theory. The theory, in addition to holding importance for theoretical debate among academics, if trustworthy, can function as a very practical predictor for school board members and superintendents. For example, the Dissatisfaction Theory should lead school boards and superintendents to pay close attention to increased voter turnout at school board elections, challengers to board seats, and an increasing number of votes cast for challengers. All of these are predicted to be indicators of a growing level of dissatisfaction among the community. Superintendents should be aware that if this trend continues and leads to politically motivated board turnover, their position is likely at risk.

Likewise, the absence of politically motivated board turnover indicates to the board and the superintendent that the community is reasonably satisfied with their actions and thus overreaction to vocal demands for school change from special interest groups may not be prudent or represent the wishes of the general populace. Similarly, general apolitical school board and superintendent turnover does not indicate community dissatisfaction and should not contribute to student achievement decline.

This study also supports the idea that school boards do operate in a democratic fashion and are controlled by the community through school board elections when they finally decide school change is needed. As such, school boards would be well advised to open communication lines if they observe the symptoms of dissatisfaction—not only to protect their political position, but to avoid negative impacts on the schools, staff, and students.

The Dissatisfaction Theory suggests that dissatisfaction in the community, through a series of causal events, eventually alters substantive school policy and thus may influence student achievement. While some criticize school boards for not representing the local public's interests and values (Rallis and Criscoe, 1993; Wirt and Kirst, 2006), this study suggests that communities and their schools exhibit a symbiotic interdependence, demonstrating a collective culture—whether positive or negative.

Leadership Stagnation or Stability?

Researchers and practitioners have long debated about the benefit of leadership stability, supporting longer tenures for school principals and superintendents (Fullan and Miles, 1992; Kowalski, 1995; Olson, 1995; Thomas, 2001). Grady and Bryant (1989) indicate that superintendents coordinate change and provide school district stability, and argue that rapid turnover makes it difficult for districts to maintain consistent goals and policy. However, the results of this study support Thomas's (2001) contention that high superintendent turnover has not been directly linked to diminishing student achievement scores. This claim is less difficult to accept when one considers that new leadership, depending on its effectiveness, may or may not create positive results in a school.

The findings in this study indicating possible detrimental effects of extended superintendent tenure in very small schools may be explained by comparing disparate superintendent leadership styles described by Carlson (1972) as place-bound and career-bound leadership patterns. Place-bound superintendents are home-grown candidates often selected by school boards who, after a period of intense change or difficulty, are looking for a leader to implement the current program and maintain stability and peace in the district. Researchers seem to agree that place-bound superintendents prefer to avoid conflict, resolving problems through techniques like changing behavior, timing the approach, direct confrontation, acquiescence and accepting, and bluffing (Bacharach, 1981; Zeigler, Kehoe, and Reisman, 1985).

In fact, many superintendents may avoid conflict by "fence-sitting," often an effective strategy (Bacharach, 1981). Other techniques for handling conflict include resisting public demands or ignoring conflict, hiding conflict, and managing conflict. Lutz and Merz (1992) contend districts that handle conflict early can avoid increasing dissatisfaction in the community. They also suggest that boards can become more open to their community, by focusing on their role as communicators (Kowalski and Keedy, 2003).

The National School Boards Association may be able to use this study's findings to reinforce the importance of board communication with the community as well as a means to detect and respond to growing dissatisfaction. While the board's role as communicator may seem obvious, recent surveys indicate that community interaction is lowest on board member priority lists (Joyce, Delagardelle, and Wolf, 2001). Unfortunately, the findings in this study seem to indicate that place-bound, extended-tenure superintendents in very small districts may be more likely to exercise peacekeeping efforts rather than promote the type of school reform and accountability that leads to student achievement gains but also creates conflict that can eventually threaten their position.

A final implication for findings in this study speaks to the recent increase in the call for the elimination of elected school boards through mayoral, city government, and state takeovers. This study confirms that school governance is indeed democratic and that the public actively influence their schools through elected school boards. Removing boards would eliminate the opportunity for communities to influence their schools and would diminish one of the last local American institutions allowing citizens to exercise democratic liberty.

REFERENCES

Agresti, A., and B. Finlay. 1997. *Statistical methods for the social sciences.* 3rd ed. Upper Saddle River, NJ: Prentice Hall.

Alsbury, T. L. 2003. Superintendent and school board member turnover: Political versus apolitical turnover as a critical variable in the application of the Dissatisfaction Theory. *Educational Administration Quarterly* 39 (5): 667–698.

———. 2004a. Does school board turnover matter? Revisiting critical variables in the Dissatisfaction Theory of American Democracy. *International Journal of Leadership in Education* 7 (4): 357–377.

———. 2004b. Democratic school governance in a changing political and social landscape: A national study. Paper presented at the annual convention of the University Council for Educational Administration, Kansas City, Missouri.

———. Forthcoming. Rural school board member and superintendent turnover and the influence on student achievement: An application of the Dissatisfaction Theory. *Leadership and Policy in Schools* 7 (2).

Bacharach, S. B. 1981. *Organizational behavior in schools and school districts.* New York: Praeger.

Best, J. W., and J. V. Kahn. 2003. *Research in education.* 9th ed. Boston: Allyn & Bacon.

Bolman, L., and T. Deal. 2000. *Escape from cluelessness.* New York: AMACOM.

Brackett, J. D. 1995. Superintendent turnover in relation to incumbent school board member defeat in Alabama from 1984-1994. *Dissertation Abstracts International* 57 (06): 2284A. (UMI No. 9635752)

Bredeson, P. V. 1996. Superintendents' role in curriculum development and instructional leadership: Instructional visionaries, collaborators, supporters, and delegators. *Journal of School Leadership* 6 (3): 2243–2264.

Bredeson, P. V., and B. Kose. 2005. School superintendents as instructional leaders: Responses to a decade of education reform, 1994–2003. Paper presented at the Annual American Educational Research Association Conference, Montreal, April 9–11.

Carlson, R. O. 1972. *School superintendents: Careers and performance.* Columbus, OH: Merrill.

Chance, E. W., and J. L. Capps. 1992. *Superintendent instability in small/rural schools: The school board perspective* (Report No. 018665). Norman: University of Oklahoma, College of Education. (ERIC Document Reproduction Service No. ED350121)

Chmara, P. N. 1989. Factors affecting superintendent turnover. PhD diss., University of Pittsburgh. (UMI No. 8921368)

Chubb, J. E., and T. M. Moe. 1990. *Politics, markets, and America's schools.* Washington, DC: Brookings Institute.

Cotter, M. E. 2001. Strategic leadership for student achievement: An exploratory analysis of school board–superintendent governance and development practices. *Dissertation Abstracts International* 62 (06), 1993. (UMI No. 3017528)

Cunningham, W. F., and G. R. Carter. 1997. *The American school superintendency: Leading in an age of pressure.* San Francisco: Jossey-Bass.

Danzberger, J. P. 1992. School boards: A troubled American institution. In *Facing the challenge: The report of the Twentieth Century Fund Task Force on school governance.* New York: The Twentieth Century Fund.

Deal, T. E., and K. D. Peterson. 1999. *Shaping school culture: The heart of leadership.* San Francisco: Jossey-Bass.

Disanti, J. S. 1988. The Dissatisfaction Theory: Framework for analysis of school district conflict. *Dissertation Abstracts International* 49 (06), 1322. (UMI No. 8815246)

Erickson, K. A., and B. Keirnes. 1978. Former members tell . . . why they left the school board. *OSSC Bulletin* 22 (4): 3–35.

Finn, C. E. 1991. *We must take charge.* New York: Free Press.

Flynn, J. L. 1984. Superintendent turnover following the election turnover of incumbent school board members in the school districts of North Carolina. *Dissertation Abstracts International* 45(08), 2327A. (UMI No. 8421108)

Fullan, M. G. 2001. *Leading in a culture of change*. San Francisco: Jossey-Bass.

Fullan, M. G., and M. B. Miles. 1992. Getting reform right: What works and what doesn't. *Phi Delta Kappan* 73 (10): 744–752.

Gliner, J. A., and G. A. Morgan. 2000. *Research methods in applied settings: An integrated approach to design and analysis*. London: Lawrence Erlbaum.

Grady, M. L., and M. T. Bryant. 1989. Critical incidents between superintendents and school boards: Implications for practice. *Planning for Change* 20:206–214.

Harrington-Lueker, D. 1996. School board at bay. *American School Board Journal* 183 (5): 18–22.

Hosman, C. M. 1990. Superintendent selection and dismissal: A changing community defines its values. *Urban Education* 25:350–369.

Iannaccone, L. 1996. Callahan's vulnerability thesis and "dissatisfaction theory." *Peabody Journal of Education* 71 (2): 110–119.

Iannaccone, L., and F. W. Lutz. 1970. *Politics, power and policy: The governing of local school districts*. Columbus, OH: Merrill.

———. 1994. The crucible of democracy: The local arena. *Journal of Educational Policy* 9 (5): 39–52.

Johnson, B. L. 1988. Sacrificing liberty for equality: The erosion of local control in American education. Occasional paper for the Louisiana LEAD Project. (ERIC Document Reproductions Service No. ED 356 531)

Johnson-Howard, D. 1991. School board member values and school district policies. Paper presented at the annual meeting of the American Educational Research Association, Chicago, April. (ERIC Document Reproduction Service No. ED 334698)

Joyce, B., M. L. Delagardelle, and J. Wolf. 2001. The Lighthouse Inquiry: School board–superintendent team behaviors in school districts with extreme differences in student achievement. Research report presented at the annual meeting of the American Educational Research Association, Des Moines.

Kirst, M. W. 1994. A changing context means school board reform. *Phi Delta Kappan* 75 (5): 378–381.

Kitchens, S. K. 1994. Superintendent turnover in relation to incumbent school board member defeat in Louisiana from 1980–1992. *Dissertation Abstracts International*, 55(04), 819A. (UMI No. 9422723)

Kowalski, T. J. 1995. *Keepers of the flame: Contemporary urban superintendents*. Thousand Oaks, CA: Corwin.

Kowalski, T. J., and J. Keedy. 2003. Superintendent as communicator: Implications for professional preparation and licensing. Paper presented at the annual conference of the University Council for Educational Administration, Portland, Oregon, November.

Krise, R. M. 1994. Incumbent school board member defeat and turnover of elected and appointed superintendents in Georgia. PhD diss., University of Georgia.

Land, D. 2002. *Local school boards under review: Their role and effectiveness in relation to students' academic achievement* (Report No. CRESPAR-R-56). Baltimore: Johns Hopkins. (ERIC Document Reproduction Service No. ED462512)

Ledoux, E. P. 1971. Outmigration: Its relation to social, political and economic conditions and to the governing of local school districts in New Mexico. *Dissertation Abstracts International* 32(11), 6047A. (UMI No. 7213774)

Lutz, F. W. 1982. Community conflict and superintendent survival. *Planning and Changing* 13:1-18.

Lutz, F. W., and L. Iannaccone, eds. 1978. *Public participation in local school districts: The Dissatisfaction Theory of American Democracy.* Lexington, MA: Lexington Books, Heath.

―――. 1986. *The Dissatisfaction Theory of American Democracy: A guide for politics in local school districts.* Paper presented at the annual meeting of the American Association of School Administrators, San Francisco, February.

Lutz, F. W., and C. Merz. 1992. *The politics of school/community relations.* New York: Teachers College Press.

Lutz, F. W., and L. Wang. 1987. Predicting public dissatisfaction: A study of school board member defeat. *Educational Administration Quarterly* 23:65-77.

Merz, C. S. 1986. Conflict and frustration for school board members. *Urban Education* 20:397-418.

Mitchell, D. E. 1978. Measurement and methodological issues related to research on incumbent defeat and superintendent turnover. In *Public participation in local school districts,* ed. F. W. Lutz and L. Iannaccone. Lexington, MA: Heath.

Mitchell, D. E., and W. G. Spady. 1983. Authority, power, and the legitimation of social control. *Educational Administration Quarterly* 19:5-33.

Mitchell, D. E., and R. R. Thorsted. 1976. Incumbent school board member defeat reconsidered: New evidence for its political meaning. *Educational Administration Quarterly* 12:31-48.

Morgan, C. L., and G. J. Petersen. 2002. The role of the district superintendent in leading academically successful school districts. In *The promises and perils facing today's school superintendent,* ed. B. S. Cooper and L. D. Fusarelli, 175-196. Lanham, MD: Scarecrow Education.

National Center of Educational Statistics (NCES). 2002. Public elementary/secondary school universe survey, common core of data. U.S. Department of Education. http://nces.ed.gov/Pubs2003/Overview03/tables/table_A2.asp.

National School Boards Foundation (NSBF). 1999. *Leadership matters: Transforming urban school boards.* Alexandria, VA: NSBF.

No Child Left Behind Act of 2001, Pub. L. No. 107-110, § 115 STAT. 1425 (2002).

Olson, L. 1992. Boards of contention: Introduction. *Education Week* 11 (32).

―――. 1995. Rapid turnover in leadership impedes reforms, study finds. *Education Week* 6.

Parelius, R. J. 1982. *The school board as an agency of legitimation and change.* Paper presented at the annual meeting of the American Educational Research Association, New York. (ERIC Document Reproduction Service No. ED 217556)

Petersen, G. J. 2002. Singing the same tune: Principals' and school board members' perceptions of the superintendent's role in curricular and instructional leadership. *Journal of Educational Administration* 40 (2): 158-171.

Petersen, G. J., and B. G. Barnett. 2005. The superintendent as instructional leader: Current practice, future conceptualizations, and implications for preparation. In

The contemporary superintendent: Preparation, practice, and development, ed. L. G. Björk and T. J. Kowalski, 107–136. Thousand Oaks, CA: Corwin.

Peterson, S. A. 2000. Board of education involvement in school decisions and student achievement. *Public Administration Quarterly* 24 (1): 46–68.

Poyourow-Ripple, R. 1990. A descriptive survey of school board member turnover and superintendent turnover in Pennsylvania, 1973–1987. *Dissertation Abstracts International* 51(03), 705A. (UMI No. 9022938)

Rada, R. D. 1984. Community dissatisfaction and school governance. *Planning and Changing* 15:234–247.

Rallis, S. F., and J. Criscoe. 1993. *School boards and school restructuring: A contradiction in terms?* Paper presented at the annual meeting of the American Educational Research Association, Atlanta, April.

Resnick, M. A. 1999. *Effective school governance: A look at today's practice and tomorrow's promise.* Denver: Education Commission of the States.

Riverside Publishing Company, and Taylor, C. S. n.d. Washington Assessment of Student Learning: Technical Reports for 1998, 1999, 2000, and 2001. http://www .kl2.wa.us/assessment/TestCoordinators.aspxttechrpt.

Robinson, N., and M. Wood. 1987. Why school board members choose to seek or not seek re-election: A test of political efficacy and trust theory. Paper presented at the annual meeting of the American Educational Research Association, Washington, DC. (ERIC Document Reproduction Service No. ED 282310)

Russell, M. 1997. A study of the relationship between school board leadership behavior and advancement of instructional quality. *Dissertation Abstracts International* 57 (08): 3349. (UMI No. 9700667)

Scott, H. J. 1991. Leadership imperatives for school board members in the reform and renewal of public schools. Paper presented at the annual meeting of the National School Boards Association, San Francisco, April. (ERIC Document Reproduction Service No. ED 336857)

Sergiovanni, T. J. 1992. *Moral leadership: Getting to the heart of school improvement.* San Francisco: Jossey-Bass.

Smoley, E. R., Jr. 1999. *Effective school boards: Strategies for improving board performance.* San Francisco: Jossey-Bass.

Streshly, W. A., and L. F. Frase. 1993. School boards: The missing piece of the reform pie. *International Journal of Educational Reform* 2 (2): 140–143.

Sullivan, P. M. 1990. The relationship between incumbent school board member replacement and superintendent turnover for selected South Carolina school districts from 1978–1988. *Dissertation Abstracts International* 52(01), 50A. (UMI No. 9117329)

Thomas, J. Y. 2001. The public school superintendency in the twenty-first century: The quest to define effective leadership (Report No. CRESPAR-R-55). Baltimore: Johns Hopkins. (ERIC Document Reproduction Service No. ED460219)

The Twentieth Century Fund/Danforth Foundation. 1992. *Facing the challenge: The report of the Twentieth Century Fund Task Force on school governance.* New York: Twentieth Century Fund Press.

Underwood, K. E., J. C. Fortune, and F. J. Cleary. 1985. Heads up: Here's how school boards are energizing public education. *American School Board Journal* 172 (1): 25–28.

Weninger, T. A., and R. T. Stout. 1989. Dissatisfaction Theory: Policy change as a function of school board member–superintendent turnover. *Educational Administration Quarterly* 25 (2): 162–180.

Whitson, A. 1998. Are local school boards obsolete? *Childhood Education* 74 (3): 172–173.

Wilson, J. C. 1994. Urban education: A board member's perspective. *Phi Delta Kappan* 75 (5): 382–386.

Wirt, F. M., and M. W. Kirst. 1992. *Schools in conflict: The politics of education.* 3rd ed. Berkeley, CA: McCutchan.

———. 2006. *The political dynamics of American education.* 2nd ed. Berkeley, CA: McCutchan.

Zeigler, L. H., and M. K. Jennings. 1974. *Governing American schools.* North Scituate, MA: Duxbury Press.

Zeigler, L. H., E. Kehoe, and J. Reisman. 1985. *City managers and school superintendents.* New York: Praeger.

13

School Boards and Raising Student Outcomes: Reflections (Confessions?) of a Former Urban School Board Member

Sam Stringfield

INTRODUCTION

The question "Can school boards make a difference in students' academic accomplishments?" is addressed through a combination of a case study and review of research on school board effects. The case study is the New Board of School Commissioners of Baltimore City (Maryland). From the spring of 1999 through June of 2005, I had the privilege of serving on the New Board of School Commissioners of the Baltimore City (Maryland) Public School System (BCPSS). The review of research on school board effects was conducted by a colleague and me (Land, 2002; Land and Stringfield, 2005). These were done because I found the experience of being on an urban school board confusing, and I wanted help in making sense of it. Alone (Stringfield, forthcoming) and with a colleague (Stringfield and Yaki-mowski, 2005), I've written "scholarly" pieces on the effects of the work of that board on students' rates of academic success. Here I wanted to describe what it was like to be on the school board of a large, historically troubled school system. I do not claim my experiences would generalize to all of the people who serve, typically for no pay, on the 15,000+ local school boards. I do hope my observations can be useful to a few of those good folks, and maybe to a few university- or foundation-based persons, too.

Twelve themes of my experience are as follows:

1. School boards can help improve the academic experiences of students.
2. Boards must have clear goals.

3. Getting accurate data and information is key.
4. Working across organizational levels is essential.
5. The work—especially the homework—required to make a positive impact is substantial, and mostly tedious.
6. Teamwork is key.
7. The environment in which school boards (and school systems) work is inherently political, not in an "evil" sense, but in the sense of diverse, often legitimate power vectors that must be addressed. If/where/when school boards didn't exist, politicians would create them to serve as political buffers.
8. Awareness of research can help. However, research on school board effectiveness is strikingly thin, and the quality of research often leaves much to be desired. Further, the guidance that can be provided by scholarly research is typically long term, and often not of use in the midst of any given fray.
9. Prior experience in relatively high-end public or private management can help.
10. The three largest levers board members hold are the superintendent's contract, the budget, and access to media.
11. A school board member's largest assets are formal and informal communications. The latter is also their Achilles heel.
12. An appreciation of the long haul, humor, and humility help.

Before delving into the data from which these twelve conclusions are reached, two sets of background data are summarized. The first is a brief post–World War II history of Baltimore and the Baltimore City Public Schools. The second is an even more brief description of my background, noted only because it had unusual components for a new school board member.

BALTIMORE AS CONTEXT

At the end of World War II, Baltimore was booming. The war effort had required steel, industrial capacity, liberty ships, and deep-water ports, and Baltimore supplied all four. In 1950, the U.S. Census reported the city had 949,000 residents. After almost continuous decline from there to the 21st century, Baltimore's population now hovers around 650,000. Over the last four decades, the BCPSS student population declined from 199,000 to below 90,000. BCPSS now has its lowest student population in nearly a century. Today's BCPSS student body is over 90 percent African American, and more than 80 percent of the students are eligible for federally supported free meals. Only a handful of other systems in the United States have similar combinations of size, percent minority, and poverty. Detroit, Cleveland, Saint Louis, Washington, D.C., and New Orleans (pre- and post-Katrina) very nearly complete the list. Chicago, Philadelphia, New York, and Los Angeles public schools don't come close in terms of prevalence of risk factors.

The de-industrialization, rise in poverty and crime, and exodus to the suburbs in all of those cities has created cultures of hopelessness, drugs, and violence. For nearly 20 years, Baltimore consistently had more than 300 murders per year, and for several years was ranked as one of the five most dangerous cities in America (these numbers improved significantly under Mayor, now Governor, Martin O'Malley). Sitting in our back yard, my wife and I occasionally heard semiautomatic weapons fire as drug dealers fought for turf. We somewhat—but not completely—got used to it.

William Manchester began his career as a city reporter on Baltimore's now defunct *Evening Sun*. He based his first novel around those experiences, and titled the book *The City of Anger*.

The effects of these social—and hence psychological—changes on the city, and especially on the school system, was multifaceted. A first response was "white flight" to the suburbs. This produced a decline in housing prices and a subsequent decline in the tax base to support the schools. The decline was such that by the mid-1990s, BCPSS was spending 18 percent less per student than any of the surrounding districts, and ranked 24th of 26 Maryland districts in per-pupil spending. This was in one of the neediest cities in America. Two other types of flight developed. One was the flight of affluent families of all races to expensive, often elitist private schools in the city. A more recent trend was "Black flight," middle-class Black families moving out of the city and into first-ring suburbs. This group included many of the teachers and administrators in BCPSS. Hence, larger and larger percentages of BCPSS educators were teaching "other people's children."

Today if one looks just a few blocks past Baltimore's beautiful Inner Harbor and sports complexes, one quickly realizes that Baltimore, like Cleveland and Detroit, is an unusually tough place in which to run a public school system.

As with most systems, BCPSS did not historically keep accurate data on such key variables as high school graduation rate, but the best available evidence was that the rate had been dropping for a generation, and by the mid-1990s was at (or possibly below) 40 percent of eighth-graders graduating in five to six years. A new authentic testing program, the Maryland School Performance Program (MSPAP) had begun in 1993, and for five consecutive years the BCPSS students' scores were not only by far the lowest in the state, but every year were falling further behind the state average. The gap was so great that in 1997, had the number of BCPSS students making reasonably adequate MSPAP scores tripled, the BCPSS percentage of students with satisfactory scores would still have been below the state's mean percentage.[1]

Further, two sets of plaintiffs had successfully worked their way through state and federal courts, demanding better education for their regular- and special education students. By the mid-1990s, the courts were threatening to take over the city's once-proud school system.

At this point the nature of the educational crisis in Baltimore had become politically intolerable. Led by Baltimore City Delegate Pete Rawlings[2] and supported by the state superintendent of schools, the state legislature negotiated a "partial state takeover" of BCPSS. The takeover had two key components. First, the state would provide additional funding for the schools. In Year 1 this would be $35 million, then $50 million in Year 2, and, in theory, the amount would rise thereafter.[3]

Second, the school board, which for generations had been appointed by the city's mayors, would be replaced by a New Board of School Commissioners. The law stipulated that the new board would be appointed through a three-way process in which the state superintendent would solicit and screen nominations, and the governor and mayor would then negotiate a final list of nine members. The board was to be representative of the larger Baltimore City community, a requirement that was universally interpreted to mean that the board should be—as the city is—majority African American.

Members' three-year terms would be staggered, with no member appointed for more than two full terms. The law that created the new board specifically prohibited the board from continuing the services of the then-current superintendent of schools.[4]

Unquestionably, the law anticipated reform driven by two forces. The first was a school board–driven reform of the Baltimore City School System. The state's lawmakers and the state school superintendent clearly viewed the then-current, mayorally appointed board and administration as hopeless and hapless. Various suggestions for new structures were floated, but none could gain politically practical traction, with the result being legislation of a new board to lead the effort.

The second presumed driver was the one on which the then-mayor and most of the state's politicians focused. This was the provision of additional money to BCPSS. Roughly one-eighth of the state's legislators lived inside Baltimore City. The other seven-eighths were being asked to allocate tax dollars to a school system that their constituents viewed as inefficient, corrupt, and, as several stated, "a black hole." (The statewide legislative coalition proved adequate for the initial funding, but it was several years before a two-party coalition could be brought together to fully fund agreed-upon reforms.[5]) Both at the time and in retrospect I believe that the added money was a necessary but not nearly sufficient condition of the subsequent improvements.

The *Baltimore Sun* and other local media ran repeated articles encouraging groups to nominate persons to the state superintendent for consideration. Dozens of people were nominated by diverse groups, and some people self-nominated. I was nominated by the American Civil Liberties Union (ACLU), in part because I had credible credentials, and in part because the education person for the ACLU was good friends with my wife's and my neighbors. I was not so much as called in for an interview by the state superintendent's screening team (the first cut).

A superb group of community leaders was chosen for the New Board, led by Dr. Tyson Tildon. Dr. Tildon had a long history of professional success and commendable service. He had been the first African American to obtain a PhD from the research side of Johns Hopkins medical institutions. He served as associate dean for research of the University of Maryland Medical Center. Dr. Tildon had a remarkable record of community service, including serving as president of the city's Public Library board, and on a variety of groups working to improve the city. As a scientist, he was continuously seeking data of all types. As a human being, he was firmly of the belief that children from virtually all backgrounds could learn at high levels.

Other persons chosen for the initial board included the dean of education at Morgan State University, a very successful co-owner of an increasingly national urban renewal group, the owner of a multi-state trucking corporation, a senior manager for the Social Security Administration, a long-term urban school reform advocate, a retired professor of counseling, and a vice president of Johns Hopkins hospitals, totaling nine community leaders.

A SCHOOL BOARD MEMBER IS CHOSEN

In the spring of 1997 I immodestly imagined I had very nearly ideal credentials to be a member of a school board in a high-poverty, troubled urban context. I was a principal research scientist at the Center for Social Organization of Schools (CSOS) at Johns Hopkins University. I'd spent my career studying various aspects of methods for creating more effective schools for students who were at substantial risk of failure. I'd directed or codirected several of the larger studies of school effects in the United States (e.g., Stringfield and Teddlie, 1991; Teddlie and Stringfield, 1993) and around the world (Reynolds, Creemers, Stringfield, Teddlie, and Schaffer, 2002); Chapter 1/Title I (e.g., Stringfield, Billig, and Davis, 1991; Borman, Stringfield, and Slavin, 2001); and whole school reform (Stringfield et al., 1997; Ross, Sanders, Wright, Stringfield, Wang, and Alberg, 2001; Datnow, Borman, Stringfield, Rachuba, and Castellano, 2003), and was founding coeditor of the *Journal of Education for Students Placed At Risk*. I codirected the systemic reform sections of two federally funded educational research centers: the Center for Research on the Education of Students Placed At Risk (CRESPAR) and the Center for Research on Excellence and Diversity in Education

(CREDE). Finally, I had been engaged in evaluations of two of the most successful school-level reforms in the city's previous decade: Success for All (Slavin and Madden, 2000) and the Barclay-Calvert experiment (Stringfield and Herman, 1995).

So when I'd been nominated to serve on Baltimore's New Board of School Commissioners in 1997 and didn't even make the first cut, I reasoned that whatever I offered, the city and state didn't want. Further, every senior scholar at CSOS advised me against even considering such service, which they viewed as a hopeless waste of energy and a diversion of talent. So, I put my energies back into a job I liked very much at Johns Hopkins.

As luck had it, 20 months later two members left the board, and I was asked by the ACLU to allow them to renominate me. I laughed and told them not only did we have ample evidence that I was unwanted, but now I was being nominated by a group that all levels of the existing power structure in the city and state despised. However, they continued asking, and I relented. I told my wife not to even think about my chances. I was chosen and sworn in, together with the daughter of the musician and actor Cab Calloway. Hence, when I began my service I was already "0 for 2" as a prognosticator, and should have known that I was in for an unpredictable ride.

"BACKWARD MAPPING"

Rather than working through details of the subsequent years, I want to "backward map" from the key data of the experience. While a wide range of local education topics can and do on occasion make front-page news, it is student outcome data that has become a constant feature of school and school system accountability in the eyes of politicians, the media, and parents. As a practical matter, for the first two groups, that means student test scores and graduation rates.[6]

As noted previously, Maryland had developed and launched (with much fanfare) statewide authentic assessments. The tests were authentic in that they relied on students' written responses to complex text and "real world"–type problems, as opposed to filling in responses on multiple choice tests. MSPAP produced a Composite Index (CI) for schools and school systems that was based on a combination of percentages of students' scores on MSPAP tests (in Grades 3, 5, and/or 8) and mean school attendance rates.[7] The Maryland School Performance Assessment Program (MSPAP) went statewide in the spring of 1993. The mean state CI rose from the initial implementation for several years. Within four years, the state's CI had risen by over 10 points, from 31.7 to 41.8. (Note that data in Table 13.1 present and contrast data from BCPSS with data from the rest of the state, removing BCPSS from the state portion of the analyses. This was done in order to heighten BCPSS ver-

Table 13.1. MSPAP

	State w/o BCPSS	BCPSS MSPAP	State–BCPSS gap
1993	35.4	10.4	24.0
1994	40.5	11.7	28.8
1995	43.9	13.8	30.1
1996	45.0	13.5	31.5
1997	46.1	13.9	32.2
			Gap widened by 8.2
BCPSS Reforms Began in the Spring of 1997			
1998	48.3	16.1	32.2
1999	47.7	17.0	30.7
2000	48.7	20.5	28.2
2001	46.5	22.5	24.0
2002	41.4	20.4	21.0
			After 5 years of reform: Gap narrowed by 11.2

sus state comparisons. Over the pre-reform years, the state CI rose 10.7 points, from 35.4 to 46.1. Comparisons involving the full state—including BCPSS—with BCPSS can be seen in Stringfield and Yakimowski, 2005.)

BCPSS's MSPAP CI began at a level by far the lowest in the state, at 10.4. This caused a great deal of political finger-pointing locally and statewide, and within the school system itself. The superintendent and the board vowed action, and the system was largely left to solve its problems. However, city scores rose only 3.5 points over the next four years. This meant that BCPSS was not only in last place by a great distance, it was falling much further behind the rest of the state. As previously described, this was politically unsurvivable, and a partial state takeover was negotiated.

In the five years following the 1997 introduction of the new board, the city-state gap shrank by 9.2 CI points (and in an analysis separating the BCPSS data from the rest of the state in Table 13.1, shrank by 11.2 points, or fully half the remaining gap), thus clearly reversing the previous multi-year trend.

One of MSPAP's limitations was that citizens, the media, and hence politicians had a hard time grasping the meaning of a concept as abstract as a CI. So, when the new board came in they re-initiated the district's historic pattern of administering nationally standardized tests. Table 13.2 presents data from the TerraNova testing of all students in Grades 1 through 8, 1998 through 2003. (Note that the test was not administered in Grades 7 and 8 in 1998, or in Grade 7 in 1999.) Especially in the early grades, Baltimore's children exhibited laudable gains on this nationally normed measure of achievement. Even at Grade 8, the students exhibited a mean improvement of 12 national percentiles in reading and 17 in mathematics.

Table 13.2.   CTBS/TerraNova Median Percentile Scores and Gains, BCPSS, 1998–2003

Subject Area	Grade							
	1	2	3	4	5	6	7	8
Total reading								
1998	25	23	25	22	16	12		
1999	37	27	26	22	16	12		21
2000	46	38	34	29	35	18	25	22
2001	55	44	41	35	41	22	28	25
2002	59	44	41	37	40	30	31	30
2003	59	50	41	40	41	31	33	33
5-year gain	34	27	16	18	25	19	8*	12**
Total mathematics								
1998	24	19	21	15	15	17		
1999	23	21	18	15	15	17		20
2000	37	32	32	26	28	21	22	20
2001	51	41	41	33	34	24	24	21
2002	54	43	43	35	36	29	28	32
2003	58	52	45	41	41	31	32	37
5-year gain	34	33	24	26	26	14	10*	17**

*3-year gain
**4-year gain

Adjusting to the requirements of No Child Left Behind (NCLB), the Maryland State Department of Education jettisoned the MSPAP and developed a set of tests targeted to new grade-level proficiency standards in reading and mathematics. The Maryland School Assessment (MSA) is described by the state as a criterion-based assessment program, with each grade's test targeted to the state's proficiency standards. The state published data at the school and district levels on the percentages of students scoring at the "basic" (e.g., not proficient), "proficient" (e.g., meeting the state criterion for the grade and academic content), and "advanced" levels. For NCLB reporting purposes, both proficient and advanced are summed as meeting standards, and hence are reported as "proficient" in Table 13.3. As with the MSPAP, for comparison purposes, Maryland State data are presented as "Maryland minus Baltimore" so that BCPSS does not influence changes in its comparison group.

As can be seen in Table 13.3, the average Maryland school and district had produced mean gain scores over time at Grades 3, 5, and 8 (and, although not reported here, Grades 4, 6, and 7 as well) in both reading and mathematics over the past five years. Across the three grades presented and two content areas, the average gain has been 15.2 percent more students obtaining a "proficient" or "advanced" score. Obviously, this is laudable.

Table 13.3.   Baltimore and Maryland without Baltimore MSA over Time (% Students Scoring Proficient or Advanced)

	Grade 3 Reading/ Math	Grade 5 Reading/ Math	Grade 8 Reading/ Math	Mean Difference (Maryland-BCPSS)
Maryland 2003 (w/o BCPSS)	60.4 / 67.9	68.2 / 57.9	63.2 / 43.0	60.1
Maryland 2007 (w/o BCPSS)	81.8 / 80.4	78.5 / 79.8	70.9 / 60.2	75.3
Maryland Improvement	21.3 / 12.5	10.3 / 21.9	7.7 / 17.2	15.2
BCPSS 2003	39.1 / 41.9	44.4 / 31.2	32.8 / 11.5	33.5
BCPSS 2007	68.8 / 62.0	30.3 / 63.9	43.8 / 24.0	53.8
BCPSS Improvement	29.7 / 20.1	15.9 / 32.7	11.0 / 12.5	20.3

Over the same five years, three grades, and two content areas, BCPSS has produced a mean gain of 20.3 percent more students achieving "proficient" or "advanced" scores. While both the city and the state have made gains, BCPSS has reduced the gap between its students and those of the rest of the state in four years by a quarter (26.6 percent to 21.5).

Elementary and middle school test scores are only valuable to the extent they indicate how well a school, school system, or state does at graduating students and preparing them for the world of work, service, and/or college. Currently Maryland lacks the integrated database necessary to chart post–high school academic success. However, the state does gather data on high school graduation rates (calculated from ninth grade forward to graduation). As can be seen in Table 13.4, before the 1997 reforms, BCPSS was graduating less than 43 percent of its ninth-graders four years later.[8] A decade ago, Maryland (without BCPSS) was graduating 84.8 percent of its students. By 2006, that percent had risen to 88.2 percent, for an increase of 3.4 percent. In contrast, pre-reform Baltimore had graduated 42.6 percent of its students, and that percentage has risen to 60.6 percent in 2006 (the last year for which data are currently available). BCPSS recorded a gain of 18.1 percent.[9] I believe this to be the largest gain in high school graduation of any large American city in the last decade. Such a gain represents a clear improvement in the potential life trajectories for literally thousands of young Americans.

Summarizing the outcome data, whether the measure is first-grade achievement, high school graduation rates, or any of several intermediate measures, BCPSS has made very significant, possibly nation-leading gains post-reform. Given that the fundamental element of the 1997 reforms was

Table 13.4.   Maryland and BCPSS Graduation Rates over Time

Year	Maryland w/o BCPSS	BCPSS	Maryland/BCPSS gap
1996	84.8	42.6	42.2
1997	85.5	46.2	39.3
1998	85.3	46.0	39.3
1999	86.1	49.5	36.6
2000	86.2	50.6	35.6
2001	86.3	58.7	27.6
2002	87.0	58.5	28.5
2003	88.4	54.2	34.2
2004	87.8	54.3	33.5
2005	87.8	59.0	28.8
2006	88.2	60.6	27.6
Gain (1996–2006)	3.6	18.0	−14.6

the creation of the New Board of School Commissioners, and that, as discussed below, the years have seen five CEOs (Baltimore's school superintendents), it is reasonable to attribute much of the gain to the actions of the city's New Board of School Commissioners.

A REFLECTION ON "WHAT WORKED" IN THE REFORMS

Assuming readers agree the four tables present a compelling case that the Baltimore City Public Schools' students made substantial academic progress in the decade post-restructuring, I devote the remainder of this chapter to discussing twelve of the themes that I believe contributed to these improvements.

1. School Boards can help improve the academic experiences of students. Indeed, sometimes the school board provides the critical link without which improvement would not happen.

BCPSS presents a straightforward existence proof of that statement. From 1997 to today BCPSS has had five CEOs. Every other major leadership position in the system has turned over at least once, and most several times. The system has had four chief academic officers (deputy superintendents for curriculum and instruction), four chief financial officers, and four directors of research and assessment. The stabilizing force throughout has been the one intended in the 1997 restructuring legislation: the New Board of School Commissioners.

The board has consistently stood for higher achievement for all students, and for fiscal responsibility. Given the declining student population, legislators demanded that the board close schools, and several tauntingly said that the board didn't have the stomach for the job. The board held hearings across the city and has led two separate cycles of school closings.

The board has stood for aggressive hiring of highly qualified teachers and more demanding curricula. It has stood for fair, tough negotiations with the various unions, and has replaced HR directors who would not or could not do so.

As the system peeled back the layers needing total overhaul (or in some cases mild refining), the board has stood behind each CEO who would take the necessary tough stands. Whether the issue was testing, budgeting, curriculum change, or professional development, the board stood for improvement. When CEOs and/or others would not take tough stands, the board calmly replaced them. When a former CEO and former Chief Academic Officer (CAO) recklessly overspent the budget, the board took the blame and worked with Baltimore's then-mayor to solve the very serious problem. When layoffs were necessary, the board took responsibility. When rising test scores were announced, the board choreographed having Baltimore's children make the key announcements.

Other examples of school boards making a large difference include the Iowa School Board Effects Study, so Baltimore's is more than simply an isolated existence proof.

2. Boards must have clear goals.

Baltimore's New Board produced a clear, bounded, multi-year master plan.

No substitute can be found for knowing what you want as a board member and as a board. Over time you can learn how to get there, but at first you have to decide, individually and as a group, where you want to go. That way, when the inevitable arrives and you must make tough choices (e.g., whether to buy new school buses, computers, more professional development, another ? percent raise for your highly deserving teachers, more library books or reading specialists; whether to budget for HR or testing or maintenance; whether to send teachers to national conferences or, indeed, whether to attend national conferences yourself), you have guiding principles. They need to be stated publicly and referenced regularly. As something more than a footnote, having more than three to five goals is the same thing as having none.

3. Getting accurate data and information is key.

Data and information are not the same things. Test scores and budget sheets can yield "hard data" to someone trained to understand them. Together with clear goals, data can often be translated into information that can at least partially address such questions as "Are we heading toward one or more of our goals?"

Board members also receive a range of other information, whether they want to or not. (I advocate for allowing all information in, and then triangulating to determine the factual nature of the incoming information and the reliability of the sources.)

First, board members need to be visiting schools. Walk the halls during and between classes. Are they clean? Orderly? Sit with students and/or teachers in the lunchrooms. Play kickball with first-graders and visit carpentry and beautician shops in high schools. Admire students' work. Tour the school kitchens. If you can smell stale urine outside the boys' bathroom, that's a very bad sign. Visit the school bus stop and the book depository. Ask and answer direct questions. There is no substitute for firsthand data.

Second, people seek you out to tell you things. Listen attentively and respectfully. Unless you know the source well, remember to triangulate what you hear. Data and facts are not the same. It is a fact that someone said something to you. What they said may or may not be factual.

A former U.S. deputy secretary of state once observed to me that the higher you go in an organization, the harder it is to get accurate data. The reason is more and more smart people who have vested interests in having you see things their way. Superintendents, many central office people, and most principals are smart people. The huge majority are not pathological liars, but they all have points of view, and those points of view may or may not be factually defensible.

Develop "drill down" skills and contacts. A lot of the things a board can help improve do not require the special skills of a rocket scientist, CPA, or psychometrician, but they almost all require excellent crud filters.

To the best of my recollection, in 5.5 years on the BCPSS school board, I rarely went a week without someone trying to influence my thinking on an upcoming issue before the board. None of the data were worthless, and some were accurate.

4. Working across organizational levels is essential.

Work with your state school board association and the National School Boards Association. Either they have experienced your specific problem before, or they probably know someone who has.

State departments of education almost always want local boards to succeed. As more of your schools fall into NCLB purgatory (whatever it is called in your state), work with the state to agree on a path forward. The path may not resolve the issue, but it demonstrates your openness and willingness to work together to solve problems.

If you live in a state that has teachers unions, the union contract is negotiated (through the administration) with the board. The board must strive for friendly, transparent relationships with the union. However, in our experience, it was almost always harmful when an individual attempted to negotiate with the union without the permission of the board chair and the knowledge of the superintendent.

The theme here is to be open to all formal lines of communication, and to be willing—as a group—to entertain potentially productive (not undercutting) informal communication across a variety of vertical and horizontal boundaries.

5. The work—especially the homework—required to make a positive impact is large, and mostly tedious.

Starting out as a new school board member who wanted to be responsible was one of the hardest tasks I ever undertook. A tremendous number of issues existed on which I knew nothing. What was a reasonable budget for heating? What is a reasonable policy on lost books among students on free lunch? How many sick days should a person be able to accrue? What happens if we ask teachers to assume a larger share of their health benefits (as I was being required to do at Johns Hopkins)? What are the (changing) black, white, and gray areas in my state's sexual harassment laws? Which reading series should the system buy and how much professional development time should we allocate to the transition from old to new? How much should the board pay a superintendent? BCPSS had a 150-page, 9-point-type budget. At what level of detail should diverse board members examine it and potentially intervene in it? How many committees should a member serve on, and in what roles? Does the board have rules and/or norms on such issues as "When should a board and/or a board member support a statement by a superintendent or fellow board member, and when should the board not? In public? In private?"

It is often valuable to remember that "if improvements were easy, somebody else would have made them already."

6. Teamwork is key.

No board member can be knowledgeable about everything. Teamwork is key. Teams only rarely evolve accidentally. Much more often they are consciously, carefully built. During the five years that Dr. Tyson Tildon was chair of the BCPSS New Board of School Commissioners, he worked constantly to create and hold together a productive, trusting team, so that even when members disagreed—which happened regularly—they did so respectfully of one another's persons and opinions.

7. The environment in which school boards (and school systems) work is inherently political, not in an "evil" sense, but in the sense of diverse, often legitimate power vectors that must be addressed. If/where/when school boards didn't exist, politicians would create them.

School boards fill a vital role in local politics and administration. School boards allocate limited public resources in ways that attempt to maximize general and specific public goods. Such tasks almost define *political*, not in a "dirty" sense, but in a responsible sense.[10]

Throughout my service on the BCPSS board, I struggled to define both my job and that of the larger board. I concluded that if America's school boards were to vaporize, within a week, local, state, and national politicians would be working hard to recreate them. The reason is that boards provide a level of public accountability for the allocation of contested public resources and the precious time of millions of our most vulnerable citizens. Elected politicians don't want to be directly responsible to parents/taxpayers/voters for the education—let alone the happiness—of every child in a city. Parents, grandparents, school neighbors, educators, political conservatives and liberals, and a range of other people want to know someone is available to whom they can complain about X (where X represents almost any of a thousand things, including dirty hallways, disrespectful students on the sidewalks after school, the need to close schools, or high school taxes). When something goes wrong in the lives of students, teachers, et cetera, mayors and other politicians want a group they can point to and demand action (as opposed to their having to take action and hence public responsibility for actions in an uncertain space themselves).

8. Awareness of research can help, though research on school board effectiveness is strikingly thin, and the quality of research often leaves much to be desired. Further, the guidance that can be provided by scholarly research is typically long-term, and often not of use in the midst of any given fray.

After a couple of years on the BCPSS board, I was struck by how many decisions I'd helped make, and how little research had influenced our board's decisions. This wouldn't be a terribly striking realization for most of America's over 90,000+ school board members, but I was a principal research scientist at Johns Hopkins University, I studied educational effectiveness for a living, and I had told myself my research background would be a core strength as I worked on the board. Clearly, it hadn't been.

Coincidentally, I had just hired a wonderfully trained young psychologist, and decided to assign to her the task of reviewing all existing research on school board effectiveness. She worked hard and reviewed all the scholarship available on the topic. She identified well over 100 books and articles on the topic, 118 of which she referenced in her scholarly review (Land, 2002). The quality of Land's scholarly effort was clear; however, the practical value of almost all previous research on school boards was obvious and frustrating.

Land concluded more effective boards focused on students' academic achievement and policy; had good relations with the superintendent, other agencies, and local and state governments and the public, as well as between school board members; and had clear goals that included students' academic achievement. They exhibited leadership (though this was poorly defined) and responsible budgeting, and they conducted adequate evaluations of themselves, the superintendent, and major initiatives. They engaged in ongoing training and development. Interestingly in the current context, Land concluded that in the entire field over 20 years of scholarship, two reasonably rigorous studies of school board effectiveness had been conducted. One was by Hoffman (1995) in the Netherlands, and the other was by the Iowa Association of School Boards (2000) in their deservedly praised "Lighthouse Study."

The shallowness of research on school boards almost defies belief. As a practicing school board member, I found some of my basic assumptions strengthened but otherwise gained only modest additional knowledge from her excellent scholarship. This chapter is written in part in the hope of helping others with something approximating more actionable advice.

9. Prior experience in the relatively high-end public or private management may help.

If nothing else, an experienced administrator may not have the shock I experienced when I was expected to help create, evaluate, and balance budgets approaching a billion dollars. Assuming it did not create a sense of helplessness, experience in dealing with large bureaucracies would be an asset.

10. The three largest levers board members hold are the superintendent's contract, the budget, and access to media.

Each of these deserves separate notice. In a strictly bureaucratic sense, the board only has one employee: the superintendent. Our experience in BCPSS was that a shortage of qualified candidates always existed, and our choices were always people who—like ourselves—had substantial areas of limitation. That said, it was important to declare annual, measurable goals for the superintendent and the system, and to hold the superintendent accountable for performance. The teachers had union contracts, but the superintendents did not. Superintendents are paid more than most of us in no small part because they can be held accountable.

Regarding the budget: Deep Throat was right. If you want to understand—
let alone control—what is happening in a school system, you have to "follow the money." An irresponsible or less than fully competent superintendent and leadership team can—and in our case did—get themselves and the
board into months and years of "crisis management" and loss of credibility
among the citizens. A budget in the red $1,000 makes the front page of the
local papers; a budget in the red by millions makes the front page for
months, perhaps years. Credibility is a very hard thing to build and is very
easy to destroy. A bad budget is a one-way ticket to trouble. It is far better to
be "forced" to spend a million dollars at the end of the year on library books
and computers than to be forced to lay off one teacher at mid-year.

Media can make or break a school board. Several BCPSS board members
had such low trust with the *Baltimore Sun* and the city's other media that
they simply refused to be interviewed. My belief was that the fourth estate
had a right and an obligation to investigate virtually everything we did and
to report on it. We were likely to get more favorable reporting if we engaged
constructively with the newspapers and the electronic media. The media
can be your friend or they can make your life miserable. Your relationship
with them is eternally somewhat/sometimes adversarial. That's okay. But on
other occasions you want a specific slant on a bad-news story or you want
a good-news story to get some coverage. Reporters understand the deal. You
give them copy when they need it, and both the reporters and the system
look a little better. Then when you need a "good news" story about an improving school, maybe you can convince them to run it. You can like 'em or
hate 'em, but a free press is part of what makes America great, and you
might as well work with them. They can make a large difference in public
perspectives on the board's work.

Do not lie to or otherwise abuse a reporter. They have long memories and
they have much more potential to "get even" in public than do school
board members.

The final two items are interrelated.

*11. A school board member's largest assets are formal and informal
communications. The latter is also their Achilles heel.*

One fiscal year I boxed every single document that came to me from the
Baltimore City Public Schools System. Twelve months later, the boxes were
stacked taller than my 6'3" frame. That's more information than an unpaid
volunteer with another, demanding job can integrate in 12 months. It also
reflects the system's inability to focus on a few key goals. In that environment, a board's ability to talk to one another and to ask focused questions
at board meetings becomes extremely important. Communication among

board members and with the CEO/superintendent, almost always focusing on key goals of the system, becomes key.

Earlier I noted the challenges in getting clear data as to ground-level realities in any large organization. In BCPSS, every member of the board had long-standing relationships with one or more employees of the system, and necessarily developed relationships with others. These become valuable "drill down" opportunities. However, information gathered through those channels is as subject to being misrepresentations as any other, and should be triangulated before being acted upon.

Having observed that, it is also important to note that the eternal enemy of decision makers is time. Decisions have to be made in real time. On the BCPSS board, as in all other leadership tasks, decisions typically have to be made in the absence of complete and clear data, and individual actors have to decide which among the contradictory data to weigh most heavily. I am aware of no simple rules for making those decisions. While I note the obvious problems with both formal and informal channels, I would hypothesize that one's systems are richer and one's decisions are more likely to be good ones if both channels carry some weight.

12. School board members should remember that appreciation of the long haul, humor, and humility all help.

In the leadership of a large organization, any person or group should be aware that day-to-day the probability of making errors is 100 percent. We are human. However, if we continue working toward clear goals, continue gathering data on our progress, and continue rechecking our initial assumptions and decisions, we are capable of moving over the long haul toward our intended goals. If the BCPSS school board–centered reforms say nothing else, they say that in spite of our multiple errors, students' progress is possible over the long haul. Get the big-picture, long-term stuff right, and do your best on the details.

Humility is critical for continuous improvement. In BCPSS it was essential we all realized that we were doing the best we could, but we could be wrong, too. That didn't mean we weren't trying hard or weren't smart: it meant that the problems we faced were long-standing and complex. Our best efforts would require regular adjustments. Decisions weren't right just because "we said so."

In that and other regards, humor—especially laughing at oneself, but also with others—is key. Successes are rare enough that they should be celebrated. Failings have to be rectified. In both cases laughter can be part of the glue that holds individuals and groups together.

SUMMARY

The United States and virtually every other country set up school boards almost as soon as they set up free public schools. Since then, a continuous discussion of the best organizing principles for school boards and debates about the effectiveness of specific boards and the general institution has emerged.

The New Board of School Commissioners of Baltimore City Public Schools was created in 1997 out of a combination of community/state dissatisfaction with the working of the old board and the universally perceived need to improve the educational opportunities provided to Baltimore's children. Over the subsequent decade, results have been clear and dramatically positive. Measured on three different testing systems, achievement scores have climbed at rates far exceeding those of the larger state. High school graduation rates have increased by a full 18 percentiles at a time when the rest of the state's rate has increased by less than 4 percentiles.

In reflecting on the experience of being a member of the BCPSS board, I've drawn 12 themes to help explain the gains. Others certainly exist, but I hope these are useful to the readers.

NOTES

1. It is important—and depressing—to remember that the state's mean rating would have been higher had it not included BCPSS, so had BCPSS improved, the state average would have risen, too. BCPSS would probably have had to quadruple its pass rate to reach the upwardly adjusted state rate.

2. Delegate Rawlings died in 2003.

3. In practice, state political will flagged, and substantial increases in state funding were not forthcoming for several years.

4. In fact, the top 14 members of the pre-1997 BCPSS administration all resigned, creating a large void at the top.

5. While any additional funding was essential to the improvement of the system, I've always felt that several aspects of the reform would only take hold when the mean pay for BCPSS teachers at least equaled, and probably exceeded, that of surrounding, easier-to-teach-in suburban districts. BCPSS had a multidecade history of hiring new college graduates, paying for their courses so that they could obtain full teacher licensure, and then having those experienced, fully licensed teachers move to the surrounding counties. As a result, BCPSS had to hire over a thousand new teachers a year. Note that research on teacher tenure is that the "value added" by teachers is lowest at first year and increases for the first several years of gained experience.

6. For individual parents, the story remains—as it should be—much more complex.

7. Additional measures were used for high schools, but these never gained prominence in state discussions.

8. Analyses conducted independently at CSOS indicated that the actual graduation rate might be as much as 4 to 5 percent lower than calculated by the state if one began measurement in the spring of eighth grade (see Stringfield and Yakimowski, 2005).

9. The difference is due to rounding of hundredths of percentages.

10. Boards can also be corrupt, and I don't want to claim otherwise. But I believe that to be a very small minority.

REFERENCES

Borman, G., S. Stringfield, and R. Slavin, eds. 2001. *Title I: Compensatory education at the crossroads.* Mahwah, NJ: Lawrence Erlbaum.

Datnow, A., G. Borman, S. Stringfield, L. Rachuba, and M. Castellano. 2003. Comprehensive school reform in culturally and linguistically diverse contexts: Implementation and outcomes from a four-year study. *Educational Evaluation and Policy Analysis* 25 (2): 143–170.

Hoffman, R. H. 1995. Contextual influences on school effectiveness: The roles of school boards. *School Effectiveness and School Improvement* 6:308–331.

Iowa Association of School Boards. 2000. IASB's Lighthouse Study: School boards and student achievement. *Iowa School Board Compass* 5 (2): 1–12.

Land, D. 2002. Local school boards under review: Their role and effectiveness in relation to students' academic achievement. *Review of Educational Research* 72 (2): 229–278.

Land, D., and S. Stringfield. 2005. Educational governance reforms: The uncertain role of local school boards in the United States. In *International handbook of educational policy,* ed. N. Bascia, A. Cumming, A. Datnow, K. Leithwood, and D. Livingstone, 260–280. New York: Kluwer.

Reynolds, D., B. Creemers, S. Stringfield, C. Teddlie, and G. Schaffer. 2002. *World-class schools: International perspectives on school effectiveness.* New York: Routledge/Falmer.

Ross, S., W. Sanders, P. Wright, S. Stringfield, L. Wang, and M. Alberg. 2001. Two- and three-year achievement results from the Memphis Restructuring Initiative. *School Effectiveness and School Improvement* 12 (3): 323–346.

Slavin, R., and N. Madden. 2000. Research on achievement outcomes of Success For All: A summary and response to critics. *Phi Delta Kappan* 82 (1): 38–40, 59–66.

Stringfield, S. Forthcoming. Improvements in academic achievement among African American students over time: National data and an urban case study. *Journal of Negro Education,* special 75th anniversary issue.

Stringfield, S., S. Billig, and A. Davis. 1991. A research-based program improvement process for Chapter 1 schools: A model and early results. *Phi Delta Kappan* 72 (8): 600–606.

Stringfield, S., and R. Herman. 1995. The Barclay/Calvert experiment: At-risk students get a highly reliable implementation of a proven program, and respond with dramatically higher achievement. Invited paper presented at the meeting of the International Congress for School Effectiveness and Improvement, Leeuwarden, The Netherlands, January.

Stringfield, S., M. A. Millsap, R. Herman, N. Yoder, N. Brigham, P. Nesselrodt, E. Schaffer, N. Karweit, M. Levin, and R. Stevens (with B. Gamse, M. Puma, S. Rosenblum, J. Beaumont, B. Randall, and L. Smith). 1997. *Urban and suburban/rural special strategies for educating disadvantaged children. Final report.* Washington, DC: U.S. Department of Education.

Stringfield, S., and C. Teddlie. 1991. Schools as affectors of teacher effects. In *Effective teaching: Current research,* ed. H. Waxman and H. Walberg, 161–179. Berkeley, CA: McCutchan.

Stringfield, S., and M. Yakimowski. 2005. The promise, progress, problems, and paradoxes of three phases of accountability: A longitudinal case study of the Baltimore City Public Schools. *American Educational Research Journal* 42 (1): 43–76.

Teddlie, C., and S. Stringfield. 1993. *Schools make a difference.* New York: Teachers College Press.

VII

REVELATION: SCHOOL BOARD'S VIABILITY AND POSSIBLE FUTURE

14

Elected versus Appointed Boards

Thomas E. Glass

THE CRITICAL MISSION OF ELECTED AND
APPOINTED URBAN BOARDS

The question of whether elected dysfunctional large urban school district boards should be replaced or substantially restructured is a serious policy question impacting the lives of million of students. A recognizable linkage clearly exists between governance at the board level and performance of students and teachers in classrooms. Although board members may not directly intervene in classrooms, they certainly control the management, budget, and operational factors impacting the daily lives of teachers and students. Governance carried out competently ensures administrators the tools to lead the instructional program and manage operations. Incompetent governance creates instability, doubt, uncertainty, and ineffective leadership on the part of the superintendent and administration.

Until the 1960s, a majority of large urban boards were appointed by mayors and other political bodies. Amidst the civil rights era, both elected and appointed urban boards ceased being populated by "community elites." New "reform" board members largely came from neighborhood groups with a sprinkling of professionals possessing organizational leadership experience. By the 1970s the power transition from community elites was completed in most cities.

With popularly elected board members came a new form of board politics. Previously, politics had been principally confined to interaction between political groups, business, civic organizations, and board members

(Tyack, 1974). New board members without ties to civic organizations saw local, state, and private groups as an enemy withholding needed resources and support. In the midst of transition to elected boards, white flight and displacement of the business tax base to suburbs occurred in many cities. Many board members became disillusioned with failures in improving achievement and did not seek reelection. In their place came a substantial number of "politicized" members running on single-issue personal agendas.

The result of three and a half decades of elected boards in many large urban districts has been massive underachievement and political chaos. It would be unfair to attribute all the chaos and underperformance to the boards. However, in district after district over a period of time elected boards have not been able to effectively lead and manage an urban institution under stress.

FLAWED GOVERNANCE

Large urban school districts are complex organizations serving communities facing a myriad of social, economic, and education problems. Lay governance systems have often been flawed due to competing political agendas, board member behavior, corruption, and lately invasive state and federal requirements. Current superintendents are frequently unable to negotiate between serving boards and meeting unrealistic community expectations. Seldom do they have the time and energy to fix the large dysfunctional bureaucracy obstructing paths to achievement gains and fiscal efficiency.

Prime evidence of flawed board governance has been in high superintendent turnover. Between 1994 and 2004, 35 urban districts serving near 11 million students appointed 135 superintendents and interim superintendents. These turnovers usually resulted in further destabilizing districts desperately attempting to raise test scores and meet state standards (Glass, 2002b, p. 1).

The tenure of individual urban superintendents varies, but a group average in the large urban districts is about three years. Most school reform policy experts agree three to five years is necessary for a superintendent to initiate reforms and see initial effects (Hess, 1999). Most urban superintendents never remain long enough to see the results of the reforms they were hired by the board to implement. Excessive superintendent turnover is sufficient evidence to justify abandonment of elected boards or seriously restructuring current boards' role and powers. It is imperative that superintendents form a functioning leadership team in these at-risk districts.

Few large urban districts in the last 10 years did not make at least three or four permanent and interim appointments: Atlanta (3), Baltimore (4), Birmingham (6), Boston (2), Broward (4), Charlotte (4), Chicago (3),

Cincinnati (3), Cleveland (7), Columbus (5), Dallas (6), Denver (5), Detroit (3), District of Columbia (5), Houston (4), Indianapolis (3), Kansas City (6), Los Angeles (2), Louisville (1), Memphis (3), Miami-Dade (6), Milwaukee (4), Minneapolis (4), Nashville (2), New Orleans (7), New York (4), Oakland (4), Philadelphia (2), Pittsburgh (3), Portland (5), San Antonio (2), San Diego (2), San Francisco (2), and Seattle (3). Importantly, superintendent turnover was stabilized in Boston, Chicago, Cleveland, and Philadelphia, where appointed boards were created in the 1990s.

ELECTED BOARD FAILURES

Coincidentally, accompanying superintendent turnover is a rapid turnover of urban board members. Several studies suggest urban board members possess nearly the same tenure as superintendents (Glass, 2002a). Success for urban districts is integrally connected to effective neighborhood school leadership. How can this occur when the district's top leadership is unstable? And, can it occur without first reforming board governance? Leadership stability may be the most critical urban education problem that can be remedied.

Policy makers neither understand nor appreciate the critical role urban school boards and superintendents can play in improving academic achievement. This is apparent as 20 years of reform efforts targeting instruction, curriculum, and building leadership have produced minimal results in most large urban districts. Almost ignored have been the daily role, actions, and possibilities of superintendents and boards. Reformers have seriously misjudged the significant influence superintendents and boards can possess over reform initiatives. Urban districts dictated to by state mandates have directed reform designed to *cure* instability at the bottom. Architects of bottom-up reforms might have examined successful restructuring of unstable corporations or governmental organizations, where change almost always begins at the governance and executive levels where policy is developed and implemented.

While the action in school districts may be in classrooms, most resource allocation and daily policy are in the hands of the board and the superintendent. State legislators, governors, the private sector and community may demand reform, but in the end the "what and how" is in the hands of the board and superintendent. Numerous legislated reforms have been needed and timely, but seldom succeed in urban districts afflicted with board turmoil and superintendent turnover. Despite over 20 years of watching reform fail in large urban districts, states have not studied the reasons for board failure. Some have taken direct action to replace boards in cases of district failure over managing finances, low achievement, corruption, or board conflict. A few such as Illinois have taken action to replace elected boards with appointed boards having different roles and responsibilities.

THE ELECTED BOARD'S LACK OF
A POLITICAL POWER BASE

Board stability, demonstrated by putting politics aside and reaching policy consensus, is the key to preventing disabling policy and superintendent "churn." Superintendents staying five to six years have a better chance to create effective management teams that can successfully lead reform initiatives. However, these teams need sufficient time to gain the trust of staff members, parents, political leaders, and citizens. The typical "churn" of three to four years is insufficient for a superintendent's team to gain the trust and establish working relationships with all district stakeholders.

Most new urban superintendents are outsiders both to the district and community. A first important challenge is building working relationships with local political and governmental leaders. Urban boards, while usually elected, have little if any citywide political power base. In most cities they have minimal if any influence in raising and distributing tax dollars. New superintendents are immediately locked in battle with state and local political power brokers for scarce resources. This high-stakes political game is complicated by board expectations for immediate financial and educational miracles. At the same time test score miracles must not create conflict inside or outside the district! Urban superintendents are often set up for political failure as quick change initiates conflict quickly brought to the attention of board members. Boards seldom take responsibility when reform conflict occurs. Successful urban superintendents are those understanding urban political processes and being adroit at keeping the district from falling into conflicts with political, community, and religious power groups.

ELECTED URBAN BOARDS:
THE RIGHT PEOPLE FOR THE JOB?

The majority of urban school boards are elected (Hess, 2002; Hoyle et al., 2004). Some board positions provide modest stipends, with all reimbursing actual expenses. Many citizens assume board positions are salaried and are amazed to find fellow citizens willing to assume a difficult and time-consuming public commitment for little or no compensation. Board members, just as superintendents, often find their positions to be more pain than gain.

In decades past, urban board members were often successful business and professional leaders. Elected urban boards today are seldom comprised of prominent "blue ribbon" business, professional, or civic leaders. A general description of current elected urban board members is that about half possess college degrees, modest financial resources, and a white-collar job (Hess, 2002). Many find board membership time requirements an interference with their regular employment. This likely is a contributing cause of increased board turnover and instability (Glass, 2001a).

Precise urban district board turnover data is not available. However, anecdotal comments and several recent superintendent studies indicate urban board turnover is increasing. The last national superintendent study conducted by the American Association of School Administrators found about half of urban board members reelected to a second term (Glass, Björk, and Brunner, 2002; Hess, 2002). Ironically, many urban superintendents do not survive the typical four-year board member term. Board turnover can easily result in superintendent turnover, as a new board majority wants a superintendent of its own choosing. This is especially true when special interest groups are successful in getting a slate of candidates elected.

THE POLITICS AND COSTS OF GETTING ELECTED TO A BOARD

Board elections in urban districts are increasingly hotly contested. Several articles describe Los Angeles and Dade County, Florida, board members spending in excess of $100,000 to be elected (Stover, 1997; Bushweller, 1996, p. 13; ASBJ, 2001, p. 5). This illustrates the high-stakes politics in getting elected to an urban board. Raising a large campaign chest can be a daunting challenge for "independent nonpolitical" board candidates (Hess, 2002, p. 35).

Various special political and conservative religious interest groups have emerged recently to elect slates of candidates. Large district superintendents report a dramatic increase in special interest group activity affecting policy and board elections (Glass, Björk, and Brunner, 2002). However, big money does not always elect board candidates. In the last Memphis board elections a candidate having little funding defeated a "corporate" candidate raising a sizable campaign war chest.

Special interest groups, when successful, expect a return on their money and time invested. Board members accepting special interest money may find themselves later compromised or in conflict with competing special interest groups. A good example of special interest group pressure occurs when hiring a superintendent. A racial minority board member may privately agree that a nonminority candidate is the best choice. However, this board member cannot openly support the candidate, fearing backlash from minority special interest groups. The necessity in some urban districts of accepting entangling support from special interest groups in order to get elected likely results in highly qualified candidates thinking twice about running for an unpaid public office (Bushweller, 1996).

Media frequently publicize negative events in the professional and personal lives of elected urban board members. This comes as a rude surprise to many urban board members never previously holding political office or being in prominent community leadership positions. Stories portraying serious legal, personal, political, and financial problems of board members are not uncommon. When this happens board stability is threatened, as the troubles of involved members become the focus of community attention. This often creates in the public mind the opinion that other board members are also miscreants.

Stories in the media frequently create the impression all urban board members possess single-issue political or personal agendas. This is certainly true in some but not all cases. Too many elected board members create this impression, immediately upon taking office, by boldly announcing they will try to convince the board to adopt policies aligning to their campaign agenda. Other media allegations are that urban board members use the position as a stepping-stone to higher and more lucrative political offices. This charge is true in some cases, as numerous former urban board members have later run for or been elected to city council or elected state positions. Fortunately, a majority of urban board members appear to be hard-working and law-abiding citizens. Unfortunately, too many frequently make the news and damage the board and district image.

THE FAILURE OF BOARDS TO CREATE
A POSITIVE LEADERSHIP ENVIRONMENT

Boards shape and create climates that may not be conducive to organizational leadership and system effectiveness. A board's attitude toward reform often encourages or discourages superintendents, principals, and teachers pursuing change. This seems often to occur in an environment where the board's rhetoric calls for reform but its actions deter reform. A typical example is approving a reform initiative but not providing sufficient funding for its success. Nearly every district program has its champion on the board and in the community. Reform initiatives usually compete in the political game of whose ox gets gored. This game can become especially vicious with elected boards as members attempt to protect programs (and neighborhood jobs) popular with their constituents. Such cases are good politics for individual board members but poor policy for the district.

Superintendents quickly learn parameters the board establishes in limiting their decision-making authority. Those with restricted decision-making parameters are encouraged to be pragmatic and maintain the status quo. The few with broad decision-making authority tend to be change agents. At risk are superintendents venturing outside the board-set parameters. This can quickly provoke a counterproductive conflict with one or more board members. Seldom, if ever, are superintendents given sufficient authority to make sweeping changes to policy, programs, and operations.

Politicized urban boards especially present superintendents with unclear and changing decision-making parameters. This is only partly attributable to board turnover and changing local political winds. Many urban boards never achieve articulation and consensus on district vision, mission, or the role of the superintendent. This often results in board members focusing on management detail rather than policy (Kowalski, 2002; Land, 2002). A confusing process of parameter setting by boards is a difficult challenge for reformist-minded superintendents and a primary cause for turnover.

Urban boards not only struggle with negative leadership district environments but also contend with severe political and private sector pressures. Some of these may produce both positive and negative effects. Most urban districts receive significant amounts of reform funding from federal, state, corporate, and foundation sources. These districts feel obligated to accept extramural funding or risk being portrayed as against reform, thus perpetuating student failure. In most cases external groups provide funding for expensive "silver bullet" programs promising to cure all the ills found in inner-city school classrooms.

Success of individual (usually lacking curriculum alignment) reform initiatives vary. Private funding agencies can become frustrated when they perceive no changes in the urban school bureaucracy. An example of displeasure with an urban board bureaucracy occurred recently in Pittsburgh. Millions of dollars in foundation funding was suddenly withdrawn as three large foundations declared the board to be incompetent and more interested in fighting with each other than working for the benefit of children (Kalson, 2002; Lee and Elizabeth, 2002).

In 2001 the Memphis board and its superintendent reacted to a perception (not supported by extensive research) that "whole school reforms" were not increasing test scores. It suddenly without notice abandoned nearly 50 reform programs. Even programs not targeted at tested basic academic skills such as Outward Bound were discontinued (Edmondson, 2001b; Viadero, 2001).

Overnight, the Memphis board changed district climate (and reputation) from being innovative and a national reform leader to that of a district in leadership drift. This sudden and unexpected action did not endear the district to local foundations and the corporate sector that invested millions of dollars on the reform packages.

ELECTED BOARD POLITICAL FAILURES

Internal board conflicts are common and publicized by the media. A good example is the Memphis board that for nearly a year in 2001 was bitterly divided over awarding a construction management contract to build a dozen badly needed new schools. Month after month media stories created the impression some board members had ties to involved firms. At the same time board members engaged in acrimonious public debate over software purchases, reform programs, hiring an private attorney for the board, and a controversial memorandum by a board member sent only to other members of the same race (Edmondson, 2001a; 2001b; Erskine, 2001).

Formal and informal racial coalitions appear in urban boards supported by citywide ethnic groups attempting to "control" the district. The activities of these coalitions are political spillage from efforts to "control" the city. The result is to further politicize a supposedly nonpartisan school district. Partisan politics always has winners and losers, and it is unfortunate when an urban school district is identified with partisan political groups. Racial politics continues to be a difficult problem for many urban boards and superintendents.

Single-issue agenda board members advocating school prayer, superintendent dismissal, school closings, budget cuts, or elimination of controversial programs are frequently a source of internal elected board conflict. Interest groups including teachers unions, religious alliances, civic groups, or corporate coalitions frequently sponsor urban board candidates and expect quick payback. This sometimes results in "their" board members behaving as ideologues unwilling to compromise on divisive issues. These ideologues can polarize a board and create serious conflict both inside and outside the district.

A number of urban board members harbor higher political ambitions. These members frequently seek any opportunity for public visibility. Their agendas focus on personal benefits rather than district benefits. Board member grandstanding alienates other board members and creates board conflict and unwanted media coverage. While some grandstanding board members seek to develop a support base for later local and state offices, others attempt to develop lucrative private employment opportunities. Internal board conflicts sooner or later involve the superintendent. Many boards divide into cliques, each working to further its agenda by contending for the superintendent's support. The superintendent quickly becomes a target for an unhappy board faction. Internal board conflicts often escape the boardroom and quickly filter into the community.

Not all elected urban boards are in constant turmoil. In the past few years the Atlanta, Las Vegas, and a few other elected urban boards, according to some observers, have worked reasonably well together. This is generally when they are elected citywide rather than from neighborhood election zones. The result has been moving away from constant superintendent churn and toward some reform. However, the length of time any urban district board can remain a viable working body is largely dependent upon future election outcomes that bring in new players and new politics. If elected board turnover is truly increasing, it is likely that superintendent churn and instability will continue.

BOARD TURMOIL CREATES FEWER APPLICANTS FOR REVOLVING CHAIRS

Recent anecdotal reports indicate applicants for urban positions are fewer today in both quantity and quality. With high turnover rates, constant conflict, and an extremely difficult job, it is no wonder some competent and experienced administrators no longer seek the large urban superintendencies in spite of salary and generous benefits exceeding $250,000 a year. Unfortunately, many urban boards naively believe increasing salary and benefit levels will attract highly qualified applicants. The bottom line unfortunately is that the urban superintendency has become a job with more pain than gain (Glass, 2001a).

Chronic superintendent churn in most large urban districts identifies a problem with the superintendent selection process and the boards that hire and fire them. The root problem appears to be highly politicized boards continually crossing the line between policy and management and in the process creating certain conflict with superintendents. Ineffective or inappropriate superintendents may be dismissed, but board elections with low voter interest may take years to remove an ineffective board member.

ELECTED BOARDS' FAILURE TO SUPPORT SUPERINTENDENT REFORM EFFORTS

Boards are often reluctant to provide superintendents reform support because new initiatives must be implemented with partial district funding, meaning that existing programs must be discontinued or cut back. This conflict-prone role for boards and superintendents as arbitrators of scarce resources has been ignored by most reformists focused on curriculum, instruction, and testing. Reform does not happen without resources, and the process to reallocate internal funds can push a board into conflict with itself and the superintendent.

Both appointed and elected urban boards have a large number of members and understandably have difficulty in reaching a majority consensus on politically charged funding issues. Often a group of board members feel the superintendent has conspired with the board majority against their pet reform initiative. Prior to reform, many opportunities for board conflict existed but today these are greater, more politically volatile, and cause superintendent churn in elected board districts. A case can be made that many reform initiatives have a negative effect on overall district effectiveness.

A lack of demonstrable results in raising test scores is frequently attributed by policy makers to an impenetrable wall of urban district bureaucracy. A superintendent new to an urban district usually finds two most immovable obstacles: board politics and an entrenched bureaucracy. Even efforts to decentralize or site-base urban districts has been unsuccessful in raising test scores or cutting through bureaucracy hardened from decades of turmoil. Unquestionably, large urban district bureaucracies are a reality and will prevail despite the displeasure of reformers, superintendents, and boards. Disjointed legislation aimed at symptoms of bureaucratic malaise will not remove roadblocks to board and superintendent performance (Hill, 2003).

A more promising strategy for successful urban reform is examining and changing the board governance model resulting in a changed organizational climate. As long as urban districts are destabilized by churning superintendents, fractious politicized board members, and suffocating bureaucracy, successful reform and change is a fantasy. The goal is for the board and superintendent to run the bureaucracy rather than it running the district.

THE FAILURE OF ELECTED BOARDS TO HOLD SUPERINTENDENTS

Data collected by the author shows that in 2001, the longest-tenured superintendent in the 10 largest urban districts was hired in 1999. This was probably the nadir of urban superintendent churn in the 20th century. Thirty-five of 135 superintendent turnovers between 1994 and 2004 were filled by interim appointments. An interim often is a retired superintendent or senior district administrator. An interim assignment is to hold the district together until a new superintendent arrives, often from another urban district. Frequently, urban districts hire interims because the board cannot agree upon selection of a new superintendent. Or, board members are involved in intra-board power struggles frequently based on racial politics or allegiance to special interest groups.

Except in the case of retirement, the employment of a long-term interim usually signals board disagreement. Few "seamless" transitions with or without an interim appointment occur. Interims worked approximately 40 of the 330 superintendent work years in the 33 urban districts between 1994 and 2004. An increasing number of interims serve a year or more and then receive a permanent appointment. Some interim superintendents serve two or three appointments.

Rapid superintendent turnover creates hesitation and confusion in the central office and neighborhood schools. With each new superintendent regime arrive new players and new rules. Rumors travel quickly in urban districts, but accurate information may takes weeks to filter down through the hierarchal bureaucracy. Old reform initiatives may be discontinued and new high-cost programs (silver bullets) purchased and implemented. Most new superintendents feel immediate public or board pressure to raise test scores. The response is another set of reform initiatives perhaps abandoned by a successor (Reid, 2001).

Most urban superintendents feel it politically smart and professionally advantageous to be known locally and nationally as a reformer. This is because most know their tenure will be only a few years and it is hard to get an urban superintendent position without a reputation as a reformer able to obtain higher test scores. This belief can result in a superintendent trying to find the quick test-score fix and national visibility while at the same time burning personal relationship bridges inside and outside the district.

Simultaneously, board members encounter pressure from legislators, parents, and the public to find the solution for low test scores. Firing a failed reformer superintendent is frequently the most expedient action for boards needing to placate the public. The board then may initiate a lengthy and expensive nationwide search to find another nationally publicized reformer. This seemingly irrational cycle occurs about every three or four years in a majority of urban districts.

THE DISCOURAGING CYCLE OF
REFORM INITIATIVES HALF COMPLETED

A typical urban district initiates three major school reform initiatives each year (Hess, 1999). New superintendents initiating reform agendas have scant chance of ever seeing long-term effects on achievement scores. A minimum of five years is required to see the effects of academic reform initiatives. Very few elected and appointed urban boards seem willing to withstand external pressures for quick fixes. Sometimes the easiest solution to solve conflict and excuse low test scores is to fire a scapegoat superintendent or hire a private-sector contractor. The constant searching, hiring, and firing of superintendents provides a very discouraging view of urban board politics at work.

The "policy churn" created by rapid superintendent turnover not only confuses and discourages staff, it communicates to parents and the public an image of district turmoil and ineptness. Political backlash occasionally follows superintendent and board member churn. In worst cases of chaos and turmoil states have intervened and appointed new boards in Chicago, Boston, Cleveland, Detroit, Prince Edward County, and Philadelphia.

In Philadelphia, failure to raise scores and provide management effectiveness led to a state takeover, a new chief executive officer, and a commission-type governance model. Mayor Michael Bloomberg in New York has gained control of New York schools and appointed a new chancellor reporting directly to the mayor. The political fallout of urban school failure is currently being keenly felt by urban mayors. The mayor's involvement varies greatly in large urban districts (Kirst, 2002).

BOARD MEMBERS AT WAR WITH DISTRICTS

The political nature of elected urban boards is often seen in members or a coalition of members declaring war on the district. Many of the acts of war are sometimes well-intentioned efforts to straighten out programs, policies, or administrative leadership. The print media gives front-page coverage and television donates sensationalized bites to attacks by these board members on districts they have been elected to be a trustee over.

Little doubt exists that elected-board urban districts are deficient in academic and administrative effectiveness, as shown by low test scores and high financial costs. The very size of the elected boards almost demands a trustee rather than elected political membership. These boards frequently engage in counterproductive behavior, for example, grilling superintendents and administrators at board meetings in front of the media. These exhibitions do not make district operations better, but instead encourage district personnel suspicions and distrust. In fact, district administrators receiving board "lashings" may make internal efforts to hide problems rather than solve them.

Board members making public war on the district by criticism and demands justify their actions by claiming to represent the wishes of constituents desiring the district be cleaned up. These board members see their role first as political officeholder and second as part of the district governance team. The business and governance of a public school district should not be conducted as a political forum. This consistently occurs in most urban districts with elected boards.

FAILING BOARDS MAKE FAILING SUPERINTENDENTS

Boards in Dallas, Seattle, Kansas City, Miami-Dade, Baltimore, Buffalo, New York, New Orleans, District of Columbia, Seattle, and other cities continually make the news hiring and firing superintendents amidst board conflict. A common excuse offered by boards for firing a failing superintendent is financial mismanagement or low test scores. Often the true reason is that the superintendent has angered a coalition of board members representing one or more special interest groups.

The urban superintendency is an incredibly difficult position full of stress and occupational paradoxes such as raising achievement scores with fewer resources. The few long-tenured urban superintendents seem to be astute and flexible politicians willing to make extensive personal sacrifices. The less successful urban superintendents seem to be bearers of curriculum "silver bullets" always preaching educational slogans. Naïve urban boards often hire these curriculum directors without understanding that skill and knowledge in being the chief executive officer of a billion-dollar enterprise is really what is needed. Many in the curriculum-director group quickly fall into conflict with boards over ethical and professional issues. The altruistic reasons given by many curriculum superintendents for entering the profession often do not closely align with politicized boards seeking personal power, control, and influence.

Occasionally, it becomes obvious a superintendent selected through an expensive national search is inappropriate. Critics rightfully accuse some urban superintendents of being experts at creating instructional slogans but lacking executive leadership to bring about results. Board members with little executive leadership experience possess a tendency to select superintendents for instructional leadership skills and community (racial) fit reasons. Boards in other urban districts seem to have previously hired the same individuals for the same reasons. The round robin of urban superintendents never achieving success as measured by achievement gains and better management seems to go on and on.

Both traditional and untraditional (backgrounds) urban superintendents seem oblivious to the fact that an urban district is a huge organization with thousands of employees and a billion-dollar budget needing competent and firm executive management leadership. Their public behavior seldom indicates concern or action toward fixing and making functional bureaucracies that would provide needed support for neighborhood schools.

Appointed urban boards hiring chief executive officers better understand the urban superintendency to be an executive leadership and management position. In response these boards (and a few elected boards such as Las Vegas) have adopted a policy board role. The hiring of noneducator

superintendents has been well publicized in cities such as Seattle, New Orleans, Kansas City, New York, Philadelphia, St. Louis, and Los Angeles. Interestingly, the tenure record of the noneducator superintendents is about
the same as traditional superintendents (Mathews, 2001).

Search consultants conducting urban searches insist the quantity and
quality of superintendent applicants is decreasing. Presently, the shallow
applicant pool of highly qualified minority applicants makes many urban
searches problematic (Glass, 2001a). Urban districts often inadvertently restrict the applicant pool by advertising for applicants with superintendent
experience in large urban districts. Some of the best superintendent talent
is found in affluent suburban districts. These superintendents have successful track records and a wide breadth of knowledge in all district administrative functions. In the past, superintendents moving from suburban districts have often been the best urban superintendents.

It is rare today when extremely successful suburban superintendents are
willing to work for elected urban boards mired in the political instability
and chaotic environments found in most urban districts. There is no doubt
elected board instability, an intensely critical media, meager resources, and
unrealistic test score expectations discourage many of the best and brightest
in the profession.

Another factor is that many candidates in the urban superintendent applicant pool possess very narrow professional backgrounds and lack experience
in supervising assistant superintendents responsible for finance, personnel,
operations, facilities, and special programs. A superintendent without experience as an assistant superintendent responsible for finance, personnel, operations, and curriculum may be at risk in hiring and supervising deputies.
These holes in competence and experience often create circumstances for conflict when boards try to fix or take over management.

MAYORS AS NEW PLAYERS

Instability and failure by large urban districts to solve achievement and
management problems has brought increasing involvement (and pressure)
on the part of big-city mayors and state governors. Mayors in Chicago, New
York, Detroit, Boston, and the District of Columbia have not been reluctant
to use political force to jar districts from complacency, turmoil, and failure.
Mayors perceive academic health ties directly to economic and social health
in their cities. More important, they do not see boards and superintendents
bringing about critically needed reform. Large cities struggling to retain
businesses, renew core areas, and attract new investment hardly need highly
publicized failing school districts led by contentious highly politicized
boards. Governors responding to political pressure in Maryland, Pennsyl-

vania, and New Jersey have sparked urban school takeovers or substantial changes in board governance.

Chicago's Richard Daley exemplifies a mayor taking direct action to improve a failing school district. After decades of board politics, financial mismanagement, crumbling buildings, and failing students, Daley was handed the Chicago schools by the Illinois legislature. After nearly 10 years of city control the Chicago schools are no longer considered the "worst in America," a title bestowed on them by former Secretary of Education William Bennett. An appointed board and superintendent under the leadership of Daley has been a model for competent urban board governance. In Cleveland voters overwhelmingly voted in 2002 to retain the appointed board system. In Hartford, Connecticut, voters approved a measure allowing the mayor to appoint five of nine board members in 2005 (Gewertz, 2002). In the District of Columbia, Mayor Anthony Williams has continually sought control of the district board for several years.

However, not all big-city mayors have sought a leadership role. The Kansas City mayor has chosen not to play a direct role in helping to salvage one of the most troubled urban districts in the country. The Kansas City schools have struggled through decades of chaos, instability, and the hiring and firing of 21 superintendents (including interims) in 25 years. The State of Missouri several times has debated taking control of the district. Detroit voted in November 2004 to return to an elected board from an appointed board. It is the first large urban district to return to an elected board. This may have occurred from displeasure with the appointed members announcing prior to the election the removal of thousands of jobs from district payrolls.

Evidence is sparse suggesting mayoral takeovers of urban districts have resulted in higher test scores. However, improvements are evident in board stability, better maintained buildings, new construction, operations management, and budget control (Viadero, 2002; Wong and Shen, 2001).

STOPPING THE ELECTED BOARD
SUPERINTENDENT CHURN

Reduction of superintendent churn in elected large urban districts might be accomplished through revision of state statutes regulating the length and terms of superintendent contracts. New legislation requiring superintendents be given six-year contracts terminated only with the permission of a state appointed third-party mediator who might put the brakes to superintendent dismissal in the midst of board conflict. Big salaries and benefit packages may lure superintendents to large urban districts, but their effectiveness depends both on board cooperation and sufficient tenure to implement systemic reform rather than a tweaking of selected programs. Six-year renewable contracts might act to restrain boards from using the superintendent as a political football.

Several experts in board-superintendent relations along with professional associations and several foundations feel a productive path to take in stabilizing boards and stopping superintendent churn is by training and convincing elected urban boards to adopt performance techniques to reduce instability (Hill, 2003). The suggested strategies are well grounded in organizational leadership literature but will be severely challenged by the political nature of the role and high board turnover. Hopefully, these board restructuring models are not to be looked upon as another silver bullet reform.

BOARD BEHAVIOR NEEDING CHANGE

Urban boards generally are comprised of nine or more members. The amount of time board members spend on district business (not personal politics) varies considerably. Some board members complain the position constitutes a full-time job. It is not hard to find data showing board members spending 20 to 30 hours a week on board business (Glass, 2002b; Hess, 2002). The pertinent question is *why* board members should spend 20 to 30 hours a week on board business. Such a time commitment suggests board members are routinely heavily involved in management.

Data do not likely exist showing how many hours per week elected versus appointed board members spend on district business. It would seem that appointed members would not have the additional time burden of attending to politics needed for reelection. The burden of elected board members mixing together hours needed for board business and personal political activity might be another strong reason to move to an appointed board.

Many large urban board members never develop a big-picture understanding of district operations and invest countless hours in reading technical reports, calling, and meeting with administrators. In general they become *too* involved in district operations and minutiae. A good example of micromanagement is a large Arizona board that met 172 times one year (Houston, personal communication, August 5, 2002). Extensive board involvement creates apprehension among administrative staff, undermining the superintendent's role. It freezes decision making as administrators wait for board approval on the smallest of matters.

Board member qualifications have been debated since the birth of public school lay governance. Complex union agreements, service contracts, tricky personnel issues, facility construction, and legal issues continually challenge decision-making competence. Few urban board members possess extensive training or experience sufficient to oversee billion-dollar enterprises. Fewer board members are experienced in competently tackling difficult and complex educational issues such as standards, high-stakes testing, instructional technology, and silver bullet reform models (Kowalski, 2002). Unfortunately, many elected urban members are effective campaigners and less effective board members.

Large lay-governed urban districts are not managed like large private corporations. One example is that urban boards meet at least twice a month, while corporate boards may meet several times a year. For the superintendent, the primary difference is that a corporate chief executive officer actually runs the corporation. An urban superintendent has no such authority. Corporations are driven by the bottom line; urban school districts are usually driven by politics.

The lay board governance model obligates superintendents and management teams to advise the board in policy and decision making. Superintendents provide boards with professional advice sometimes received in a contentious and disrespectful manner, undercutting the superintendent's credibility. The ensuing board debate provides the public with a view of a board in conflict rather than a public body discussing policy alternatives. Importantly, disregarding professional advice diminishes the stature of the superintendent and management team in the public's eye.

If this occurs frequently a probable result is serious superintendent-board conflict. Politically, superintendents cannot withstand numerous instances where the board openly disregards a recommendation. This is particularly true in hiring and firing personnel, establishing budgets, and instructional decisions. When it is apparent the board is "running" the district superintendent, turnover is usually close at hand. Many urban superintendents joke they begin looking for the next job the day after they are hired.

Several superintendents who have served appointed boards have candidly told the author that their experiences have been dramatically different than with previous elected boards. In their opinion the appointed boards were much easier to work with, less contentious, and goal directed.

THE NEED TO REFORM ELECTED URBAN BOARDS

State accountability statutes mandating high-stakes testing and standards are aimed at failing large urban districts. Reform or replacement of more elected boards in future years is likely as states react to a lack of progress in raising urban achievement scores needed to meet the requirements of No Child Left Behind. Despite the all-pervasive influence of urban unemployment, underemployment, impoverished families, poor housing, inadequate health services, crime, and financially strapped schools, politicians continue to expect all children to score above average (or be proficient) on state standardized tests.

Many states have accountability legislation allowing state takeovers of failing districts. State takeovers in California, Illinois, New Jersey, West Virginia, Pennsylvania, and Ohio have resulted both from failing test scores and ineffective board leadership. State takeover is not a panacea for failing urban schools. In fact, state education departments are ill equipped and unenthusiastic about operating local school districts.

The options available to states in urban takeovers are limited. Replacing thousands of teachers and principals is next to impossible amidst a teacher shortage. However, boards, superintendents, and management personnel might be replaced with state appointees or private contractors. Whether or not the public in large cities will allow school boards to be replaced by private companies is questionable. Currently, districts like Philadelphia make extensive use of school contracting. But replacing the total management and governance structure of an urban district is yet to occur. The public school board has always been a true American icon, believed by many to be the government agency closest to the people (Danzberger, Kirst, and Usdan, 1992). Minority communities in urban areas might also resist losing control of a social institution they have struggled to control for decades.

A good argument is whether an elected urban board member representing 150,000 residents is "close" to the public. Board member name recognition accompanied by pathetically low voter turnout generally describes urban board member elections. Another argument made for retaining elected urban boards is racial minority participation. Some policy makers argue that if mayors appoint boards they favor nonminorities due to education and professional experience. This is a lame excuse because the number of minority citizens possessing advanced college degrees and professional (management) experience is steadily increasing in urban communities.

Current political processes in urban districts discourage many highly qualified citizens from running for board positions. Raising campaign funds, securing political allies, and serving on a politicized board (often in perpetual conflict with itself) is not an alluring prospect to many highly skilled management professionals, community leaders, or even retired educators. Board members owning businesses or those with sensitive employers may risk their livelihoods through participation in public board conflicts. Prominent business and professional leaders serving on boards most likely do not welcome seeing their names in the newspaper and on television in the midst of "school wars."

The stakes are very high that states and cities feel compelled to give serious consideration to reforms ensuring high-quality urban board leadership. The present haphazard system is simply not resulting in a functional system of lay governance for many districts. In fact, it is so dysfunctional in some cities that the likelihood of moving the district forward is moot (unless future elections bring a sufficient number of constructive board members). The challenge in these cities is to prevent further deterioration of educational services.

Recent surveys of chief state school officers, leading superintendents, administrator and school board associations show roughly two-thirds feel the present board governance model needs substantial reform (Glass, 2001b). On the other hand, nearly three-fourths of board presidents believe the present model needs no reform (Glass, 2002a). The question is whether boards are part of the solution or part of the problem. How might the urban public react to a plebiscite guaranteeing structural reform of the board governance model?

A NEW BOARD SELECTION MODEL: A KEY TO REFORM

Who might best serve on urban boards? How might they be selected? What constraints should there be on board behavior and actions? Two paths are evident toward ensuring competent selection of urban board members. The first is through a restructured electoral process. The second is through mayoral or special nonpartisan commission appointment.

Reforms considered for the electoral process might include a set of qualifications of formal education, training, and prior leadership or management experiences. Sets of qualifications currently exist for public offices such as judgeships, assessors, coroners, district attorneys, engineers, and public health officers. A nonpartisan commission appointed by the (a) governor, (b) mayor, (c) city council, or (d) a citywide commission might select a number of best-qualified candidates to contest vacant positions. The candidates' limited campaign expenses might be reimbursed with public funding. A proviso might limit providing public funding for candidates running as a member of a coalition partially financed by special interest groups.

Once elected, board members might be subject to removal by the nominating commission or the mayor nominating or appointing them. The qualifying commission or mayor might remove a board member for absenteeism, unprofessional conduct, conflict of interest, or behavior subject to civil or criminal prosecution. In some states voters currently have the right to remove elected board members through the recall process.

A second path of mayoral (or governor) initiative might be direct or indirect appointment. Direct appointment by the mayor is very straightforward. In Chicago, Mayor Richard Daley selects five members to serve on the board. The same system exists in New York, where Mayor Bloomberg has recently taken control of the schools. Another direct appointment model is

Hartford, where in 2005 the mayor appointed five of nine members. Detroit presently has a dual appointment system. Boston and Cleveland boards are appointed by mayors and city councils.

A second option for mayoral appointment might be through a nominating commission comprised of members recommended by various community sectors. Such a nominating commission would screen qualified applicants and make recommendations to the mayor. Only approved candidates could be selected by the mayor.

The success of either model is dependent on well-qualified citizens seeking board positions. Mayors or highly qualified nominating commissions might have a better chance of encouraging quality applicants than the present self-selection model. Present electoral systems sometimes identify good candidates, but sometimes less-than-qualified candidates are elected by default.

A third and more drastic model is abandoning the urban school board model and replacing it with a superintendent sitting as a member of the mayor's cabinet. Selected advisory boards might be appointed by the mayor to provide input to the superintendent on major or selected decisions and policy. In this model the superintendent and mayor work closely both in policy and operations. Successes or failures would rest with the mayor and superintendent.

Action must be taken very soon in many cities to make school systems functional. In about 20 years almost half of the nation's schoolchildren may be attending urban schools. The future of American democracy may reside in urban classrooms. Critics of appointed boards claim school board membership is a democratic right, but they offer no substantive rescue plan other than board training. In-service training or even adoption of "board policy models" does not permanently change ingrained basic member disruptive behaviors or solve the problems of a flawed system. Most elected urban boards simply do not function in the long term due to neighborhood politics, leadership inexperience, and board members' attitudes. Those that do function well over a period of time should be carefully studied to identify enabling factors such as superintendent leadership, board chair leadership, members' expertise carried over from their jobs, or special conditions of the electoral process.

BOARD EVALUATION: A KEY TO REFORM

Teachers, administrators, and superintendents are required by law to be evaluated. No state currently requires school boards to be independently evaluated. And no state requires superintendents and board members to be evaluated together as a team. A few boards pass through a type of self-evaluation each year as recommended by the National School Boards Association and its state affiliates. This self-evaluation is usually perfunctory.

If board and board member performance were evaluated and made public, many board members might be a bit more restrained in some of their actions. Currently, the only external board evaluation is provided by the media, not always an impartial or qualified evaluator. Urban school boards especially should be held publicly accountable, as they employ thousands of workers and spend billions of tax dollars. Most important, they are responsible for the education of the nation's most valuable future resource.

Today, urban school boards are not accountable to the public, seemingly possess modest skills, are very conflict-prone and politicized, and demonstrate they often cannot work successfully in tandem with superintendents. The electoral process is proving to be an inadequate evaluator for urban boards.

Legislation should be implemented at the state level to require external evaluations of all large urban school districts in a state. This external evaluation should be conducted by state and national evaluation experts working with community groups, governmental officials, and parents to ensure the governance model is working and management is effective. Evaluation of academic achievement is already required by state accountability models and No Child Left Behind. It is well past time that governance and management should be evaluated.

SUMMARY

Unfortunately, the "school reform industry" has distracted urban boards and districts from focusing on what is most important. Every urban district has raising test scores as its mission. However, becoming an effective and efficient organization should be the primary mission. If this goal is met test scores will go up, dollars will be prudently spent, and leadership will be stabilized. Basic to this mission is an appropriate governance model.

The national importance is high for urban school districts to show substantial improvement in test scores, achievement, and preparing students for the world of work. The past history of failure, instability, and fractured leadership must not be allowed to continue. State governors, legislators, and urban mayors need to cooperate in finding and implementing strategies to stabilize urban boards and the superintendency. These actions are the real first step to successful urban school reform. The current strategy of tinkering with staff development, silver bullets, and punitive high-stakes testing will not solve the crisis. When elected large urban boards fail in the future, replacement may be the only effective action for policy makers.

REFERENCES

Bushweller, K. 1996. How to get elected. *American School Board Journal* 83 (July): 20–23.

Cooper, B., and L. Fusarelli. 1999. *Career crisis in the school superintendency?* Arlington, VA: American Association of School Administrators.

Danzberger, J., M. Kirst, and M. Usdan. 1992. *Governing schools: New times, new requirements.* Washington, DC: Institute for Educational Leadership.

Edmondson, A. 2001a. Two firms bid for contract to build schools. *Memphis Commercial-Appeal,* July 2.

———. 2001b. Committee set up to examine legal needs. *Memphis Commercial-Appeal,* August 7.

Erskine, M. 2001. Stink within school board: Only Black members got messages before vote. *Memphis Commercial-Appeal,* June 22.

Gewertz. C. 2002. Voters send varied messages in races. *Education Week* 22 (January): 5–6.

Glass, T. 2001a. *Superintendent leaders look at the superintendency, school boards and reform.* Denver: Education Commission of the States.

———. 2001b. *State education leaders view the superintendent crisis.* Denver: Education Commission of the States.

———. 2002a. *School board presidents view superintendent selection.* Denver: Education Commission of the States.

———. 2002b. Is it time to do away with elected boards? Paper presented to the National Policy Board on Education Administration, Washington, D.C., February.

Glass, T., L. Björk, and C. Brunner. 2002. *The study of the American school superintendency 2000: Superintendents in the new millennium.* Arlington, VA: American Association of School Administrators.

Hess, F. 1999. *Spinning wheels: The politics of urban school reform.* Washington, DC: Brookings Institution.

———. 2002. *School boards at the dawn of the 21st century.* Alexandria, VA: National School Boards Association.

Hill, P. 2003. *School boards: Focus on school performance, not money and patronage.* Seattle: Progressive Policy Institute.

Hoyle, J., L. Björk, V. Collier, and T. Glass. 2004. *The superintendent as CEO.* Thousand Oaks, CA: Corwin Press.

Kalson, S. 2002. Shock therapy for a dysfunctional public school system. *Pittsburgh Post-Gazette,* July 10.

Kirst, M. 2002. *Mayoral influence, new regimes, and public school governance.* Philadelphia: Consortium for Policy Research in Education.

Kowalski, T. 2002. *The future of local school district governance: Implications for school boards and superintendents.* Paper presented at the annual meeting of the American Educational Research Association, New Orleans.

Land, D. 2002. Local boards under review: Their role and effectiveness in relation to students' academic achievement. *Review of Education Research* 72 (Summer): 229–278.

Lee, C., and J. Elizabeth. 2002. Foundations yank Pittsburgh school grants. *Pittsburgh Post-Gazette,* July 15.

Mathews, J. 2001. An end to school boards. *Washington Post*, February 13.

National School Boards Association. 1997. Some board candidates are turning to political consultants. *School Board News*, September 5, 4.

Reid, K. 2001. Chicago chief named amid urban turnover. *Education Week*, September 14, 14.

Sack, J. 2001. K–12 enrollment sets another record. *Education Week*, June 15, 24.

Stover, D. 1997. School board candidates contend with rising costs. *School Board News*, September 2, 2.

Tyack, D. 1974. *The one best system: A history of American urban education.* Cambridge, MA: Harvard University Press.

Viadero, D. 2001. Memphis scraps redesign models in all its schools. *Education Week*, September 14, 3–4.

———. 2002. Big-city mayors' control of schools yields mixed results. *Education Week*, January 10, 3–4.

Wong, K., and F. Shen. 2001. Does school district takeover work? Assessing the effectiveness of city and state takeover as a school reform strategy. Paper presented at the annual meeting of the American Political Science Association, Chicago, August.

15

Education Mayors and Big-City School Boards: New Directions, New Evidence

Kenneth K. Wong and Francis X. Shen

Is an elected school board the best system of governance for America's large urban school systems? Can elected boards turn around chronic underperformance and manage budgetary crises? Or might another model of governance be more effective? Can mayoral-appointed boards shed their historical stigma of patronage politics and bring about better teaching and learning for city students?

Most Americans don't think the mayor should get involved, but this perception is starting to change rapidly. In 2006 and 2007, the Gallup poll asked Americans if they favored mayoral control. In 2006, only 29 percent were in favor, but in 2007 that number had jumped to 39 percent, with 42 percent of parents in favor.[1] Such trends in public opinion, combined with increased interest from mayors, make mayoral control a frequently debated topic in today's education policy circles.

In summer 2007, for instance, the issue was raised in Albuquerque, New Mexico, when Mayor Martin Chavez expressed a desire to play a role in the search for a new Albuquerque Public Schools (APS) superintendent.[2] While members of the APS school board were open to listening, they and an editorial in the Albuquerque paper made clear that the mayor should have no direct role in superintendent hiring. The editorial expressed support for the separation of mayor and city school board: "The Albuquerque mayor is elected by the citizens of Albuquerque, not APS, whose constituents elect school board members to represent them in all school matters."[3]

In this chapter we offer a contrasting view, arguing on the basis of recently completed empirical research that for many big-city school districts, an education mayor can serve as a catalyst for district improvement (Wong et al., 2007). Our goal in this chapter is to provide an introduction to, and evaluation of, the emerging trend of using mayoral-appointed school boards to govern big-city school systems.[4] Following the high-profile introduction of mayoral governance in Boston (1992) and Chicago (1995), cities such as Cleveland (1998) and New York (2002) have followed suit, and many others have explored the possibility of doing the same. While each city has mapped out its own policy agenda, the success of each reform centers on two interrelated elements: (a) a legal change to formally enable the mayor to appoint a majority of the school board members, and (b) an equally important personal commitment from the mayor to use political capital to improve school district performance.

Some observers fear that mayoral-appointed school boards at the start of the 21st century will act as mayoral-appointed boards did at the turn of the last century: as vehicles for patronage politics. Critics also argue that mayoral-appointed boards reduce democratic participation in school governance (Chambers, 2006). While valid, we believe that too often this criticism conflates mayoral-appointed boards with state takeovers of failing districts, and overlooks the new style of integrated governance practiced by today's education mayors.

The chapter is divided into three sections that may be thought of as (a) where we've come from, (b) what we know, and (c) where we're going with mayoral-appointed school boards. First, we introduce the concept of mayoral leadership in the context of big-city school systems. We emphasize the unique challenges faced by large urban systems, and note how the performance of these districts can have not only local but also statewide and national implications. The second part of the chapter summarizes the research base on mayoral-appointed school boards. We focus on the results from our recently completed five-year empirical study of mayoral leadership, with evaluations of student achievement, district financial management, and human capital. We find that mayoral control is associated with roughly a .15 standard deviation increase in student performance in both reading and math. We also find that mayoral control is linked to new spending priorities aimed at teaching and learning.

Having summarized the history and current research, the third part of the chapter explores the future of mayoral control through a discussion of education governance transformations in three cities in 2006 and 2007: Los Angeles, Albuquerque, and Washington, D.C. The recent experiences of mayors and school boards in these cities are illustrative of the political and legal complexities involved in any challenge to existing school board governance arrangements. In analyzing these cases, we suggest that proper timing and strong political partnerships are prerequisites for the future success of mayoral involvement in city schools.

I. MAYORAL LEADERSHIP IN CONTEXT

In this first section we consider the unique challenges of big-city school districts, and the historical context in which new mayoral education leadership has arisen. We first clarify that mayoral control is appropriate for a small number of school districts, but these districts merit special consideration because they serve such large student populations. We then discuss how the new-style education mayor stands in marked contrast to an older-style mayor, who looked to the city schools primarily as a source of patronage jobs.

A Big-District Phenomenon

Mayoral-appointed school boards, in which a mayor appoints the majority of a school board, are designed to address the unique governance challenges faced by big school districts. When discussing our empirical analysis, we make further distinctions, but it is useful at first blush to consider just variations in district size. If we define "big" to mean 40,000+ students (128 districts as of 2005–2006 data), less than 1 percent of all school districts are big. Even if "big" is defined as 20,000+ students (approximately 375 districts), only 2.7 percent of all districts qualify. Thus, even if every big school district were suddenly transformed to an appointed board, more than 97 percent of America's "10,000 democracies" would remain untouched (Berkman and Plutzer, 2005).[5]

These statistics raise a question: If mayoral control is not a possibility for so many local school boards, why has it gained so much attention? The answer can be found by looking not at the number of school boards, but at the number of *students* potentially affected by such a governance shift. Based on data from the Common Core of Data for 2005–2006, more than a quarter (26.6 percent) of the nation's K–12 students are served by the largest 129 districts, and nearly 41 percent are taught in the 375 largest.

The implication of these demographic realities for school board governance is that some school boards and mayors—those that operate in our nation's largest cities—bear a larger burden than others. The differences between large and small district governance are vast. Consider first the student-to-board-member ratio at the bottom and top of the distribution. At the top, the seven members of the Los Angeles Unified School District are responsible for governing the education of 727,319 students, a ratio of 103,903 students per board member. By contrast, the seven members of the Blue Valley board in Randolph, Kansas, govern a district of 226 students, for a ratio of 32 students per board member.[6] The board member/student ratio is thus over 3,000 times as large in Los Angeles.

More than just size differences, small and large district boards must deal with qualitatively different issues. Sticking with our illustrative comparison between Los Angeles and Blue Valley, the minutes of the two school boards are revealing.[7] Blue Valley board meetings rarely stretch longer than two and a half hours, and begin with "positive comments," such as: "The tile design the Art Department created in the high school hall floor is very impressive" and "The Christmas party was a huge success."[8] Board meetings in the LAUSD are day-long affairs, broadcast on local television, and filled with layers of finance and management business. We raise these differences not to make light of the important work of school boards in small districts, but rather to emphasize that mayoral-appointed boards arise in a unique context: enormous urban districts built on layers of bureaucracy. Our understanding and evaluation of mayoral control must be made within this particular context.

New-Style Education Mayors:
From Patronage to Integrated Governance

Mayors have always had an interest in their city's school system, but not all mayors' interests have been for the public good. Especially in the first half of the 20th century, mayoral involvement in education was often driven by the logic of patronage politics. As discussed in detail by accounts such as Peterson's (1976) *School Politics, Chicago Style*, mayors' involvement in the school system was not driven by a genuine desire to improve teaching and learning.

Over the course of the 20th century, reforms initiated in the turn-of-the-century Progressive Era movement attempted to address the problem of patronage by instituting more professionalized management of America's school systems. Two important characteristics of this movement were to consolidate school districts and to "take the politics out of schools" (Tyack, 1974; Just, 1980; Peterson, 1976). On both counts, the reformers were quite successful. Berry's study of school consolidation notes: "Between 1930 and 1970, nine out of every ten school districts were eliminated through consolidation" (Berry, 2007, p. 49). Similarly, previously appointed school boards in big-city districts were almost all replaced with elected boards. In a 1938 study, Henry and Kerwin found that of the 191 cities with populations over 50,000, 43 (over 20 percent) of the city school systems had appointed school boards. Over the next 50 years that number would drop precipitously. Before Boston turned to mayoral control in 1992, only a handful of appointed school boards remained.[9] Resistance to mayoral involvement is also connected to a split between the views of different stakeholders. The opening words of Henry and Kerwin's book remain relevant today:

> The majority of school administrators subscribe to the view that the nature and importance of education are such that the schools should be adminis-

tered under an authority entirely free from the control or influence of local public officials . . . The majority of political scientists, on the other hand, are of the opinion that effective administration . . . can best be obtained by the closer coordination of schools and municipal governments. (Henry and Kerwin, 1938, p. vii)

The theory of "integrated governance" explains why, from a political science perspective, mayoral control of education is a promising reform strategy (Wong, 1999). The theory recognizes that big-city school systems involve many stakeholders. Students, teachers, administrators, parents, city and state taxpayers, the business community, and the state department of education all have a legitimate interest in the health and success of the city schools. Similarly, integrated governance recognizes that student success is linked to many factors outside the schoolhouse; local economic conditions, safety, public confidence, and local and state politics can all help (or hinder) school district progress.

With so many stakeholders and interested parties, school board politics in large urban school systems is likely to become fragmented and overly bureaucratic. Indeed, much dissatisfaction with urban school boards is fueled by the perception that board members spend too much time arguing with one another, and not enough time engaging in meaningful reform. It is difficult in such contexts to engage in systemwide reform, because individual stakeholders are more closely tied to the concerns of their particular constituent group. Mayoral control addresses this problem of local fragmentation and competing interests by consolidating decision making. The school system is integrated into broader municipal governance, allowing for citywide interests to prevail over parochial ones.

Integrated governance involves both a formal, legal change and a change in priorities. Legally, integrated governance is enabled when a mayor is given the power to appoint a majority of school board residents. This legal process can been carried out in one of three ways: (a) state legislatures can pass a new law permanently giving the mayor school board appointment powers (e.g., Chicago); (b) state legislatures can pass a law temporarily giving the mayor school board appointment power, with a popular referendum (e.g., Boston and Cleveland) or sunset clause included (e.g., New York); or (c) if it has the authority to do, the city can change its charter to allow for appointed board members (e.g., Oakland). In crafting a new law, state legislatures enjoy flexibility in the specific provisions, including duration of control, oversight, and board member nominating processes. Table 15.1 summarizes the types of mayoral control governance that have been put in place. It is evident from the table that states and cities have partnered in different ways to produce unique pieces of legislation. While sharing common elements, no two mayoral-appointed governance structures look exactly the same.

Table 15.1.   Summary of Mayoral Control of School Districts (as of August 2007)

City	Start Date	End Date	New/ Old	Mayor Appoints Majority of Board	Mayor Appoints All of Board	Mayor Has Full Appt. Power
Boston, MA	1992	Ongoing	New	Yes	Yes	No
Chicago, IL	1995	Ongoing	New	Yes	Yes	Yes
Baltimore, MD[a]	1997	Ongoing	New	Joint Appt. w/ Gov.		
Cleveland, OH	1998	Ongoing	New	Yes	Yes	No
Detroit, MI[b]	1999	2004	New	Yes	No	Yes
Oakland, CA	2000	Ongoing	New	No	No	Yes
Harrisburg, PA^	2000	Ongoing	New	Yes	Yes	Yes
Washington, DC[c]	2007	2012	New	Full Governance Authority		
Philadelphia, PA[d]	2001	Ongoing	New	Joint Appt. w/ Gov.		
New York, NY	2002	2010	New	Yes	No	Yes
Hartford, CT^e	2005	Ongoing	New	Yes	Yes	Yes
Los Angeles, CA[f]	2008	2013	New	No	No	No
St. Louis, MO[g]	2006	2008	New	No	No	Yes
New Haven, CT	Pre-1990	Ongoing	New	Yes	Yes	Yes
Providence, RI	Pre-1990	Ongoing	New	Yes	Yes	No
Trenton, NJ^	Pre-1990	Ongoing	New	Yes	Yes	Yes
Jackson, MS	Pre-1990	Ongoing	Old	Yes	Yes	No

NOTES: ^These small and mid-size districts are not included in our empirical analysis. a. Before 1997, the school board in Baltimore was appointed by the mayor. b. The governance description for Detroit in this table refers to the period 1999–2004. Detroit reverted to an elected school board in 2004. c. The elected board in D.C. remains, but its substantive governing powers have been transferred to the mayor. d. Before 2001, the school board in Philadelphia was appointed by the mayor. e. The governance description for Hartford refers to the period 2005–. Before 2005, the school board was appointed by a mix of mayoral and state authorities. See text for discussion. f. Under the proposed (August 29, 2007) Partnership for Los Angeles Schools plan, L.A. Mayor Villaraigosa would take control of two underperforming high schools and associated feeder schools, starting in 2008. g. In a special, temporary arrangement a three-member "Special Administrative Board of the Transitional School District of the City of St. Louis" was established in 2007. The mayor appoints one member, the board of aldermen a second, and a third is appointed by the state.

In addition to a legal change, a change in priorities is also necessary. Integrated governance is "driven by a focus on student performance and is characterized by district-level capacity and willingness to intervene in failing schools" (Wong, 1999; Wong et al., 1997, p. 148). Under integrated governance, new-style mayors are more likely to encourage fiscal discipline and remain open-minded to innovative practices that blend bureaucratic and market approaches focused on outcome measures. Integrated governance has emerged in a climate in which policy makers have placed a greater emphasis on building human capital as a form of economic development. Schools are increasingly seen as critical to attracting businesses and retaining middle-class families in the city.

Mayors, School Boards, and Democracy

In addition to concerns over patronage, an oft-repeated concern with mayoral control is that it is anti-democratic, reducing public participation in school district governance. Chambers (2006) argues that in Chicago and Cleveland academic achievement gains and management efficiency came at the cost of public discussion and deliberation. In thinking about the democratic nature of mayoral control, it is important to distinguish a *mayoral-appointed* school board from a state-led "takeover" of a school district. Typically in a state takeover the local school board is stripped of its substantive powers, and a state-appointed board or committee runs the school district until it reaches certain management, achievement, or financial benchmarks (Wong and Shen, 2003). State takeovers are open to criticism on the grounds of democracy because they replace an elected board with a non-elected governing body. In contrast, mayoral control in the form of a mayoral-appointed school board retains electoral accountability, but shifts it from school board elections to mayoral elections. Some variations of mayoral control, such as those recently implemented in Washington, D.C., maintain an elected school board but redefine the scope of its powers.

The political incentive structure at the heart of integrated governance is the alignment of the mayor's electoral fate with school district performance. As Boston Mayor Thomas Menino said in his 1996 State of the City address, "I want to be judged as your mayor by what happens in the Boston public schools. If I fail to bring about these specific reforms by the year 2001, then judge me harshly."[10] If city residents are unhappy with school district management or performance, they can express their views by voting against the mayor. Indeed, that's exactly what happened in Detroit in 2004, when city residents voted to return to a traditional elected school board.

Two important differences between mayoral and school board elections exist. First, voter turnout is significantly higher in mayoral elections. While variation exists, a review of the literature suggests that school board turnout hovers around 20 percent (Shen, 2003). Mayoral elections, with higher voter participation, actually enhance democracy in the sense that more voters participate. The higher voter participation levels also make mayoral elections less susceptible to the influential groups that are overrepresented in school board elections (Zeigler, 1977; Moe, 2004; Taebel, 1974).[11]

The second difference between school board and mayoral elections concerns the scope of the performance being evaluated. In school board elections, voters evaluate school performance specifically. In mayoral elections, the schools are seen as one component of the bundle of services that the city provides. From the perspective of integrated governance theory, this type of citywide evaluation is encouraged because schools are seen as necessarily integrated with the city's economy, tax base, housing, and social services.

Mayoral control of school introduces a new type of accountability. As described by Mayor Michael Bloomberg: "The Mayor should have sole control over the appointment of the Schools Chancellor, and the Chancellor should report directly to the Mayor. That establishes democratic accountability—and if democracy can be trusted to safeguard our social services, police forces and other essential services, why wouldn't it work to protect our most precious resource, our children?" (Bloomberg, 2002).

II. EVALUATING MAYORS AND SCHOOLS: EMPIRICAL EVIDENCE

Researchers have much more data with which to objectively evaluate today's education mayors than previous analysts had to evaluate their patronage predecessors. Having provided an introduction to the contours of mayoral control, we now summarize what we know about the performance of integrated governance in practice.

Evaluating Mayoral Control: A New Approach

The scholarly literature on mayoral-appointed school boards has consisted primarily of small-N case studies, relying on interviews, surveys, and document analysis (Henig and Rich, 2004; Cuban and Usdan, 2003; Kirst, 2002). These studies provide us with rich detail about the nature of mayoral control, and in some cases track outcomes in particular districts. Using this methodology, however, makes it difficult to link governance changes to changes in student achievement and financial/management outcomes at a systematic level. In our study we designed a mixed-methods analytic approach to complement existing research with new quantitative, empirical assessment. The hallmark of our analysis is moving beyond district-level summary statistics to conduct more systematic intra- and inter-district statistical analysis.

In designing the study, we addressed several preliminary issues. Our methodological challenge was to develop a purposeful sample allowing us to generalize to the population of interest (King, Keohane, and Verba, 1994). In our case, we want to make inferences about the impact of new-style mayor-led integrated governance in large urban cities, *relative to the old style of elected school boards* that would have been operating in its place.

We identified a population of interest: those school districts that are big and coterminous with the city. Using data from the National Center for Education Statistics' Common Core of Data and a series of decision rules, we identified districts in the nation that (a) are not a component of a supervisory union, (b) primarily serve a central city of a Metropolitan Core Based

Statistical Area (CBSA), (c) have at least 40 schools, (d) receive at least 75 percent of their students from a principal city, and (e) send at least 75 percent of their city's public school students to the same school district. The first three decision rules restrict our analysis to large districts serving big population centers.

The last two decision rules are designed to address the requirement of a coterminous city/district boundary. Mayoral-appointed school boards are not an appropriate policy reform when the boundaries of the school district vary significantly from those of the mayor's city. This disconnect between district and city can arise in one of two ways. First, a single city may be served by multiple school districts. Dallas and Indianapolis are examples of this situation. Second, a single school district may serve students coming from multiple cities. This is more common, as large city districts may also serve some smaller, surrounding municipalities. When the percentage of students in the district gets too small, the mayor may have less influence because the district listens to officials in those other municipalities as well. We chose 75 percent for each of these decision rules because it is generally accepted as a high, supermajority bar. Putting these decision rules into place produced a sample of 104 school districts, spanning 40 states.[12]

Once a sample has been chosen, an equally important and challenging question arises: What outcomes are we concerned about and how can we measure them? Mayor-led integrated governance is designed to bring about change along many dimensions. We can think of these as broadly falling into four categories:

1. Productivity, e.g., student achievement
2. Management and governance, e.g., financial and organization operations
3. Human capital, e.g., characteristics of teachers and leadership
4. Building public confidence, e.g., public opinion and awareness about the school district

In this chapter we focus on the first three categories, though in our larger study we examine public confidence as well.

Comparing Student Achievement across Districts and States

As Diane Ravitch has observed, "50 states, 50 standards, 50 tests" are seen across the country (2005). Without a uniform testing system, the 50-state, 50-test reality leaves us with three distinct methodological challenges:

1. It is easiest to look only at a single district, but what generalized conclusions can we draw from single-district studies?

2. If we want to examine districts in multiple states, how can we collect such a diverse set of student achievement measures?
3. How can comparisons be made across different measures to isolate the effects of mayor-led integrated governance?

In order to carry out this analysis, we had to construct a dependent achievement outcome variable that is comparable across districts. As discussed by Robert Yin and his colleagues, this is difficult when trying to compare districts that employ different standardized tests (Yin, Schmidt, and Besag, 2006). Because the tests are not uniform, it is not appropriate to simply compare across states. We cannot, for instance, say that a Boston school with 75 percent of its students proficient on the Massachusetts Comprehensive Assessment System (MCAS) is performing at the same level as a St. Louis school with 75 percent of its students proficient on the Missouri Assessment Program (MAP). Comparisons are made more difficult still when states choose different measures (e.g., percentile ranks, percent passing) to report.

The problem is analogous to finding a common language to allow people of different countries to speak with one another. Our "universal language" solution in this case is the statistical language of "standard deviations." The process of translating each state's test into standard deviations is called standardization. Standardization is a statistical method used to compare two (or more) scores that have been measured using different scales. The resulting standardized measures allow us to see how many "standard deviations" each district in the country is above/below its own state mean. This measure of standard deviations is called a "z-score." We can compare any two (or more) districts with each other by comparing their z-scores. Statistically, we calculate a standardized "z-score" that is defined as follows:

$$Z = \frac{X - \mu}{\sigma}$$

where X is the district's average performance, μ is the mean state performance, and σ is the standard deviation within the population of all districts in the state. The resulting z-scores have a mean of 0, a standard deviation of 1, and are measured in "standard deviations." A z-score of positive 1.5 for a district means that the district is achieving at 1.5 standard deviations above the state mean. A z-score of -0.6 for a district means that the district is achieving at .6 standard deviations below the state mean.

The standardization approach has been used in a number of other situations involving education data being compared across different measures. A Brookings study, for instance, used z-scores when comparing the performance of charter schools across different states. Z-scores have also been used to adjust for different scales on spelling and reading tests. An Idaho study used the approach when it was felt that the data they were working with were not comparable as raw scores (Allinder et al., 1992; Loveless, 2003; Ravitz, Mergendoller, and Rush, 2002).

Our process of standardization can be best understood as two related sets of comparisons that are being made. First, we compare each of our sample districts to other districts in the same state. Utilizing the mean and standard deviation within the state, we are able to calculate z-scores representing "the number of standard deviations District A is above/below the mean in State 1." It's important to recognize that in this first round, comparisons are only being made between the *same measure of achievement* on the *same achievement test*. We are comparing Boston's percent proficient on the MCAS to other Massachusetts districts' percent proficient on the MCAS. We are comparing Detroit's percent proficient on the MEAP to other Michigan districts' percent proficient on the MEAP. We never compare MEAP with MCAS, or with any other state's test.

In this study, we make extensive use of the National Longitudinal School-Level State Assessment Score Database (NLSLSASD), supplemented by data provided by state departments of education when the NLSLSASD data was missing.[13]

Quantifying Mayoral Control

Quantifying mayoral control is essential for conducting the type of cross-district regression analysis we carry out in this study. We focus on formal, legal authority. This has several advantages. First, the degree of formal power is a measure that is available for each district. Printed in black-and-white statutes, institutional governance can be readily coded. Second, formal powers are what state legislatures and city residents (via charter amendments) can directly change. From a policy perspective, then, these are the legal tools available.

We have identified three key dimensions in which mayoral control can be institutionalized: the presence of a new-style mayor, formal authority for that mayor to appoint a majority of the school board, and whether the appointive power is legally restricted in any way. Because we are not sure which aspect of mayoral control may be most salient, we consider each aspect independently before summing them up into an index. Based on these three dimensions, we create three dichotomous variables. Each variable measures a unique aspect of mayoral control. We use this method—a series of yes/no questions about mayors' formal powers—because it avoids the almost impossible task of specifying a mayor's precise "level of control." For instance, it is not possible to accurately assess whether a mayor has "a lot" or "a little" power. Instead, we try to get at this by thinking about factors likely to be highly correlated with mayoral power in the education realm. We consider three factors:

1. *NEW_STYLE:* A dichotomous variable, coded as 1 if the mayor has *adopted a new style of governance*, integrating electoral accountability and school performance. The variable is coded 0 if the school system remains governed within an old-style regime.
2. *MAJORITY:* A dichotomous variable, coded as 1 if the mayor has the power to *appoint a majority* of the school board. The variable is coded 0 if the mayor can appoint zero or any submajority of the board.
3. *FULL:* A dichotomous variable, coded as 1 if the mayor has *full appointment power* for school board, with no requirement of council, aldermen, or other approval. The variable is coded 0 otherwise.

Because the effectiveness of mayoral control may also depend on the cumulative effect of these powers, we add an additional index variable that sums up the three dimensions above. This index variable, labeled *MAYOR_INDEX*, has a low value of 0, and a high value of 3. We run two sets of models. In "Model A" we include the three measures of mayoral control independently. This allows us to test their relative contribution to student achievement and other outcomes. We then run "Model B," in which we replace the three individual measures with the composite Mayor Index.

Our data set allows us to look over many districts and across multiple years. This means that our unit of observation is not simply the district (as it would be if we had only data from one year), but the "district-year." The values of the mayoral control variables change, over time, within the same district. In New York, for example, the value of the *MAJORITY* variable is 0 for the years 1999–2001, and 1 for the years 2002 and 2003. Similar changes are seen when a governance shift is made.

In addition to mayoral control, other district-level factors are likely to affect student achievement. To address each of the following alternative explanations, we develop a quantifiable measure entered into our regression equation as a control variable. We present a summary of these measures in Table 15.2, and we can think of these alternative explanations as falling into three broad categories: (a) school district characteristics, (b) student background, and (c) governance.

How Does Mayoral Control Affect Achievement?

The first step in setting up a proper evaluation of mayors and educational outcomes is to ask exactly how it is that mayors are likely to affect student performance. It might be helpful here to think about what mayors are *not* doing. Mayors are not jumping into the classroom, choosing the books for

Table 15.2.   Measurement of Contributing Factors to Student Achievement in Big-City School Districts

Factors to Be Considered	How We Measured It in Our Analysis
Governance	
Mayoral involvement in education	Three variables (coded as 0 or 1) that measure whether the mayor has (a) adopted a new style of education governance, (b) formal powers to appoint a majority of the school board, and (c) full discretion to appoint. We also combine these three individual factors into an index (0–3) measuring overall mayoral involvement.
Mayor-council form of government	Variable (coded as 0 or 1) noting if the city government has a mayor-council form of government
School board politics	Percentage of school board seats that are elected in a single-member fashion
School District Characteristics	
Size of school district	Student enrollment in school district[a]
Strength of private school market	Percentage of the city's children, aged 3–18, who are attending private schools[b]
Financial ties to state	Percentage of school district's education revenue that comes from the state[c]
	Dollars per student spent on instruction, adjusted for inflation and geography
Student Background	
Minority representation in student body	Percentage of district students who are Hispanic; percentage who are African American[b]
Special needs population	Percentage of district students who are special education students[b]
Student poverty	Percentage of children living within the school districts boundaries who are identified as living beneath the poverty line[b]

NOTES: Source for this table is Table 3.2 in *The Education Mayor* (Wong et al., 2007, p. 67). a. Variable constructed using data from the U.S. Department of Education's Common Core of Data. b. Variable constructed using data from the 2000 U.S. Census. c. Variable constructed using data from the Annual Survey of Government Finances conducted by the United States Bureau of the Census.

students to read, or poring over school budgets to see if more money should be spent on supplies. Mayors are operating at a *systemwide* level. In what we describe elsewhere as a politics of partnership, mayors are providing a political shield for the school district central office to operate with less partisanship influencing decisions. Because they operate at districtwide levels, we need to think about outcomes at the district level. We also need to recognize that mayoral influence may not be immediate. Unlike a new superstar teacher who may walk into a classroom and raise student achievement in a month, mayoral-led reforms are designed to be long term and systemic. Because of this long-term vision, our analysis must be longitudinal as well as carried out at the district level.

Using statistical language, we can say our unit of observation in this analysis is the "district-year" and that we have "panel data." This means we look year-to-year at districtwide performance. We analyze student achievement over the period 1999–2003 in each of the 101 districts for which we have achievement data from the National Longitudinal School-Level State Assessment Score Database (NLSLSASD). We study reading and math outcomes separately. In keeping with the economics literature on the relationship between educational inputs and outputs, we use a district-level production function (Hanushek 1979; 1986).

Using the NLSLSASD achievement time series (1999–2003) and cross-sectional (N=101) data, we use Equation 1 and employ the following base OLS regression model:[1]

[1] $ACHIEVE_{it} = \beta_0 + \beta_1 ACHIEVE_{it-1} + \beta_2 MAYORAL\_CONTROL_{it} + \beta_3 MAYOR\_COUNCIL_i + \beta_4 PCT\_SINGLE\_MEMBER_{it} + \beta_5 PCT\_PRIVATE_{it} + \beta_6 PCT\_STATE\_REV_{it} + \beta_7 PPE\_INSTRUCT_{it} + \beta_8 ENROLL_{it} + \beta_9 PCT\_HISPANIC_{it} + \beta_{10} PCT\_AFR\text{-}AMERICAN_{it} + \beta_{11} PCT\_KIDS\_POVERTY_{it} + \beta_{12} PCT\_SPECIAL\_ED_{it} + \delta_i + \gamma_t + \epsilon_{it}$

where $ACHIEVE_{it}$ is the standardized (z-score) achievement for school district i in year t; $ACHIEVE_{,,i,\,t\text{-}1}$ is the district's previous year's standardized (z-score) achievement; $MAYORAL\_CONTROL_{it}$ is either the composite $MAYOR\_INDEX$ or the individual three measures: NEW_STYLE, $MAJORITY$, and $FULL$; $MAYOR\_COUNCIL_{it}$ is a dichotomous variable indicating whether or not the city uses a mayor-council form of government; $PCT\_SINGLE\_MEMBER_{it}$ is the percentage of city school board seats that are voted on in a single-member fashion; $PCT\_PRIVATE_{it}$ is the percentage of K–12 students in the city enrolled in private schools; $PCT\_STATE\_REV_{it}$ is the percentage of school district revenue from state sources; $PPE\_INSTRUCT_{it}$ is the district's per-pupil expenditures on instruction, adjusted for inflation and regional cost differences; $ENROLL_{it}$ is the district student enrollment; $PCT\_HISPANIC_{it}$ is the percentage of Hispanic students in the district; $PCT\_AFR\text{-}AMERICAN_{it}$ is the percentage of African American students in the district; $PCT\_KIDS\_POVERTY_{it}$ is the percentage of city residents, age 3–18, who were living below the poverty level in 2000; $PCT\_SPECIAL\_ED_{it}$ is the percentage of district students who have an Individualized Education Plan (IEP); δ_s captures State Fixed Effects; γ_t captures Year Fixed Effects, and ϵ_{ti} is an error term.[14]

In addition to our base model, we consider two models that investigate the possibility of lagged effects from mayoral control. In these alternative models, we make one adjustment to the model presented in Equation 1. Instead of including *MAYORAL_CONTROL* for year *t*, we include the measure for year *t-1*. This is our "Lag 1" Model. We then run a series of models using *MAYORAL_CONTROL* for year *t-2*. This is our "Lag 2" Model. The results from these models with lagged mayoral control variables are presented alongside the results from the baseline achievement model.

Results: Integrated Governance Raises Elementary School Performance

With the details of the statistical methods now laid out, we turn to the central question of our study: Does mayoral control work in raising student achievement? The answer, simply put, is yes. The answer, more nuanced, is that majority appointment power of school board members and the presence of a new-style education mayor are effective tools for raising achievement, but that a lack of oversight on the mayor's choices may actually work against this progress. Our analysis suggests that mayors can steer the ship in the right direction, but they still have a long way to go before their districts achieve acceptable levels of student achievement.

Let us turn now to the specific evidence for our conclusions. All of the results for elementary achievement are presented in Table 15.3. Due to space considerations, we report only reading results, but note that the findings for math are substantively the same. In the first model, labeled "Model A," we include all three measures of mayoral control: whether a new style of mayor emerges; whether the mayor has formal power to appoint a majority of the school board; and whether the mayor has the power to select school board members without any oversight. In the second model, labeled "Model B," we replace the individual components with the composite Mayor Control Index.

How does mayoral control relate to standardized elementary reading achievement? Looking at the results we see that giving the mayor power to appoint a majority of the city's school board is associated with an increase of .15 in standardized elementary reading achievement (Table 15.3). New-style mayors are associated with a similar .11 increase in reading (Table 15.3). These relationships are similar in both the one- and two-year lag models, where we consider the relationship between present year achievement and governance arrangements in previous years. Driven by these two aspects of mayoral control, the composite mayoral control index is significantly and positively related to standardized reading achievement in both the baseline and two-year lag models (Table 15.3). At the same time, however, allowing the mayor full power to appoint school board members, without oversight from a nominating committee, is inversely related to elementary reading achievement (Table 15.3).

Table 15.3. Results from Linear Regression Models for Standardized Elementary Reading Achievement, 1999–2003, Year and State Fixed Effects; Coeff. and Robust Std. Errors Reported

	No Lag		1-Year Lag		2-Year Lag	
	A	B	A	B	A	B
New-Style Mayor	.11**	.	15***		.15***	
	(.05)		(.06)		(.05)	
Majority Appointment Power	.15***	.07	.10**			
	(.05)		(.05)		(.05)	
Full Appointment Power	−.15**		−.19**		−.10	
	(.07)		(.09)		(.06)	
Mayor Control Index	.05*		.03		.07***	
	(.03)		(.03)		(.02)	
Previous Achievement	.85***	.86***	.86***	.86***	.86***	.86***
	(.03)	(.03)	(.03)	(.03)	(.03)	(.03)
Mayor Council	−.03		−.02		−.03	
	(.03)		(.03)		(.03)	
% Single-Member School Board	.009	.005	.002	.002	.004	.006
	(.035)	(.035)	(.035)	(.035)	(.035)	(.035)
% Private Schools	−.52*	−.49*	−.54*	−.49*	−.51*	−.49*
	(.30)	(.29)	(.30)	(.28)	(.31)	(.29)
% Revenue from State	.28**	.22*	.27**	.23*	.27**	.25**
	(.13)	(.12)	(.13)	(.12)	(.12)	(.12)
PPE Current Instruct.	.02	.01	.02	.01	.02	.02
	(.02)	(.01)	(.02)	(.01)	(.02)	(.01)
Enroll (100,000)	.01	.01	.06	.04	.04	.03
	(.10)	(.10)	(.10)	(.10)	(.10)	(.10)
% Hispanic	−.49***	−.45**	−.46***	−.43**	−.48***	−.46***
	(.18)	(.17)	(.17)	(.17)	(.17)	(.17)
% Black	−.50***	−.50***	−.46***	−.46***	−.50***	−.51***
	(.12)	(.12)	(.12)	(.11)	(.12)	(.12)
% Kids in Poverty	−.54*	−.51*	−.57*	−.52*	−.52*	−.5*
	(.29)	(.28)	(.30)	(.29)	(.29)	(.28)
% Special Ed.	.25	.50	.20	.42	.24	.43
	(.69)	(.70)	(.70)	(.71)	(.69)	(.69)
Constant	.07	.08	.07	.07	.06	.05
	(.14)	(.14)	(.14)	(.14)	(.14)	(.14)
Observations	451	451	451	451	451	451
R-squared	0.95	0.95	0.95	0.95	0.95	0.95

NOTES: Source for this table is Table 4.2 in *The Education Mayor* (Wong et al., 2007, pp. 84–85). All models employ state and year fixed effects. Robust standard errors by clustering on school districts. Two-tailed significance denoted as: *** for p<.01, ** for p<.05, * for p<.1. Enrollment measured in 1,000,000s.

From this evidence it's clear that mayoral leadership has made a difference in the early grades. Districtwide achievement levels, relative to other districts in the state, is positively associated with new-style education mayors and giving the mayor the power to appoint a majority of the local school board. At the same time, not putting any restrictions on whom the mayor appoints to the school board seems to dampen achievement levels. In light of these findings, a few policy implications are immediately evident. First, optimal systems should design mayoral control systems to include nominating committees that provide the mayor with a slate of candidates from which to choose school board members. Second, evaluation of mayoral control should recognize that improvements from mayoral control may take at least two years to become evident in aggregate statistics.

Although we do not have space to include the analysis here, we find a similar relationship at the high school level. Many reforms, such as reducing central office bureaucracy, can be thought to be grade-level neutral. Less red tape in the central office benefits all schools, regardless of the grades they serve.

What is particularly encouraging about the achievement results is that they are the *marginal effects of mayoral control*, holding all else constant. In other words, even if poverty levels remain the same, funding levels don't improve, and private school competition holds constant, our model predicts that a governance change leads to significant, positive improvements in overall district achievement. If mayors can work simultaneously to reduce poverty and increase funding, the overall effect of mayoral control may be even larger in the longer run.

Financial Management and Human Capital

Mayoral-led integrated governance as a reform policy is distinguished by its broad reach. Mayors are in a position not only to improve teaching and learning, but to fundamentally alter the financial and management conditions in which teaching and learning occur. In addition to improving fiscal stability, integrated governance allows the central decision-making authorities more flexibility in terms of resource allocation. In particular, mayors may be able to reduce school district central office inefficiencies, thereby allowing for greater investments in teaching, learning, and student service provision. At the same time, however, they are operating in an environment that is often hostile to change. Whether or not mayors can make good on their promise to improve fiscal efficiency remains an open question for which we conducted extensive additional rounds of statistical analysis to address.

To consider the relationship between mayoral-appointed school boards and measures of effective management and improvements in human capital, we once again employed a panel data approach. We obtained financial and staffing data for all of our 104 sample districts, and for the entirety of our 11-year period of observation, 1993–2003. The financial outcome data comes from the Annual Survey of Government Finances conducted by the U.S. Bureau of the Census. The Annual Survey gathers data on revenues, expenditures, and debt from over 15,000 school districts. In addition to this financial data, we use the National Center for Education Statistics' Common Core of Data (CCD) as a source for our demographic control variables, as well as data on district staffing patterns. Both data sources provide data that is comparable across time and across districts.[15]

Using our time series (1993–2003) and cross-sectional (104 districts) data, we employ a fixed-effects regression model similar to the achievement model. The base model for our finance and staffing regressions takes the form of:

[2] $OUTCOME_{it} = \beta_0 + \beta_1 MAYORAL\_CONTROL_{it} + \beta_2 MAYOR\_COUNCIL_i + \beta_3 PCT\_SINGLE\_MEMBER_{it} + \beta_4 PCT\_PRIVATE_{it} + \beta_5 ENROLL_{it} + \beta_6 PCT\_HISPANIC_{it} + \beta_7 PCT\_AFR-AMERICAN_{it} + \beta_8 PCT\_KIDS\_POVERTY_{it} + \beta_9 PCT\_SPECIAL\_ED_{it} + \delta_i + \gamma_t + \epsilon_{it}$

where $OUTCOME_{it}$ is the financial or staffing outcome measure for school district i in year t; and the other variables are the same as defined previously.[16]

Results: Mayors' New Strategic Spending Priorities

Does mayoral control lead to greater per-pupil revenues? Our results suggest that they do not.[17] The power to appoint a majority of school board members is significantly and negatively related to per-pupil revenues. The presence of a new-style mayor is not related in a statistically significant way with per-pupil revenues. Returning to the general question of whether a mayor can overcome institutional inertia and broader economic trends, the negative relationship between mayoral control and per-pupil revenues suggests that factors beyond the mayor's control may determine revenue levels. Faced with limited options for raising new funds themselves, and dealing with urban districts that already rely heavily on state and federal compensatory funding, mayors may have to reframe their financial aims. Rather than infuse the school district with new money, they may be forced to work more efficiently with the same or even fewer resources.

Our analysis finds that at baseline, mayoral control is inversely associated with the level of per-pupil spending on instruction and support, but given five years, the percentage spent on instruction and support increases. The distinction between percentage allocation and overall expenditure levels is an important one. Mayoral-led districts aren't spending more, but they're spending differently. Mayoral-led districts are reallocating resources to instruction and instructional support.

While mayors may be able to institute changes in school district financial management, it appears that district employees may be insulated from sweeping changes brought in by mayoral-control regimes. Mayoral-control measures are not statistically significantly related to increases in the percentage of district staff that are teachers, administration, or student support.

Synthesizing the findings of our analysis of mayors and school finances, we believe that the big-picture story is one in which new-style mayors are becoming more strategic in prioritizing their resource allocation and management. Central to this strategy is the notion of fiscal discipline in constraining labor costs. We see this in the inverse relationship between mayoral control and expenditures. Education mayors, while continuing to partner with labor unions, seem able to leverage cooperation (or concessions) from the school employees' unions. In Chicago, for instance, the 1995 Act precluded a teachers' strike during the first 18 months of mayoral control.

Another aspect of mayors' strategic priorities seems to be improving bureaucratic efficiency by reducing expenditures on general administrative purposes. Mayoral control lowered the level spending on general administration and also reduced the percentage of expenditures on general administration. By reducing general administrative costs, mayors free up more money for instructional purposes and may improve public confidence that wasteful spending is not occurring in the district. The trend of mayors spending more on instructional purposes is also seen in their decision to prioritize this type of spending over noninstructional services such as support services, transportation, and some operations costs.

A third aspect of mayoral control emerging from our analysis is the need for leadership to "do more with less," presumably by improving district efficiency. While we do not have a direct measure of efficiency, we find some circumstantial evidence to suggest new spending priorities under mayoral control systems. Given five years to implement their strategies, mayoral-led systems allocate more salaries and wages to instruction, thus prioritizing the resources that most directly affect quality teaching. Another indicator we see are allocations for "other" nonelementary and secondary programs declining at both baseline and five years.

Summing Up: Mayors Make a Difference

The results of our empirical analyses, the most comprehensive to date on the impact of mayors on student achievement and financial management in school districts, supports the claim of integrated governance that mayoral-appointed school boards can have a significant, positive effect on district performance. The first wave of mayoral control has proven that integrated governance is a viable policy reform in urban education. The success of mayoral control has attracted the attention of many mayors who are dissatisfied with their city school systems. We turn now to an analysis of this possible "second wave" of mayoral control.

III. SECOND WAVE OF MAYORAL CONTROL:
REFORM AND RESISTANCE

The first wave of mayoral control has proved that mayors can make a difference. But the transition from an elected to a mayoral-appointed board is not an easy one. Mayoral control fundamentally challenges existing power arrangements by formally changing the legal governance of city school systems. It is not surprising, therefore, that proposals to increase the mayor's power vis à vis the school board are often met with resistance. In this section we discuss the contentious relationships between mayors and school boards in three cities: Los Angeles, Albuquerque, and the District of Columbia. To varying degrees from 2005 through 2007 these cities attempted to change the governance structure of their schools. The experiences of mayors in these cities teach us important lessons about the politics of mayoral control.

Los Angeles: Failure to Launch

The changing relationship between Los Angeles Mayor Antonio Villaraigosa and the Los Angeles Unified School District (LAUSD) is a lesson to other mayors about the importance of timing and partnership. In Table 15.4 we provide a timeline of important dates in Mayor Villaraigosa's ultimately failed attempt to transform LAUSD into a mayor-appointed board.[18]

One of the premises of mayoral control is that without an intervention, the school district will continue to underperform or potentially perform even worse. This premise, however, may be challenged by those interested in maintaining the status quo. This is exactly what happened in Los Angeles, when Mayor Villaraigosa pushed forward his plan for a mayoral-appointed school board. Reacting to the mayor's moves, Los Angeles School Board president Marlene Canter responded, "I think the mayor's entire conversation is based on an assumption that the district is moving in the wrong direction, and that is flat-out wrong."[19]

This conflict between the school board president and mayor was a conflict over the objective state of the present school system. It calls attention to the importance of properly evaluating the school district's performance.

Table 15.4. Chronology of Important Events Related to Mayoral Control of the Los Angeles Unified School District (LAUSD), April 2005–August 2007

Date	Event
Prior to March 2005	EdVoice, with philanthropist Eli Broad, approaches California State Legislature with proposal that would allow for mayoral control in failing urban school districts.
Prior to March 2005	The Small Schools Alliance develops.
Prior to March 2005	Neither sitting mayor James Hahn nor challenger Antonio Villaraigosa publicly state their interest in appointing school board members.
March 15, 2005	Both mayoral candidates align themselves with the Small Schools Alliance's "Contract to Transform L.A. Schools," but neither candidate offers a mayoral-appointed school board as a reform option.
April 20, 2005	Mayor Hahn announces his proposal for a change in the L.A. city charter that would allow for mayoral appointment of three board members, and the creation of five new charter schools.
April 21, 2005	Councilman Villaraigosa announces his support for the mayor having "ultimate control and oversight" over the school district.
April 27, 2005	The "Joint Commission on LAUSD Governance" is established by the Los Angeles City Council to serve for one year to "determine the best manner in which to align the L.A.U.S.D. governance structure."
April 27, 2005	California Senator Dianne Feinstein officially announces her support for the concept of mayoral-appointed school boards.
May 6, 2005	California Senator Barbara Boxer officially announces her support for the concept of mayoral-appointed school boards.
May 17, 2005	Mayor Hahn (41.4%) is defeated by challenger Antonio Villaraigosa (58.6%) in the General Election.
June 17, 2005	Before the Senate Select Committee on Urban Governance, Mayor-Elect Villaraigosa states that, "I think the mayor should be able to appoint all the members of the school board."
July 1, 2005	Mayor Villaraigosa officially takes office.
July 18, 2005	State Senator Gloria Romero (D-Los Angeles) amends CA Senate Bill 767 to establish the "Mayoral Leadership to Improve Education in Los Angeles Act," which would allow for mayoral appointment of school board members in Los Angeles if the district does not meet certain benchmarks.
July 18, 2005	Mayor Villaraigosa backs away from SB 767, instead saying he wants to focus on "the areas we can work on now."
July 20, 2005	Los Angeles Times Op-Ed, "A mayor for the schools," argues in support of mayoral control of schools.

(*continued*)

Table 15.4. (*continued*)

Date	Event
July 24, 2005	Robert M. Hertzberg, former speaker of the California Assembly, writes an Op-Ed in the Los Angeles Daily News, supporting mayoral control.
July 29, 2005	Mayor Villaraigosa announces the formation of a 30-member "Council of Education Advisors," composed of teachers, principals, and education experts.
August 3, 2005	EdVoice begins its campaign to build support for SB 767.
November 2005	Mayor Villaraigosa steps up his public appeals for mayoral control.
November 20, 2005	Los Angeles Times editorial, "ABCs of school reform," argues again in support of mayoral involvement in the LAUSD.
December 1, 2005	City Controller Laura Chick proposes to conduct an audit of the Los Angeles Unified School District.
January–April 2006	Mayor Villaraigosa speaks out on education issues.
March 9, 2006	Controller Chick's report on LAUSD financial documents finds "there is a disturbing lack of transparency and accountability."
April 18, 2006	Mayor Villaraigosa delivers his State of the City speech and proposes "giving the superintendent . . . not the school board . . . the authority to direct personnel decisions, grant charters, develop the budget, and design and manage the instructional program" with "a council of mayors, whose members will be proportionally represented" to "oversee the hiring and firing of the superintendent and approve the budget."
April–June 2006	Opponents voice criticism of mayor's plan; mayor works with legislatures, teachers union, district officials, and civic leaders to draft legislation allowing for mayoral control.
June 21, 2006	Compromise plan announced in which Council of Mayors retains some power, but not as much as originally proposed.
July 31, 2006	Independently commissioned report, The Final Report of the Presidents' Joint Commission on LAUSD Governance, is released and calls for more decentralization.
August 28, 2006	Assembly Bill 1381 passes the Senate on a vote of 22 to 14.
August 29, 2006	Assembly Bill 1381 passes the House on a vote of 42 to 20.
September 18, 2006	Governor Schwarzenegger signs AB 1381 into law, scheduled to go into effect on January 1, 2007.
October 10, 2006	LAUSD files a lawsuit in Superior Court challenging the new law as unconstitutional.
December 21, 2006	Superior Court Judge Dzintra Janavs rules in favor of LAUSD, finding that AB 1381 is unconstitutional; mayor's legal team quickly appeals the decision.
April 2, 2007	2nd District Court of Appeal in Los Angeles hears the appeal of Mayor Villaraigosa, challenging the lower court's decision declaring AB 1381 unconstitutional.

Date	Event
April 17, 2007	Court of Appeal rules against Mayor Villaraigosa, effectively closing this pathway toward mayoral control.
May 15, 2007	Two mayor-backed school board candidates, Tamar Galatzan and Richard A. Vladovic, win their run-off elections for the LAUSD school board, giving the mayor four "reform" board members.
August 29, 2007	Mayor and LAUSD announce the Partnership for Los Angeles Schools, to take effect in 2008, allowing the mayor to govern two low-performing high schools and associated feeder schools.

It also makes clear that the *timing* (or mis-timing) of an evaluation can affect the way that mayoral control is perceived.

Looking at Table 15.4, what's interesting to note is that specific evaluation of the LAUSD came *after* the initial statement of interest from Mayor Villaraigosa, and after a piece of legislation was introduced into the California State Senate. Ideally, this evaluation groundwork should be laid *before* public pronouncements by city officials, and certainly before legislation is proposed.

Evaluating school district performance is important for two reasons. First, it is important to know exactly what the district needs to improve. Anecdotes and reputation alone are not enough to support reform. Instead, empirical evidence, properly analyzed and interpreted, must form the foundation of reform. It may turn out, for instance, that a school district is doing much better in reading than in math, or is challenged more on the expenditure than the revenue side of the ledger.

Second, from a political perspective, it is important that the mayor and those interested in promoting mayoral control can point to hard evidence to support their positions. When a substantial change in education governance is proposed, the plan will be closely scrutinized. Citizens want to know what sort of *results* they can expect. In Los Angeles, for instance, a November 2005 article in the *Los Angeles Times* suggested to its readers that "the takeovers in Chicago and New York have yielded mixed results."[20] In the face of such scrutiny, the more relevant data mayors have at their fingertips, the better they are able to respond.

After the evaluation stage, the next step is building political support. Five factors outside of city government are most powerful in affecting the development of mayoral control: (a) school board opposition; (b) municipal, regional, and state political climate; (c) strength of interest groups, especially the teachers' union; (d) support of civic and business community; and (f) local media.

The process in Los Angeles illustrates how both the state legislature and policy entrepreneurs can shape the debate about mayors and public education. During his first term, and through the majority of his campaign, former Mayor Hahn did not publicly voice interest in running the Los Angeles schools. In fact, in the initial press materials on education the governance distinction was made clear: "*Although the Los Angeles School Board runs the public schools*, Mayor Hahn is working to improve educational opportunities for Los Angeles students by expanding after-school programs, making schools safer, promoting literacy and working with the school district to build schools more quickly to relieve overcrowding."[21] No mention is made of any intention by Mayor Hahn to change the school district governance structure. Mayor Hahn had not even chosen to do what his predecessor, Mayor Riordan, did in 1999: actively campaign for a slate of candidates in the school board elections.[22]

It wasn't until March 2005 that Mayor Hahn spoke out in favor of appointing school board members.[23] Using different education rhetoric than he had at the beginning of the campaign, Hahn said, "Every day, everywhere I go, people talk to me as if I have control over the schools." Hahn went on to argue that "if people are going to hold me accountable . . . it seems to me the mayor ought to have some say about what's going on in the school district."[24] In response, challenger Antonio Villaraigosa pointed out that this was an abrupt change of direction: "The mayor continues to make last-minute campaign proposals about ideas that he never discussed or delivered on in four years as mayor."[25]

But just a few days later, Villaraigosa said that the mayor should have "ultimate control and oversight" over the school district.[26] Although it was not clear exactly what Villaraigosa had in mind as a governance structure for "ultimate control," the sentiment of both mayoral candidates had changed markedly. Mayoral control of the Los Angeles public schools was now on the table. To understand how it got there, we must look beyond the two candidates. Two sources—a group of philanthropists and a policy entrepreneur—played prominent roles.

At the state level, even before it became an issue in the mayor's race, the groundwork for mayoral control was being laid by the state's leading educational philanthropists, principally through the nonprofit and bipartisan education advocacy group EdVoice.[27] One philanthropist in the group, Eli Broad, had been active in Riordan's 1999 push for the slate of four school board candidates.[28] In that race, Broad helped raise over $200,000 to fund the campaign work.

In 2005, the advocacy efforts of these philanthropists would eventually lead to the creation in June 2005 of a "Senate Select Committee on Urban Governance," chaired by State Senator Gloria Romero.[29] Senator Romero, a Democrat from Los Angeles, said that the formation of this committee was "not about assigning blame, it's about taking responsibility."[30] EdVoice's initial proposal was designed to target not only Los Angeles, but Oakland and Fresno as well.

At the same time that the state senate was considering the issue, the idea of changing to mayoral control became tied to the work of innovative Los Angeles policy entrepreneur Steve Barr, Chairman/CEO of Greendot Public Schools and President of the Small Schools Alliance (SSA).[31] Barr founded Greendot Public Schools in 1999, operating five charter high schools with over 1,500 students. Greendot, based on a model of small schools, has been incredibly successful in improving student performance, graduation rates, and college attendance.[32]

An outgrowth of the small schools model, the SSA developed a "Contract to Transform L.A. Schools," and starting in February 2005 invested in a $2 million campaign to promote the idea.[33] The SSA pushed to have both mayoral runoff candidates sign the pledge, and by March 2005 both candidates were on board. Although mayoral control was not one of the primary tenets of the pledge, Barr said, "If the board rejects it and drags their feet, then it's time to have a discussion in this city, just like New York and Chicago, where the mayor says, 'This is too important for me not to get involved. I will be accountable and I will take over the schools.'"[34] As noted in a postelection analysis by the *Los Angeles Times*, it was Barr's SSA that "forced the mayoral candidates to address radical school reform."[35]

The Los Angeles example alerts us to the possibility of disjointed timing. In the Los Angeles case, different interests pushed for different aspects of mayoral control independently of the mayor's own actions. The consequences of this disjointed timing can be problematic for the development of strong partnerships that are needed for successful reform. Looking at subsequent developments in Los Angeles provides evidence that shaky foundations can lead to problematic policy development.

During the first few months of 2006, Mayor Villaraigosa became more vocal on education issues. In a speech before the U.S. Conference of Mayors in January 2006, Mayor Villaraigosa emphasized education reform, stating that "we need to take the issue of education reform to the front and center of the debate about poverty and opportunity."[36] At the same time, the mayor was developing his plan for a governance change. On April 18, in his State of the City speech, the mayor proposed "giving the superintendent . . . not the school board . . . the authority to direct personnel decisions, grant charters, develop the budget, and design and manage the instructional program" with "a council of mayors, whose members will be proportionally represented" to "oversee the hiring and firing of the superintendent and approve the budget."[37] Even though the mayor's plan maintained an elected school board, it stripped the board of much of its power for district oversight. In response, the board and a number of organizations were vocal in criticizing the plan. Some warned of patronage. Others felt it was a political power grab. For the next few months, the mayor worked with opponents, members of the legislatures, and civic leaders to craft a compromise bill.

The compromise was reached on June 21, and by the end of the summer the legislature had passed the bill. The governor signed it into law on September 18, with a scheduled effective date of January 1, 2007. Within a month, however, the LAUSD board filed suit in court alleging that the law was unconstitutional. On December 21, Superior Court Judge Dzintra Janavs agreed. The mayor appealed to the Court of Appeal, but after a hearing on April 2, the Court of Appeal ruled against the mayor on April 17.

Stymied by the courts, Mayor Villaraigosa chose a tactic that had been attempted by Mayor Riordan before him: backing a slate of school board candidates. It was reported that the mayor spent $3.5 million to support his three candidates (each of whom won) in spring 2007 school board races.[38] Although the mayor had no formal power over these board members, his informal influence could be considerable given the support he offered during their campaigns. On August 29, the first signs of this new partnership appeared in the form of the Partnership for Los Angeles Schools. Under the agreement, the mayor would take control of two low-performing high schools and the associated feeder schools. While this latest development is a small step in the right direction, the bigger picture shows a mayor initially hesitant to get into education policy, then unable to build the prerequisite partnerships required for long-term success.

Albuquerque: Seeking Formal Powers

In 2006, Albuquerque Mayor Martin Chávez made public his desire to appoint a majority of the Albuquerque Public Schools (APS) school board. Citing the need for more accountability, Mayor Chávez expressed his view that "the system is broken."[39] The mayor found political partners in the state legislature, as State Senator Ortiz y Pino proposed a bill that proposed "a special school district election prior to June 30, 2008, in which the question shall be submitted to the qualified electors of the district of whether the school district should have a local school board consisting of four members elected from single-member districts and three members appointed by the mayor of the largest municipality of the district and confirmed by the city council."[40] Neither this bill, nor two similar bills that would have had the same effect, were passed during the 2007 regular session, leaving Mayor Chávez without any new authority.[41]

Mayor Chávez, who subsequently chose to run for U.S. Senate, was an education mayor in waiting. As indicated in his 2005 State of the City speech, the mayor believed that "no Mayor can be successful unless the schools are successful, no city succeeds without its educational system and schools need cities as well."[42] But without the formal powers, Mayor Chávez was limited in what he could accomplish. He had to settle for informal means such as offering advice on superintendent hiring. In the meantime, he moved his immediate priorities to other policy areas.[43]

As in Los Angeles, Mayor Chávez's experiences remind us that mayoral desires for leadership must be matched by support from the state legislature. Without a new law or amendment to the state constitution, Mayor Chávez remained an education mayor without formal powers.

Washington, D.C.: New Leadership

The story of the school board and mayoral control in Washington, D.C., in the last decade is a cyclical one.[44] Following Congressional action in 1995, the Board of Trustees was relegated to an essentially advisory position. In 2001, then-Mayor Anthony Williams was given, by approval of city voters, the power to appoint a majority (four of seven) of the school board. This law had a sunset provision, however, and was not renewed after 2004. As Mayor Williams's earlier appointees finished their terms, new members would be elected and no longer appointed. It seemed as if mayoral control in D.C. had run its course.

That changed, however, when Adrian Fenty was elected mayor in November 2006. At age 35, Fenty was the city's youngest elected mayor and immediately set out to make education a priority. In his first week as mayor, Fenty released his education proposal and echoed the sentiments of Mayors Daley, Menino, and Bloomberg when he explained that his "proposal changes one critical piece of the puzzle—increased accountability and action. I am asking today for that responsibility to be placed squarely on my shoulders."[45] The bill was submitted as the District of Columbia Public Education Reform Amendment Act of 2007 (Bill 17-001).[46]

Bolstering the mayor's proposal was the release of analysis carried out by the consulting firm, the Parthenon Group.[47] The analysis explicitly examined the feasibility of reform success with and without mayoral control, arguing that "ultimately mayoral control is required to exercise direct influence over the full range of DC's greatest pain points."[48] Consistent with the theory of integrated governance articulated in this chapter, the Parthenon Group's analysis argued that streamlining governance of state and local functions would improve accountability and management efficiency.

In response, the D.C. school board produced its own alternative plan, "The Student Achievement Emergency Act of 2007."[49] The months of February and March 2007 saw political positioning on both sides, as much testimony was given and partnerships were forged. The mayor was able to obtain key endorsements from the teachers union and an interfaith network. At the same time, however, two reports by the Council of Great City Schools called into question the effectiveness of the plan.[50] After the political debate, the bill was adopted by the D.C. Council and signed by the mayor on April 23 as D.C. Law 17-9. After review by Congress, the law became effective on June 12, 2007.

The new structure relegated the board of education to an advisory role, and gave the mayor full authority to run the district.[51] As stated in the law, "The Mayor shall govern the public schools in the District of Columbia. The Mayor shall have authority over all curricula, operations, functions, budget, personnel, labor negotiations and collective bargaining agreements, facilities, and other education-related matters, but shall endeavor to keep teachers in place after the start of the school year and transfer teachers, if necessary, during summer break."[52] Once approved by Congress, Mayor Fenty immediately named Michelle Rhee as Acting Chancellor of DCPS and started his transition program which continues as of this writing in late 2007.

The law gives the mayor five years to show progress. Although each year the mayor must submit a progress report, "On September 15, 2012, in lieu of the annual evaluation . . . the Mayor shall submit to the Council a 5-year assessment of the public education system established by D.C. Law 17-9, including: (a) A comprehensive evaluation of public education following the passage of D.C. Law 17-9; and (b) A determination as to whether sufficient progress in public education has been achieved to warrant continuation of the provisions and requirements of D.C. Law 17-9 or whether a new law, and a new system of education, should be enacted by the District government."[53] It remains to be seen what Mayor Fenty's effect is on the DCPS over the next five years, but our analysis of other cities suggests that he will be successful. By forging partnerships and gaining full control, Mayor Fenty is taking steps to join Daley, Menino, and Bloomberg as a successful education mayor.

CONCLUSION

In this chapter we have attempted to introduce integrated governance and mayoral-appointed school boards as an alternative to the traditional elected school board in struggling big-city school districts. Our empirical analysis suggests mayoral-appointed school boards can raise student achievement by at least .15 standard deviations. Mayors can also bring fiscal stability and new spending priorities into the system. The effects of mayoral control go beyond those we have discussed in this article. In our larger study, for instance, we discuss at greater length the relationship between mayoral control and race, civic participation, leadership, and public confidence. We encourage readers who would like to know more to review the larger body of research.

From a policy perspective, those interested in a possible transition to mayoral control can draw an important lesson from the contrast between Mayor Villaraigosa's failure to achieve control and Mayor Fenty's quick success in Washington, D.C. Mayor Fenty's legislative success relied on objective analysis as the groundwork, a well-thought-out plan, and brokering of important political partnerships. Mayoral control cannot be forced upon a city. City residents, school district officials, state legislatures, and other stakeholders must become convinced that mayoral control is an appropriate policy solution.

A Range of Mayoral Involvement

Although we have focused in this chapter solely on mayoral-appointed school boards, we close with a reminder that mayors have a variety of ways to influence the public school system even if they do not appoint members of the school board. Mayoral control is a flexible reform option that can and should adapt itself to particular local conditions. Integrated governance does not force policy makers to accept cookie-cutter regulations, but instead allows for creative implementation that best matches up with what politicians and educators see in their district. Looking at Table 15.5 it is evident that cities must make two decisions: (a) How much involvement should the mayor have at this time? and (b) How much involvement is politically feasible at this time?

The options we lay out are not exhaustive, but they do span the range of possible options cities and school districts have available. Moving from low to high mayoral involvement (left to right on Table 15.5), the options are:

1. *Mayoral-led "blue-ribbon panel."* This is almost always a politically feasible option because the panel does not have any legal authority. Its recommendations are just that—recommendations. A panel may be a good way to generate discussion, but a concern is that the panel's recommendations will not be followed with real action.
2. *Permanent mayoral office/department for education.* Because expert panels and commissions are typically dissolved after the release of their study, creating a permanent office or department within city government to look at education is more substantial. Some political resistance may emerge if the mayor's office is seen as encroaching on school district territory, but the mayor's office of education can focus on complementary programs such as after-school programs and facilities maintenance. While an office such as this would not affect fundamental school district operations, it could provide the basis for a solid partnership going forward, demonstrating that the city is capable of successfully operating educational programs.

Table 15.5. Range of Mayoral Involvement in Urban Education

	Low Involvement		Medium Involvement		High Involvement	
	Traditional Governance Arrangement	Mayoral-Led "Blue-Ribbon Panel"	Permanent Mayoral Office / Dept. for Education	Mayoral-Supported School Board Slate	Partially Mayoral-Appointed School Board	Fully Mayoral-Appointed School Board
Description	Mayor responsible for city government; school district governance is wholly separate	Traditional governance system is not changed, but mayor selects a blue-ribbon committee to study the city's schools and produce a report; the report is not binding and the committee is not standing	Traditional governance system is not changed, but mayor establishes a standing office to promote city schools and advise the mayor's office on issues related to education	Mayor becomes more active in school governance by actively endorsing or campaigning on behalf of a slate of school board candidates	Traditional governance system is altered, and mayor is given power to appoint some of the school board members	Traditional governance system is replaced by a fully mayoral-appointed school board
Example districts	Majority of U.S. school districts	Pittsburgh (Report issued by the Mayor's Commission on Public Education in 2003)	Minneapolis ("Capital City Education Initiative")	St. Louis (Mayor Slay backed a slate of 4 candidates in 2003)	Oakland (minority appointed) New York (majority appointed)	Chicago Boston

	Legal changes required?					
	No	No	Maybe	No	Yes	Yes
Major design considerations	Little to no mayoral involvement, so few design options available	Who should be on panel? How should they be selected? Scope of the panel's study. Timeline for panel's work. How involved should the school district be with this assessment? What outcome indicators will the panel look at? How will findings be presented?	What issues will the new office focus on? How will the office coordinate with the school district? Funding for the office? Who will lead the office?	How will school board candidates be identified for endorsement? Will mayor actively recruit the candidates? Will mayor give tacit endorsement, or actively campaign? Once on the board, what relationship will exist between mayor and supported school board members? What relationship with the rest	Should mayor appoint a majority or a minority of the board members? Should mayor be able to choose from any qualified candidate, or choose instead from a slate of candidates screened by independent commission? How long should mayor retain this power? How long will appointed members serve for?	In addition to questions in the previous column: When should mayor be given this power? Will appointing power be indefinite? Subject to vote? How large should the new school board be? How long should school board members serve for? How will superintendent be selected?

(continued)

Table 15.5. *(continued)*

	Low Involvement		Medium Involvement		High Involvement	
	Traditional Governance Arrangement	*Mayoral-Led "Blue-Ribbon Panel"*	*Permanent Mayoral Office / Dept. for Education*	*Mayoral-Supported School Board Slate*	*Partially Mayoral-Appointed School Board*	*Fully Mayoral-Appointed School Board*
				of the school board? Should endorsements be made each school board election?	What additional checks and balances can be introduced to ease concerns about the transfer of power?	

NOTE: Source for this table is Table 9.2 in *The Education Mayor* (Wong et al., 2007, pp. 194–195).

3. *Mayoral-supported school board slate.* Mayoral-supported school board slates are a twist on mayoral control. Rather than trying to *change* the system, in this reform approach, mayors try to *utilize* the system in a new way. Mayors can take advantage of low-salience school board elections, and try to back a majority of the school board candidates. If successful, the mayor should have great informal influence over the board. Because of this increased informal influence, the strategy is likely to draw much resistance from entrenched interests. It may also create a schism on the board, between the mayoral- and nonmayoral-supported candidates.

4. *Partially mayoral-appointed school board.* Adopting the mayoral control notion, but taking a middle-of-the-road approach, this "hybrid" model allows for some, but not all, power to be shifted to the mayor. Depending on the specific proposal, the mayor may appoint a minority (e.g., Oakland) or majority (e.g., New York) of the school board. Because power is distributed, this option is more politically feasible. But for the same reason, the mayor may be more limited in what she or he can accomplish because potential exists for more opposition on the board to the mayor's vision.

5. *Fully mayoral-appointed school board.* In this model, the mayor is given full power to appoint school board members. This type of reform has gained the most attention, despite the fact that it has only occurred in a few districts, because it involves an institutional restructuring of school system governance. It shakes up the status quo, and demands real reform.

This broad range of reform options, considered together with the themes of timing and partnerships, leaves many questions for cities, school boards, and mayors to explore. It is hoped the research in this study helps policy makers as they answer those questions.

NOTES

1. Lowell C. Rose and Alec M. Gallup, *The 39th annual Phi Delta Kappa/Gallup poll of the public's attitudes toward the public schools,* 2007, p. 38.

2. "Mayor wants voice in choosing APS leader," *Albuquerque Tribune,* July 18, 2007.

3. "Editorial: Leave superintendent search to school board," *Albuquerque Tribune,* July 24, 2007. http://www.abqtrib.com/news/2007/jul/24/editorial-leave-superintendent-search-school-board/.

4. For a more thorough background discussion and more detailed empirical results, readers are encouraged to consult our online reference: http://www.Education Mayor.com.

5. Calculations based on district-level analysis of the Common Core of Data, 2005–2006. Size estimated here by number of students in the school district.

6. Current board members for these two districts are noted online: http://www.lausd.k12.ca.us/lausd/board/secretary/ and http://www.usd384.k12.ks.us/directory/Board.html. Enrollment figures based on NCES Common Core of Data for 2005–2006.

7. Both boards post minutes of their meeting online: http://www.usd384.k12.ks.us/boe/home.html and http://www.lausd.k12.ca.us/lausd/board/secretary/html/agendas/agendas.html.

8. USD #384 Blue Valley-Randolph, January 2007 minutes. http://www.usd384.k12.ks.us/boe/jan.html.

9. One long-standing appointed board, for instance, is Jackson, Mississippi. In Jackson, the mayor appoints the school board with approval of the city council. While this appointive process puts it in Group 1, Jackson differs from the rest of the districts in Group 1. Unlike the other districts where new legislation has been required, long-standing Mississippi law allows districts such as Jackson to choose their own method of board selection. Because the mayor's appointive power is historical, and not part of a new wave of reform, Jackson does not fit as well into our category of "new-style" mayoral governance. The mayor also works in conjunction with the city council, whose approval is required. In terms of accountability, then, Jackson may be more analogous to Baltimore's older mode of joint control under the mayor and state. The mayor's appointive power is also limited to appointments, and does not extend to removal.

10. Thomas Menino, State of the City address, 1996.

11. Low school board turnout and associated susceptibility to special interests have been recognized for decades in the literature. Taebel (1977), for instance, developed a theory of "constituent voters and clientele voters." Constituent voters are theorized to be those who are "direct beneficiaries of local government," e.g., government employees. Clientele voters are those whose benefits from local government "are generalized in nature." Peterson (1981) makes a similar point about the incentives for municipal employees to exercise political power. Taebel's data comes from observation of a 1974 school board election "in a moderately sized city in the Southwest." He finds that "out of 55,000 registered voters, only 2,525 voters actually cast ballots . . . for a voter turnout rate of 4.6 percent." But Taebel's most interesting finding is the disproportionate representation of constituent voters in the election. Using surveys administered to voters, Taebel finds that only 68.8 percent are clientele voters. In other words, even though teachers and public school employees are not 32 percent of the electorate, in this election they were. Taebel's conclusion is that "elected officials would be well off if they merely attain the support of the constituent voters."

12. See Chapter 3 of *The Education Mayor* (Wong et al., 2007) for a more detailed discussion of our methodological approach.

13. See our online supplement at http://www.EducationMayor.com for more information on construction of the data set.

14. Our data is clustered around school districts, e.g., we have five observations (1999, 2000, 2001, 2002, and 2003) for a single school district (Chicago). Our clusters (the districts) are independent, but the individual observations are not. To ac-

count for this feature of the data, in our OLS regressions, we cluster around the district to obtain robust standard error estimates that adjust for the within-cluster correlation.

15. In analyzing the financial data, we construct two general types of variables from the raw Annual Survey of Government Data. The first type is a measure of allocation, examining financial subcategories as a percentage of the whole. The second type is a measure of magnitude, exploring the amount (dollars per student) being spent in various subcategories. All of our allocation measures are reported as percentages, and all of our magnitude measures take into account enrollment and are therefore reported as dollars per student. For each of the revenue and expenditure measures, we consider both allocation and magnitude.

16. In addition to this baseline model, we consider models with five-year lagged governance. We cluster on the school district to provide for robust standard errors.

17. We do not reproduce results tables in this chapter, but readers interested can obtain more detailed information at our online supplement.

18. The RAND Corporation has also chronicled these events through late 2006. See Catherine H. Augustine, Diana Epstein, and Mirka Vuollo, *Governing urban school districts: Efforts in Los Angeles to effect change* (Santa Monica, CA: RAND Corporation, 2006).

19. Joel Rubin and Richard Fausset, "Mayor talks tough to push school takeover," *Los Angeles Times*, November 21, 2005. http://www.latimes.com/news/local/la-me-takeover21nov21,1,4562336.story?coll=la-headlines-california.

20. Joel Rubin and Richard Fausset, "Mayor talks tough to push school takeover," *Los Angeles Times*, November 21, 2005. http://www.latimes.com/news/local/la-me-takeover21nov21,1,4562336.story?coll=la-headlines-california.

21. Emphasis added. "Mayor Hahn on education." http://www.smartvoter.org/2005/05/17/ca/la/vote/hahn_jk/paper2.html (accessed October 2005).

22. Jill Darling Richardson, "Poll analysis: Riordan endorsements could influence school board votes," *Los Angeles Times*, April 4, 1999.

23. Melissa Milios and David Zahniser, "Hahn looks to improve schools," *Los Angeles Daily Breeze*, March 2005.

24. Melissa Milios and David Zahniser, "Hahn looks to improve schools," *Los Angeles Daily Breeze*, March 2005.

25. Melissa Milios and David Zahniser, "Hahn looks to improve schools," *Los Angeles Daily Breeze*, March 2005.

26. Noam N. Levey and Jessica Garrison, "Big win, but little time to deliver," *Los Angeles Times*, May 18, 2005. David Zahniser, "Villaraigosa backs LAUSD reform," *Copley News Service*, March 2005.

27. As described on their Web site, EdVoice "was established by our state's leading educational philanthropists who understand that the future of California will be shaped by the quality of education our public schools deliver." http://www.edvoice.org/edvoice/ev_about.html (accessed October 2005).

28. John Buntin, "Sugar daddy government," *Governing*, June 2004.

29. "Senate committee discusses mayoral involvement in urban school governance," *California School News*, June 10, 2005.

30. "Senate committee discusses mayoral involvement in urban school governance," *California School News*, June 10, 2005.

31. As described on their Web site, "The Small Schools Alliance (SSA) is a coalition of Los Angeles education, community, business and political leaders dedicated to transforming Los Angeles Unified School District (LAUSD) into the best public school system in the nation within the next 10 years." http://www.smallschools.org/ (accessed October 2005).

32. See http://www.greendot.org/home/index.html.

33. The contract rested on six tenets: (1) school sizes of 500 students or less; (2) curriculum designed by UC and Cal State educators to ensure students that graduate are prepared to go on to college or trade schools; (3) key decisions at each school, including budgets, are made by staff and teachers; (4) teachers benefit from better-run schools with increased salaries and benefits; (5) parents become more involved in their child's school by agreeing to dedicate at least 30 hours per year to school activities; and (6) all schools remain open until 5:00 p.m. to fit working families' schedules.

34. David Zahniser, "Cutting LA school sizes would be no easy task," *Los Angeles Daily News*, April 4, 2005.

35. Noam N. Levey and Jessica Garrison, "Big win, but little time to deliver," *Los Angeles Times*, May 18, 2005.

36. Antonio Villaraigosa, speech to U.S. Conference of Mayors, January 25, 2006. http://www.lacity.org/mayor/myrspeechold/mayormyrspeech246935126_01252006.pdf.

37. Antonio Villaraigosa, State of the City speech, April 18, 2006. http://www.scpr.org/features/2006/school_governance/mayorspeech.html.

38. David Zahniser and Joel Rubin, "Mayor spent millions on school board races," *Los Angeles Times*, August 1, 2007.

39. Amy Miller, "Chávez targets school system; Mayor seeks right to appoint board," *Albuquerque Tribune*, March 15, 2006. http://www.abqjournal.com/news/metro/441921metro03-15-06.htm.

40. Senate Bill 928. Text as introduced. http://legis.state.nm.us/Sessions/07percent20Regular/bills/senate/SB0928.html.

41. In addition to SB928, a pair of bills that would have the same effect (but through a different legal route) were also introduced by Senator Gerald Ortiz y Pino. The alternative pair of bills included Senate Joint Resolution 18 to amend the New Mexico Constitution, and SB959 to then produce the same changes in school district governance.

42. Susie Gran, "Albuquerque mayor seeks a role in school superintendent search," *Albuquerque Tribune*, August 8, 2007. http://www.abqtrib.com/news/2007/aug/08/albuquerque-mayor-seeks-role-school-superintendent/.

43. In August 2007, the six items listed under the heading "Mayor's Office Priorities" were Extreme Sports Park, Sustainability, Autism Town Hall, Mayor's Office of Volunteerism and Engagement, Mayor's A+ Award Nomination, San Juan Chama Diversion Project, and Mayor's Press Conferences.

44. Readers interested in more details on the Washington, D.C., story should consult the online magazine *D.C. Watch*: http://www.dcwatch.com/, and especially their page devoted to mayoral control: http://www.dcpswatch.com/mayor/index.html.

45. District of Columbia Government Media Advisory, "Mayor Adrian M. Fenty announces education initiative," January 4, 2007. http://www.dcwatch.com/mayor/070104.htm.

46. http://dc.gov/mayor/pdf/DC_Public_Education_Reform_Act_final.shtm.

47. Parthenon Group, "Fact-base for D.C. reform," December 2006. dc.gov/mayor/DCPS_Reform_report.shtm.

48. Parthenon Group, "Fact-base for D.C. reform," December 2006. dc.gov/mayor/DCPS_Reform_report.shtm.

49. http://www.saveourschoolsdc.org/pdf/boeplan.pdf.

50. Council of Great City Schools, "The mayor's plan for achieving success in the DCPS: Is the implementation likely to match the vision?" March 2007. http://www.cgcs.org/pdfs/DC_Instructional.pdf, and "Analysis of Mayor Adrian Fenty's plan for the District of Columbia public schools," February 2007. http://www.cgcs.org/images/Publications/DC_Analysis.pdf.

51. The law created a new state board of education: "Beginning at 12:01 p.m. on January 2, 2009, the Board shall consist of 9 elected members. One member shall be elected from each of the 8 school election wards created pursuant to section 2 of the Boundaries Act of 1975, effective December 16, 1975 (D.C. Law 1-38; D.C. Official Code § 1-1011.01), and one member shall be elected at-large. The Board shall select its president from among the 9 members of the Board."

52. D.C. Code § 38-172(a) (2007).

53. D.C. Code § 38-193(b) (2007).

REFERENCES

Allinder, R. M., L. S. Fuchs, D. Fuchs, and C. L. Hamlett. 1992. Effects of summer break on math and spelling performance as a function of grade level. *Elementary School Journal* 92 (4): 451–460.

Berkman, M. B., and E. Plutzer. 2005. *Ten thousand democracies: Politics and public opinion in America's school districts.* Washington, D.C.: Georgetown University Press.

Berry, C. 2007. School consolidation and inequality. In *Brookings papers on education policy: 2006–2007*, ed. T. Loveless and F. Hess, 49–75. Washington, D.C.: Brookings Institution.

Bloomberg, M. R. 2002. School reform: Putting our kids first. July 10. www.ci.nyc.ny.us/html/om/html/2002a/weekly/weekly_061002.html (accessed August 15, 2007).

Chambers, S. 2006. *Mayors and schools: Minority voices and democratic tensions in urban education.* Philadelphia: Temple University Press.

Cuban, L., and M. Usdan. 2003. *Powerful reforms with shallow roots: Improving America's urban schools.* New York: Teachers College Press.

Hanushek, E. A. 1979. Conceptual and empirical issues in the estimation of educational production functions. *Journal of Human Resources,* Summer, 351–388.

———. 1986. The economics of schooling: Production and efficiency in public schools. *Journal of Economic Literature,* September, 1141–1177.

Henig, J. R., and W. C. Rich, eds. 2004. *Mayors in the middle: Politics, race, and mayoral control of urban schools.* Princeton, NJ: Princeton University Press.

Henry, N. B., and J. G. Kerwin. 1938. *Schools and city government: A study of school and municipal relationships in cities of 50,000 or more population.* Chicago: University of Chicago Press.

Just, A. E. 1980. Urban school board elections: Changes in the political environment between 1950 and 1980. *Education and Urban Society* 12 (4): 421–435.

King, G., R. Keohane, and S. Verba. 1994. *Designing social inquiry.* Princeton, NJ: Princeton University Press.

Kirst, M. W. 2002. *Mayoral influence, new regimes, and public school governance.* CPRE Research Report Series RR-049. Philadelphia: Consortium for Policy Research in Education, University of Pennsylvania Graduate School of Education.

Loveless, T. 2003. *Brown center report on American education 2003.* Washington, DC: Brookings Institution.

Moe, T. M. 2004. Teacher unions and school board elections. In *Besieged: School boards and the future of education politics,* ed. W. G. Howell. Washington, DC: Brookings Institution.

Peterson, P. E. 1976. *School politics, Chicago style.* Chicago: University of Chicago Press.

Ravitch, D. 2005. Every state left behind, *New York Times,* November 7.

Ravitz, J., J. Mergendoller, and W. Rush. 2002. What's school got to do with it? Cautionary tales about correlations between student computer use and academic achievement. Paper presented at annual meeting of the American Educational Research Association, New Orleans, Louisiana, March.

Shen, F. X. 2003. Spinning the schools: Political incentives and mayoral takeover of urban schools districts. Paper presented at the annual meeting of the American Educational Research Association, Chicago, April.

Sutton, M. 2005. The push for mayor appointed school boards bypasses San Diego. *For Now: Voice of San Diego,* June 15. http://www.voiceofsandiego.org/site/apps/s/content.asp?c=euLTJbMUKvH&b=291837&ct=1010937 (accessed October 2005).

Taebel, D. A. 1977. Politics of school board elections. *Urban Education* 12 (2): 153–166.

Tyack, D. B. 1974. *The one best system: A history of American urban education.* Cambridge, MA: Harvard University Press.

Wong, K. K. 1999. *Funding public schools: Politics and policy.* Lawrence: University Press of Kansas.

Wong, K. K., R. Dreeben, L. Lynn Jr., and G. L. Sunderman. 1997. *Integrated governance as a reform strategy in the Chicago public schools.* Chicago: University of Chicago.

Wong, K. K., and F. X. Shen. 2003. Measuring the effectiveness of city and state takeover as a school reform strategy. *Peabody Journal of Education* 78 (4): 89–119.

Wong, K. K., F. X. Shen, D. Anagnostopoulos, and S. Rutledge. 2007. *The education mayor: Improving America's schools.* Washington, D.C.: Georgetown University Press.

Yin, R. K., J. Schmidt, and F. Besag. 2006. Aggregating student achievement trends across states with different tests: Using standardized slopes as effect sizes. *Peabody Journal of Education* 81 (2): 47–61.

Zeigler, L. H. 1975. School boards research: The problems and prospects. In *Understanding school boards: Problems and prospects,* ed. P. J. Cistone. Lexington, MA: Lexington Books.

About the Editor and Contributors

Thomas L. Alsbury, Editor, *assistant professor of educational administration, North Carolina State University*

Dr. Alsbury earned his B.S. in Molecular Biology, B.A. in Chemistry Teaching, M.Ed. in Curriculum and Instruction, post-master's and M.Ed. in Educational Administration with principal credentials from the University of Washington. He earned his superintendent credentials and Ed.D. in Educational Administration at Washington State University. Dr. Alsbury completed the only national study related to one of the major theories on school governance and has received numerous distinguished awards for his research. Dr. Alsbury's line of research is in organizational theory, the superintendency, and school board governance. Over the past five years he has been the chair of the American Educational Research Association's special interest group called Research on the Superintendency, and is widely published on the topic. He has consulted and presented to several international, national, and state school board and superintendent associations, and to universities and school districts. Dr. Alsbury chaired the 2007 national school board symposium *School board research: Main lines of inquiry* and served as editor of this volume.

Lars G. Björk, *professor, director of the Institute for Education Research, University of Kentucky*

Dr. Björk holds a Ph.D. and an Ed.S. in Educational Administration, an M.Ed. in Public Administration, an M.Ed. in Secondary Education, and a B.A. in Education from the University of New Mexico. He served on the faculties of the University of New Mexico, University of South Carolina, and Georgia Southern University. Dr. Björk serves as the codirector of the University Council for Educational Administration's Center for the Study of the Superintendency.

William Lowe Boyd, *distinguished professor, Harry L. Batschelet Chair of Educational Administration, Penn State University*
Dr. Boyd earned his Ph.D. from the University of Chicago and is the editor of the *American Journal of Education*. A specialist in educational administration and education policy and politics, he has published over 130 articles and has coedited 15 books. He has researched education reform efforts in the United States, Australia, Britain, Canada, and Sweden. As a researcher, Dr. Boyd has studied school reform; school effectiveness; efforts to achieve coordinated, school-linked services for at-risk children and their families; and the politics of parental choice in education.

Peter J. Cistone, *dean, professor, College of Education, Florida International University*
Dr. Cistone holds an M.A. in Education from Lehigh University and a Ph.D. in Educational Administration from Pennsylvania State University. A member of the faculty at Florida International University since 1982, he served as dean of the College of Education for five years. Previously, he held academic appointments at the Ontario Institute for Studies in Education/University of Toronto and Temple University. The author of numerous publications, he is noted for his seminal contribution to school governance theory in his book *The Politics of Education* (1974) with Laurence Iannaccone, and his edited book *Understanding School Boards* (1975). Dr. Cistone chaired the first national symposium on school board research in 1972, which resulted in the 1975 publication of an edited book compiling the papers from the symposium and provided the first state-of-the-research synthesis on school governance.

Barbara DeHart, *dean, School of Educational Studies; director, Urban Leadership Program; Claremont Graduate University, Claremont, California*
Dr. DeHart is a recent professor and director of the cohort-based Urban Leadership Center. Her research focuses on the areas of educational leadership; organizational theory; and educational politics, policy, and governance (at the macro and micro levels). She holds a Ph.D. from the University of California at Santa Barbara. Dr. DeHart has served public education for 33 years, most recently as superintendent of schools in Westminster School District, Orange County, California. She recently completed a study on California school board governance following up on Iannaccone's research.

Mary L. Delagardelle, *director, Iowa School Boards Foundation*

Dr. Delagardelle holds a Ph.D. in Educational Leadership and Policy Studies from Iowa State University. She has served as a school board member and educator for over 30 years and is currently the deputy executive director of the Iowa Association of School Boards and executive director of the Iowa School Boards Foundation. Dr. Delagardelle's dissertation. Role and Responsibilities of Local School Board Members in Relation to Student Achievement, won the College of Human Science Research Excellence Award. Dr. Delagardelle recently led a multi-year research project on school board training and governance approaches that positively influence student achievement.

Lance D. Fusarelli, *associate professor, educational leadership and policy studies, Educational Administration Coordinator, North Carolina State University*

Dr. Fusarelli earned an M.A. in Government and a Ph.D. in Educational Administration from the University of Texas at Austin, where he was a university Fellow. He won the Dissertation of the Year award from the Politics of Education Association and held a faculty position at Fordham University. As an expert in school policy, school boards, and superintendents, he has written or coauthored five books, including *Effective Communication for School Administrators: A Necessity in an Information Age* (2007). Dr. Fusarelli has written numerous articles on school governance and policy implications in the *Journal of School Leadership, Journal of Educational Administration, Peabody Journal of Education,* and *Educational Policy.*

DeLacy D. Ganley, *codirector, Teacher Education Internship Program; assistant professor, School of Educational Studies; Claremont Graduate School*

Dr. Ganley holds an M.A. in English and a Ph.D. in Educational Leadership. Since 2004, she has codirected Claremont Graduate University's Teacher Education Internship Program, serving as the Director of Curriculum and Research. Dr. Ganley's background as a K–16 English teacher gives her experience working with linguistically and culturally diverse populations and an understanding of how technology can facilitate student learning. Dr. Ganley's research interests are eclectic but can be grouped into four main categories: (a) the beliefs, characteristics, and practices that interrupt cycles of academic failure and promote student success; (b) teacher preparation; (c) systems theory and its application to educational institutions; and (d) school leadership and reform.

Thomas E. Glass, *professor of leadership, University of Memphis*

Dr. Glass holds an M.A. and Ph.D. in Educational Sociology from Wayne State University. He held faculty positions at Northern Illinois University, Washington State University, the University of Detroit, and Indiana University. Dr. Glass served public schools as a superintendent and administrator in Michigan, Washington, and Arizona. Recently, he was lead author of *The Study of the American School Superintendency 2000: A Look at the Superintendent of Education in the New Millennium*. For 10 years he served as editor of the *Journal of School Business Management* and has been a frequent contributor to numerous education journals. For over 25 years, Dr. Glass has served as a consultant to nearly one hundred school districts, assisting them in public opinion polling, strategic planning, facilities, demographics, communications, and management review.

Frederick Hess, *director, Educational Policy Studies, American Enterprise Institute (AEI)*

Dr. Hess holds a B.A. in Political Science, M.A. in Government, M.Ed. in Curriculum and Instruction, and a Ph.D. in Government from Harvard University. A former public high school social studies teacher, Dr. Hess previously taught education and politics at the University of Virginia. He is a faculty associate at the Harvard University Program on Education Policy and Governance and serves on the review board for the Broad Prize in Urban Education. At AEI, Dr. Hess works on a diverse range of K–12 and higher education issues including educational politics, administrative preparation and licensure, and school governance. He has been the executive editor of *Education Next* since 2001 and has recently released a book entitled *Educational Entrepreneurship: Realities, Challenges, Possibilities* (2006).

Laurence Iannaccone, *retired, professor emeritus, University of California at Santa Barbara*

Dr. Iannaccone was associate dean and department chair of the Graduate School of Education at the University of California at Santa Barbara and program leader in educational administration. He has been on the faculties of the Ontario Institute for Studies in Education, the University of Toronto Educational Theory Department, Harvard University, The Claremont Graduate School, Washington University, and New York University. During Dr. Iannaccone's tenure, he served as editor of the journal *Educational Researcher*. Dr. Iannaccone is author of innumerable books and articles on school board governance. His most recent research article was "The Crucible of Democracy: The Local Arena," in the *Journal of Education Policy* (1994). Dr. Iannaccone is known for his development of the Dissatisfaction Theory of American Democracy.

Michael W. Kirst, *professor emeritus, School of Education, Stanford University*

Dr. Kirst received his bachelor's degree in economics from Dartmourth College and his M.P.A. and Ph.D. in political economy and government from Harvard University. He was twice selected as chairman of the Politics of Education Special Interest Group in the American Educational Research

Association. He is codirector of the Policy Analysis for California Education (PACE) Center and was president of the California State Board of Education. A former staff director of the U.S. Senate Subcommission on Employment, Manpower, and Poverty, Dr. Kirst has also held several major positions in the U.S. Office of Education. He was twice selected as chairman of the Politics of Education Special Interest Group in Politics of Education. He is editor for the McCutchan series in educational administration and policy analysis. Dr. Kirst's seminal Decision Output Theory led to the book *The Political Dynamics of American Education* (2005) with Frederick Wirt.

Theodore J. Kowalski, *Endowed Professor, Kuntz Family Chair in Educational Administration, University of Dayton*

Dr. Kowalski is a former public school teacher, principal, associate superintendent, and superintendent. He earned an M.A. and Ph.D. in Educational Administration from Indiana State University. He held faculty positions at Saint Louis University and Ball State University, where he was the dean of the Teachers College. Dr. Kowalski is the author of more than 160 publications including 17 books, as well as the editor of the *Journal of School Public Relations.* His most recent book is the second edition of *The School Superintendent,* a book frequently used in university superintendent courses. His most recent journal article is entitled "Evolution of the School Superintendent as Communicator" (2005).

Frank W. Lutz, *retired, emeritus professor, Texas A&M–Commerce*

Dr. Lutz received his B.S., M.S., and Ed.D. from Washington University at Saint Louis. He directed the Center for Policy Studies in Education at Texas A&M, served as dean of Education at Eastern Illinois, director of Education Policy Studies at Pennsylvania State University and director of Institute of Staff Relations at NYU. With Laurence Iannaccone, he founded the Dissatisfaction Theory of American Democracy. After retirement, Dr. Lutz joined the new doctoral faculty at the University of Texas–Pan American and was influential in establishing their program in education leadership. He has written, coauthored, or edited 7 books, 23 chapters, 14 monographs, 107 articles, and has presented over 100 papers at scholarly and professional organizations.

Carol Merz Frankel, *dean, professor emeritus, School of Education, University of Puget Sound*

Dr. Merz has been dean of the School of Education at the University of Puget Sound since 1987. She holds a B.A. and an M.A. in Education from Stanford University and an Ed.D. from Washington State University in Educational Administration. She previously served as a school principal and teacher for nearly 20 years. Dr. Merz has done seminal theoretical research on school board governance with notable contributions in her books *Schools and Community: Promise and Paradox* (1997), and *The Politics of School Community Relations* (1992). Dr. Merz also did key research on school boards and school board governance in journals including *Urban Education* and *Planning & Changing*.

Meredith Mountford, *associate professor, director for the Center for Educational Leaders, Florida Atlantic University*

After eight years as a teacher, one year as a principal, and three years as a superintendent in Wisconsin, Dr. Mountford earned her Ph.D. in educational administration at the University of Wisconsin–Madison. Mountford's dissertation, Motivations for School Board Membership, Conceptions of Power, and Their Affect on Decision-Making, won the Dissertation of the Year award for American Educational Research Association's special interest group called Research on the Superintendency. Dr. Mountford also held faculty positions at the University of Missouri–Columbia and was director of the Ed.D. Program in Educational Leadership. Dr. Mountford's most recent publications include *Conceptions of Power Held by Educational Leaders: The Impact on Collaborative Decision-Making Processes* (2005) with Rose Ylimaki and *Motives and Power of School Board Members: Implications for School Board-Superintendent Relationships* (2004).

George J. Petersen, *professor and chair of the Department of Graduate Studies in the College of Education at California Polytechnic State University, San Luis Obispo*

Dr. Petersen earned his Ph.D. in Educational Policy from the University of California–Santa Barbara and held a faculty position at the University of Missouri–Columbia. He also served as the associate director of UCEA. He is the author of several books on educational policy, including *The Politics of Leadership: Superintendents and School Boards in Changing Times* (2005) with Lance Fusarelli. His journal articles include "School Leader, Advocate, and the Good Neighbor: The Superintendent's Complex Relationship with the Board President, the School Board, and the Rest of the Community" (2006) and "The Board President and Superintendent: An Examination of Influence through the Eyes of the Decision Makers" (2005).

Francis X. Shen, *Inequality Fellow, Harvard Kennedy School of Government*

Francis Shen is a graduate of Harvard Law School and a licensed attorney in Missouri. He recently coauthored *The Education Mayor* (2007), and is completing a Ph.D. in the Harvard University Government Department. He has published on a wide range of education policy issues, including school finance, charter schools, and school governance.

Sam Stringfield, *professor and Distinguished University Scholar, codirector, Nystrand Center of Excellence in Education, College of Education and Human Development, University of Louisville*

Dr. Stringfield earned his Ph.D. in Educational Psychology from Temple University. In addition to his current position he is also director of the Grawemeyer Award in Education, acting chair of the Department of Educational and Counseling Psychology, and a faculty member of the Department of Teaching and Learning and the Department of Leadership, Foundations, and Human Resources Education. Dr. Stringfield is the author of numerous publications including *Educational Governance Reforms: The Uncertain Role of Local School Boards in the United States* with Deborah Land (2005). His articles frequently appear in educational policy journals such as *American Educational Research Journal* and *Educational Evaluation and Policy Analysis.*

Kenneth K. Wong, *The Walter and Leonore Annenberg Professor in Education Policy; professor of education, political science, and public policy; director of Urban Education Policy Program at Brown University*

Dr. Wong holds M.A. and Ph.D. degrees in Political Science from the University of Chicago and has been director of the National Research Center on School Choice, Competition and Student Achievement. He held faculty positions at Peabody College and Vanderbilt University and was the associate director of the Peabody Center for Education Policy. Author of numerous publications, he currently has a book under contract entitled *How Mayors Improve School Performance.*

Made in the USA
Monee, IL
07 June 2022

97652655R00213